Intermediate German

FOR

DUMMIES®

by Wendy Foster

WILEY

Wiley Publishing, Inc.

Intermediate German For Dummies®

Published by
Wiley Publishing, Inc.
111 River St.
Hoboken, NJ 07030-5774
www.wiley.com

Copyright © 2008 by Wiley Publishing, Inc., Indianapolis, Indiana

Published by Wiley Publishing, Inc., Indianapolis, Indiana

Published simultaneously in Canada

For general information on our other products and services, please contact our Customer Care Department within the U.S. at 800-762-2974, outside the U.S. at 317-572-3993, or fax 317-572-4002.

For technical support, please visit www.wiley.com/techsupport.

Wiley also publishes its books in a variety of electronic formats. Some content that appears in print may not be available in electronic books.

Library of Congress Control Number: 2008921681

ISBN: 978-0-470-22624-7

Manufactured in the United States of America

10 9 8 7 6 5 4 3 2 1

WILEY

About the Author

Wendy Foster was born in Connecticut and grew up in Scituate, Massachusetts. While studying in France, she traveled around Europe, and became curious about the German language and culture. After graduating with a teaching certificate and a degree in French, she decided to return to Europe to study German. Her love of the Alps inspired her to live in Munich, where she spent 30 years. During that time, she studied German, completed her MA in French at Middlebury College in Paris, and later learned Spanish in Spain. Her professional experience includes teaching Business English, German, French, and intercultural communication skills, as well as writing and translating. She recently returned to her New England roots, where she works from her home overlooking a spectacular salt marsh that constantly beckons her to go kayaking, walking, bird watching, and swimming.

Dedication

This book is dedicated to the marsh, its wildlife, Wingaersheek Beach, the Annisquam River, and the man I share it with, Phil Kehoe.

Author's Acknowledgments

I must thank several people for their unwavering encouragement and support as I worked on this project. I thank my international friends Sandra Waller, Peter Hirschmann, Crista Zecher, Adrienne Clark-Ott, Ludwig Ott, and Udo Alter. I thank my American friends Barb and Neil Murphy, Holly and Franck Fleury, and Willie and Darrell Wickman.

In addition, I would like to thank the editorial staff at Wiley for their insight, patience, and expertise, especially my project editor Chad Sievers, copy editor Danielle Voirol, acquisitions editor Michael Lewis, and technical editor Brian Tucker at Wabash College. A special thanks to my literary agent Marilyn Allen.

Publisher's Acknowledgments

We're proud of this book; please send us your comments through our Dummies online registration form located at www.dummies.com/register/.

Some of the people who helped bring this book to market include the following:

Acquisitions, Editorial, and Media Development

Project Editor: Chad R. Sievers

Acquisitions Editor: Michael Lewis

Senior Copy Editor: Danielle Voirol

Editorial Program Coordinator: Erin Calligan Mooney

Technical Editor: Brian Tucker, PhD

Editorial Manager: Michelle Hacker

Editorial Assistants: Joe Niesen, David Lutton

Cartoons: Rich Tennant (www.the5thwave.com)

Composition Services

Project Coordinator: Kristie Rees

Layout and Graphics: Carl Byers, Carrie Cesavice, Stephanie D. Jumper, Laura Pence, Erin Zeltner

Proofreaders: Laura Albert, John Greenough, Joni Heredia

Indexer: Broccoli Information Management

Publishing and Editorial for Consumer Dummies

> **Diane Graves Steele,** Vice President and Publisher, Consumer Dummies
>
> **Joyce Pepple,** Acquisitions Director, Consumer Dummies
>
> **Kristin A. Cocks,** Product Development Director, Consumer Dummies
>
> **Michael Spring,** Vice President and Publisher, Travel
>
> **Kelly Regan,** Editorial Director, Travel

Publishing for Technology Dummies

> **Andy Cummings,** Vice President and Publisher, Dummies Technology/General User

Composition Services

> **Gerry Fahey,** Vice President of Production Services
>
> **Debbie Stailey,** Director of Composition Services

Contents at a Glance

Table of Contents

Introduction

You may be standing in the aisle of a bookstore at the mall perusing this book. Maybe the mail carrier has dropped *Intermediate German For Dummies* on your doorstep, so you've decided to rip open the bubble pack envelope because you love popping those bubbles. No matter how you came across this book, acquiring more German helps you in a myriad of ways. Like it or not, globalization is taking place at an ever-increasing pace. German is spoken by more members of the European Union than any other language, and Germany plays a leading economic role in the European Union. You may be a businessperson, adventurer, or student — it doesn't matter. But unless you plan to live as a hermit, then in some way or another you're bound to come in contact with German. So get a head start and be ready to speak, write, travel, and most of all, have fun **auf Deutsch** (*in German*).

Using this book builds your confidence in no time — well, okay, you do need some free hours here and there, but the time you do spend using this book will pay off down the road. Consider what you can gain from *Intermediate German For Dummies* as the equivalent of having invested a huge chunk of money, time, and effort at the local health club to become super fit for a trek across the Alps. The obvious difference is that you have to plunk out only a small chunk of change and some time and effort in order to reap personal and professional gain.

About This Book

Intermediate German For Dummies is your key to success in becoming confident in both written and spoken German. In this book, you get straight talk, the nitty-gritty, and enough detail to see you successfully through any major and minor roadblocks to communicating in German.

You'll find this book very user-friendly because you can go through it in any order you choose, zeroing in on your priorities. You can skim or, better yet, skip over the grammar you don't need. Use the book to find answers to specific questions you may have on a topic that comes up while you're writing. All the chapters have ample practice exercises following the grammar explanations so you can check whether you've grasped the material. Flip to the end of the chapter, and you find the Answer Key for the exercises with explanations pertinent to problematic usage. Without even realizing it, your German vocabulary expands as you cruise through the book. The example sentences and exercises use practical, everyday German so you can flex your vocabulary muscles as you complete the tasks. Most important, as you go through this book, **Viel Spaß!** (*Have a lot of fun!*)

Conventions Used in This Book

To make your progress go as smoothly as possible, I use some conventions in this book. They can help you spot essential elements in the text and exercises:

- ✔ I **boldface** the essential elements in verb tables, which may be information like verb endings or irregular conjugations. Elsewhere, I bold German words and example sentences.

- ✔ I *italicize* English translations that accompany German words and sentences. I also italicize English terms that I immediately follow with a definition.

- ✔ The Answer Key at the end of each chapter has not only the solutions to the practice exercises (in **bold**) but also *italicized* English translations. Answers have explanations where I feel it's important to clarify why the answer given is the correct one.

- ✔ Before each group of practice exercises, I provide an example exercise in Q&A format to show you how to complete the task. The example (Q.) is followed by the answer (A.) and an explanation for that answer, as needed.

Foolish Assumptions

In writing *Intermediate German For Dummies*, I made the following assumptions about you, dear reader:

- ✔ You've acquired at least a smattering of spoken and written German, or better yet, more, and you're acquainted with some basics of German grammar.

- ✔ You're willing to jump into German at the deep end and start swimming, even if you do need some water wings at first.

- ✔ Your goal is to expand your knowledge of German so that you feel comfortable in both speaking and writing the language. (Alternatively, you want to dream in German.)

- ✔ You don't want to be burdened by long-winded explanations of unnecessary grammatical terms, nor do you care to hold a scholarly discussion in German about Goethe's *Faust*. You just want to you express yourself in clear and reasonably accurate German.

- ✔ You're enthusiastic about having some fun while honing your German skills because the last thing you want from this book is to be reminded of boring school days where success meant figuring out how to: a) sleep and learn at the same time b) skip class and not be missed c) wrap the teacher around your little finger so that no matter what you did, you still got good grades.

If any or all of these statements describe you, then you're ready to get started using this book. **Willkommen!** (*Welcome!*) If you don't have at least a basic understanding of German, I suggest you first check out *German For Dummies* by Paulina Christensen, Anne Fox, and Juergen Lorenz (Wiley).

How This Book Is Organized

This book is divided into six parts on general topics. In turn, these six parts are divided into several chapters containing explanations, tables, and exercises. Each chapter and appendix addresses a different aspect of the specific part. Here's the preview.

Part I: The Basic Building Blocks of German

In this part, you reacquaint yourself with the world of nouns and verbs, numbers and dates, word order and more fundamentals. See the mysteries of gender and case unveiled. Part I also contains a practical guide to increasing your word power exponentially. You understand how to retrieve newly acquired vocabulary and expressions.

Part II: Getting Started Now: Writing in the Present

Here you get the tools needed to construct sentences in the present tense. I give you ample practice combining nouns and pronouns with verbs. I include info on asking and answering questions, as well as agreeing and disagreeing. You see how to express certainty and uncertainty and how to make wishes and requests using subjunctive verbs. This part also shows you the six modal verbs that help you be polite, ask for help, and talk about what you can do, want to do, should do, or must do.

Part III: Fine Tuning Your Writing with Flair

You want to sound like a native, right? This part helps you find out how to express yourself using two-part verbs and reflexive verbs. It also delves into the finer points of expressing yourself using adjectives of description. The chapters here show you how to put adjectives and adverbs to work for you by making comparisons, show how to connect shorter ideas with conjunctions, and touch on using prepositions.

Part IV: Looking Back and Ahead: Writing in the Past and the Future

In this part, you practice expressing yourself using past and future verbs. You become familiar with the difference between the conversational past and the simple (narrative) past, and you see how to choose the correct verb form to express yourself in the future.

Part V: The Part of Tens

Here you find my top ten easy and useful tips on the following topics: optimizing your German (in other words, how to make your German writing the best it can be), and avoiding pitfalls.

Part VI: Appendixes

The four appendixes provide an assortment of references to help you in your writing and speech. The first appendix includes verb tables for conjugating verbs. The second appendix covers case-ending tables to help you use nouns, pronouns, and adjectives correctly. Two mini-dictionaries allow you to find the meaning of a German word you don't understand or the German equivalent of an English word.

Icons Used in This Book

Consider these icons as key points as you take the journey through this book. You find them in the left-hand margin throughout. The icons include the following:

Helpful hints like these would've made it a whole lot easier for me to feel more comfortable using German when I was living in Bavaria way back in the Dark Ages.

The Warning icon points out the hidden dangers you may encounter as you journey through the deep forest of tangled words, slippery sentence structure, and the like.

This icon alerts you to key information that's worth revisiting. You want to stash this info in your mind because you'll end up using it again and again.

Pay attention to these key points. By noticing similarities and differences between German and English, you see patterns that show you how to assemble German into meaningful statements.

This icon marks the core learning tool in this book: a set of exercises designed for you to check your progress. Go ahead — grab a pencil and get started.

Where to Go from Here

Try scanning the Table of Contents for starters. Select a chapter that piques your interest and take it from there. Read the section that presents a concept, point of grammar, or guidelines. Study the example at the beginning of the practice section and write your answers to a few of the exercises. You'll soon find out what you know or don't know by checking your answers in the Answer Key at the back of the chapter. When you're satisfied with your results in one section, flip back to the Table of Contents and find another section you're ready to tackle.

Part I helps you assess what you already know. The other parts build up the confidence you need in order to successfully expand your German horizons. Work at your own pace, proceeding in any order you choose. Skip over sections you're not ready to do yet. If you don't get the hang of a section, reread the grammar explanation, check out the example sentences, or look at the first couple of solutions in the Answer Key.

Anytime you feel like you're losing steam, **mach eine Pause** (*take a break*), close your eyes, and dream about **die Romantische Straße** (*the Romantic Road* — an enchanting route through some of the most picturesque parts of southern Germany). Before you realize it, you'll be dreaming of storybook castles and court jesters **auf Deutsch** (*in German*)!

Part I
The Basic Building Blocks of German

The 5th Wave   By Rich Tennant

"Wait! Wait! I want to find out what gender 'eggplant' is so I know how to pick it up."

In this part . . .

*I*magine you're building a house. Regardless of whether it's made of bricks, wood, or cards, a well-designed house all boils down to whether the foundation is solid enough to support the structure above it. So it is with Part I: This is where you get a solid foundation for building your German. Chapter 1 assembles the basic tools you need for construction. Following this groundwork is Chapter 2; there, you gain confidence in case and gender, which act as the mortar that sets words into meaningful sentences. With Chapter 3, you're in the process of laying out some supporting beams of German, including numbers, time, dates, and nationalities. So far, so good. Chapter 4 adds sparkle to your otherwise mundane construction job. You get a jump start on increasing your word power by recognizing groups of words that fit together logically.

Chapter 1

Assembling the Basic Tools for German Sentences

*Y*ou need some basic grammar tools to help you assemble winning sentences. In this chapter, I explain the roles of the grammar tools — such as your trusty cases, clauses, and cognates — to help you boost your confidence in German. Next, you need to find some parts to build a sentence: parts of speech such as a noun, or better yet, a couple of nouns, a verb, an adjective or two, and a maybe a preposition. These spare parts, er, words, are easy to find in a big dictionary. At the end of this chapter, I give you pointers on how to navigate your way through a bilingual dictionary.

Throughout *Intermediate German For Dummies*, you encounter the terms I describe in this chapter. I use these terms to explain grammar, vocabulary, and the idiosyncrasies of building sentences in German. If you're not familiar with such terms, getting the hang of the exercises in later chapters will take longer. Lingering here before jumping ahead can save you time in the future. At the very least, scan the headings and tables in this chapter quickly; when you see a term that you're fuzzy about, stop there and have a look.

If English is your native language, chances are you don't need to bother with deciding whether the words you're using are verbs, nouns, or adjectives because you know how to fit words together. Along the path to success in German, it's a different story. You're prone to roadblocks caused by not knowing which word to use, how to use it, or where to place it in a sentence. This chapter removes the barriers to your progress with German.

Grasping German Grammar Terms

To get a firm grasp on German grammar, you need to make sure you can keep track of the many terms you encounter. This section clears up any fuzzy ideas you may have about the names for tools of German grammar, such as *gender, case,* and *tense.* (I use terms for parts of speech in this section, but I give a fuller explanation of nouns, verbs, adjectives, and so on in a separate section of this chapter.)

Conjugating verbs and understanding tenses

Verbs are the words of action, and a verb that isn't yet part of a sentence is an *infinitive* or is *in infinitive form*. This is the verb as it's seen in a dictionary entry, as in **wohnen** (*to live*). In English, the *to* indicates that the word is in infinitive form; the German equivalent is the **-en** ending on the verb.

When you *conjugate* a verb, you change the verb form so it fits in your sentence to convey information such as which subject is doing the action and when something happens. Conjugation involves breaking the verb down into its usable parts. Look at the conjugation of the verb *to work: I work, you work, he/she/it works, we work, you work, they work.* English has only two different spellings of *work* (with and without *s*). The same conjugation in German — **ich arbeite, du arbeitest, er/sie/es arbeitet, wir arbeiten, ihr arbeitet, sie arbeiten, Sie arbeiten** — reveals four different verb endings: **-e**, **-est**, **-et**, and **-en**.

Verbs are conjugated in different *tenses,* which describe time. The three main descriptions of time are past, present, and future. Here's a briefing on the tenses I cover in this book, with the relevant verbs underlined:

- ✔ **Present tense:** This tense describes an action that's happening now, habitual actions, or general facts. Look at the following sentence, which uses the verb **wohnen** (*to live*) in the present tense: **Ich wohne in den U.S.A.** You can translate it as *I live in the U.S.A.* or *I'm living in the U.S.A.* (See Chapter 5 for details on the present.)

- ✔ **Present perfect (conversational past):** In German, the present perfect describes something that happened in the past, whether finished or unfinished. It's used in conversational German. **Ich habe in den U.S.A. gewohnt** can mean *I have lived in the U.S.A.* or *I lived in the U.S.A.* (See Chapter 16.)

- ✔ **Simple past:** The simple past is used in formal language to describe past actions. **Ich wohnte in den U.S.A.** means *I lived in the U.S.A.* (See Chapter 17.)

- ✔ **Future:** The future, obviously, describes events that haven't yet occurred. **Ich werde in den U.S.A. wohnen** means *I will live in the U.S.A.* or *I'm going to live in the U.S.A.* German makes much less use of the future tense than English, often opting for the simple present instead. (Check out Chapter 18.)

English uses continuous (progressive) tenses — verbs with a form of *to be* and *-ing,* as in *am living* or *have been living* — to describe a temporary or ongoing action. But because German has no continuous forms, you can simply use the basic German tenses you see in the preceding list for the continuous form in English. German also uses other tenses slightly differently from English.

The subjunctive is not a tense but rather a *mood,* something that indicates *how* you describe an action — for example, as a fact, a possibility, or an uncertainty; but as with tenses, the subjunctive gets its own conjugation. (See Chapter 8 for the subjunctive.)

It's a proven fact that you don't retain vocabulary, grammar, or what-have-you the first time you're exposed to it. Or the second or third time. To combat this, use a system of recording important information that works well for you: Try making flashcards, creating an alphabetical word list, writing new expressions in meaningful sentences, and incorporating new grammar points into a short dialogue. You can also copy the questions you need to review, leaving the answers blank, so that you can redo them later.

In the following exercise, the verb is indicated in bold. Decide which verb tense it is and write your answer in the space provided (refer to the bold, underlined verbs in this section for help). Then translate the verb. The example shows the English translation of the complete sentence. You find the complete translations to the exercises like this in the Answer Key at the end of every chapter.

Q. Ich **kaufte** ein neues Auto.

A. Ich kaufte ein neues Auto. (*I bought a new car.*) **Simple past, *bought.*** The **-te** ending signals the simple past tense.

1. Ich **werde** ins Restaurant **gehen.** _____, _____.

2. Ich **habe** den Film **gesehen.** _____, _____.

3. Ich **fahre** morgen nach Chemnitz. _____, _____.

4. Ich **arbeite** dort an einem Projekt. _____, _____.

5. Ich **studierte** Mathematik an der Universität. _____, _____.

Getting gender, number, and case

The trio of gender, number, and case are closely linked to each other to help you make sense out of single words and to connect them into sentences. You need to know how to use gender, number, and case to express your ideas in understandable language. Check out the following explanations:

- ✔ **Gender:** People are one of two genders, masculine or feminine, right? Dogs and cats are, too. But do stones and water have a gender? In German, yes indeed! Every noun has a gender; the triumvirate **der** (*masculine*), **die** (*feminine*), **das** (*neuter*) are the choices. All three are the gender-specific versions of the English word *the.* (If this were a soccer game, the German team would've already won by a margin of two.)

  When looking at German, don't confuse gender. Gender has to do with the word itself, not the meaning of the word.

- ✔ **Number:** Number refers to singular and plural, like *one potato, two potatoes, three potatoes.* German plurals are more intricate than English plurals. In fact, German offers five major different types of plural endings. Some plurals compare with the irregular English plurals, like *man, men* (**der Mann, die Männer**). (Check out Chapter 2 for more on making nouns plural.)

- ✔ **Case:** There are four cases in German: nominative, accusative, dative, and genitive. But what does that actually mean? Cases help tell you what role the word plays in the sentence. They have to do with the difference between *I* and *me* or *she* and *her*. Cases deal with the significance of the *to* in *give it to me* or the apostrophe *s* in *dog's Frisbee.*

  German case endings are numerous, and they show the relationship between the words having those cases. English uses case far less often. (Chapter 2 has more info on case.)

Understanding word order

In many respects, German word order is more flexible than English word order because case plays a key role in clarifying the meaning of a sentence, something that's not nearly as powerful of a tool in English. When positioning words in a German sentence, however, there are a few major points to keep in mind.

- The simplest word order looks like English word order:

    1. Subject in first position: **Meine Wohnung** (*My apartment*)

    2. Verb in second position: **hat** (*has*)

    3. Other information follows: **einen großen Balkon** (*a large balcony*)

- Yes/no type questions have inverted word order; flip the conjugated verb with the subject: **Hat deine Wohnung einen Balkon?** (*Does your apartment have a balcony?*)

- More complex sentences — for example, a sentence with two verb parts — require more understanding of where to position the verbs in a sentence. In various sections of this book, you find out more about correct word order.

Grammar terms that describe words, parts of words, and word groupings

You need to know several terms that are used to describe words that you put together to convey meaning — *sentence, clause, phrase,* and so on. The following list shows the most important key words I use in this book:

- **Phrase:** A group of words without a subject or a verb; most often used to describe a prepositional phrase, such as **ohne Zweifel** (*without a doubt*)

- **Clause:** A group of related words that has subject and a verb, such as **wir arbeiten . . .** (*we're working . . .*)

- **Sentence:** A group of words that represents a complete thought and has a complete sentence structure: subject, verb, and punctuation, such as **Gehen wir!** (*Let's go!*)

- **Prefix:** A "word beginning" attached to the front of a word that alters the word's meaning, such as **un** (*un-*) + freundlich (*friendly*) = **unfreundlich** (*unfriendly*)

- **Suffix:** A "word ending" attached to the back of a word that alters the word's meaning, such as (der) Kapital + **ismus** = Kapital**ismus** (*capital* + *ism* = *capitalism*)

- **Cognates:** Words that have the same meaning and the same (or nearly the same) spelling in two languages, such as **der Hammer** (*the hammer*) or **die Melodie** (*the melody*)

    Note: Technically, *cognates* are simply two words that come from a common ancestor.

Write the name of the term that describes the word(s) in the exercises.

0. in der Nacht _____

A. in der Nacht (*in the night*) **phrase**

6. der Safe _____

7. Ich schwimme oft im Sommer. _____

8. die <u>Vor</u>arbeit _____

9. sie möchte gehen . . . _____

10. mit meiner Familie _____

11. wunder<u>bar</u> _____

Identifying Parts of Speech

In order to build a sentence, you need to figure out which words to use and how to put them together. To do this, you figure out what you want to say, identify the parts of speech you need to express your ideas, and then decide which words you want to use. Word order in a German sentence can depend on the parts of speech that you're using. In Table 1-1, I explain what these terms mean.

Table 1-1		Parts of Speech	
Name	*Definition*	*Examples*	*Notes*
Noun	A person, place, animal, thing, quality, concept, and so on	**Dracula** **Hotel California** **Känguruh** (*kangaroo*) **Liebe** (*love*)	In German, they're always capitalized. (See Chapter 2.)
Pronoun	A word that replaces, or stands in for a noun	**er** (*he*) **sie** (*she*) **uns** (*us*)	German has far more pronoun variations; the four cases influence pronoun endings. (See Chapter 2.)
Article	A word that indicates the gender of a noun	**der/die/das** (*the*) **ein/eine/ein** (*a/an*)	German has three differ- ent genders, so it uses three different articles for *the* — **der/die/das** — and *a/an* — **ein/eine/ ein.** (See Chapter 2.)

(continued)

Table 1-1 (continued)

Name	Definition	Examples	Notes
Verb	A word that shows action or a state of being	**denken** (*to think*) **haben** (*to have*) **reisen** (*to travel*)	Verbs are conjugated according to person (I, you, he, and so on), tense (present, past, and future), and mood (for example, the difference between *it is* and *it would be*).
Adjective	A word that modifies or describes a noun or a pronoun	**schön** (*beautiful*) **praktisch** (*practical*) **interessant** (*interesting*)	Adjectives may or may not have case endings. (See Chapters 12 and 13.)
Adverb	A word that modifies or describes a verb, an adjective, or another adverb	**schnell** (*fast, quickly*) **sehr** (*very*) **schrecklich** (*terribly*)	In German, adjectives and adverbs can be the same word. (See Chapter 13.)
Conjunction	A word that connects other words or sentence parts together	**und** (*and*) **aber** (*but*) **weil** (*because*)	In German, some conjunctions affect the word order of the sentence. (See Chapter 14.)
Preposition	A word that shows a relationship between its object (a noun or pronoun) and another word in a sentence	**mit (mir)** (*with [me]*) **ohne (mich)** (*without [me]*) **während (des Tages)** (*during [the day]*)	In German, a preposition uses case (dative, accusative, or genitive) to show the relationship to its object. (See Chapter 15.)

In the sentences that follow, identify the part of speech in boldface and write it next to the sentence. Then try your hand at writing the sentence in English.

Q. Wo **sind** meine Schlüssel?

A. Wo sind meine Schlüssel? **verb.** A clue is that the verb is in second position, as is typical in German word order. *Where are my keys?*

12. Sie sind auf dem Tisch. _____

13. Im Zoo gibt es viele **exotische** Tiere. _____

14. Ich mag die Pinguine, **aber** die Elefanten sind noch interessanter.

_____

15. Im Zoo sind **die** Tiere nicht glücklich. _____

16. Ich möchte **im** Park spazierengehen. _____

17. Hast du meine schwarzen **Schuhe** gesehen? _____

18. Deine Schuhe **liegen** unter dem Sofa. _____

19. Fahre bitte nicht so **schnell!** _____

Finding Meaning through Context

One essential tool for making sense of a foreign language is to consciously look for meaning through the context of the words. You probably do the same thing in your own language. Imagine you're reading a text that's not in your field of expertise. You instinctively look at any headings, scan the text rapidly, and get more clues from any illustrations, charts, or tables. When you're looking at a text in German, you can meet the challenge by employing the techniques you already use in your native language.

To understand what a whole sentence means, see how the words fit together. Identify the verb or verbs and a noun or pronoun, and that's the meat of your sentence. Check out how the other words are related to the subject and verb — for example, look for a prepositional phrase or a conjunction. (See the preceding section for the parts of speech.) In short, use all the tools at your disposal to understand German sentences.

The following exercise combines the tools and parts explained in the previous sections of this chapter. Each sentence has one word missing. Decide which word of the four choices is the correct one, and write your answer in the space.

0. Viele Leute _____, dass München "die heimliche Hauptstadt Deutschlands" ist.

    a) behaupten   b) Sonne   c) der   d) vorwärts

A. Viele Leute **a) behaupten,** dass München die heimliche Hauptstadt Deutschlands ist. (*Many people claim that Munich is "the secret capital of Germany."*) The verb **behaupten** is in second position in the clause; next comes a second clause that is set apart by a comma.

20. Es gibt noch _____ Bezeichnungen für München.

    a) der   b) Personen   c) zwei   d) das

21. Die Einwohner sagen, München ist "die Weltstadt mit Herz," _____ "das Millionendorf."

    a) in   b) arbeiten   c) oder   d) interessant

22. In der Tat _____ die Stadt voller Überraschungen.

    a) von   b) ist   c) in   d) können

23. Jedes Jahr wird das grösste Volksfest der Welt in München _____.

    a) gehabt   b) Stein   c) geworden   d) gefeiert

24. Millionen Touristen kommen zum Oktoberfest, aber _____ Leute kommen zu spät. Warum?

    a) manche   b) haben   c) die   d) grün

25. Leider geht _____ Oktoberfest am ersten Sonntag im Oktober zu Ende.

    a) nur   b) in   c) das   d) von

Using a Bilingual Dictionary

Horses are only as good for riding as their training is. And dictionaries are only as useful for finding words as their owners' knowledge of how to use a dictionary. Except for the terms *breaking in a horse* and *breaking in a book,* that's about it for parallels (unless, of course, you want to speak German to your horse).

A bilingual dictionary is a challenge at first; take on the challenge and read the information at the front of the dictionary on how to use the dictionary. The symbols and abbreviations are your key to successful scouting for the right word. This section helps you sort out this handy tool.

Making the right choice (at the bookstore)

When choosing a bilingual dictionary, your first task is selecting the right dictionary. First and foremost is the size and quality. Don't scrimp here. Take your bathroom scales to a serious bookstore at the mall and weigh all the German/English bilingual dictionaries. Pick the two heaviest ones. (Okay, just kidding. You don't need to bring your scales, but do consider the obvious: that you'll be able to find more information in larger dictionaries.) Then compare three different entries. Start with a frequently used verb like **machen**. The following shortened dictionary entry for the verb **machen** shows you how a good dictionary organizes the information on the first two lines:

> **machen 1** *vt* (**a**) to do; (*herstellen, zubereiten*) to make. **was ~ Sie (beruflich)?** what do you do for a living?; **gut, wird gemacht** right, I'll get that done *or* will be done (*coll*).

You may notice two abbreviations and a symbol in this entry:

- The abbreviation *vt* stands for *transitive verb;* that's a verb that can take a direct object. Other verbs have the abbreviation *vi,* which stands for an *intransitive verb;* that's a verb without a direct object.

- The second abbreviation *coll* stands for *colloquial;* expressions or words marked by this abbreviation are used in informal conversation.

- The ~ symbol represents the *headword* (the first word) **machen.** The complete expression is **Was machen Sie (beruflich)?**

Start your dictionary comparison task by following these steps:

1. **Look at how comprehensive the entries are.**

   Check for commonly used phrases, such as **was machst du denn da?** (*what in the world are you doing here?*), **mach schneller!** (*hurry up!*), or **mach's gut** (*take* *care*), and compare their translations for detail and content. You should be able to find complete sentences and phrases using **machen.** Comprehensive dictionaries should offer alternative words in German (at least for frequently used verbs such as **machen**), along with possible translations. For example, after **machen,** you may find **herstellen** (*to produce, manufacture*) or **zubereiten** (*to prepare*), as in the example entry.

2. **Ask yourself which dictionary is more user-friendly.**

   In other words, does the dictionary provide plenty of helpful abbreviations to help you understand the entries? Do you see clearly marked sections under the headword **machen?** They should be marked by numbers and letters in bold; in the example entry, you find **1** and (**a**). Some quality dictionaries indent the numbered sections to make them even easier to locate. You can compare whether there's a phonetic pronunciation for tricky words. Also, check that the dictionary makes ample use of symbols like *coll* to indicate usage of the word.

   Apart from the abbreviations that show part of speech, gender, number, case, and so on, you find many more details in any large, quality dictionary. A (very) short list of such abbreviated terms should include *fig* (figurative), *lit* (literal), *esp* (especially), *sl* (slang), *Tech* (technology), *Psych* (psychology), *Prov* (proverb), *Jur* (law), *spec* (specialist term), *Aus* (Austrian usage), *Sw* (Swiss usage), and many more.

Make your choice wisely, and start enjoying your new **Wörterbuch** (*dictionary*). Oh, and don't forget to take the scales home with you, too.

If you prefer an online dictionary and you're not sure about how to make a good selection, follow the same criteria. Select a couple of reputable dictionary publishers, go to their online dictionaries, and find out how extensive and (hopefully accurate) they are. If you're not familiar with dictionary publishers, go to `www.google.de` and check out the dictionaries listed under "deutsch-englisches wörterbuch." Do a thorough Web search to find what's available and compare the sources you find.

Performing a word search

Maybe you didn't buy a paper dictionary because you found a nifty online alternative. That's all right. Online dictionaries are a good backup for finding out about words if you're on a limited budget. No matter whether you're using a hard copy or an online dictionary, you still have to know how to find the right word.

Familiarize yourself with the symbols and abbreviations used by looking up a few nouns, verbs, adjectives, and so on. See whether you understand them in the context of the dictionary entry. Instead of trying to memorize the meaning of all the abbreviations, make a photocopy of the list and keep it as a bookmark in your dictionary. Better yet, laminate it. That way you can use it as a mouse pad, a table mat, or whatever. You can then cross-check definitions to get more information on words you're looking up.

When you look up a word that has several definitions, read beyond the first or second entry line and try to decide which one suits your needs. Think about context, and decide which word fits best into the rest of the sentence. Besides meaning, here are some other factors that may affect your word choice:

✔ **Nouns:** Think of gender and number as the vital statistics of a noun.

   • Gender is indicated by *m, f,* and *nt* (for masculine, feminine, and neuter) in some dictionaries.

- Number is indicated with the plural ending form for that noun. There are five main groups of noun endings. A common ending is **-en;** other nouns add **-s.** With some nouns, you see the genitive case ending indicated for that noun in addition to the plural ending.

✔ **Verbs:** Verbs also have vital statistics you need to know.

- A verb is transitive or intransitive (symbols like *vt* and *vi*). A *transitive verb* takes a direct object; an *intransitive verb* doesn't.

- A transitive verb may have a separable prefix (*vt sep*) or an inseparable prefix (*vt insep*). If the prefix is separable, it usually gets booted to the end of the sentence when the verb is conjugated.

- Some verbs are reflexive (*vr*), meaning they require a reflexive pronoun.

- The simple past form and the past participle are also indicated (in some dictionaries with *pret* and *ptp,* respectively).

✔ **Prepositions:** Prepositions in German dictionary entries show which case they have: accusative (*prep + acc*), dative (*prep + dat*), or genitive (*prep + gen*). Some prepositions have more than one case, and most prepositions have more than one meaning.

✔ **Pronouns:** Pronouns include personal pronouns (*pers pron*), such as **ich** (*I*); demonstrative pronouns (*dem pron*), such as **denen** (*them*); relative pronouns (*rel pron*), such as **das** (*that*); and reflexive pronouns (*reflexive pron*), such as **mich** (*myself*). See Chapter 2 for details on pronoun types.

Adjectives and adverbs may be the same word in German. Memorize both, and you have two words for the effort of looking up one.

Look at the dictionary entries and answer the questions about the words and abbreviations.

Reise-: ~**pafl** *m* passport: ~**scheck** *m* travellerís cheque *(Brit),* traveler's check *(US);* ~**spesen** *pl:* travelling *(Brit)* or traveling *(US)* expenses *pl;* ~**versicherung** *f* travel insurance: ~**ziel** *nt* destination.

Key for abbreviations: *m* = masculine, *(Brit)* = British usage, *(US)* = North American usage, *pl* = plural, *f* = feminine, *nt* = neuter

Q. In the entry for **Reise-,** which word is feminine? Is it one word or two words in German?

A. **Reiseversicherung** is feminine, and it's **one word** in German.

26. The headword (first one) has a hyphen at the end of the word like this: **Reise-:** What does the hyphen mean?

_____

27. What's the word for *destination,* and which gender is it?

_____

Answer Key

1 Ich werde ins Restaurant gehen. (*I'm going to go to the restaurant.*) **Future, *will go/am going to go.*** Either translation is appropriate; *am going to go* sounds more natural here because it expresses an intention. **Werde** plus the verb at the end signals the future tense.

2 Ich habe den Film gesehen. (*I have seen/saw the film.*) **Present perfect, *have seen/saw.* Habe** plus the participle at the end of the sentence signals present perfect tense.

3 Ich fahre morgen nach Chemnitz. (*Tomorrow I'm driving to Chemnitz.*) **Present, *am driving.*** The ending **-e** signals the present tense.

4 Ich arbeite dort an einem Projekt. (*I'm working on a project there.*) **Present, *am working.*** The infinitive is **arbeiten.** The simple present is formed by adding **-e** to the end of the stem **arbeit-.** The simple past would be **ich arbeitete = arbeit- + -ete.**

5 Ich studierte Mathematik an der Universität. (*I studied math at the university.*) **Simple past, *studied.*** The **-te** ending signals the simple past tense.

6 der Safe (*the safe/vault*) **cognate**

7 Ich schwimme oft im Sommer. (*I often swim in the summer.*) **sentence**

8 die Vorarbeit (*the preliminary work*) **prefix**

9 sie möchte gehen . . . (*she'd like to go . . .*) **clause**

10 mit meiner Familie (*with my family*) **phrase**

11 wunderbar (*wonderful*) **suffix**

12 **pronoun; *They're on the table.* Sie** is a pronoun. The usual German word order is subject + verb. Here, the subject is a pronoun.

13 **adjective; *There are a lot of exotic animals in the zoo.* Exotische** describes the plural noun **Tiere.** The suffix ending **-isch** is often comparable to the suffix *-ic* or *-ical* in English.

14 **conjunction; *I like the penguins, but the elephants are more interesting.*** The two sentence parts are joined by the conjunction **aber** (*but*).

15 **definite, plural article; *In the zoo, the animals aren't happy.* Die** is the plural article in nominative case, indicating that **Tiere** is plural.

16 **preposition; *I'd like to go for a walk in the park.* Im** is a **preposition.** The prepositional phrase is **im Park** (*in the park*).

17 **noun; *Have you seen my black shoes?* Schuhe** is a plural noun.

18 **verb; *Your shoes are lying under the sofa.* Liegen** is a verb. It's in second position in the sentence after the subject **deine Schuhe.**

19 **adverb; *Please don't drive so fast!* Schnell** is an adverb in this sentence because it describes how the person is driving (**fahre**), and *driving* is the verb.

20 **c. zwei;** Es gibt noch **zwei** Bezeichnungen für München. (*There are two other names for Munich.*)

21 **c. oder;** Die Einwohner sagen, München ist "die Weltstadt mit Herz," **oder** "das Millionendorf." (*The inhabitants say [that] Munich is the "friendly city" or "the village with a million inhabitants."*) Literally, the **Weltstadt mit Herz** is the *world city with a heart*.

22 **b. ist;** In der Tat **ist** die Stadt voller Überraschungen. (*Indeed, the city is full of surprises.*) Many tourists aren't aware of another celebration of beer known as **das Starkbierfest.** The Munich carnival season is also very lively, with people taking to the streets to celebrate Mardi Gras.

23 **d. gefeiert;** Jedes Jahr wird das grösste Volksfest der Welt in München **gefeiert.** (*Every year, the largest folk fest in the world is celebrated in Munich.*)

24 **a. manche;** Millionen Touristen kommen zum Oktoberfest, aber **manche** Leute kommen zu spät. Warum? (*Millions of tourists come to the Oktoberfest, but some people come too late. Why?*)

25 **c. das;** Leider geht **das** Oktoberfest am ersten Sonntag im Oktober zu Ende. (*Unfortunately, the Oktoberfest ends on the first Sunday in October.*) It's actually better to get there before the Oktoberfest begins if you don't like crowds and just want to see the enormous venue. You may even be able to drink a beer with the workers constructing the tents.

26 The hyphen means that all the words in that entry are connected to **Reise-,** in this case as compound words.

27 **Das Reiseziel** (*destination*) is neuter (*nt*).

Chapter 2

Sorting Out Word Gender and Case

* *

In This Chapter

▶ Getting word genders going

▶ Articulating the articles

▶ Subjects, objects, or possessions: Casing out noun and pronoun cases

▶ Doing some pronoun practice

* *

Most words in a German sentence take their cues from the nouns (or their esteemed representatives, the pronouns). When studying German, you really don't know a new noun unless you know its characteristics, which include gender. So for each new noun you come across, you need to accept its gender as a part of the word and commit it to memory. In order to use nouns and pronouns (as well as adjectives and prepositions) in a German sentence, you need to know how they fit together; this is the role of case. Case and gender are closely linked together, and I consider them pieces of a puzzle in making German sentences. Case and gender may look complicated at first, but as soon as you start fitting the pieces in, the picture becomes clearer. In this chapter, you get the lowdown on how gender and case work hand in hand to form various endings on the members of two large families of words: the article family and the pronoun family.

Rounding Up Grammatical Genders

Not everything with gender lives and breathes. Listen to people talk about inanimate objects, and you may hear them refer to the faithful bicycle they cherish, the noncompliant computer they want to throttle, or the old jalopy they're trying to coax up a hill as *he* or *she.* Like these other things you may have a love-hate relationship with, German *words* have gender.

In German grammar, *gender* is the classification of a noun or a pronoun into one of three categories: masculine, feminine, or neuter. These genders often have nothing to do with the meaning of the word; they're simply an identity bracelet. Note that *gender* refers to the word, not whatever the word represents. You need to know a word's gender because it can dictate the spelling of other words in the sentence.

So how can you get a grasp of gender so you can form a word correctly? Each time you come across a new noun, be firm with yourself; find out its gender (and how to form its plural form). With a little time, you can master the concept. This section helps you identify a word's gender, form plural nouns (and note the effects on gender), eye indefinite articles, and identify when not to use articles.

Identifying German genders and figuring out which one to use

In English, you mark a noun as one of three genders: male (masculine), female (feminine), or inanimate/neither (neuter). The descriptions *male, female,* and *inanimate* refer to living beings and things. The words in parentheses — *masculine, feminine,* and *neuter* — refer to grammatical distinction, which is how German describes *noun gender.*

Gender distinction in English is *natural,* which means you need to know only whether the noun refers to a female being, a male being, or an inanimate object (neither male nor female). You can refer to the nouns as *he, she,* or *it.* And the articles you use — such as *the, a,* and *an* — don't tell you anything about gender at all. Look at these examples:

✔ *Can you see the girl over there? She's really tall.* (You know the word *girl* refers to a female, so you use *she* when you refer back to her in the second sentence.)

✔ *The new German teacher is Herr Mangold. I think he comes from Bremen.* (The teacher is male, so you refer to him as *he.*)

✔ *Have you seen the cool guitar in the shop window? It has 12 strings.* (You refer to an inanimate object as *it.*)

In German, you likewise have three genders, but gender distinction isn't *natural* as it is in English. It's like a marker that refers to the word, not its meaning. The three markers for *the* (singular) in German are **der** (*masculine*), **die** (*feminine*), and **das** (*neuter*). For example, look at the words for eating utensils, where you have all three bases covered: **der Löffel** (*the spoon*), **die Gabel** (*the fork*), and **das Messer** (*the knife*). Why should a a spoon be masculine, a fork feminine, or a knife neuter? See any logical pattern here? I don't. Much of the gender designation in German is unnatural, which means there's no silver bullet to help you remember the gender of a word in German. German dictionary entries identify nouns as **der, die,** or **das.** (Have a look at Chapter 1 for more information on using a dictionary.)

The three gender markers, the definite articles **der, die,** and **das,** all mean *the.* Compare the three following German sentences, which are the same as the three English example sentences.

✔ **Kannst du das Mädchen da drüben sehen? Es ist sehr groß.** (*Can you see the girl over there? She's really tall.*) *The girl* in German is **das Mädchen,** a neuter gender noun, as are all nouns ending in **-chen.** The ending indicates that a person or thing is small or young. You refer to the girl as **es,** which means *it.* Remember, this is simply a grammatical reference. It's not an affront to you girls out there!

✔ **Der neue Deutschlehrer ist Herr Mangold. Ich glaube, er kommt aus Bremen.** (*The new German teacher is Herr Mangold. I think he comes from Bremen.*) You refer, grammatically speaking, to **Herr Mangold** as **er** (*he*). In most (but not all) cases in German, male beings are **der** nouns, and female beings are **die** nouns.

✔ **Hast du die tolle Gitarre im Schaufenster gesehen? Sie hat zwölf Seiten.** (*Have you seen the cool guitar in the shop window? It has 12 strings.*) Strange but true: Grammatically speaking, a guitar is feminine, so you refer to it as **sie** (*she*). Most nouns ending in **-e** are feminine nouns.

So how do you know exactly how to form/use genders correctly in German? First, remember that gender is an integral part of each noun; it's like a piece of the noun's identity. When you see a new noun, there are several ways to find out its gender. A dictionary can help, and some of the following noun gender categories can offer you a reasonable guess.

Some categories of nouns are consistently masculine, feminine, or neuter. For instance, noun gender usually does follow the gender of people: **der Onkel** (*the uncle*), **die Schwester** (*the sister*). Most often, the noun groups have to do with the ending of the noun. Look at some fairly reliable groups in Tables 2-1 and 2-2 (note, however, that there are exceptions).

Table 2-1	Common Genders by Noun Ending (or Beginning)	
Usually Masculine (der)	*Usually Feminine (die)*	*Usually Neuter (das)*
-er (especially when referring to male people/jobs)	**-ade, -age, -anz, -enz, -ette, -ine, -ion, -tur** (if foreign/borrowed from another language)	**-chen**
-ich	**-e**	**-ium**
-ismus	**-ei**	**-lein**
-ist	**-heit**	**-ment** (if foreign/borrowed from another language)
-ner	**-ie**	**-o**
	-ik	**-tum** or **-um**
	-in (when referring to female people/occupations)	Starting with **Ge-**
	-keit	
	-schaft	
	-tät	
	-ung	

Table 2-2	Common Noun Genders by Subject	
Usually Masculine (der)	*Usually Feminine (die)*	*Usually Neuter (das)*
Days, months, and seasons: **der Freitag** (*Friday*)	Many flowers: **die Rose** (*the rose*)	Colors (adjectives) used as nouns: **grün** (*green*) → **das Grün** (*the green*)
Map locations: **der Süd(en)**(*the south*)	Many trees: **die Buche** (*the beech*)	Geographic place names: **das Europa** (*Europe*)
Names of cars: **der Audi** (*the Audi*)		Infinitives used as nouns (gerunds): **schwimmen** (*to swim*) → **das Schwimmen** (*swimming*)

(continued)

Table 2-2 *(continued)*

Usually Masculine (der)	Usually Feminine (die)	Usually Neuter (das)
Nationalities and words showing citizenship: **der Amerikaner** (*the American*)		Young people and animals: **das Baby** (*the baby*)
Occupations: **der Arzt** (*the doctor*)		

Note: Compound nouns (nouns with two or more nouns in one word) always have the gender of the last noun: **die Polizei** (*the police*) + **der Hund** (*the dog*) = **der Polizeihund** (*the police dog*).

Corralling plurals

When you want to make a noun plural in English, all you usually need to do is add an *-s* or *-es*. However, you have five ways to choose from when forming plural nouns in German. But before you throw your hands up in dismay, think about how English varies from the one standard form of making plurals with *-s* or *-es*. Think of *mouse/mice, tooth/teeth, child/children, shelf/shelves, phenomenon/phenomena, man/men,* or *country/countries.* Better yet, you can form the plural of some words in two different ways. Think about *hoof/hoofs/hooves.* See what I mean? Many English plurals are also a matter of memorization. So with both languages, you have a variety of plural endings and/or changes in the noun.

Here's the good news: You don't have to worry much about gender in plural definite articles in German because **die** (*the* in plural form) is all you need. Remember that **die** corresponds to all three singular definite article forms: **der** (*the,* masculine), **die** (*the,* feminine), and **das** (*the,* neuter).

Although **die** has a double duty of a singular feminine definite article and a plural definite article for all three genders, you can distinguish between singular and plural. First, find out the difference in noun endings for each feminine noun in its singular form and its plural form. Next, the context in the sentence may help you see whether you're dealing with a singular or plural form of the noun. You do have one more very important factor that enters into the equation, and that's case. Check out the section "Calling all Cases: The Role Nouns and Pronouns Play."

Table 2-3 shows you the five main ways of forming plural nouns in German. There's no hard and fast method of knowing which plural ending you need, but you can recognize some patterns as you expand your vocabulary. At any rate, you need to place high priority on knowing plural forms. Look at some patterns for forming plural nouns (and keep in mind that there may be exceptions):

✔ Feminine nouns with (feminine) suffixes **-heit, -keit,** and **-ung** usually have an **-en** plural ending: **die Möglichkeit** (*the possibility*) → **die Möglichkeiten** (*possibilities*).

✔ Singular nouns ending in **-er** may not have any ending in plural: **das Fenster** (*the window*) → **die Fenster** (*the windows*).

- Many nouns have an umlaut in the plural form, including many one-syllable words: **der Kuss** (*the kiss*) → **die Küsse** (*the kisses*); **der Traum** (*the dream*) → **die Träume** (*the dreams*).

- Some German nouns are used only in the plural or in the singular: **die Ferien** (*the [often: school] vacation*) is always plural; **die Milch** (*the milk*) is always singular.

Table 2-3	The Five German Plural Groups		
Change Needed	*English Singular and Plural*	*German Singular*	*German Plural*
Add **-s**	*the office(s)*	**das Büro**	**die Büros**
	the café(s)	**das Café**	**die Cafés**
	the boss(es)	**der Chef**	**die Chefs**
	the pen(s)	**der Kuli**	**die Kulis**
No change, or add umlaut (**··**)	*the computer(s)*	**der Computer**	**die Computer**
	the window(s)	**das Fenster**	**die Fenster**
	the garden(s)	**der Garten**	**die Gärten**
	the girl(s)	**das Mädchen**	**die Mädchen**
	the father(s)	**der Vater**	**die Väter**
Add **-e** or umlaut (**··**) + **-e**	*the train station(s)*	**der Bahnhof**	**die Banhöfe**
	the friend(s) (singular is male)	**der Freund**	**die Freunde**
	the problem(s)	**das Problem**	**die Probleme**
	the city/cities	**die Stadt**	**die Städte**
	the chair(s)	**der Stuhl**	**die Stühle**
Add **-er** or umlaut (**··**) + **-er**	*the book(s)*	**das Buch**	**die Bücher**
	the bicycle(s)	**das Fahrrad**	**die Fahrräder**
	the house(s)	**das Haus**	**die Häuser**
	the child/children	**das Kind**	**die Kinder**
	the castle(s)	**das Schloss**	**die Schlösser**
Add **-n, -en,** or **-nen**	*the idea(s)*	**die Idee**	**die Ideen**
	the boy(s)	**der Junge**	**die Jungen**
	the sister(s)	**die Schwester**	**die Schwestern**
	the student(s) (female)	**die Studentin**	**die Studentinnen**
	the newspaper(s)	**die Zeitung**	**die Zeitungen**

Lassoing indefinite articles

Just like English has two indefinite articles — *a* and *an* — that you use with singular nouns, German also has two indefinite articles (in the nominative case): **ein** for masculine and neuter-gender words and **eine** for feminine-gender words. An indefinite article has many of the same uses in both languages. For example, you use it before a singular noun that's countable the first time it's mentioned — **Ein Mann geht um die Ecke** (*A man is walking around the corner*) — or when a singular countable noun represents a class of things: for example, **Ein Elefant vergisst nie** (*An elephant never forgets*). You can also use **ein/eine** together with a *predicate noun* (a noun that complements the subject): **Willy Brandt war ein geschickter <u>Politiker</u>** (*Willy Brandt was a skillful <u>politician</u>*).

Another similarity with English is that there's no plural form of the German indefinite article **ein/eine**. (Also, depending on how you're describing something plural, you may or may not need to use the plural definite article.) Look at the following generalized statement, which requires no article: **In Zermatt sind Autos verboten** (*Cars are forbidden in Zermatt* [Switzerland]).

The following shows you the definite articles and the corresponding indefinite articles (nominative case):

Gender/Number	Definite (the)	Indefinite (a/an)
Masculine	**der**	**ein**
Feminine	**die**	**eine**
Neuter	**das**	**ein**
Plural	**die**	(no plural form)

With German nouns, the gender functions only as a grammatical marker. Table 2-4 shows some words for animals and other things you see on the farm. I chose this vocabulary to illustrate how German noun gender appears random, but in effect, you need to keep in mind that it's *grammatical,* not *natural* gender — that is, the gender of the word, not the animal itself. You find the English translation in the left-hand column and the German noun in the column corresponding to its gender. For instance, **ein Pferd** (*a horse*) appears in the neuter column. ***Note:*** However, a word that specifically describes a male or female type of animal has the same gender as the animal; for example, genders match in **eine Stute** (*a mare*) and **ein Hengst** (*a stallion*).

Table 2-4	Indefinite Articles and Things on the Farm		
English Words	**Masculine**	**Feminine**	**Neuter**
a barn		eine Scheune	
a calf			ein Kalb
a cat		eine Katze	
a chicken			ein Huhn
a cow		eine Kuh	

English Words	Masculine	Feminine	Neuter
a fence	ein Zaun		
a horse			ein Pferd
an ox	ein Ochse		
a tractor	ein Traktor		

Missing absentee articles

In a few instances in German, you don't use an article in the sentence. First of all, you don't use the indefinite article when you mention someone's profession, nationality, or religion. Look at the three examples:

>**Mein Onkel war General bei der Bundeswehr.** (*My uncle was [a] general in the army.*)

>**Sind Sie Australier oder Neuseeländer?** (*Are you [an] Australian or [a] New Zealander?*) Nationalities are nouns in German.

>**Ich glaube, sie ist Lutheranerin.** (*I think she's [a] Lutheran.*) Members of a religious affiliation (or an affiliation such as a political party) are nouns in German.

Secondly, just as in English, you don't use the definite article in generalized statements using plural nouns in German. But you do use the plural definite article when you're not making a generalization: **Die Bäume haben keine Blätter** (*The trees have no leaves*).

Thirdly, names of countries have genders in German, most often **das,** or *neuter* (see Chapter 3), but you generally don't include the definite article, such as in **Viele berühmte Komponisten sind aus Deutschland oder Österreich** (*Many famous composers are from Germany or Austria*).

However, a small number of exceptions exist (see Chapter 3 for more countries that are exceptions):

>**Die Schweiz gehört nicht zur Europäischen Union.** (*Switzerland doesn't belong to the European Union.*) Note **die,** the feminine definite article.

>**Die Vereinigten Staaten sind die größte Volkswirtschaft der Welt.** (*The United States has the largest economy in the world.*) Note **die,** the plural definite article.

Fill in the missing German words as indicated by the English in parentheses. Refer to the earlier tables for help in deciding whether you need **der, die, das, ein,** or **eine** and for help selecting the correct endings for plurals.

Q. _____ (*a window*) im Wohnzimmer ist kaputt.

A. Ein Fenster im Wohnzimmer ist kaputt. (*A window in the living room is broken.*)

1. _____ (*the piano*) ist brandneu.

2. Haben _____ (*the two female students*) einen Nebenjob?

3. _____ (*the hotels*) in der Stadtmitte sind laut.

4. Siehst du? _____ (*the cat*) sitzt auf deinem Auto.

5. Ist das _____ (*a barn*) oder ein Haus?

6. Können _____ (*the boys*) gut Fußball spielen?

7. _____ (*the horse*) ist zu jung zu reiten.

8. _____ (*computers*) sind heutzutage relativ billig.

Calling All Cases: The Roles Nouns and Pronouns Play

Cases indicate the role or function of nouns and pronouns in the sentence. English and German both have cases, as do most languages. Cases allow you to know the function of these words and how they connect with other words in a sentence. This section identifies the four German cases and how they're used, as well as how English and German cases compare.

Identifying the four cases

German has four cases, and you need to know the ins and outs of them because they're the reason nouns, pronouns, articles, and adjectives all go through changes in spelling the way a chameleon changes its color. Here are the four cases:

✔ **Nominative case (nom.):** This case is for the subject of the sentence. The *subject* is a person or thing acting like the quarterback and calling the shots. In a sentence, it's who or what carries out the action. In **Brady wirft den Ball** (*Brady throws the ball*), Brady is the subject.

   Note: You use the nominative case for *predicate nouns* as well; these are nouns (or noun phrases) that express more about the subject, such as a description or an identification. For example, in *he's a remarkable football player*, both the subject (*he*) and the predicate noun phrase (*a remarkable football player*) are in the nominative case.

✔ **Accusative case (acc.):** This case is for the direct object of the sentence. The *direct object* is a bit similar to the quarterback's ball — the subject is acting on it. In **Ein Zuschauer fängt den Ball** (*A spectator catches the ball*), the ball is the direct object. *Note:* Prepositions also use the accusative case for the words they connect. (See Chapter 15 for prepositions.)

✔ **Dative case (dat.):** This case is for the indirect object of the sentence. The *indirect object* receives the direct object — it's like the person the spectator gives the ball to. In **Der Zuschauer gibt seinem Sohn den Ball** (*The spectator gives his son the ball*), **seinem Sohn** (*his son*) is the indirect object, so it's in the dative case. In both German and English, you generally use the verb **geben** (*to give*) the same way; you *give* (the verb) something (**den Ball,** accusative case) to someone (**seinem Sohn,** dative case). *Note:* Prepositions also use the dative case for the words they link with. (See Chapter 15 for prepositions.)

✔ **Genitive case (gen.):** This case shows possession. A person or thing can be the possessor, or owner. In **Die Mutter des Sohnes jubelt** (*The mother of the son cheers*), the son belongs to his cheering mother; **des Sohnes** is in the genitive case. *Note:* Prepositions also use the genitive case for the words they link with. (See Chapter 15 for prepositions.)

The word endings alter slightly according to the case. These changes are necessary to identify what you want to express in a German sentence. (The case ending tables in Appendix B come in extremely handy when you want to find the correct word and its word ending.)

Eyeing the similarities and differences

When dealing with case, English and German have their share of similarities and differences. Before you can tackle the differences in cases, you first need to understand that German and English do look at case in similar fashions. They include the following:

✔ **The two languages share the same system of marking cases of personal pronouns.** In other words, pronouns have different forms (spellings) according to the case they're taking in a sentence. For example, in **er lebt dort** (*he lives there*), the pronoun **er** (*he*) is the subject, so it's in the nominative case. However, in **ich kenne ihn gut** (*I know him well*), **ihn** (*him*) is the direct object, so it's in the accusative case. Spelling changes indicate the role the pronoun is playing: **ich** changes to **mich** (*I* changes to *me*) and **wir** changes to **uns** (*we* changes to *us*).

The same is even true for relative pronouns: **Der** changes to **dessen** (*who* changes to *whose*). I discuss relative and personal pronouns later, in "Putting Pronouns in Place."

✔ **They use the nominative case — the same case you use for subjects — when you have a predicate noun as the object of a sentence.** A *predicate noun* is a person, thing, or a concept that you place on equal footing with the subject. Such nouns state more about the subject. For English and German, the verb **sein** (*to be*) is the prime example of a verb that's followed by the predicate nominative. German also uses the predicate nominative with the verbs **bleiben** (*to stay, remain*), **heißen** (*to be named, called*), and **werden** (*to become*). (In English, people often call these verbs *linking verbs.*) Look at this example: **Mein Zahnarzt ist auch der Zahnarzt meiner Eltern** (*My dentist is also my parent's dentist*). **Mein Zahnarzt** and **der Zahnarzt** are both nominative case.

As for differences, English doesn't have case endings for nouns, so it relies on word order to indicate which grammar hat the noun wears (English has case markers for pronouns only). You usually have the following word order: subject-verb-object (or other information, such as a prepositional phrase). Typically, you can recognize what the subject of the sentence is because you see it at the beginning of the sentence.

German does have different case spellings/endings for both articles and nouns, so word order can be more flexible. Look at the word order of the two sentences that follow:

Der Junge liebt den Hund. (*The boy loves the dog.*)

Den Hund liebt der Junge. (*The boy loves the dog.*)

In both sentences, **der Junge** (*the boy*) is the subject and **den Hund** (*the dog*) is the object of the sentence; you have no difference between the two sentences as far as meaning goes. In German, however, you do have a different case ending for the definite article. In the nominative singular case, it's **der (Hund),** but in the accusative case, it's **den (Hund).** So why put **den Hund** (the direct object) at the beginning of the sentence? Because in German, you can use that word order to emphasize that it's **den Hund** (and not some other house pet) that the boy loves. To get that type of emphasis in English, you need to say something like *It's the dog that the boy loves.* English speakers tend to create this kind of emphasis vocally, whereas in German, you can accomplish such a nuance in both writing and speech.

Table 2-5 shows how the definite article *the* changes in both gender and case. You see the four cases and the three genders, plus the plural form of the definite article *the*.

Table 2-5	German Words That Mean *The*			
Case	*Masculine*	*Feminine*	*Neuter*	*Plural*
Nominative (subjects, predicate nouns)	der	die	das	die
Accusative (direct objects)	den	die	das	die
Dative (indirect objects)	dem	der	dem	den
Genitive (owned objects)	des	der	des	der

You have a grand total of six different definite articles in German and one lonely word, *the*, in English. Practice makes perfect, so set your standards high for mastering the definite article in German. Try your hand at the following exercises.

Put in the missing German definite articles. Use Table 2-5 for help in deciding whether you need **der, die, das, den, dem,** or **des.** The grammar information in parentheses offers you help in doing the exercises. You see these abbreviations: m. = masculine, f. = feminine, n. = neuter, pl. = plural, nom. = nominative, acc. = accusative, dat. = dative, and gen. = genitive. These abbreviations refer to the noun that directly precedes them.

Q. _____ Mannschaft (f., nom.) spielt sehr gut Fußball.

A. Die Mannschaft spielt sehr gut Fußball. (*The team plays soccer very well.*)

9. Brauchst du _____ Kuli (m., acc.)?

10. Ich möchte _____ Auto (n., acc.) kaufen.

11. Was kostet _____ Lampe? (f., acc.)

12. _____ Radio (n., nom.) läuft nicht sehr gut.

13. Das ist _____ Freund (m., nom.) meiner Schwester.

14. Ich schreibe _____ Firma (f., dat.) einen Brief.

15. _____ Leute (pl., nom.) sind sehr freundlich.

16. _____ Film (m., acc.) finde ich sehr lustig.

Putting Pronouns in Place

What's the big deal about pronouns like *you, me, it, them, this, that*, and more? First of all, these plentiful, useful, and essential critters are lurking in various corners of many sentences. Second, they're great for replacing or referring to nouns elsewhere in a sentence. Third, like articles, they also need to change spelling/endings according to the role they're playing in a sentence (case) and the noun for which they may be doing the pinch hitting.

This section discusses the three types of pronouns: personal, demonstrative, and relative pronouns. (See Chapter 11 for reflexive pronouns.) In German, they're all more affected by the gender/case patterns than in English, so I put them into tables for your reference. These case tables help you to do the corresponding exercises in the chapter, and you can also go to Appendix B for reference. I arrange such tables in order of frequency of use: nominative, accusative, dative, and genitive.

Note: One more group of pronouns, called the possessive pronouns — such as **mein** (*my*), **dein** (*your*), **unser** (*our*), and so on — are, technically speaking, classified as adjectives; they have endings that resemble those of descriptive adjectives such as *interesting, tiny,* or *pink.* (See Chapter 12 for more details on possessive adjectives/pronouns.)

Personal pronouns

The personal pronoun family comes in very handy in all kinds of situations when you want to talk (or write) about people, including yourself, without repeating names all the time. You use the nominative case very frequently in most any language (every sentence, after all, needs a subject), and German is no exception. (See the earlier "Identifying the four cases" section for more on cases.)

Try to memorize the personal pronouns as soon as possible, and be sure you know all three cases (no genitive here). With German personal pronouns, the biggest difference is that you have to distinguish among three ways to formulate how to say *you* to your counterpart: **du, ihr,** and **Sie.** Other personal pronouns, like **ich** and **mich** (*I* and *me*) or **wir** and **uns** (*we* and *us*), bear a closer resemblance to English. *Note:* The genitive case isn't represented among the personal pronouns because it indicates possession; the personal pronoun **mich** (*me*) can represent only a person, not something he or she possesses.

Check out Table 2-6 for the personal pronouns. Notice that *you* and *it* don't change, and the accusative (for direct objects) and dative (for indirect objects) pronouns are identical in English. I've added the distinguishing factors for the three forms **du, ihr,** and **Sie** in abbreviated form: singular = s., plural = pl., informal = inf., formal = form.

Table 2-6	German Personal Pronouns	
Nominative (nom.)	*Accusative (acc.)*	*Dative (dat.)*
ich (*I*)	**mich** (*me*)	**mir** (*me*)
du (*you*) (s., inf.)	**dich** (*you*)	**dir** (*you*)
er (*he*)	**ihn** (*him*)	**ihm** (*him*)
sie (*she*)	**sie** (*her*)	**ihr** (*her*)
es (*it*)	**es** (*it*)	**ihm** (*it*)
wir (*we*)	**uns** (*us*)	**uns** (*us*)
ihr (*you*) (pl., inf.)	**euch** (*you*)	**euch** (*you*)
sie (*they*)	**sie** (*them*)	**ihnen** (*them*)
Sie (*you*) (s. or pl., form.)	**Sie** (*you*)	**Ihnen** (*you*)

You have this exercise with the personal pronoun left out, followed by what you need to insert in parentheses (the pronoun in English/the case/directives for *you* if that's the word needed). Go ahead and refer (liberally!) to Table 2-6.

Q. Wohnen _____ in der Nähe? (*you*/nom./s., form.)

A. Wohnen **Sie** in der Nähe? (*Do you live nearby?*)

17. Ich glaube, _____ arbeitet zu viel. (*you*/nom./pl., inf.)

18. Nein, _____ arbeiten nicht genug. (*we*/nom.)

19. Spielst _____ gern Karten? (*you*/nom. /s., inf.)

20. Ja, _____ spiele gern Poker. (*I*/nom.)

21. Kennst du _____? (*him*/acc.)

22. Ich gehe ohne _____ in die Stadt. (*you*/acc./pl., inf.)

23. Wirklich? Ich dachte, du gehst mit _____. (*us*/dat.)

24. Wie gefällt _____ der neue Bürgermeister? (*you*/dat./s., form.)

Relating to relative pronouns

You use relative pronouns (*who, whom, whose, that,* and *which*) to include extra information about a noun or pronoun expressed beforehand. You typically see relative pronouns at the front of a relative clause where they refer back to the noun in the main clause. And what is a *main clause?* It's a sentence fragment that can stand on its own and still make sense. A *relative clause* is a type of *subordinate clause,* which, as you can probably guess, is the type of sentence fragment that can't stand alone. (If you find the terminology here — main clause and subordinate clause — confusing, then refer to Chapter 1 for clarification.)

Look at the three key points for understanding what relative pronouns are all about:

- ✔ **In German, you must use a relative pronoun to connect the two clauses.** In English, you don't always have to. For example: **Ist das der Mann, den du liebst?** (*Is that the man [whom, that] you love?*). In this sentence, the main clause is followed by the relative clause, **den du liebst.** The second **den** is the relative pronoun connecting the two parts of the sentence.

- ✔ **You place a comma between the main clause and the relative clause.** In English, people usually include this comma only before the relative pronoun *which.* Remember that the relative clause begins with the relative pronoun. For example: **Bestellen wir die Pizza, die wir meistens essen** (*Let's order the pizza that we usually eat*). No comma needed in English, but you do have a comma separating the main clause **Bestellen wir die Pizza** from the relative clause **die wir meistens essen,** which begins with the relative pronoun **die.**

- ✔ **Word order comes into play in relative clauses.** You push the conjugated verb to the end of the clause. For example: **Gestern habe ich eine gute Freundin getroffen, die ich seit Jahren nicht gesehen habe** (*Yesterday I met a good [female] friend whom I haven't seen for years*). In the relative clause **die ich seit Jahren nicht gesehen habe,** the verb has two parts, **gesehen,** the past participle, and **habe,** which is the conjugated part of the verb. **Habe** is the last word in the sentence. (For in-depth information on the present perfect verb tense, go to Chapter 16.)

Table 2-7 shows the breakdown of the relative pronouns (*who, whom, whose, that*) by gender and case.

Table 2-7	Relative Pronouns			
Gender/Number of the Noun Being Replaced	*Nominative Case*	*Accusative Case*	*Dative Case*	*Genitive Case*
Masculine (m.)	der	den	dem	dessen
Feminine (f.)	die	die	der	deren
Neuter (n.)	das	das	dem	dessen
Plural (pl.)	die	die	denen	deren

For this relative pronoun exercise, correct the mistakes in the sentences. You have only one mistake in each sentence. Here are three types of errors to look for:

- ✔ The wrong relative pronoun — think about gender and case

- ✔ No comma or a comma in the wrong place

- ✔ Wrong word order for verb(s) in the relative clause

Take your time as you hunt for the mistake. Check out Table 2-7. If you lose patience, just guess. You find an explanation for the mistakes in the Answer Key.

Q. Sie sind die Kinder, den so viel Lärm machen.

A. Sie sind die Kinder, **die** so viel Lärm machen. (*They're the children who are making so much noise.*) The correct relative pronoun is **die** because you need the plural nominative form; it refers to the plural **die Kinder,** and it functions as the subject (nominative case) of the relative clause.

25. Hast du eine Hose, die passt besser? _____

26. Ich kenne den Supermarkt, der du meinst. _____

27. Ist das die Frau, die arbeitet bei der Polizei? _____

28. Wie gefällt dir das Hemd, die ich anhabe? _____

29. Du hast die CDs die mir gehören. _____

30. Italien ist das Land das ich besuchen möchte. _____

Demonstrating demonstrative pronouns

You use a *demonstrative pronoun* when you want to emphasize or point out the pronoun that's replacing a noun. Besides the demonstrative pronouns *he, it, they,* and so on, which are the translations (in parentheses) that you see in Table 2-8, you can also translate these pronouns with the demonstratives *this, that, these,* or *those.* Similar to English, the demonstrative pronoun generally comes at the beginning of a phrase. You use demonstrative pronouns in the nominative case to emphasize the subject or in the accusative case to emphasize the object.

There's only a single difference between the nominative case and the accusative case, and that's with the masculine pronouns. **Der** is the nominative, and **den** is the accusative case. With the exception of the accusative **den,** you need to know only the gender of the noun that you're replacing — or whether it's plural — and then use that form of the demonstrative pronoun.

Table 2-8	Demonstrative Pronouns	
Gender/Number of the Noun Being Replaced	*Case (for Subjects and Predicate Nouns)*	*Accusative Case (for Direct Objects)*
Masculine (m.)	**der** (*he/it*)	**den** (*him/it*)
Feminine (f.)	**die** (*she/it*)	**die** (*her/it*)
Neuter (n.)	**das** (*it*)	**das** (*it*)
Plural (pl.)	**die** (*they*)	**die** (*them*)

The words in bold are the nouns and the demonstrative pronouns that are standing in for the noun to show emphasis:

> ✔ Ist **der Flug** ausgebucht? (*Is the flight completely booked?*) **Der Flug** is a masculine singular noun.
>
> Ja, **der** ist voll. (*Yes, it's full.*) **Der** is the subject of the sentence, so it's in the nominative case, and it replaces **der Flug,** which is masculine singular. **Der** is the masculine singular demonstrative pronoun in the nominative case.
>
> ✔ Wie findest du **die Trauben**? (*How do you like the grapes?*) **Die Trauben** is plural.
>
> **Die** finde ich herrlich! (*I think they're terrific!*) **Die** is the direct object of the sentence, so it's accusative. **Die** pinch hits for **die Trauben,** which is plural, so you use the plural accusative demonstrative pronoun, **die.**

In the following exercise, decide which demonstrative pronoun is missing and write it in the space provided. You need to determine whether the pronoun is replacing the subject or the object in the sentence and which gender it takes.

Q. Ist die Straße relativ ruhig? Ja, _____ ist absolut ruhig.

A. Ist die Straße relativ ruhig? Ja, **die** ist absolut ruhig. (*Is the street relatively quiet? Yes, it's absolutely quiet.*) **Die Straße** is a feminine singular noun. In the second sentence, **die** is the subject (nominative case) that replaces **die Straße,** a feminine singular noun, so you use **die,** the feminine singular nominative case demonstrative pronoun.

31. Kaufst du den Kuchen für das Geburtstagsfest? Nein, _____ backe ich heute Nachmittag.

32. Ist das Fahrrad da drüben kaputt? Nein, _____ ist in Ordnung.

33. Kennen Sie diese Frauen? Ja, _____ kenne ich sehr gut.

34. Wie findest du den Film? _____ finde ich ganz schlecht.

35. Sind die Pferde freundlich? Ja, _____ sind freundlich.

36. Ist Frau Lachner im Büro? Nein, _____ ist im Urlaub.

Answer Key

1. **Das Klavier** ist brandneu. (*The piano is brand new.*)

2. Haben **die zwei Studentinnen** einen Nebenjob? (*Do the two students have a side job/part time job?*)

3. **Die Hotels** in der Stadtmitte sind laut. (*The hotels in the middle of the city are loud.*)

4. Siehst du? **Die Katze** sitzt auf deinem Auto. (*Do you see? The cat is sitting on your car.*)

5. Ist das **eine Scheune** oder ein Haus? (*Is that a barn or a house?*)

6. Können **die Jungen** gut Fußball spielen? (*Can the boys play soccer well?*)

7. **Das Pferd** ist zu jung zu reiten. (*The horse is too young to ride.*)

8. **Computer** sind heutzutage relativ billig. (*Computers are relatively cheap these days.*)

9. Brauchst du **den Kuli?** (*Do you need the pen?*)

10. Ich möchte **das Auto** kaufen. (*I'd like to buy the car.*)

11. Was kostet **die Lampe**? (*What/how much does the lamp cost?*)

12. **Das Radio** läuft nicht sehr gut. (*The radio doesn't work very well.*)

13. Das ist **der Freund** meiner Schwester. (*That's my sister's friend.*)

14. Ich schreibe **der Firma** einen Brief. (*I'm writing the company a letter.*)

15. **Die Leute** sind sehr freundlich. (*The people are very friendly.*)

16. **Den Film** finde ich sehr lustig. (*I find the film very funny/I think the film's very funny.*)

17. Ich glaube, **ihr** arbeitet zu viel. (*I think you work too much.*)

18. Nein, **wir** arbeiten nicht genug. (*No, we don't work enough.*)

19. Spielst **du** gern Karten? (*Do you like to play cards?*)

20. Ja, **ich** spiele gern Poker. (*Yes, I like to play poker.*)

21. Kennst du **ihn**? (*Do you know him?*)

22. Ich gehe ohne **euch** in die Stadt. (*I'm going downtown without you.*)

23. Wirklich? Ich dachte, du gehst mit **uns**. (*Really? I thought you were going with us.*)

24. Wie gefällt **Ihnen** der neue Bürgermeister? (*How do you like the new mayor?*)

25. Hast du eine Hose, die besser **passt**? (*Do you have a pair of pants that fits better?*) Watch out for word order. If you translate in your head word for word, you may fall into the trap of thinking

that the sentence looks okay. However, the verb (**passt**) needs to be at the end of the sentence, even though in English, you usually place the adverb (**besser**) after the verb you're describing.

26 Ich kenne den Supermarkt, **den** du meinst. (*I know the supermarket you mean/are talking about.*) You need **den** as the pronoun in the accusative because you're talking about a masculine noun, **der Supermarkt,** and **den** is the direct object of the verb **meinen** (here: **meinst**), which is in the relative clause **den du meinst.**

27 Ist das die Frau, die bei der Polizei **arbeitet**? (*Is that the woman who works for the police?*) The word order is incorrect because the verb **arbeitet** needs to be at the end of the relative clause.

28 Wie gefällt dir das Hemd, **das** ich anhabe? (*How do you like the shirt [that] I'm wearing?*) I promise not to lay too many traps. You need **das** because it replaces a neuter noun (**das Hemd**) and it refers to the direct object [accusative case] of **anhaben** in the relative clause.

29 Du hast die CDs, die mir gehören. (*You have the CDs that belong to me.*) Mind your commas. Even though English doesn't need a comma between **CDs** and **die,** German does.

30 Italien ist das Land, das ich besuchen möchte. (*Italy is the country [that] I'd like to visit.*) Once again, the comma is missing. However, in English, you don't even need the word *that* in the relative clause.

31 Kaufst du den Kuchen für das Geburtstagsfest? Nein, **den** backe ich heute Nachmittag. (*Are you buying the cake for the birthday party? No, I'm baking it this afternoon.*) **Der Kuchen** is masculine singular. In the second sentence, **den** is the object of the sentence, so it's accusative; it refers to a masculine singular noun, **der Kuchen.** You need **den,** the masculine singular accusative demonstrative pronoun.

32 Ist das Fahrrad da drüben kaputt? Nein, **das** ist in Ordnung. (*Is that bicycle over there broken? No, it's [working] all right.*) **Das Fahrrad** is neuter and singular. In the second sentence, **das** is the subject, so it's nominative. It replaces **das Fahrrad,** a neuter singular noun. You need **das,** the neuter singular nominative demonstrative pronoun.

33 Kennen Sie diese Frauen? Ja, **die** kenne ich sehr gut. (*Do you know these women? Yes, I know them well.*) **Diese Frauen** is plural. In the second sentence, **die** is the direct object, so it's accusative. **Die** pinch hits for **die Frauen,** which is plural, so you use the plural accusative demonstrative pronoun **die.**

34 Wie findest du den Film? **Den** finde ich ganz schlecht. (*What do you think of the film? I think it's really bad.*) **Der Film** is masculine singular. In the second sentence, **den** is the object, in accusative case, and it punts for a masculine singular noun, **der Film.** You need the masculine singular accusative demonstrative pronoun **den.**

35 Sind die Pferde freundlich? Ja, **die** sind freundlich. (*Are the horses friendly? Yes, they're friendly.*) **Die Pferde** is plural. In the second sentence, **die** is the subject, so it's nominative. **Die** pinch hits for **die Pferde,** which is plural, so you use the plural nominative demonstrative pronoun **die.**

36 Ist Frau Lachner im Büro? Nein, **die** ist im Urlaub. (*Is Frau Lachner in the office? No, she's on vacation.*) **Frau Lachner** is feminine. In the second sentence, **die** is the subject, so it's nominative, and it's the placeholder for **Frau Lachner,** which is feminine singular. You use **die,** the feminine singular demonstrative pronoun in the nominative case.

Chapter 3

Laying the Foundations of German

● ●

In This Chapter

▶ Using ordinal and cardinal numbers

▶ Discussing dates

▶ Telling time

▶ Talking about countries, citizens, and languages

● ●

In German-speaking countries, I love seeing **die Bedienung** (*the server*) in street cafés walking around with a bulging black leather change purse either tucked in the back of the pants (the male version) or attached at the waist in front, neatly camouflaged under a starched white apron (the female version). When you say **die Rechnung, bitte,** or its more informal version, **Zahlen, bitte** (*the check, please*), they have a crafty way of whipping it out of hiding and opening it wide, ready for action. The next part is my favorite: watching the seasoned **Kellner** (*waiter*) take a quick look, add up the tab without pen and paper, and blurt out, **"Das macht siebenundzwanzig Euro"** (*That'll be twenty-seven euros*). That's the moment of reckoning: How good are you at understanding numbers in German?

In this chapter, you work with basic building blocks: numbers, dates, time, countries, and nationalities. Feeling confident that you can use these elements without any hesitation means you're ready to feed the waiter's portable cash wallet. You can likewise understand which **Bahnsteig** (*track*) the train is leaving from (and at what time) and jump on the correct train when there's been a last-minute track change.

Doing the Numbers

Forming and using German **Zahlen** (*numbers*) isn't difficult. In fact, barring a few exceptions — notably the one I call the cart-before-the-horse — most numbers follow a logical pattern. This section covers cardinal and ordinal numbers as well as a few other number situations so you can write and speak numbers in German without any problems.

Counting off with cardinal numbers

Cardinal numbers have nothing to do with religious numbers colored red or a songbird that can sing numbers. These numbers are just plain, unadulterated numbers like 25, 654, or 300,000. In this section, you get a list of cardinal numbers, details on differences, and practice using these numbers.

Table 3-1 shows numbers 1–29. Notice a couple of points about numbers 21 and up:

- They're written as one word: **einundzwanzig** (*21*), **zweiundzwanzig** (*22*).

- They follow the cart-before-the-horse rule — that is, you say the ones digit before the tens digit, linking the words with **und**: for example, **vierundzwanzig** (*24; Literally: four and twenty*). Does that remind you of the "four and twenty blackbirds" from the nursery rhyme "Sing a Song of Sixpence"?

Table 3-1	Cardinal Numbers 1–29	
Numbers 0–9	*Numbers 10–19*	*Numbers 20–29*
0 **null**	10 **zehn**	20 **zwanzig**
1 **eins**	11 **elf**	21 **einundzwanzig**
2 **zwei**	12 **zwölf**	22 **zweiundzwanzig**
3 **drei**	13 **dreizehn**	23 **dreiundzwanzig**
4 **vier**	14 **vierzehn**	24 **vierundzwanzig**
5 **fünf**	15 **fünfzehn**	25 **fünfundzwanzig**
6 **sechs**	16 **sechzehn**	26 **sechsundzwanzig**
7 **sieben**	17 **siebzehn**	27 **siebenundzwanzig**
8 **acht**	18 **achtzehn**	28 **achtundzwanzig**
9 **neun**	19 **neunzehn**	29 **neunundzwanzig**

In spoken German, people commonly use **zwo** instead of **zwei.** This avoids the confusion — acoustically speaking — with **drei.** To double-check that you heard **zwei** and not **drei** in credit card numbers, prices, telephone numbers, room numbers, and so on, simply ask, or repeat the number(s) using **zwo.** Say, for example, **Ich wieder-hole vier-zwo-acht** (*I'll repeat four-two-eight*). If you're still not sure of the numbers even after repeating them back to the speaker, try the failsafe route — ask for them via e-mail: **E-mailen Sie mir bitte diese Zahlen/ihre Telefonnummer** (*Please e-mail me these numbers/your telephone number*). In writing, the number *two* is always **zwei.**

Table 3-2 shows representative numbers spanning 30–999. Double-digit numbers follow the same pattern as 20–29 do in Table 3-1: **einunddreißig** (31; literally: *one and thirty*), **zweiunddreißig** (32; literally: *two and thirty*), and the like. Numbers with more digits likewise flip the ones and tens digits: For instance, you'd read 384 as **drei-hundertvierundachtzig,** which literally means *three hundred four and eighty.*

Note that 30, unlike the other multiples of ten (40, 50, and so on) is spelled slightly differently. **Dreißig** has no **z** in its ending, whereas the other double-digits do (**vierzig, fünfzig,** and so on). This spelling difference affects pronunciation. **Dreißig** has an *s* sound, and **vierzig** has a *ts* sound in the ending.

Table 3-2	Cardinal Numbers 30–999	
Numbers 30–100	*Numbers 101–114*	*Numbers 220–999*
30 **dreißig**	101 **hunderteins**	220 **zweihundertzwanzig**
40 **vierzig**	102 **hundertzwei**	348 **dreihundertachtundvierzig**
50 **fünfzig**	103 **hundertdrei**	452 **vierhundertzweiundfünfzig**
60 **sechzig**	104 **hundertvier**	573 **fünfhundertdreiundsiebzig**
70 **siebzig**	111 **hundertelf**	641 **sechshunderteinundvierzig**
80 **achtzig**	112 **hundertzwölf**	767 **siebenhundertsiebenundsechzig**
90 **neunzig**	113 **hundertdreizehn**	850 **achthundertfünfzig**
100 **hundert**	114 **hundertvierzehn**	999 **neunhundertneunundneuzig**

In German, people often say telephone numbers in double digits, so that's when you need to be super careful to get the sequence right as you write the number. The number 76 20 93 88 would be **sechsundsiebzig, zwanzig, dreiundneunzig, achtundachtzig** (*six and seventy, twenty, three and ninety, eight and eighty*). You may find it easier to write the second digit first like this: You hear **fünfundvierzig,** so you write 5 (**fünf**), leaving room in front of the digit (_5). Then write the 4 (**und vierzig** [*and forty*]) in the tens place (4̱5). German native speakers don't do this, however, in case you were wondering!

Especially in spoken German, you can use **einhundert** (*one hundred*) instead of **hundert** (*hundred*). This makes the number clearer to the listener.

When referring to currency, you can talk about the bills like this: Imagine you're cashing 400€ in traveler's checks and you want three 100€ bills and five 20€ bills. You say **Ich möchte drei Hunderter und fünf Zwanziger** (*I'd like three hundreds [euro bills] and five twenties*). The numbers **Hunderter** and **Zwanziger** are nouns, and you form them like this: Take the number, for example **hundert,** and add **-er** to the end of the number: **hundert + -er = Hunderter.**

For numbers higher than 999, look at Table 3-3. Notice that the decimal point in German numbers represents the comma in English (see the "Other number-related info" section later in this chapter).

Table 3-3	Numbers over 999	
English Numerals	*German Numerals*	*Numbers Written in German*
1,000	**1.000**	**tausend** or **ein tausend**
1,000,000	**1.000.000**	**Million** or **eine Milllion**
1,650,000	**1.650.000**	**eine Million sechshundertfünzigtausend**
2,000,000	**2.000.000**	**zwei Millionen**
1,000,000,000	**1.000.000.000**	**eine Milliarde**
2,000,000,000	**2.000.000.000**	**zwei Milliarden**

In English, you use a comma to indicate thousands and a period to show decimals. German (and many other languages) does the reverse: It uses a period (**Punkt**) for indicating thousands, and the comma (**Komma**) works as a decimal point. Look at these examples:

English	*Deutsch*
1 inch = 2.54 centimeters	**1 Zentimeter** (*centimeters*) **= 0,39 Zoll** (*inches*)
	0,39 is read as **null Komma drei neun**
Mount Everest is 29,029 feet high.	**Mount Everest ist 8.848 Meter hoch.**
	8.848 is read as **achttausendachthunder-tachtundvierzig**

You're hearing numbers on the phone, and you have to write them down. Write each number in numerical form the German way, remembering that the comma and decimal point are switched in German.

Q. zweiundneunzig _____

A. 92

1. siebenundvierzig _____

2. achthundertdreiundsiebzig _____

3. eintausenddreihunderteinundsiebzig _____

4. vierzehn Komma fünf _____

5. zwanzigtausendzweihundertneunundsechzig _____

6. siebzehntausendneunhundertachtunddreißig _____

7. vierundachtzigtausendzweihundertsieben _____

Getting in line with ordinal numbers

Ordinal numbers are the kinds of numbers that show what order things come in. (Was that a duh moment for you?) You need ordinal numbers when you're talking about **das Datum** (*the date*), **die Feiertage** (*the holidays*), **die Stockwerke in einem Hotel** (*the floors in a hotel*), and stuff like that.

Ordinal numbers function as adjectives, so they have the adjective endings you normally use in a sentence. (Go to Chapter 13 for specifics on adjectives.) The general rule for forming ordinal numbers is to add **-te** to the numbers 1 through 19 and then **-ste** to the numbers 20 and above. For example, **Nach der achten Tasse Kaffee, ist er am Schreibtisch eingeschlafen** (*After the eighth cup of coffee, he fell asleep on the desk*).

This rule has three exceptions: **erste** (*first*); **dritte** (*third*); and **siebte** (*seventh*). For example, **Reinhold Messner war der erste Mensch, der Mount Everest ohne Sauerstoffmaske bestieg** (*Reinhold Messner was the first person to climb Mt. Everest without an oxygen mask*).

Here are two other adjectives you need to know when putting things in order: **letzte** (*last*) and **nächste** (*next*). You can use them to refer to a sequence of numbers, people, things, or the like:

> **Könnten Sie bitte die letzte Nummer wiederholen?** (*Could you repeat the last number please?*)

> **2006 wurde Bruno, der letzte wildlebende Bär in Deutschland, erschossen.** (*In 2006, Bruno, the last wild bear in Germany, was shot.*)

In order to write dates as numerals, write the digit followed by a period: **Der 1. Mai ist ein Feiertag in Deutschland** (*May 1st is a holiday in Germany*). If you say the same sentence, it's **Der erste Mai ist ein Feiertag in Deutschland.**

Look at the examples of ordinal numbers in Table 3-4. The first column shows the ordinal numbers as digits, the second column shows the same ordinal numbers as words, and the third column shows how to say *on the (fifth floor, sixth of December, and so on).*

Note: In Table 3-4, you see how to formulate the expression *on the (first)*. It's **am** + *ordinal number* + **en. Am** is the contraction of **an** (*on*) + **dem** (*the*); it's formed by taking the preposition **an,** which uses the dative case here plus **dem,** the masculine dative of **der.** You need to show dative case agreement with the adjective **erste,** so you add **-n: erste** + **n** = **ersten.** (See Chapter 15 for more on prepositions.)

Table 3-4	Ordinal Numbers	
Ordinals as Numerals	*Ordinals as Words*	*On the (First . . .)*
1st	**der erste** (*the first*)	**am ersten** (*on the first*)
2nd	**der zweite** (*the second*)	**am zweiten** (*on the second*)
3rd	**der dritte** (*the third*)	**am dritten** (*on the third*)
4th	**der vierte** (*the fourth*)	**am vierten** (*on the fourth*)
5th	**der fünfte** (*the fifth*)	**am fünften** (*on the fifth*)
6th	**der sechste** (*the sixth*)	**am sechsten** (*on the sixth*)
7th	**der siebte** (*the seventh*)	**am siebten** (*on the seventh*)
18th	**der achtzehnte** (*the eighteenth*)	**am achtzehnten** (*on the eighteenth*)
22nd	**der zweiundzwanzigste** (*the twenty-second*)	**am zweiundzwanzigsten** (*on the twenty-second*)

Was Ist das Datum? Expressing Dates

To make sure you know how to express dates correctly, you need to know how to correctly use **die Tage der Woche** (*the days of the week*), **die Jahreszeiten** (*the seasons*), and **die Monate** (*the months*) in your writing and speech. That way, you can clearly and correctly ask and answer **Was ist das Datum?** (*What is the date?*).

Die Tage der Woche (*the days of the week*), their short forms used in calendars, and some pertinent notes are as follows:

- **Montag (Mo)** (*Monday*)
- **Dienstag (Di)** (*Tuesday*)
- **Mittwoch (Mi)** (*Wednesday*)
- **Donnerstag (Do)** (*Thursday*)
- **Freitag (Fr)** (*Friday*)
- **Samstag (Sa)** (*Saturday;* used in most of Germany, as well as Austria and German-speaking Switzerland) or **Sonnabend (Sa)** (*Saturday;* used in eastern and northern Germany)
- **Sonntag (So)** (*Sunday*)

Note: In German-speaking countries, calendars begin with **Montag.**

You also need to have a firm grasp of the seasons and months when writing and speaking German because they're major parts of dates. (The last thing you want to do is invite someone to your July barbeque and tell them it's in the winter.) The following outlines **die Jahreszeiten** (*the seasons*):

- **der Frühling** or **das Frühjahr** (*the spring*); you can use either term interchangeably in German speaking regions
- **der Sommer** (*the summer*)
- **der Herbst** (*the autumn*)
- **der Winter** (*the winter*)

The following list lays out **die Monate** (*the months*) of the year:

- **Januar** (*January*) or **Jenner** (*January;* often used in Austria)
- **Februar** (*February*)
- **März** (*March*)
- **April** (*April*)
- **Mai** (*May*)
- **Juni** (*June;* some German speakers say **Juno** to distinguish it, acoustically speaking, from **Juli**)
- **Juli** (*July;* some German speakers pronounce it as "you *lie*" instead of "*ju* lee" to avoid confusion with **Juni**)
- **August** (*August*)
- **September** (*September*)

✔ **Oktober** (*October*)

✔ **November** (*November*)

✔ **Dezember** (*December*)

When you refer to each day of the week, season, and month, remember that they're all masculine (**der**), except for **das Frühjahr.** When speaking or writing days of the week and months, you generally leave out the article **der.** However, some combinations with the dative prepositions **an** (*on*) and **in** (*in*) do include **der** in its dative form (see Chapter 15 for more on prepositions). Also, seasons use the definite article. Take a look at the examples, two of which include **an** and **in** with the article **der:**

> **Gestern war Dienstag, heute ist Mittwoch, und morgen ist Donnerstag.** (*Yesterday was Tuesday, today is Wednesday, and tomorrow is Thursday.*) The article **der** isn't used; you're referring to the name of the day of the week.

> **Am kommenden Freitag fahre ich nach Flensburg.** (*I'm driving to Flensburg this coming Friday.*) **An + dem = am; an** is a dative preposition, and **dem** is the dative masculine article derived from **der.** (The phrase **am kommenden Freitag** describes the specific Friday; Literally: *on this coming Friday.*)

> **Im Frühling gibt es viele Feiertage in Deutschland.** (*In [the] spring there are a lot of holidays in Germany.*) **In + dem = im; in** is a dative preposition, and **dem** is the dative masculine article.

> **Warum trägst du Sommerkleidung bei herbstlichen Temperaturen?** (*Why are you wearing summer clothes during fall-like temperatures?*) **Bei** is a dative preposition, so to form the dative plural ending to the adjective **herbstlich,** you add **-en.** *Note:* **Sommerkleidung** is a combination of two nouns. Because the last word of any noun combination determines the gender, you have **der Sommer + die Kleidung = die Sommerkleidung.** In the prepositional phrase **bei herbstlichen Temperaturen,** the preposition **bei** takes the dative case, so the adjective **herbstlichen** is in the dative plural.

Dates are written in the order of day-month-year in German (and in the other European languages as well), such as **Die Berliner Mauer ist am 09.11.1989 gefallen** (*The Berlin Wall fell on 11/09/1989,* or *The Berlin Wall fell on November 9, 1989*). You need the periods in dates in German, just as you need to write the date in English with a slash between the month, day, and year. If you said the date with ordinal numbers, it'd be like this: **Die Berliner Mauer ist am neunten elften neunzehnhundertneunundachtzig gefallen.** Alternatively, you could say, . . . **am neunten November.**

Fill in the missing information shown in English in parentheses. Write the numbers as words, remembering to include **am** (*on the*) if necessary. (For more info on numbers, see "Doing the Numbers," earlier in this chapter.)

0. Er hat Geburtstag _____. (*on February 29th*)

A. Er hat Geburtstag **am neunundzwanzigsten Februar.** (*It's his birthday on February 29th.*)

8. Morgen ist _____. (*Saturday*)

9. _____. ist meine Lieblingsjahreszeit. (*spring*)

10. Nikolaustag ist _____. (*on December 6th*)

11. Haben Sie _____ gesagt? (*March*)

12. Wir fliegen am kommenden _____ nach
    Mallorca. (*this [coming] Sunday*)

On the Clock: Expressing Time

You're in **Interlaken (in der Schweiz)** (*Interlaken, Switzerland*) and you want to know what time it is. You have four choices: Look at your own watch; look at the nearest clock tower (most are absolutely stunning — many have four clocks, one for each side) and find out how accurate the Swiss are in keeping time (very!); buy a Rolex for 1,399 Swiss francs (no euros in Switzerland); or practice understanding German clock time by asking someone on the street, **Wie viel Uhr ist es?** (*What time is it?*). You're just about guaranteed he or she will tell you the precise time.

In conversational German, you use the system comparable to English, in which **nach** (*past*) refers to times past the hour up until half past. **Vor** (*to*) refers to the times from half past to the next hour.

You use **Halb** (Literally: *half*) to refer to half past the hour. However, in German, you name the next hour; for example, **halb acht** (Literally: *half eight*) means *half past seven*, or 7:30.

For official time, such as train or plane schedules (and frequently in everyday German), you use the 24-hour system, reading the numbers as you'd read a digital clock. In other words, for 1 p.m. and later, you add 12; 2 p.m. + 12 is therefore **14 Uhr: Unser Zug fährt um 14.45 Uhr** (pronounced **vierzehn Uhr fünfundvierzig**) (*Our train leaves at 2:45 p.m.*). Table 3-5 shows the German time expressions and their English equivalents.

Table 3-5		Expressing Time	
German (Conversational Language)	*English Equivalent*	*German (Official Time)*	*English Equivalent*
drei (Uhr)	*three (o'clock)*	**drei (Uhr)**	*three (o'clock)*
zehn (Minuten) nach drei	*ten (minutes) past three*	**drei Uhr zehn**	*three ten*
Viertel nach drei	*quarter past three*	**drei Uhr fünfzehn**	*three fifteen*
fünf (Minuten) vor halb vier	*no equivalent; Literally: five minutes before half four*	**drei Uhr fünfundzwanzig**	*three twenty-five*
halb vier	*half past three*	**drei Uhr dreißig**	*three thirty*
fünf (Minuten) nach halb vier	*no equivalent; Literally: five minutes past half four*	**drei Uhr fünfunddreißig**	*three thirty-five*
Viertel vor vier	*quarter to four*	**drei Uhr**	*three forty-five*

		fünfundvierzig	
German (Conversational Language)	**English Equivalent**	**German (Official Time)**	**English Equivalent**
zehn vor vier	*ten to four*	**drei Uhr fünfzig**	*three fifty*
vier (Uhr)	*four (o'clock)*	**vier (Uhr)**	*four (o'clock)*

Note: You say **es ist ein Uhr** (*it's one o'clock*) the same way as in English, but you say **es ist eins** (*it's one*) when you leave out the word **Uhr.** All other clock times are the same number with or without the word **Uhr,** as seen in Table 3-5.

The numerical method of telling time may be the easiest. German traditionally uses a period where English uses a colon. Note that when you read the time, you say **Uhr** (*o'clock*) where the period appears. Alternatively, you can leave it out, just as you can leave out the *o'clock* in English. For example, **Um wie viel Uhr kommst du? Um sechs oder um sieben?** (*What time are you coming? At six or at seven?*). Note also that the use of **Uhr** in the question means the word *time* in English. You can also say **Die Bank öffnet um 8.30 Uhr** (pronounced **acht Uhr dreißig**) (*The bank opens at 8:30 a.m.*).

Read the times given in words in the sentences that follow, and write the correct time, German style (using the 24-hour system) as numerals. To help you out, some examples have two German alternatives for the time given. Then write the English translation of the sentence.

0. Der Flug 629 landet um _____. (einundwanzig Uhr fünfundzwanzig)

A. Der Flug 629 landet um **21.25 Uhr. (*Flight 629 lands at 9:25 p.m.*)**

13. Die Geschäfte schließen schon um _____. (sechzehn Uhr)

_____

14. Der erste Anruf kam um _____. (sieben Uhr fünfundvierzig/Viertel vor acht)

_____

15. Wir kommen um _____ in Dortmund an. (siebzehn Uhr zwanzig)

_____

16. Am Donnerstag spiele ich Tennis um _____. (vierzehn Uhr)

_____

17. Gestern Abend sind sie um _____ ins Bett gegangen. (ein Uhr dreißig/halb zwei)

_____

Naming Countries, Nationalities, and Languages

As the world appears to be shriveling up in size due to telecommunication, English seems to be relentlessly pushing its way into other languages. That may be true in some respects, but one area in which countries and nationalities are holding their own is that of place names. Each country has its own spelling, pronunciation, and even a different word altogether for one-and-the-same place. One of my favorites is Munich, the capital of **Bayern** (*Bavaria*). In German, it's called **München,** and it's world-famous for its **Oktoberfest** (no translation: think beer). So far, so good.

In **Frankreich** (*France*), Munich is pronounced the distinctive French way, with the stress on the last syllable (Mu *neek*). Yet the Italians call it *Monaco*, which can be really confusing if you've just come to Munich from the French Riviera (luckily, that's called the *Côte d'Azur* in French *and* German) and you've passed through a tiny country you thought was the home of the Grimaldi dynasty and not the home of the **Oktoberfest.** The point is that place names often change between languages; for example, one of the largest lakes nestled in the Alps, Lake Constance, is called **Bodensee** (Literally: *ground/bottom lake*) in German, although there is a town of **Konstanz** situated on **Bodensee.**

Take heart! In this section, I get you off the ground with a simplified bird's-eye view of names in German. You have an overview of the German names for countries, nationalities, languages, and some regions that are relevant to German-speaking Europeans, both geographically and economically. As you go through this section, imagine you're traveling through Europe. By the end, you should understand a lot about which places German speakers are referring to.

When traveling in Europe, looking at maps is likely to be very confusing when you're not aware of what a place is called in English, let alone how it's named in other languages. Using maps that have both English and the place names in their own language is a huge help when you're not familiar with different spellings of place names.

Eyeing German-speaking countries

Deutschsprachige Länder (*German-speaking countries*) are mostly located in the center of western Europe. In the countries in Table 3-6, German is the dominant language. You see the English and German names, nationalities, and adjectives.

Table 3-6	German-Speaking Countries		
Country Name in English (Country)	*Country Name in German (Land)*	*Nationality (Nationalität)*	*Adjective (Adjektiv)*
Germany	**Deutschland**	**der/die Deutsche**	**deutsch**
Austria	**Österreich**	**der/die Österreicher/-in**	**österreichisch**
Switzerland	**die Schweiz**	**der/die Schweizer/-in**	**schweizer(isch)**
Liechtenstein	**Liechtenstein**	**der/die Lichtensteiner/-in**	**lichtensteinisch**

In Table 3-7, German has an official status alongside another language or languages in that country. Some of the people in these places speak German.

Table 3-7	Other Countries That Speak German		
Country Name in English (Country)	**Country Name in German (Land)**	**Nationality (Nationalität)**	**Adjective (Adjektiv)**
Luxembourg	**Luxemburg**	**der/die Luxemburger/-in**	**luxemburgisch**
Italy (in South Tyrol, a region in the north of Italy bordering on Austria)	**Italien (Südtirol)**	**der/die Italiener/-in (Südtiroler/-in)**	**italienisch (südtirolisch)**
Belgium	**Belgien**	**der/die Belgier/-in**	**belgisch**

More than a million French in the region of Alsace speak a dialect of German. Large numbers of people still speak German in the countries under the influence of the former Soviet Union. And there are German-speaking people in Namibia, the former German Southwest Africa.

Grammatically speaking about countries, nationalities, and languages

When dealing with languages, terms for citizens, and adjectives of countries, use the standard rules for making sentences. Nouns and adjectives need to follow rules on gender (**der, die, das**), case (nominative, accusative, dative, and genitive), and number (singular or plural). (For these rules, see Chapter 2 for nouns and Chapter 12 for adjectives.) Notice that the adjectives aren't capitalized but names of languages are capitalized, as are terms for citizens because they're nouns.

> **BMW, Mercedes, und VW sind deutsche Autos.** (*BMW, Mercedes, and VW are German cars.*) The adjective **deutsche** is plural, in the nominative case.

> **Sie sprechen fließend Deutsch.** (*You speak fluent German.*) Here, **Deutsch** is the language, so it's capitalized.

For the most part, countries in German, such as **Kanada** (*Canada*) or **Mexiko** (*Mexico*), are neuter. You don't need **das** (*the*) if you want to say something like **Mein Schwager kommt aus Brasilien** (*My brother-in-law is from Brazil*). You need the article **das** only when an adjective comes in front of the name of the country, as in **Das grüne Grönland gibt es nicht** (*There is no green Greenland*).

A few countries have plural, feminine, or masculine gender. You need to know them because you always include the article when you name such countries:

- A few plurals are **die Vereinigten Staaten, die Philippinen,** and **die Niederlande** (*the United States, the Philippines,* and *the Netherlands*).

- A few countries with feminine gender are **die Schweiz, die Türkei,** and **die Ukraine** (*Switzerland, Turkey,* and *Ukraine*).

  ✔ Masculine-gender countries are usually Muslim countries: **der Irak** (*Iraq*) and **der Iran** (*Iran*).

TIP

As for the actual languages, remember that a language is a noun, so it's capitalized. To form the name of a language, you generally take the country name, add or subtract a few letters (mostly for pronunciation purposes), and put **-isch** onto the end: **Portugal → Portugiesisch** (*Portugal → Portugese*). Of course, there are a few oddballs like **Aseri,** spoken in Azerbaijan.

German neighbors and trading partners

Germany enjoys a solid reputation for its high quality of **Exportartikel** (*export goods*) and **Dienstleistungen** (*services*). With the introduction of the euro in 2002 and the recent expansion of the **Europäische Union** (*European Union*) to 27 members in 2007, Germany's major trading partners are still — for the most part — its European neighbors. Table 3-8 lists Germany's major trading partners in alphabetical order, showing the country name in English and German, the nationalities, and the adjective for that country.

Table 3-8	Major German Trading Partners		
Country	*Country (Land) in German*	*Nationality (Nationalität)*	*Adjective (Adjektiv)*
Belgium	**Belgien**	**der/die Belgier/-in**	**belgisch**
China	**China**	**der Chinese/die Chinesin**	**chinesisch**
France	**Frankreich**	**der Franzose/die Französin**	**französisch**
Great Britain	**Großbritannien**	**der Brite/die Britin**	**britisch**
Italy	**Italien**	**der/die Italiener/-in**	**italienisch**
the Netherlands	**die Niederlande** (plural)	**der/die Niederländer/-in**	**niederländisch**
Spain	**Spanien**	**der/die Spanier/in**	**spanisch**
the United States	**die Vereinigten Staaten** (plural)	**der/die Amerikaner/-in**	**amerikanisch**

PRACTICE

Read the following sentences and fill in the correct country, nationality, language, or adjective. Using the preceding information, together with the occasional help in parentheses, you should be able to come up with the correct solutions.

Q. Frankreich ist das Land, in dem man _____ spricht.

A. Frankreich das Land, in dem man **Französisch** spricht. (*France is the country where French is spoken.*)

18. Die "Union Jack" ist die _____ Flagge.

19. Südtirol ist eine Gegend in Italien, wo man _____ spricht.

20. Viele Produkte aus Plastik kommen aus _____. (**_Hint:_** This country has the largest population in the world.)

21. Sie kommt aus Spanien; sie ist _____.

22. In _____ spricht man Deutsch. (**_Hint:_** Its capital is Vienna.)

Answer Key

1 siebenundvierzig: **47**

2 achthundertdreiundsiebzig: **873**

3 eintausenddreihunderteinundsiebzig: **1.371**

4 vierzehn Komma fünf: **14,5**

5 zwanzigtausendzweihundertneunundsechzig: **20.269**

6 siebzehntausendneunhundertachtunddreißig: **17.938**

7 vierundachtzigtausendzweihundertsieben: **84.207**

8 Morgen ist **Sonnabend/Samstag**. (*Tomorrow is Saturday.*)

9 **Der Frühling** ist meine Lieblingsjahreszeit. (*Spring is my favorite season.*)

10 Nikolaustag ist **am sechsten Dezember**. (*St. Nicholas Day is on the sixth of December.*) Instead of getting a visit from Santa Claus on December 24, German children awaken on December 6 to find that St. Nikolaus has filled their shoes with small gifts and sweets (assuming good behavior, of course).

11 Haben Sie **März** gesagt? (*Did you say March?*)

12 Wir fliegen **am kommenden Sonntag** nach Mallorca. (*We're flying to Mallorca this coming Sunday.*)

13 Die Geschäfte schließen schon um **16 Uhr**. (*The stores close [already] at 4 p.m.*)

14 Der erste Anruf kam um **7.45 Uhr**. (*The first call came at 7:45 a.m.*)

15 Wir kommen um **17.20 Uhr** in Dortmund an. (*We're arriving in Dortmund at 5:20 p.m.*)

16 Am Donnerstag spiele ich Tennis um **14 Uhr**. (*I'm playing tennis at 2 p.m. on Thursday.*)

17 Gestern Abend sind sie um **1.30 Uhr** ins Bett gegangen. (*Last night they went to bed at 1:30 a.m.*)

18 Die "Union Jack" ist die **britische** Flagge. (*The Union Jack is the British flag.*)

19 Südtirol ist eine Gegend in Italien, wo man **Deutsch** spricht. (*South Tyrol is a region in Italy where German is spoken.*)

20 Viele Produkte aus Plastik kommen aus **China**. (*Many products made of plastic come from China.*)

21 Sie kommt aus Spanien; sie ist **Spanierin**. (*She's from Spain; she's Spanish.*)

22 In **Österreich** spricht man Deutsch. (*People speak German in Austria.*)

Chapter 4

Building Your Word Power

In This Chapter

▶ Picking out combination words

▶ Grasping word families and friends

▶ Understanding word structure

*U*nless you want to confine your conversations to things like *The girl is pretty, I'm hungry,* and *Do you speak English?* you probably want to develop your German vocabulary. Luckily, paying attention to how words are related to each other can boost your word power exponentially. As you discover how words are formed, you can categorize and store them in logical groups, such as word families, word categories, opposites, prefixes, and suffixes. You can also practice identifying *cognates* (words with a common source that mean the same thing in two languages), *near cognates* (words with a common source that mean nearly the same in two languages), and *false friends* (words that look the same but mean something different in two languages).

Even when you encounter a word you don't know, if you can identify something about that word, you may be able to figure out its meaning. For example, the word **das Reisefieber** has two easily recognizable parts, **Reise** (*travel*) and **Fieber** (*fever*); together they approximate the idea of *excitement about traveling*. This chapter takes a look at word structures specific to the German language, providing great opportunities for interesting word storage, among them compound nouns and picture language.

Working with Word Combinations

Word combinations are the kinds of words that have two or more parts, some of which may be separate words combined into one; others may be combinations of a prefix together with a noun, adjective, or verb. You find them frequently in both English and German, and in the case of German nouns, they can sometimes look daunting from the standpoint of sheer length, yet when you're familiar with one or more parts of the word, you can often piece the others together.

Your key to increasing your vocabulary beyond the basics is getting the hang of recognizing the separate parts that fit together to form word combinations. Before you know it, you'll be feeling comfortable with the likes of words like **das Außendienstverkaufspersonal** (*field sales force/personnel*) without thinking twice because you're able to figure out what the separate parts mean: **außen** = *external, outside,* **Dienst** = *service, employment,* **Verkauf** = *sales* (the verb **verkaufen** = *to sell,* **kaufen** = *to buy*), and **Personal** = *personnel, staff*. Each word element is useful as a separate word, so you're getting five words for the price, er, effort of one. This section takes a closer look at word combinations, including compound nouns, picture compound nouns, and verb combinations.

Spotting compound nouns

At times, German looks like a language made up of complicated, extremely long words. In fact, some people say it not only *sounds* heavy and ponderous but also *looks* heavy and ponderous. Most of these culprit words, called *compound words,* are really quite innocuous. After all, they're nothing more than a few smaller words strung together. German is rife with compound words that may or may not be two or more separate words in English: **Der Geschäftsmann** (*the businessman*) is one word in both languages, but **der Kugelschreiber** (*the ballpoint pen*) is two words in English.

Recognizing the parts of compound words is a great way to increase your vocabulary threefold, sometimes more, depending on how many words combine to form a single word. When you break down a long word into its parts, you can generally make a very accurate guess about what the compound means.

A *compound noun* is a combination of two or more words, usually both nouns. Some compound nouns are the exact equivalent of two words in English. For instance, **das Fotoalbum** (*photo album*) is a combination of **das Foto** (*photo*) + **das Album** (*album*). Others have a slightly different meaning when compared to their usage as separate words: **Der Ruhetag** (*closing day*) is **die Ruhe** (*quiet, calm*) + **der Tag** (*day*); **"Montag Ruhetag"** could be a sign outside a restaurant indicating that it's closed on Monday.

My personal favorites among the compound nouns are what I call *picture words*; they describe the meaning of the word in visual language that differs from the descriptions in English. I deal with picture words in the next section of this chapter.

There are a small number of changes in spelling in some compound words. The most common added letter you find is **s;** for example, it appears in the middle of **die Arbeitszeit** (*the working hours*), a combination of **die Arbeit** (*the work*) and **die Zeit** (*the time*). In the word **der Orangensaft** (*the orange juice*) the **n** added in the middle indicates the plural of **die Orange** (**die Orangen**). Sometimes a letter or two are dropped: **Das Fernsehprogramm** (*the TV program*) is comprised of **der Fernseher** or **das Fernsehen** (both mean *TV*) with the last two letters dropped (**-en** or **-er**) plus **das Programm.**

Compound nouns take the gender of the last word in the combination. Note that the following combination is feminine: **der Sport** (*sport*[s]) + **die Abteilung** (*department*) = **die Sportabteilung** (*sports department* in a department store).

> Wo sind meine **Tennisschuhe?** (*Where are my tennis shoes?*) **Die Tennisschuhe** = **das Tennis** (*Tennis*) + **die Schuhe** (*shoes*).
>
> Sie sind im **Wohnzimmer.** (*They're in the living room.*) **Das Wohnzimmer** = **wohnen** (*to live*) + **das Zimmer** (*room*).
>
> Was ist deine **Lieblingsspeise?** (*What's your favorite food?*) **Die Lieblingsspeise** = **Lieblings** (*favorite,* combined with other words) + **die Speise** (*food*).
>
> Ich liebe **Himbeereis.** (*I love raspberry ice cream.*) **Das Himbeereis** = **die Himbeere** (*raspberry*) + **das Eis** (*ice cream*).

There's no easy test to determine whether a word is in fact a compound noun. Just look at the word, try to see where it breaks down, figure out what the parts mean, and put it back together again, making a reasonable stab at the meaning of that compound word. You may recognize one part as the noun form of a verb you know, or you may see a prefix that you're familiar with. The context of the word in a sentence is usually a good means of making an educated guess. And good dictionaries are your best bet if you're still stumped.

Combine the words from the word bank with the words in the exercise to form compound nouns in the exercise. Include the definite article. Some words undergo a slight change. Then write the English definition of the word next to the compound noun.

_0._ der Rock _____.
_____.

_A._ **das Rockkonzert (_the rock concert_)**. The definite article is **das** because **das Konzert** is the last word in the combination.

~~das Konzert~~	das Eis	die Stadt	die Tasche	der Knödel	das Spiel
das Essen	die Zeit	das Zimmer	der Kasten	das Brot	

1. der Käse _____.
_____. (**_Hint:_** The Earl of . . . may have invented them.) Literally, it means _cheese bread_.

2. Haupt _____.
_____.

3. die Erdbeere _____.
_____.

4. der Brief _____.
_____. (**_Hint:_** You find letters in it.)

5. essen _____.
_____. (**_Hint:_** Look at the examples in this section)

6. der Computer _____.
_____.

7. das Jahr _____.
_____. (**_Hint:_** There are four every year. Add **-es** between the two words.)

8. die Kartoffel _____.
_____. (**_Hint:_** It's a southern German/Austrian specialty often served with **Schweinebraten** [_roast pork_].)

9. die Hand _____.
_____.

10. der Mittag _____.
_____.

Describing picture compound nouns

With most compound nouns, you can easily get the general idea of what they mean by putting the meanings of the two (or more) parts together to form one meaning. However, with picture compound words, meaning isn't exactly obvious at first glance. These nouns may be only single words in English or English words that appear to be descriptive, making it a challenge to figure out their meaning.

> **das Haus** (*house*) + **die Schuhe** (*shoes*) = **die Hausschuhe** (*slippers,* shoes you wear in the house)

The key to understanding the meaning of a picture compound word is using your imagination to think figuratively if the literal meaning doesn't make sense. Alternatively, try thinking (way) outside the box. For example, take the word **der Zahnstein**. It's made up of two reasonably common nouns, **Zahn** (*tooth*) and **Stein** (*stone*). So what in the world is a *tooth stone*? You may first conjure a picture of a stone that looks like a tooth. Good idea; close, but no cigar. Now imagine what it would look like to have stones, or stone-like material attached to a tooth. Does that sound like a possible description of *tartar*? That's it! **Zahnstein** is the reason the dental hygienist is always reprimanding you!

Read the hints in the following exercise; each hint is for the picture compound noun that follows. Try to translate words of the compound noun separately, and then guess the meaning of the compound word.

Q. (Ich gebrauche ihn mit einer Nadel und Faden.) der Fingerhut _____ + _____ = _____.

A. *finger* + *hat* = **thimble** (*I need it with a needle and thread.*)

11. (Ich brauche sie im Winter.) die Handschuhe _____ + _____ = _____.

12. (Ich brauche sie in der Nacht.) die Taschenlampe _____ + _____ = _____.

13. (Früher waren sie alle schwarz/weiß.) das Fernsehen _____ + _____ = _____.

14. (Damit kann ich gut schreiben.) der Kugelschreiber _____ + _____ = _____.

15. (Darin lese ich interessante Artikel.) die Zeitschrift _____ + _____ = _____.

16. (Ich trage ihn wenn ich ins Bett gehe.) der Schlafanzug _____ + _____ = _____.

Checking out verb combinations

Nouns aren't the only ones that can combine to form long words; verbs are guilty of the same habit. Figuring out the meaning of a verb combination is just as easy when you can break down the parts, which may be prefixes, prepositions, or verbs that combine with another verb.

How do you figure out the meaning of the verb? You need to break down the verb into its parts, try to figure out what each part means, and put it back together again. The following tips can help:

- ✔ **Try to recognize the discrete parts of the verb.** Look for prefixes or prepositions at the beginning of the word.

- ✔ **Find out what these prefixes or prepositions mean if you don't know already.** (Chapter 10 deals with separable- and inseparable-prefix verbs, Chapter 15 handles prepositions, and Chapter 11 includes a section on verbs and prepositions.)

    Some prefixes or prepositions have equivalents in English. Take the example of **vor:** It usually means *before*, and as far as pronunciation goes, it resembles the prefix *fore-* in words like *foreshadow* or *foresight*. With others, you may need to find out what they mean: **Zusammen** (*together*) doesn't resemble English, but it has the same number of syllables, so that may be a method of remembering its meaning.

Take the verb **regenerieren.** Break it down into **re- + gener- + -ieren.** The prefix **re-** has the same meaning in English (*to repeat an action*), and **-ieren** is a variation on the regular infinitive verb ending **-en;** it often means *-ate* or *-ify* in English. Putting the word together, you can make a correct guess that **regenerieren** means *to regenerate*.

> Ich möchte zum Hotel **zurückgehen.** (*I'd like to go back to the hotel.*) The prefix **zurück** means *back* or *return*, and the verb **gehen** is *to go* or *walk*.

> Die Familie **ist** zum Erntedankfest **zusammengekommen.** (*The family gathered together for Thanksgiving.*) The verb **zusammenkommen** is in present perfect tense; the prefix **zusammen** means *together*, and **kommen** means *to come*.

Furthermore, many nouns are derived from the verb combinations. Most have different endings. Look at these examples:

> The verb is **fortsetzen** (*to continue*); the noun is **die Fortsetzung** (*continuation, sequel*).

> The verb is **zubringen** (*to take to*); the noun is **der Zubringer** (*feeder*). **Ein Zubringerbus** is a *shuttle bus*.

Match the English definitions of the verbs with the given German verb. Look at the prefix/preposition/verb tables in Chapters 10 and 11 first, or try to make an educated guess. Refer to the English word bank; if you want to challenge yourself more, cover the list — now! Then write the English definition without looking.

Q. zusammenbrechen _____

A. **to collapse, break down**

~~to collapse, break down~~   to require, presume   to plan   to spend [money]

to leave, take off   to arrive   to be fond of   to assemble

to go for a drive

17. ankommen _____   21. spazierenfahren _____

18. abfahren _____   22. ausgeben _____

19. vorhaben _____   23. zusammensetzen _____

20. voraussetzen _____   24. liebhaben _____

Grasping Word Families and Word Categories

Memory works best when your brain can make lots of connections, so grouping German words in word families and word fields can help you remember vocab for the long term. This is good news because enhancing your vocabulary dramatically increases the ways you can express yourself.

When you come across a new verb, especially a frequently used verb, find out some other words related to it. Use a good German-English dictionary as a reference (see Chapter 1 for information on using a bilingual dictionary). You often find related words and expressions under the headword (main dictionary entry), especially if it's a frequently used verb. Scan for words in bold under that headword, and record new words in groups using the headword for reference. For example, under the headword **kommen** (*to come*), you find **ankommen** (*to arrive*), **herkommen** (*to come over*), **hervorkommen** (*to come out*, like the sun or blossoms), and a large number of expressions using **kommen;** for example, **Wie komme nach Wien?** (*How do I get to Vienna?*) or **auf etwas kommen** (*to think of something, to get into something*).

This section discusses how you can use word families and word categories to your advantage to strengthen your German vocabulary.

Working with word families

Picture a family seated around a bountiful table at Thanksgiving. Replace the family members with words, put the family elder(s) at the head of the table, and there you have it: a *word family*. It's made up of words that have the same root or origin. Some word families are very numerous, including ten or more nouns (descendants of the elders), a verb (family elder), adjectives, and maybe even an adverb that are all related. Some word families have an extended family: cousin words that have the same root but are words combined from other families.

Nouns and verbs in an English word family may be exactly the same or slightly differ-ent: *to heat* and *the heat, to live* and *the life.* German follows suit, but it puts an infini-tive ending, **-en,** on verbs: **arbeiten, die Arbeit.** Some English and German words have *suffixes* — endings to words. English adjective endings include *-able, -y,* and *-al,* as in *likeable, windy,* and *critical.* Some German adjective endings are **-lich, -ig,** and **-isch,** as in **lieblich** (*delightful,* or *sweet* as in wine), **windig** (*windy*), and **kritisch** (*critical*). (See Chapter 13 for more on adjectives.)

Consider, for example, the verb **arbeiten** (*to work*). It's pretty much the same as the noun **die Arbeit** (*the work*). Other words in the same family include **der Arbeiter** (*the worker*) and **die Arbeiterin** (*the female worker*). The extended family includes word combinations like **die Arbeiterschaft** (*the workforce*), **der Arbeitsablauf** (*the work-flow*), **arbeitswütig** (*workaholic* — an adjective in German), and so on.

Match the English definitions in the word bank to the German words in the exercise. Some hints are indicated in parentheses; *adj.* is the abbreviation for *adjective.* The root (family elder) is **arbeiten** (*to work*).

0. das Arbeitsamt _____

A. **the employment office; das Amt** means *the (public) office.*

the employment office	labor saving	the employer
the attitude to work	the employee	the working class
the place of work, workstation	the workroom	the unemployment compensation
jobless		

25. die Arbeiterklasse _____

26. der Arbeitgeber (**geben** = *to give*) _____

27. das Arbeitslosengeld _____

28. arbeitsparend (adj.) _____

29. arbeitslos (adj.) _____

30. der Arbeitnehmer (**nehmen** = *to take*) _____

31. der Arbeitsplatz _____

32. die Arbeitsmoral _____

33. der Arbeitsraum _____

Write each English translation from the word bank next to its German equivalent. Some hints are indicated in parentheses; *adj.* is the abbreviation for *adjective.* The root is **fahren** (*to drive, go*).

Q. die Fahrbahn (of traffic on a highway) _____

A. **the lane**

~~the lane~~	the direction of traffic	the exit
itinerant (for example, folk)	the ticket	the driving instructor
negligent, reckless	the passenger	the entrance
the schedule		

34. die Fahrkarte _____

35. die Einfahrt (here: to a highway) _____

36. der Fahrgast (**der Gast** = *the guest*) _____

37. die Fahrtrichtung _____

38. fahrend (adj.) _____

39. fahrlässig (adj.) _____

40. der Fahrlehrer _____

41. der Fahrplan _____

42. die Ausfahrt (here: from a highway) _____

Picture that! Working with word categories

Imagine a traditional family farm scene: succulent green fields with horses and cows grazing contently in them. Next to the fields is a pond with a few ducks and geese paddling around in it. Over by the barn is a cat on the prowl for mice hiding in the straw, and the farmer is climbing onto his tractor. So is this section about German farms? Not quite. It's about helping you organize words into logical categories or groups to make it easier to retrieve them at a later time. In the case of this scene, if you start with the category **der Bauernhof** (*the farm*), you'd include a list of farm animals and the words for *barn, farmer, tractor,* and so on.

To record new vocabulary in categories, use the techniques that work best with that category. For example, draw a picture of a farm scene and label it in as much detail as you can. You won't need to use any English translations at all. (Even if your rendition of a duck does look like a seagull, *you* know what it is.) The types of categories are practically limitless, and they can include wherever your interests in German lie.

The key to successful word storage is choosing the best means of organizing words. By organizing the words well, you usually don't need to translate them into English. You're now on the road to thinking in German. Select meaningful categories that correspond to any interests you have, personal or professional, sports or hobbies, intellectual or mundane — the sky's the limit. When you're motivated by such topics, you're bound to find it extremely easy and fun to find and store words in your area of interest.

Here are some great ways to store new words:

- ✔ **List related words in an order that's meaningful to you.** For instance, write the names of vegetables from best to worst tasting, or arrange colors from light to dark: white, beige, yellow, orange, red, and so on. Or tell a story — put words describing your morning routine in sequential order.

- ✔ **Write words in a way that reflects their meaning.** For instance, write color words in German in the color they represent.

- ✔ **Develop a "word fan" showing the spectrum of words in a range of description,** such as verbs of speed starting with **kriechen** (*to crawl*) on up to **laufen** (*to run*). Other categories of words that work well arranged in this fashion are adverbs of frequency, arranged from **niemals** (*never*) to **immer** (*always*), and a range of emotions, starting with **deprimiert** (*depressed*) on up to **entzückt** (*delighted*).

- ✔ **Describe how to do simple tasks or routines** like making coffee, hanging a picture on the wall, or getting ready to go to work, using as many verbs as possible.

- ✔ **Label words describing location where they belong on a picture or a map.** To remember prepositions like *over, under, beside,* and *in front of,* draw a picture of a living room, and write the word **über** (*above*) over the coffee table. Or draw an object, say a cat under the table, and write a sentence like **Die Katze ist unter dem Tisch** (*The cat's under the table*). Use a street map for labeling **links** (*left*), **rechts** (*right*), **an der Kreuzung** (*at the intersection*), and so on.

- ✔ **Make a web or chart to show how ideas relate.** For instance, if you're listing words related to air travel, write the word **der Flughafen** (*the airport*) in the middle. Then add several branches for word groups like **die Abfertigung** (*check-in*), **die Sicherheitskontrolle** (*security check*), **im Flugzeug** (*in the airplane*), and so on.

- ✔ **Create a diagram.** Sketch a computer and label the parts (most are the same in English and German). Remember to include the articles **der/die/das.**

- ✔ **For individual words within a group, draw a picture of that word and incorporate the word into the picture.** Nouns, adjectives, and even verbs lend themselves well to this storage method. Take, for example, **der Berg** (*the mountain*). Draw the outline of a mountain and fill it with the word **der Berg** inside it. Draw adjectives to resemble what they mean: Write **gross** and **klein** (*large* and *small*) using huge letters and tiny letters. Picture-compound nouns are great fun to draw. With **der Leckerbissen** (*the treat*; Literally: *tasty + bite*), draw someone licking their lips or whose mouth is watering, add a plus sign (+), and draw some teeth biting down on something you love to eat.

Write **die Farben** (*the colors*) in the exercise, listed in order from light to dark. The hints can help you get the order I've come up with.

0. _____ (die Farbe von Schnee)

A. **weiß** (*white*) (*the color of snow*)

43. _____ (dasselbe Wort auf Englisch)

44. _____ (die Farbe von Osterglocken [*daffodils*])

45. _____ (ich esse sie gern)

46. _____ (eine Farbe von Nelken [*carnations*])

47. _____ (ich sehe . . .)

48. _____ (im Frühling sind die Blätter der Bäume . . .)

Streamlining Word Storage

In reading and listening to German, you're likely to find a surprisingly large number of words that are comparable in the two languages (words that have the same common source and mean the same thing); they're called *cognates.* Their cousins are the *near cognates:* Words that have a common source, mean nearly the same in two languages, and may be spelled somewhat differently. And then you run across the *false friends,* the ones that have a surprisingly different meaning in the other language, even though they look the same.

Half the battle of vocabulary acquisition is a matter of knowing how a word fits into a larger group, and of course, how to use it. Imagine a chest of many drawers marked *cognates, near cognates,* and *false friends.* As you open the drawers of this section one by one, you find hands-on opportunities to increase your awareness of storing words in ways that you can easily retrieve them.

Recognizing cognates and near cognates

Cognates and *near cognates* are words with a common source that mean the same or nearly the same thing in two languages. In the case of German and English, many words have the same roots, although some have undergone spelling changes over time. Aside from **der Arm, der Kindergarten, der Rucksack, die Wanderlust, die Zeitgeist,** and other such classics, you can discover a plethora of others, many of which you can group by the similarity of their structure. As you recognize the similarities, place the words accurately into their groups. Some minor spelling changes are easy to recognize; for instance, the letter *c* in English is usually **k** in German, *sh* in English is **sch** in German, and so on.

Here's a small sampling of characteristics that signal English/German cognates:

- ✔ Nouns ending in **-er** often denote a person who works doing the job that word describes. Someone who designs is a *designer,* which is a cognate — **der Designer.**

  Nouns ending in **-or** build a similar group of cognates: **der Professor.**

- ✔ Adjectives ending in **-al** are often cognates: **liberal.**

- ✔ Verbs ending in **-ieren** are often near cognates: **vibrieren** = *to vibrate.*

- ✔ French words used in English and German are sometimes cognates: **das Portrait.**

- ✔ German words used in English aren't exactly cognates because they're the same word, but why not make use of this precious resource? **der Ersatz** = *the alternative, replacement*

Here are some verbs that are near cognates: **denunzieren** (*denounce*), **existieren** (*exist*), **fotografieren** (*photograph*), **frustrieren** (*frustrate*), **reformieren** (*reform*), **regulieren** (*regulate*), and **simulieren** (*simulate*).

Arrange the following words from the word bank into groups according to five characteristics for categorizing cognates described in this section: nouns ending in **-er,** nouns ending in **-or,** adjectives ending in **-al,** French words, and German words. To challenge you, the words that belong to the three categories with endings (**-er, -or,** and **-al**) are written without the ending. Add the ending to the word after the hyphen, and list the word in the correct category.

Q. Nouns ending in -er

A. **der Jogger**

~~der Jogg~~	norm-	das Café	der Reakt-	kitschig
form-	der Priest-	der Direkt-	das Restaurant	der Design-
gemütlich	diagon-	der Report-	optim-	der Chauffeur
der Profess-	der Fisch-	das Dekolleté	der Poltergeist	liber-
das Portrait	der Ventilat-	kaputt	die Angst	der Radiat-

49. Nouns ending in -er

der Jogger _____ _____

_____ _____

50. Nouns ending in -or

_____ _____ _____

_____ _____

51. Adjectives ending in -al

_____ _____ _____

_____ _____

52. French words

_____ _____ _____

_____ _____

53. German words

_____ _____ _____

_____ _____

False friends: Bad buddies

The following can easily happen: You start getting chummy with some words that are the same in both languages. You're borrowing English words left and right, plopping them into German phrases with great success. Along comes a word in German that *looks* like an English word, so you decide to use it. It's your new German colleague's birthday, so you buy a little present, walk up, and say **"Ein Gift für Sie."** You've just offered him some poison! (Yes, it's a unique gift, but did you have to blurt it out and ruin the surprise?) That's right: **Das Gift** means *poison*. The word for *present* is **das Geschenk.**

If you assume that you can blithely use a word you read in German without being sure of what it actually means, watch out! German is rife with potential bloopers, called *false friends* or *false cognates,* like **das Gift.** Conversely, German has borrowed words from English, using them differently. A cellphone is called **ein Handy** in German. When cellphones were new on the market, some German speakers would swear up and down that *handy* was the correct expression in English as well. Without a handy bilingual dictionary, leave any questionable words out of your active vocabulary for the time being. Better safe than sorry.

Take a look at some words that can potentially lead to mix-ups. For example, **Das ist ein bekanntes Gymnasium.** A famous gym? Strange, you think, as the tour guide points out a large building that looks an awful lot like a school. That's because **das Gymnasium** is a *high school* in German. Another one: **Das ist ein grosses** (*large*) **Bad.** What, a big bad somebody, like big bad John? Well, that's one way to remember what it means; **das Bad** is a *bathroom, john, loo, head,* whatever you want to call it.

To remember some tricky false friends, draw a picture of what the word means and label it, show what the word means by incorporating the word into the picture itself, or make the letters of the word take the shape of an object. You may be visualizing something slightly bizarre, and that's the fun part of it, which will probably help you remember the word more readily. **Der Herd** (*stove, range*) may work if in your mind's eye, you see a whole bunch of *stoves* with horns out on the *range* in Texas. (***Note:*** **Die Herde** means *the herd,* as in a group of cows. It's a different entry in the dictionary, however, because it has a different meaning, spelling, and gender.)

The following 12 German words embedded in sentences have a different meaning from their English lookalikes. Read the word in the context of the sentence, look at the English definitions in the word bank, and write the definition that logically fits.

Q. Ich arbeite am Samstag, **also** schlafe ich am Sonntag. _____

A. **so, therefore, thus** (*I'm working on Saturday, so I'll sleep on Sunday.*)

~~so, therefore, thus~~	daily special	vintage car	friendly, likeable
consistent, logical	good, well behaved	condom	sensitive
prescription	advice	soon	dung
perhaps, possibly			

54. Ich komme **bald** — warte nur fünf Minuten. _____

55. Diese Kinder sind **brav.** Sie gehorchen (*obey*) ihren Eltern. _____

56. Ein Präservativ hilft gegen Schwangerschaften (*pregnancies*). _____

57. Du bist sehr logisch und **konsequent** — bravo. _____

58. Was ist **das Menü** heute im Restaurant? _____

59. Ich habe **Mist** unter meinen Schuhen. Es stinkt! _____

60. Kommen Sie? Ich weiß nicht — **eventuell.** _____

61. Er geht zum Arzt; er braucht **ein Rezept.** _____

62. Was soll ich tun? Ich brauche **einen Rat.** _____

63. Sie hat viele Freunde; sie ist sehr **sympathisch.** _____

64. Das ist ein schönes Auto — **ein** echtes **Oldtimer.** _____

65. Sie sind zu **sensibel;** das ist nicht gut. _____

Answer Key

1 **das Käsebrot** (*cheese sandwich*) Literally, it means *cheese bread*.

2 **die Hauptstadt** (*capital city*) Literally, it means *main city*.

3 **das Erdbeereis** (*strawberry ice cream*) The last **-e** from **Erdbeere** is dropped for pronunciation purposes.

4 **der Briefkasten** (*mailbox*)

5 **das Esszimmer** (*dining room*) The verb **essen** drops the **-en** infinitive ending.

6 **das Computerspiel** (*computer game*)

7 **die Jahreszeit** (*season*)

8 **der Kartoffelknödel** (*potato dumpling*)

9 **die Handtasche** (*handbag*)

10 **das Mittagessen** (*lunch*) Literally, it means *noon meal*.

11 die Handschuhe: **hand + shoes = gloves** (*I use them in the winter.*)

12 die Taschenlampe: **pocket + light = flashlight** (*I use it in the night.*)

13 das Fernsehen: **distance + see = TV** (*They all used to be black and white.*)

14 der Kugelschreiber: **ball/sphere + writer = ballpoint pen** (*I can write well with it.*)

15 die Zeitschrift: **time + script/text = magazine** (*I read interesting articles in it.*)

16 der Schlafanzug: **sleep + suit = pajamas** (*I wear it when I go to bed.*)

17 ankommen: **to arrive**

18 abfahren: **to leave**

19 vorhaben: **to plan**

20 voraussetzen: **to require, presume**

21 spazierenfahren: **to go for a drive,** like a Sunday drive

22 ausgeben: **to spend (money)**

23 zusammensetzen: **to assemble**

24 liebhaben: **to be fond of;** there's also **lieben** (*to love*)

25 die Arbeiterklasse: **the working class**

26 der Arbeitgeber: **the employer**

27 das Arbeitslosengeld: **the unemployment compensation**

28 arbeitsparend: **labor-saving**

29 arbeitslos: **jobless**

30 der Arbeitnehmer: **the employee**

31 der Arbeitsplatz: **the place of work, workstation**

32 die Arbeitsmoral: **the attitude to work**

33 der Arbeitsraum: **the workroom**

34 die Fahrkarte: **the ticket**

35 die Einfahrt: **the entrance**

36 der Fahrgast: **the passenger**

37 die Fahrtrichtung: **the direction of traffic**

38 fahrend: **itinerant** (for example, folk); the suffix **-end** means *-ing*

39 fahrlässig: **negligent, reckless; lässig** can also mean *casual*

40 der Fahrlehrer: **the driving instructor**

41 der Fahrplan: **the schedule**

42 die Ausfahrt: **the exit**

43 **beige** (*beige*) (*the same word in English*)

44 **gelb** (*yellow*) (*the color of daffodils*)

Ostern (*Easter*) + **Glocken** (*bells*) is literally *Easter bells*. Daffodils tend to appear around Easter time.

45 **orange** (*orange*) (*I like to eat them*); same word in German for the fruit

46 **rosa** (*pink*) (*a color of carnations*)

47 **rot** (*red*) (*I see . . .*)

48 **grün** (*green*) (*In spring, the leaves on the trees are . . .*)

49 Nouns ending in -er: der Jogger, **der Designer, der Fischer, der Priester, der Reporter**

50 Nouns ending in -or: **der Direktor, der Professor, der Radiator, der Reaktor, der Ventilator**

51 Adjectives ending in -al: **diagonal, formal, liberal, normal, optimal**

52 French words: **das Café, der Chauffeur, das Decolleté, das Portrait, das Restaurant**

53 German words: **die Angst, gemütlich, kaputt, kitschig, der Poltergeist**

54 bald: **soon** (*I'm coming soon, wait just five minutes.*)

55 brav: **good, well-behaved** (*These children are well-behaved. They obey their parents.*)

56 Ein Präservativ: **condom** (*A condom helps against pregnancies.*)

57 konsequent: **consistent, logical** (*You're very logical and consistent.*)

58 das Menü: **daily special** (*What's the daily special in this restaurant today?*)

59 Mist: **dung** (*I've got dung under my shoes. It stinks!*)

60 eventuell: **perhaps, possibly** (*Are you coming? I don't know.*)

61 ein Rezept: **prescription** (*He's going to the doctor; he needs a prescription.*)

62 einen Rat: **advice** (*What should I do? I need advice.*)

63 sympathisch: **friendly, likeable** (*She has many friends; she's very friendly.*)

64 ein Oldtimer: **vintage car** (*That's a beautiful car — a vintage car.*)

65 sensibel: **sensitive** (*They're too sensitive; that's not good.*)

Part II

Getting Started Now: Writing in the Present

The 5th Wave   By Rich Tennant

"I'd ask for directions in German, but I don't know how to form a question into the shape of an apology."

In this part . . .

This part explains how to express yourself in the here and now. The present tense is a versatile workhorse in German, standing in for a variety of past, present, and future English tenses in a surprising array of situations; Chapter 5 deals with the particulars. Chapters 6 and 7 provide you with the nuts and bolts you need to formulate questions, and they tell you how to give reasonably accurate and understandable answers. Wondering what comes next? Speculation is one part of Chapter 8. That chapter also lets you practice expressing doubt, hope, uncertainty, and hypothetical situations.

Chapter 9 is where you find the lowdown on modal verbs, the kind that help you say things such as *may I, I'd like to, should we,* and *I can.* In Chapter 10, you get the hang of separable and inseparable prefix verbs. Separable prefix verbs have two parts that sometimes get separated in a sentence. Easy? Sort of. In a dictionary, the verb is listed with the two parts stuck together, so you need to be able to recognize such verbs in their stuck and unstuck usage.

Chapter 5

Grasping the Present Tense

*Y*ou*'re driving* down the road when you *see* a small herd of cows. Some *are grazing,* others *are chewing* their cud. Okay, so they *might be drooling,* too, but even so, it *gets* you on to thoughts about milk, and the idea *hits* you: You*'re going to get* some ice cream. You *say* to yourself, "I *think* I*'ll go* to Jan and Berry's because I really *do owe* myself a treat. After all, I*'ve been working* hard, and —" you *wake up* and realize you*'ve been dreaming* for the past five minutes. Darn!

Believe it or not, this isn't a plug for ice cream. It is, however, a superb example of how streamlined German can be, because you can put all the verbs in the preceding paragraph (marked in italics) in the present tense in German. This multitalented player stands in for the plain old simple present tense (*gets, wake up*), the present continuous (*are driving, are chewing*), an emphatic form (*do owe*), some futures (*are going to get, will go*), and even references to actions that started in the past (*have been working, have been dreaming*). **Das hört sich gut an, oder?** (*That sounds good, doesn't it?*) (For more information on the terminology of verb tenses, see Chapter 1.)

And all along, you thought I was going to start out with something along the lines of "First things first: The *present tense* is the verb form you use to talk about the present. Period." Well, that's true for sure, but there's more to it. In this chapter, you see how to use subject pronouns with the present tense and how to conjugate regular and irregular verbs. You also see how versatile the present tense is.

Simplifying Subject Pronouns and Their Relationship to Verbs

Before you can understand the present tense (and all other verb tenses), you need a firm grasp of the subject pronouns. These pronouns stand in for long-winded nouns and pop up everywhere in any language, and they play a key role in helping you get your verbs in shape. You always see them in tables that conjugate verbs, so get them down pat before you start work on the verbs that accompany them.

You use *subject pronouns* — **ich** (*I*), **du** (*you*), **er** (*he*), **sie** (*she*), **es** (*it*), and so on — to express who or what is carrying out the action or idea of the verb. They refer to the noun without naming it, which means they can serve as placeholders so you don't have to sound redundant by repeating the noun. (For more discussion on pronouns, check out Chapters 1 and 2.) In order to use subject pronouns, you need to know which *person* (first, second, or third) and *number* (singular or plural) the pronoun represents; for example, **ich** (*I*) = first person, singular. To connect the correct subject pronoun to a present-tense verb, you need to know which conjugated verb form to use. I lay out this information in "Getting Your Verbs in Shape: Present-Tense Conjugations."

Table 5-1 shows you the breakdown of subject pronouns in German and English. Notice the format with singular on the left, plural on the right, and the pronoun **Sie** (*you*) at the bottom. I use the same setup throughout the verb tables in this book.

Table 5-1	Subject Pronouns	
Person	*Singular*	*Plural*
First	**ich** (*I*)	**wir** (*we*)
Second (familiar)	**du** (*you*)	**ihr** (*you*)
Third	**er** (*he, it*) **sie** (*she, it*) **es** (*it*)	**sie** (*they*)
Second (formal)	**Sie** (*you,* both singular and plural)	

Think of the subject pronouns as *persona* because they im*person*ate the subject that they represent. You characterize them by their grammatical *person* (based on who's speaking and listening), number (singular or plural), and sometimes formality (which I discuss in the next section). Here's a closer look at the three persons:

- ✔ **First person:** The one(s) speaking: **ich** (*I*) or **wir** (*we*).

- ✔ **Second person:** The one(s) spoken *to:* **du, ihr, Sie.** All three mean *you* in English; **du** is the singular, familiar form, which you'd use with a friend; **ihr** is the plural, familiar form, which you'd use with a group of friends; and **Sie** is the formal form, whether singular or plural, which you'd use with the chancellor of Germany and her cabinet ministers (and everyone else you're not on a first-name basis with).

- ✔ **Third person:** Who or what is spoken *about:* **er** (*he, it*), **sie** (*she, it*), or **es** (*it*); **sie** (*they*). If you're talking about an inanimate object (*it*), the choice among **er, sie,** and **es** depends on the gender of the noun — see Chapter 2 for details.

Making sure "you" dresses for the occasion: The formality of du/ihr and Sie

Hopefully, if you're hobnobbing with some business moguls, the mayor, and a throng of socialites at the charity benefit of the year, you're on your best behavior. On the other hand, most people do and say whatever they feel like while hanging out with their buddies at a backyard barbecue on a Saturday afternoon. That formality/informality factor is what you need to keep in mind when you address people in German because there are three ways to say *you*: **du, ihr,** and **Sie.**

Use **Sie,** which is always capitalized, to speak to one or more people with whom you have a more distant, formal relationship. It's appropriate

- ✔ When you aren't sure about whether **du/ihr** or **Sie** is correct
- ✔ When you're not yet on a first-name basis with someone (for example, using Herr Kuhnagel or Frau Zitzelsberger, not Sigmund or Hildegard)
- ✔ When you're talking to adults you don't know well
- ✔ In business or at your place of work
- ✔ In public situations to a person in uniform (police officer, airport official, and other such individuals)

Use **du** when you talk to one person (or animal) in an informal way, and use **ihr,** the plural version of **du,** to address more than one person (or animal) informally. An informal pronoun is appropriate

- ✔ When a German speaker invites you to use **du**
- ✔ For talking to a close friend or relative
- ✔ For addressing children and teens younger than 16 or so
- ✔ When you talk to pets

You may hear **du** among close working colleagues, students, members of a sports team, or people hiking in the mountains, but unless someone asks you, **"Wollen wir uns dutzen?"** (*Shall we say du to each other?*), try to stick with **Sie.**

Using first names and addressing people with **du** (or **ihr**) when it isn't appropriate can turn German speakers off — fast. Language and culture are bonded together with superglue, so avoid pasting your culture on the German-speaking world. Be careful with recent crossover scenarios at the workplace: people addressing each other with **Sie,** although they use first names: **Heinz, haben Sie meine E-mail gelesen?** (*Heinz, have you read my e-mail?*). If you use last names (**Frau Dinkelhuber** and **Herr Sternhagel**), using **Sie** is best.

Distinguishing among sie, sie, and Sie

I have a threesome tangle to help you unravel, and then you're on your way to success with subject pronouns. Look back at Table 5-1, and you find the Three Musketeers, **sie** (*she*), **sie** (*they*), and **Sie** (*you*), lurking in their separate boxes. Seeing them in what looks like random places may seem daunting, but a few clues can help you sort them out. First, you know the meanings by their context. The conjugated verb and capitalization also help reveal the meaning. Here's what to watch:

- ✔ **Conjugation:** When **sie** means *she,* its verb form is distinct; in the present tense, the conjugated verb usually ends in **-t.** When **sie/Sie** means *they* or *you,* the present-tense verb ends in **-en.** (For more on conjugation, see the next section.)

✔ **Capitalization:** The *they* and *you* forms of **sie/Sie** have identical conjugations, but only the *you* version, which is formal, is capitalized.

The following examples show how you figure out which one to use when:

Wo wohnt sie? (*Where does she live?*) The verb is in third-person singular form.

Wo wohnen sie? (*Where do they live?*) The verb is in third-person plural form, and **sie** isn't capitalized.

Wo wohnen Sie? (*Where do you live?*) The verb is in second-person plural form (which is identical to the third-person plural form), and **Sie** is capitalized.

When you're speaking, listen carefully for cues in the context that help you distinguish between sentences like **Wo wohnen sie?** and **wo wohnen Sie?** If you're still not sure, just ask, **"Meinen Sie mich?"** (*Do you mean me?*). If you're on a first-name basis with the speaker, then you're all set; no confusion here because if someone asks you where you live, you hear the informal version: **Wo wohnst du?**

In the following situations, decide which subject pronoun you would use (**ich, du, er, sie, es, wir, ihr, sie,** or **Sie**) and write it in the space provided. Refer to Table 5-1 on subject pronouns.

0. Someone talking about his father uses _____.

A. **er**

1. Friends talking to each other use (plural form) _____.

2. You're talking about your friends, so you use _____.

3. An adult meeting another adult for the first time uses _____.

4. When you talk about yourself, you use _____.

5. An adult talking to three children aged 8, 11, and 14 uses _____.

6. You're talking to an animal, so you use _____.

7. A man talking about his wife uses _____.

8. When you talk about your cousin and yourself, you use _____.

9. You're talking about your colleagues, so you use _____.

10. A teenaged customer talking to a sales assistant uses _____.

11. When you talk to someone on a ski lift in Switzerland, you use _____.

12. A military comrade talking to another comrade uses _____.

Getting Your Verbs in Shape: Present-Tense Conjugations

I love to talk — about myself, family, friends, job, and what's going on in my life. Talking (and writing) about all these things and more in German is usually a matter of knowing how to construct a verb in the present tense with the help of a noun (subject) and a few other elements. Most German verbs are *regular*, meaning they follow a standard pattern of conjugation. Think of conjugation as activating a verb from its sleepy infinitive form found in dusty dictionaries (**leben, lachen, lieben**) and its English equivalent with that pesky *to* (*to live, to laugh, to love*) into a form that's compatible with the subject.

This section shows how to put verbs through their paces by conjugating them and combining them with nouns, pronouns, and other grammar goodies so you can start talking and writing with confidence in German.

Agreeing with the regulars

Regular verbs don't have any change in their basic form, which I call the *stem*. You conjugate a verb by taking the stem — which is almost always the result of lobbing off **-en** from the infinitive form of the verb (the not-yet conjugated form) — and adding the right ending to the verb. In the present tense, English has only the ending *-s* or no ending at all (*I live, you live, he lives*), whereas German has four endings (**-e, -st, -t,** and **-en**).

To conjugate a regular verb in the present tense, just drop the **-en** from the infinitive and add the appropriate ending to the stem. The endings are **-e, -st, -t, -en, -t, -en,** and **-en.** The following verb table shows how to conjugate the verb **kommen** (*to come*). I've simply added the present-tense endings, marked in bold, onto the stem **komm-**. (Make sure you know the meanings of the subject pronouns by checking Table 5-1 earlier in this chapter.)

kommen (*to come*)	
ich komm**e**	wir komm**en**
du komm**st**	ihr komm**t**
er/sie/es komm**t**	sie komm**en**
Sie komm**en**	
Er **kommt** aus Irland. (*He comes from Ireland.*)	

If the verb stem ends in **-d** or **-t,** place an **e** in front of the verb endings **-st** and **-t.** The following table shows how you conjugate the regular verb like **arbeiten** (*to work*) in the present tense. The endings are marked in bold. The stem **arbeit-** ends in **-t,** so you add an **e** before the verb endings for the second- and third-person singular (**du arbeitest, er/sie/es arbeitet**) and the second-person plural familiar form (**ihr arbeitet**).

arbeiten (*to work*)	
ich arbeit**e**	wir arbeit**en**
du arbeit**est**	ihr arbeit**et**
er/sie/es arbeit**et**	sie arbeit**en**
Sie arbeit**en**	
Du **arbeitest** sehr schnell. (*You work very fast.*)	

Both English and German sometimes insert extra vowels to make a verb understandable. Just try saying *she teachs* as one syllable — it's not easy. English adds an *e* before the *-s* so *teaches* expands to two syllables; the listener can then recognize that the speaker is using the third-person singular. German adds **-est** and **-et** to **du arbeit-** and **er/sie/es arbeit-** for the same reason: pronunciation. Adding the **e** lets speakers pronounce **arbeitet** with three syllables.

With a few verbs that don't have an **-en** infinitive ending, notably **wandern** (*to hike*) and **tun** (*to do*), drop **-n** from the infinitive and add only **-n** to

✔ The first-person plural form: **wir wandern** (*we hike*) and **wir tun** (*we do*)

✔ The third-person plural form: **sie wandern** (*they hike*) and **sie tun** (*they do*)

✔ The formal second-person singular and plural form: **Sie wandern** (*you hike*) and **Sie tun** (*you do*)

The following lists other common regular German verbs. You can use the regular conjugation on all of them:

✔ **arbeiten** (*to work*)

✔ **bringen** (*to bring*)

✔ **finden** (*to find, have an opinion*)

✔ **gehen** (*to go, walk*)

✔ **heißen** (*to be called, named*)

✔ **kaufen** (*to buy*)

✔ **kennen** (*to know [a person]*)

✔ **kommen** (*to come*)

✔ **kosten** (*to cost*)

✔ **lernen** (*to learn*)

✔ **reisen** (*to travel*)

✔ **sagen** (*to say*)

✔ **schreiben** (*to write*)

✔ **spielen** (*to play [a game, cards]*)

✔ **wandern** (*to hike, wander*)

✔ **wohnen** (*to live*)

In the following exercise, decide which verb conjugation to insert in the space provided. The English verb is at the end of the phrase, and the personal pronoun provides the clue for the German ending. If you don't see the personal pronoun, think which one would replace the noun(s) or name(s) that you do see and conjugate as you would for that pronoun.

Q. Was _____ ihr? (*to play*)

A. Was **spielt** ihr? (*What are you playing?*)

13. Sabina und Moritz _____ nach Australien. (*to travel*)

14. Der Computer _____ 599€. (*to cost*)

15. Meine Großmutter und ich _____ beide Monika. (*to be named, called*)

16. _____ du oft Briefe? (*to write*)

17. Ich _____ sehr gern in den Bergen. (*to hike*)

18. Wo _____ Sie? (*to live*)

19. Manfred _____ heute Abend spät nach Hause. (*to come*)

20. _____ ihr den Mann da drüben? (*to know*)

21. Ja, mein Mann _____ mit ihm in derselben Firma. (*to work*)

22. Wohin _____ Sie? (*to go*)

23. Heute _____ Florian und Maria ein Auto. (*to buy*)

24. Ich _____ Deutsch sehr leicht zu lernen. (*to find, have the opinion*)

Conjugating verbs with spelling changes

The verbs in this section are more or less regular, but their stems undergo a few small changes in spelling. Luckily — or unluckily, depending on how you see it — many of the spelling-change verbs are frequently used, so perhaps you can acquire them by osmosis! You may notice that some of the verbs here are *cognates,* words that come from a common ancestor and are often similar in meaning and spelling. For instance, **fallen** and *to fall* are the same, taking into account the German infinitive ending **-en,** and **helfen** and *to help* closely resemble each other (check out Chapter 4 for more about cognates).

These verbs with spelling changes are technically classified as verbs with stem-vowel changes because — you guessed it — the vowel(s) in the stem changes when you conjugate the verb. The *stem* is the part of the infinitive left after you slice off the **-en** ending: **Sprechen** (*to speak*) is the infinitive, and **sprech-** is the stem.

The stem-vowel changes take place in the **du** and **er/sie/es** forms (and in one verb type, the **ich** form). When dealing with these types of verbs, you encounter the following changes:

- ✔ **a→ä; au→äu** (very small group including **laufen** [*to run*])
- ✔ **e→i**
- ✔ **e→ie**
- ✔ **e→i** (**nehmen**); also, consonant change **hm** to **mm** (see the **nehmen** verb table)
- ✔ **i→ei** (**wissen**); also, **ich** and **er/sie/es** forms have no endings (see the **wissen** verb table)

The next five tables show each of these stem-vowel changes, along with the additional changes in **nehmen** (*to take*) and **wissen** (*to know as a fact*) groups. In these tables, only the stem-vowel changing verb forms are in bold.

fahren (*to drive*): a→ä	
ich fahre	wir fahren
du **fährst**	ihr fahrt
er/sie/es **fährt**	sie fahren
Sie fahren	
Du **fährst** sehr vorsichtig. (*You drive very carefully.*)	

Other **a→ä** verbs include the following:

- **backen** (*to bake*)
- **fallen** (*to fall*)
- **gefallen** (*to like, enjoy*)
- **halten** (*to stop, think about*)
- **laufen** (*to run*)
- **schlafen** (*to sleep*)
- **tragen** (*to carry, wear*)
- **waschen** (*to wash*)

sprechen (*to speak*): e→i	
ich spreche	wir sprechen
du **sprichst**	ihr sprecht
er/sie/es **spricht**	sie sprechen
Sie sprechen	
Adrienne **spricht** fließend Englisch, Deutsch, und Französisch. (*Adrienne speaks fluent English, German, and French.*)	

Here are some other **e→i** verbs:

- **essen** (*to eat*)
- **geben** (*to give*)
- **helfen** (*to help*)
- **vergessen** (*to forget*)

lesen (*to read*): e→ie	
ich lese	wir lesen
du **liest**	ihr lest
er/sie/es **liest**	sie lesen
Sie lesen	
Das Kind **liest** schon Romane. (*The child already reads novels.*)	

Sehen (*to see*) is also an **e→ie** verb.

nehmen (*to take*): e→i, hm→mm	
ich nehme	wir nehmen
du **nimmst**	ihr nehmt
er/sie/es **nimmt**	sie nehmen
Sie nehmen	
Du **nimmst** zu viele Kekse! (*You're taking too many cookies!*)	

wissen (*to know as a fact*): i→ei	
ich **weiß**	wir wissen
du **weißt**	ihr wisst
er/sie/es **weiß**	sie wissen
Sie wissen	
Weißt du, wer das ist? (*Do you know who that is?*)	

When you use **wissen** to refer to information in the sentence, you use a comma to separate the two sentence parts.

Try your hand at mastering the fine art of stem-vowel changes: In the following exercise, decide which verb conjugation to insert in the space provided. Remember, the stem-vowel changes take place in the **du** and **er/sie/es** (second-person singular familiar and third-person singular). You may have to make a few other changes, so make sure you refer to the preceding tables.

0. _____ du eine Jacke zum Abendessen? (*to wear*)

A. **Trägst** du eine Jacke zum Abendessen? (*Are you wearing a jacket to dinner?*)

25. Helena _____ am schnellsten. (*to run*)

26. Ich _____ sehr schlecht ohne meine Brille. (*to see*)

27. Mein Vater _____ mir viel Geld. (*to give*)

28. Was _____ ihr zum Frühstück? (*to eat*)

29. Meistens _____ die Kinder nur bis 6.00 Uhr. (*to sleep*)

30. Wohin _____ du am Wochenende? (*to drive*)

31. Ludwig _____ Deutsch mit einem schwäbischen Akzent. (*to speak*)

Conjugating the irregulars haben and sein: To have and to be

To have and to be: It sounds like a cross between a book title by an adventurous journalist turned author and a famous quote in English literature or a remake of a movie from the '40s. Whatever comes to mind when you think of these two verbs, **haben** (*to have*) and **sein** (*to be*) are stars in their own right.

These two common verbs are irregular. Just as in English, you come across them as full-fledged, free-standing, autonomous verbs and as auxiliary (helping) verbs. (For more on auxiliary verbs, see Chapter 9.) The auxiliary verb function of **haben** and **sein** is to work with other verbs in a frequently used verb tense: the *present perfect,* which I discuss in Chapter 16. For now, I simply show you what **haben** and **sein** look like in the present tense and explain how the English and German uses of these verbs compare.

Haben: Let me have it

Look at the conjugation of **haben** in the present tense. Notice that the verb actually has only two irregular verb forms: **du hast** and **er/sie/es hat.** The rest follow the regular verb conjugation pattern of taking the stem (in this case **hab-**) and adding the usual ending.

haben (*to have*)	
ich **habe**	wir **haben**
du **hast**	ihr **habt**
er/sie/es **hat**	sie **haben**
Sie **haben**	
Sie **hat** eine grosse Familie. (*She has a large family.*)	

German, like English, has many expressions that involve the verb *to have.* Many of them are the same in German and in English: **Zeit haben** (*to have time*). Others aren't — for example, English has two ways to express that something is absolutely necessary, *must* and *have to.* German has only one, **müssen** (*must*): **Ich muß anfangen** (*I have to start*). In other cases, German uses the verb **haben** when English has a different construction:

✔ **Expressing likes with haben and the adverb gern: Gern** means *gladly, with pleasure* when you use it alone. When expressing likes, **gern** is usually placed at the end of the sentence: **Hast du klassische Musik gern?** (*Do you like classical music?*). You find more on this expression in Chapter 11.

✔ **Talking about your birthday:** You say **Ich habe am achten Oktober Geburtstag** (*My birthday is on the eighth of October*).

✔ **With expressions that describe a physical condition, an emotional condition, or a state of being:** Five common expressions are

- **Angst haben** (*to be afraid*)

- **Durst haben** (*to be thirsty*)

- **Glück haben** (*to be lucky, fortunate*)

- **Hunger haben** (*to be hungry*)
- **Recht haben** (*to be right*)

Try these exercises using the verb **haben.** First, write the sentence in German. You have the elements you need to form the sentence (or question) separated by a slash (/). Combine the parts, making sure you use the right conjugated form of **haben.** Second, try to write the same sentence in English. If you find this task difficult, look at the Answer Key at the end of this chapter.

Q. Haben / du / einen Hund?

A. **Hast** du einen Hund? (*Do you have a dog?*)

32. Nein, ich / haben / eine Katze.

_____

33. Wann / haben / ihr / Zeit?

_____

34. Wir / haben / kein Wasser.

_____

35. Ein Polizist / haben / immer Recht.

_____

36. Ihr / haben / viele CDs.

_____

Sein: To be or not to be

Look at the conjugation of **sein** (*to be*) in the present tense. Notice that all the verb forms are irregular, although **wir sind, sie sind,** and **Sie sind** are identical. Regular verb conjugations in the present tense also have the same endings for **wir, sie,** and **Sie** pronouns. For comparison, consider the regular verb **gehen** (*to go, walk*): **wir gehen, sie gehen,** and **Sie gehen.**

sein (*to be*)	
ich **bin**	wir **sind**
du **bist**	ihr **seid**
er/sie/es **ist**	sie **sind**
Sie **sind**	
Sind Sie Herr Schumpich? (*Are you Mr. Schumpich?*)	

The verb **sein** is a true workhorse in German. Not only does it tell you what is and what isn't, but you also use it to form the present perfect — although **haben** is the main auxiliary verb for that task. (For more information on the present perfect tense, see Chapter 16.)

German and English use the verb **sein** (*to be*) in similar ways (*What's your boss like? Is it time yet? Who's that? Is it quiet? Are you ready? No, we're not. Am I too old? How much is that? What's up? Where are we? Isn't she funny? Where are you? I'm lost.*). Here's how you can use **sein**:

✔ **With an adjective:** This way is the most common:

> **Du bist sehr lustig.** (*You're very funny.*)

> **Mein Sohn ist nicht musikalisch.** (*My son is not musical.*)

Some expressions in German use the verb **sein** with an adjective plus a noun or pronoun in the dative case. (For more information on cases, refer to Chapter 4.) A couple of common expressions are

> **Mir ist kalt/warm.** (*I'm cold/warm.*) **Mir** is the dative case of the pronoun **ich.**

> **Ihm ist schlecht/übel.** (*He's feeling sick/sick to his stomach.*) **Ihm** is the dative case of the pronoun **er.**

✔ **With an adverb:**

> **Wir sind morgen nicht hier.** (*We're not here tomorrow.*)

> **Sie ist dort.** (*She's there.*)

✔ **With nouns:**

> **Sind Sie Kanadier?** (*Are you a Canadian?*)

> **Ich bin Bauingenieur.** (*I'm a civil engineer.*)

Note that German leaves out the article **ein** (*a*) for professions. (See Chapter 4 for more information.)

A few expressions using **sein** are expressed slightly differently from their English equivalents:

✔ **Wie ist ihre Telefonnummer/Adresse?** (*What's your phone number/address?* Literally, **wie** means *how.*) Chapter 7 deals with questions.

✔ **Hier ist Frau Becker.** (*I'm Mrs. Becker.* — to identify yourself on the telephone)

✔ **Ihr seid hier richtig.** (*You're in the right place.*)

Try these exercises using the verb **sein.** First, write the sentence in German. You have the elements needed to form the sentence (or question) separated by a slash (/). Combine the parts, making sure you use the right conjugated form of **sein.** Then try to write the same sentence in English. Remember that in some situations, the present tense in German is used for continuous and future tenses, as well as actions that started in the past in English.

Q. Unser Haus / sein/ nicht sehr groß.

A. Unser Haus **ist** nicht sehr groß. (***Our house isn't very large.***)

37. Wie alt / sein / die Kinder?

_____

38. Nächste Woche / sein / ihr in Freiburg.

_____

39. Du / sein / sehr ruhig.

_____

40. Uns / sein / kalt.

_____

41. Seit wie lange / sein / Sie schon fertig?

_____

Using the Very Versatile Present Tense

When you want to gain confidence speaking and writing in any language, you work on polishing your verb skills so you feel competent using the present, the past, and the future tenses. In German, grasping the present tense opens the door to several ways of expressing yourself. Knowing how versatile the present tense is in German means that you economize with this handy verb tense.

When you want to talk about something in German, first figure out whether you can use the present tense. In virtually all the situations where you use the present in English, you also use the present in German. In addition, you have a lot of opportunities in German to use the present tense when you have to use other verb tenses in English. It certainly makes your life easier when you know these various situations!

The primary difference in usage is that English has a continuous verb form and German doesn't. English uses the present continuous (Our guests *are staying* until Sunday) to indicate that an action is happening now, and it uses the present tense for habitual actions or facts without expressing whether the action is going on at the time (My brother *lives* on a lake). Because German doesn't verbally express such time distinctions, the listener can interpret sentences such as **Was denkst du?** in two ways: *What are you thinking?/What's on your mind?* or *What do you think?/What's your opinion?*

Look at Table 5-2 for three ways to translate one German sentence into English.

Table 5-2	English Present Tense Translations for German Present	
German Present Tense	*Possible English Translations*	*Intended Idea*
Jörg spielt sehr gut Basketball.	*Jörg plays basketball very well.*	Stating a general fact, common knowledge (simple present)
Jörg spielt sehr gut Basketball.	*Jörg is playing basketball very well.*	Happening now, today, this week, and so on (present continuous)
Jörg spielt sehr gut Basketball.	*Jörg does play basketball very well.*	Showing emphasis, or to contradict someone's opinion (simple present with auxiliary *do*)

Hold on — there's more to come on the versatility of the simple present tense in German. You even use it to talk about future plans, predictions, spontaneous decisions made at the time of speaking, and for activities that started in the past and are still going on. Table 5-3 shows how German uses the present tense for talking about the future and the past.

Table 5-3	Future and Present Perfect Tense Translations for German Present	
German Present Tense	*English uses other tenses*	*Intended idea*
Wir treffen uns um acht Uhr, oder?	*We're meeting/going to meet at eight o'clock, aren't we?*	Stating a plan or intention
Vielleicht regnet es morgen.	*Maybe it'll rain tomorrow.*	Predicting or speculating
Warte mal, ich helfe dir. (colloquial)	*Wait a sec, I'll help you.*	Making a spontaneous decision at the time of speaking, such as offering help or promising
Sie arbeitet seit 20 Jahren bei der Firma.	*She's been working at the company for 20 years.*	Expressing an action that started in the past and is still going on

Answer Key

1 Friends talking to each other use (plural form) **ihr.** *Talking to* is your key for second person, and *friends* is your key for the informal, plural form.

2 You're talking about your friends, so you use **sie.** *Talking about* tells you that you need third person, and *friends* is your key for plural form.

3 An adult meeting another adult for the first time uses **Sie.** You show respect and formality with **Sie.**

4 When you talk about yourself, you use **ich.**

5 An adult talking to three children aged 8, 11, and 14 uses **ihr.**

6 You're talking to an animal, so you use **du.**

7 A man talking about his wife uses **sie.** He says *she,* so you need **sie,** the third-person singular form.

8 When you talk about your cousin and yourself, you use **wir.**

9 You're talking about your colleagues, so you use **sie.** Here, **sie** stands for *they.*

10 A teenaged customer talking to a sales assistant uses **Sie.** The teen's age doesn't matter; saying **Sie** is polite and respectful. Even an adult would use **Sie.**

11 When you talk to someone on a ski lift in Switzerland, you use **Sie.** Start out with **Sie;** you're always safe. However, maybe you'll hear the person using **du.** Or you may hear something like, **"Sollen wir uns dutzen?"** (*Shall we say **du** to one another?"*) That's your opportunity to answer, **"Gern!"** (*Yes, I'd like to!* or *Gladly!*).

12 A military comrade talking to another comrade uses **du.** Especially in times of stress, people working side by side need the support of each other, and familiarity and closeness are indicated by **du.**

13 Sabina und Moritz **reisen** nach Australien. (*Sabina and Moritz are traveling to Australia.*)

14 Der Computer **kostet** 599€. (*The computer costs 599€.*)

15 Meine Großmutter und ich **heißen** beide Monika. (*My grandmother and I are both named Monika.*)

16 **Schreibst** du oft Briefe? (*Do you often write letters?*)

17 Ich **wandere** sehr gern in den Bergen. (*I like to hike in the mountains.*)

18 Wo **wohnen** Sie? (*Where do you live?*)

19 Manfred **kommt** heute Abend spät nach Hause. (*Manfred is coming home late this evening.*)

20 **Kennt** ihr den Mann da drüben? (*Do you know the man over there?*)

21 Ja, mein Mann **arbeitet** mit ihm in derselben Firma. (*Yes, my husband works with him in the same company.*)

22 Wohin **gehen** Sie? (*Where are you going?*)

23 Heute **kaufen** Florian und Maria ein Auto. (*Florian and Maria are buying a car today.*)

24 Ich **finde** Deutsch sehr leicht zu lernen. (*I find it very easy to learn German/I think it's very easy to learn German.*)

25 Helena **läuft** am schnellsten. (*Helena runs the fastest.*)

26 Ich **sehe** sehr schlecht ohne meine Brille. (*I see very poorly without my glasses.*)

27 Mein Vater **gibt** mir viel Geld. (*My father gives/is giving me a lot of money.*)

28 Was **esst** ihr zum Frühstück? (*What do you eat/are you eating for breakfast?*)

29 Meistens **schlafen** die Kinder nur bis 6.00 Uhr. (*The children usually sleep only until 6 a.m.*)

30 Wohin **fährst** du am Wochenende? (*Where are you driving to/going on the weekend?*)

31 Ludwig **spricht** Deutsch mit einem schwäbischen Akzent. (*Ludwig speaks German with a Swabian accent.*) Swabia is a region in the southwest of Germany, where the inhabitants have a distinct accent somewhat similar to Swiss German.

32 Nein, ich **habe** eine Katze. (***No, I have a cat.***)

33 Wann **habt** ihr Zeit? (***When do you have time?***)

34 Wir **haben** kein Wasser. (***We don't have any water.***)

35 Ein Polizist **hat** immer Recht. (***A policeman is always right.***) This is one that's expressed differently in English.

36 Ihr **habt** viele CDs. (***You have a lot of CDs.***)

37 Wie alt **sind** die Kinder? (***How old are the children?***)

38 Nächste Woche *seid* ihr in Freiburg. (***Next week you'll be in Freiburg.***) In German, you can express this type of future using the present tense.

39 Du **bist** sehr ruhig. (***You're very quiet.***)

40 Uns **ist** kalt. (***We're cold.***) **Uns** is the dative case pronoun; it's like saying *to us it's cold.*

41 Seit wie lange **sind** Sie schon fertig? (***How long have you been ready?***) In German, you use the present tense (*are*) here, not the present perfect (*have been*), as you do in English.

Chapter 6

Are You Asking or Telling Me? Questions and Commands

In This Chapter

▶ Asking yes/no questions

▶ Calling all question words: Who, where, what, why?

▶ Tagging questions: You can do it, can't you?

▶ Commanding the imperative: Do it!

*A*sking questions puts you in the conversational driver's seat. You use questions to initiate dialogues, find out what you need to know, and clarify information you're not sure about. When you're studying a new language, you may find that your counterpart is speaking so fast that you can barely understand the first word, let alone the barrage that follows. So you ask the person to slow down: **Langsamer, bitte** (*Slower, please*). This isn't bad for a start, but you still don't know what the person just said. You feel like asking where the stop button (or at least the rewind button) is, but instead you ask, **Können Sie das bitte wiederholen?** (*Could you repeat that, please?*). But you're still in the back seat, and your goal is to get behind the wheel. How you achieve that is simple: You implement effective question techniques.

This chapter gets you up to speed on formulating questions. At the end of each section, you can go for a test drive (not exactly racing on the Nürburgring, **leider** [*unfortunately*]) and see how skillful you are at making questions. (Refer to Chapter 7 for detailed practice in answering questions.) **Verstehen Sie, was ich meine?** (*Do you understand what I mean?*)

In addition to questions, you also need to know how to tell someone to do something. You use the imperative form for giving commands, giving instruction, persuading people, and offering encouragement. This chapter also gives you tools for understanding and using the imperative. Read on.

Inverting Word Order for Yes/No Questions

German word order is easy to follow when you form a question that merits a yes or no answer. You simply flip the subject and the conjugated (main) verb: The verb is in first place, and the subject is in second place (where the verb usually goes in statements). English is more complicated because you usually use the auxiliary (helping) verb *to do* or *to be* together with the main verb; in English, only the auxiliary verb goes in first place. Take a look at the German and its translations:

Leben Sie in einer Großstadt? (*Do you live in a large city?*)

Bleibt sie hier? (*Is she staying here?*)

Ist es kalt bei Ihnen im Winter? (*Is it cold where you live in the winter?*)

The German present tense encompasses two English verb tenses (and more). The present continuous doesn't exist in German, so in the second question here, you use the present. (See Chapter 5 for more on the present tense.) The inverted word order in German is the same for both the present tense and present-continuous tense in English.

Am Bahnhof (*at the train station*): Imagine you're in **München** (*Munich*), and you're planning an **Ausflug** (*outing, excursion*) to Berlin. You decide to take the train, so you go the window marked **Reiseauskunft** (*travel information*). In this exercise, you see a list of questions followed by a dialogue. Write the questions in the correct spaces provided. Read everything before you start to fill in the questions so you get the gist of the conversation.

Haben Sie viel Gepäck dabei?

Fährt ein Zug am Nachmittag?

~~Kann ich Ihnen helfen?~~

Ist das Ticket 1. Klasse sehr teuer?

Gibt es ein gutes Hotel am Bahnhof in Berlin?

Wollen Sie ein Ticket 1. Klasse oder 2. Klasse nehmen?

Fahren Sie innerhalb Deutschlands?

Ist der Transport für das Fahrrad sehr teuer?

Kann ich aber ein Fahrrad mitnehmen?

Reisen Sie nach Berlin hin und zurück?

0. Bahnhofsangestellter (*train station clerk*): Grüß Gott. _____?

Reisender (*traveler*): Ja, ich brauche eine Auskunft. Kann ich hier Tickets kaufen?

A. Grüß Gott. **Kann ich ihnen helfen?** (*Hello. Can I help you?*)

R: Ja, ich brauche eine Auskunft. Kann ich hier Tickets kaufen? (*Yes. I need some information. Can I buy tickets here?*)

1. B: Ja. _____?

R: Ja. Ich möchte nach Berlin fahren.

2. B: _____?

3. R: Ich weiß nicht. _____?

4. B: Nein, es kostet nur 45€ mehr. _____?

R: Ja, genau.

5. B: _____?

6. R: Nein, nur eine Tasche. _____?

B: Sicher, kein Problem.

7. R: _____?

B: Nun, Sie müssen 20€ für das Rad bezahlen.

8. R: _____?

B: Ja, Sie können um 13.30 Uhr oder um 15.15 Uhr abfahren.

9. R: Gut, dann nehme ich den Zug um 13.30 Uhr. _____?

B: Ja, es gibt mehrere Hotels.

R: Sehr freundlich, vielen Dank für ihre Auskunft.

Gathering Information with Question Words: Who, What, Why, and More

When kids reach the age of asking why, it's marvelous at first, but after weeks of non-stop questioning, you may wonder whether they're practicing for a career in some government spy agency. Asking *why* is a kid's way of engaging an adult in conversation just as much as it is a way of gathering information. As you progress in German, you need question words (interrogative pronouns) such as *who, what, where,* and *when* to gather specific information, but you can also use the kid's tactic of asking **wer** (*who*), **was** (*what*), **warum** (*why*), and so on as a tool for engaging people in conversation. Doing so is a useful tactic because it gives you more control over the direction of the discussion.

The inverted word order for yes/no questions (see the preceding section) is the same for information-gathering questions, only the question word (or phrase) comes first. Thus, the word order for info-gathering questions is question word + verb + subject, such as **Warum ist der Himmel blau?** (*Why is the sky blue?*) or **Wann fahren wir nach Hause?** (*When are we driving home?*).

Table 6-1 lists 12 German question words and phrases, the English equivalent in alphabetical order, and an example question in English with its German equivalent.

Table 6-1	Question Words and Example Questions	
Question Word	*Example Sentence*	*Translation*
wie (*how*)	**Wie heißen Sie?**	*What is your name?*
wie viele (*how many*)	**Wie viele Personen arbeiten in Ihrer Firma?**	*How many people work in your company?*
wie viel (*how much*)	**Wie viel kostet die Karte?**	*How much is the ticket?*

(continued)

Table 6-1 (continued)

Question Word	Example Sentence	Translation
was (*what*)	**Was machen wir nach der Pause?**	*What are we doing after the break?*
was für (*what kind of*)	**Was für ein Auto fahren Sie?**	*What kind of car do you drive?*
wann (*when*)	**Wann beginnt das Konzert?**	*When does the concert begin?*
wo (*where*)	**Wo wohnen Sie?**	*Where do you live?*
woher (*where . . . from*)	**Woher kommen Sie?**	*Where are you from?*
wohin (*where . . . [to]*)	**Wohin fährt der Bus?**	*Where does the bus go (to)?*
welcher/welche/ welches (*which*)	**Welche Straßenbahn soll ich nehmen? (die Straßenbahn)**	*Which tram should I take?*
wer (nominative)(*who*), **wen** (accusative)(*whom, who*), **wem** (dative)(*who*), **wessen** (genitive)(*whose*)	**Wer ist Ihr Chef?**	*Who is your boss?*
warum (*why*)	**Warum hält der Zug jetzt (an)?**	*Why is the train stopping now?*

Welcher/welche/welches (*which*) is an interrogative pronoun with three versions to correspond with the three noun genders **der/die/das: welcher Computer** (*which computer*), **welche Frau** (*which woman*), **welches Auto** (*which car*). You need to remember that it has adjective endings — in other words, the case endings of the noun it's describing. For example, consider **Mit welchem Bus soll ich fahren?** (*Which bus should I take?* Literally: *With which bus should I drive/travel?*). The preposition **mit** uses the dative case, and **der Bus** is masculine, so **mit welchem Bus** uses the masculine dative singular form of **welch-** in the prepositional phrase.

Wer (*who*) is an interrogative pronoun that has three other forms. **Wer** is the nominative case, **wen** (*whom, who*) is accusative, **wem** (*who*) is dative, and **wessen** (*whose*) is genitive.

In the following dialogue, Julian is interested in language courses for his company. He telephones Angelika, the coordinator at Interface Sprachenschule, who answers his questions. Put the appropriate question words from Table 6-1 into the spaces.

Q. _____ Buch benutzen Sie in Ihrer Sprachenschule? (das Buch)

A. **Welches** Buch benutzen Sie in Ihrer Sprachenschule? (*Which book do you use in your language school?*)

10. Angelika: Interface Sprachenschule, guten Morgen!

Julian: Guten Morgen, Julian Stromberger von der Firma Nordstern.

A: Kann ich Ihnen helfen?

J: Ja, wir möchten einen Sprachkurs für Spanisch machen.

A: Kein Problem, sehr gerne.

J: _____ kostet so ein Sprachkurs?

11. A: _____ Personen machen den Kurs?

J: Wir sind vier Personen.

A: Dann kostet der Kurs 500€ pro Person.

12. J: _____ Stunden sind es?

A: Es sind 40 Stunden.

13. J: _____ ist es so teuer?

A: Weil es nur vier Personen sind.

14. J: _____ ist der Unterricht?

A: Der Unterricht kann in Ihrer Firma sein.

J: Oh, in Ordnung, einverstanden.

15. A: _____ soll die Lehrerin fahren?

J: Sie muß nach Starnberg fahren.

A: Einverstanden.

16. J: _____ macht den Unterricht?

A: Eine junge Lehrerin.

17. J: _____ heißt die Lehrerin?

A: Sie heißt Cristina.

18. J: _____ kommt sie?

A: Sie kommt aus Santiago de Chile.

19. J: _____ können wir anfangen?

A: Sie können nächste Woche am Montag anfangen.

J: Ah, gut, vielen Dank. Auf Wiederhören.

A: Danke für Ihren Anruf. Auf Wiederhören.

Checking Information: Tag! You're It, Aren't You?

When you're talking to someone and you want to check some information, you may say something like this, expecting the listener to agree with you: *The mall opens at 10, doesn't it?* The same tactic is handy when you're not sure whether the other person is actually listening to you or is more engrossed in the game on TV.

As you delve into the depths of the German language, you can easily wonder at how much more complicated German grammar seems than English grammar. Then you stumble upon the realm of tag questions, and you can giggle at how simple it is to play tag in German. A *tag question* is simply what you tack onto the end of a statement to make it into a question. In English, the tag depends on the subject and verb in the statement. The possibilities are practically endless in English: *isn't she?, do you?, can't you?, wasn't it?, were you?, wouldn't it?, are you?,* and so on. The German equivalent is far simpler.

To form a tag question in German, just add **nicht?** (Literally: *not?*) or **nicht wahr?** (Literally: *not true?*) to the end of the sentence. Both expressions serve the same function as the long list of tag question equivalents in English: to shake out a sign of agreement, disagreement, or even just a grunt of acknowledgement from the listener. You can use tag questions interchangeably. They aren't grammatically linked to the first part of the sentence, as they are in English, so any time you want to elicit a response from someone as a means of checking your information, to show agreement or disagreement, and so on, you can use **nicht** or **nicht war,** even if you're talking about something in the past, present, or future or something that is negative or positive.

> **Sie fahren morgen nach Düsseldorf, nicht wahr?** (*You're going/driving to Düsseldorf tomorrow, aren't you?*)

> **Der Film war nicht besonders gut, nicht?** (*The movie wasn't especially good, was it?*)

Other tags abound in colloquial German. One common tag is **oder?** (Literally: *or?*), and another one you may hear in the southern German-speaking regions is **gell?** (loosely translated as *right?*). Sticking with the two "official" tag elements is best, but if you hear people around you using **oder?** or **gell?,** you may want to try them out as well, keeping in mind that they're colloquial and regional German. Both of these tags are used the same way as **nicht** and **nicht wahr** — in other words, to check that you understand some information, to elicit a response from someone, to show agreement or disagreement, and so on.

If you're using the **Sie** form, stick to the standard German tags, **nicht** and **nicht wahr.**

In this exercise, you're checking some information. Add on your choice of the four German tags — **nicht? nicht wahr? oder? gell?** — to the end of the statement.

Q. Sie wohnen in Graz, _____?

A. Sie wohnen in Graz, **nicht wahr?** (*You live in Graz, don't you?*)

20. Der Mann da drüben heißt Herr Storch, _____?

21. Wir haben noch eine Stunde Zeit, _____?

22. Hier regnet es oft im Frühling, _____?

23. Sie sind morgen im Büro, _____?

24. Sie hat uns alle wichtigen Informationen gegeben, _____?

Combining Question Words: Compounds with Wo-

You're listening to the German businessman sitting next to you on the plane telling you something like **Ich bin gegen höhere Benzinpreise** (*I'm against higher gas prices*). You hear the first part of the statement, **ich bin gegen,** but you don't catch the rest — what's he against? That one song about Benzin by Rammstein? You ask, **Sie sind gegen was?** (*You're against what?*). The businessman can understand your question, but it sounds as though you're challenging his opinion. It's a bit like saying, *Just what is it that you claim you're against?!* and insinuating that you don't agree at all. How do you communicate that you don't want to challenge his judgment, but you do need a repeat of the statement? You ask, **Wogegen sind Sie?** (*What are you against?*).

The question **Wogegen sind Sie** literally means *What against are you?* **Wogegen** asks for the object of the preposition **gegen** (*against*). In German, you stick **wo-** in front of the preposition. The **wo-** signals to the listener that a question is coming up and that it's going to be about the object of the preposition. The listener gets the most important information first in the question.

The German word order in questions beginning with **wo-** compounds like **worüber** (*what about, what over*) may seem odd at first: **Worüber spricht sie?** (*What's she talking about?* Literally: *What over [about] is she talking?*). However, compare it to a similar structure in really formal English: *To whom am I speaking?* instead of the far more natural sounding, *Who am I speaking to?* Remember: Such word order may seem odd in English, yet it's standard fare in German.

A second important function of the compound question words using **wo-** is to prompt the listener that the question you're asking allows an open-ended answer: **Wofür sind Sie?** (*What are you for?*). The listener may answer like this: **Ich bin für den Frieden** (*I'm for peace*) or **Ich bin für einen Spaziergang im Park** (*I'm [up] for a walk in the park*).

The meaning of the preposition in the compound with **wo-** may be different from the original meaning. Remember that many German verbs require particular prepositions in particular contexts (check out Chapter 15 for more on prepositions), which sometimes can determine which preposition you choose to combine with **wo-,** such as **Worauf warten Sie?** (*What are you waiting for?*) or **Ich warte auf den Bus** (*I'm waiting for the bus*). The person posing the question uses the phrase **warten auf . . .** in question form. The reply contains the complete phrase (**ich warte auf**) with the object of the preposition (**den Bus**).

When you know the most common verb-preposition combinations, you're on the road to success at forming **wo-** compounds. (Chapter 11 and Chapter 15 help you with such combinations.) However, you also need to know which grammatical case to use with prepositions. Most important is being aware that prepositions can change meaning depending on the context of the sentence, so it's wise to know fixed expressions.

Table 6-2 shows the most common compounds formed by adding **wo-** to the prepositions. The English equivalents can help you to get a feel for the preposition, but they
change meaning according to the context of the sentence. When the preposition
begins with a vowel, the letter **r** is inserted between the two elements of the question
word (for instance, **wo + r + in = worin**).

Table 6-2	Questioning Using wo- Compounds	
German Preposition	*Translation*	*Wo- Compound*
an	*on, at, to*	**woran**
auf	*on top of, to*	**worauf**
aus	*out of, from*	**woraus**
durch	*through, by*	**wodurch**
für	*for*	**wofür**
gegen	*against*	**wogegen**
in	*in, inside of*	**worin**
hinter	*behind, after*	**wohinter**
mit	*with, by*	**womit**
nach	*after, to*	**wonach**
über	*over, above*	**worüber**
um	*around*	**worum**
unter	*under*	**worunter**
von	*from, by*	**wovon**
vor	*in front of, before*	**wovor**
zu	*to, at*	**wozu**

The following exercise provides two tasks. First, you see a question with the **wo-** question
compound missing; use the answers for each question to help you decide which **wo-**
word you need to insert. Then try your hand at translating the reply into English.

Q. _____ haben Sie Respekt? Ich habe Respekt vor anderen Menschen.

A. **Wovor** haben Sie Respekt? (*What/Whom do you have respect for?*)

Ich habe Respekt vor anderen Menschen. (***I have respect for other people.***)

25. _____ wartest du? Ich warte auf meine Freundin.

_____

26. _____ ist er? Er ist für mehr Freiheit.

_____

27. _____ bitten Sie? Ich bitte um einen Stift.

_____

28. _____ werden Sie krank? Durch schlechten Fisch werde ich krank.

_____

29. _____ halten Sie sich? Ich halte mich an die Gesetze.

_____

Making Choices: Asking What Kind of . . . ?

You're looking at a ticket machine for the public transportation system in a major German city. You know the system is really extensive because on the wall next to the machine is a huge subway/light rail map, the **U-Bahn/S-Bahn Netzplan** (**U-Bahn** is short for **Untergrundbahn** [*subway*], and **S-Bahn** stands for **Schnellbahn** [*commuter rail/light rail*]). The shiny blue and silver ticket machine is a real gem from a technical standpoint, but it doesn't look very user-friendly to **Ausländer** (*foreigners*) like you. The machine must provide lots of ticket choices because there are all kinds of buttons to push and various slots for inserting money and taking out tickets; still, no one seems to be having any trouble. You have two choices: Pretend you're at a slot machine in Las Vegas, press a few buttons, and hope you'll get a ticket out of the deal, or use the phrase **was für (ein)** and ask a likely victim, **"Was für eine Karte brauche ich?"** (*What kind of ticket do I need?*) — or, pointing to the ticket in her hand, ask, **"Was für eine Karte ist das?"** (*What kind of a ticket is that?*).

Obviously, I suggest you try the second option: To form this type of question, you use the phrase **was für (ein)** with a noun as the subject (nominative case) or the direct object (accusative case) of a question. I break down two questions to show you how this works. First, **Was für eine Karte ist das?** (*What kind of a ticket is that?*). In this question, you start as always with **was für.** Next, add the subject of the sentence, **eine Karte** (*a ticket*), and then the verb **ist** (*is*) and **das** (*that,* indicating the ticket the passenger is holding). The second question, **Was für eine Karte brauche ich?** (*What kind of ticket do I need?*) starts the same way with **was für,** followed by **eine Karte,** which is the object of the sentence. The verb **brauche** (*need*) follows, and then comes the subject of the question, **ich** (*I*).

If you're having trouble figuring out what a subject (nominative case) is and what a direct object (accusative case) is, turn the question into a normal, declarative sentence. To **Was für eine Karte ist das?** you may hear the answer **Das ist eine Streifenkarte** (*That's a strip ticket*). **Eine Streifenkarte** is nominative case; you use it with the verb **sein** (*to be*). To answer **Was für eine Karte brauche ich?** you may hear **Sie brauchen eine Streifenkarte** (*You need a strip ticket*). The subject is **Sie,** in nominative case, and the object is **eine Streifenkarte,** in accusative case.

Table 6-3 shows the breakdown of the grammatical structure for asking **was für ein . . .?** (*what kind of . . .?*) Notice the case and gender endings of the subject and object in each question; remember that the preposition **für** in **was für** doesn't determine the case; rather, the other information in the question does so.

Table 6-3	Was Für: Showing Case and Gender Endings			
Gender/ Number	Nominative (Was Für . . .?)	Translation	Accusative (Was Für . . .?)	Translation
Masculine	**Was für ein Fahrschein ist das?**	*What kind of ticket is that?*	**Was für einen Fahrschein brauche ich?**	*What kind of ticket do I need?*
Feminine	**Was für eine Fahrkarte ist das?**	*What kind of ticket is that?*	**Was für eine Fahrkarte brauche ich?**	*What kind of ticket do I need?*
Neuter	**Was für ein Bier ist das?**	*What kind of beer is that?*	**Was für ein Bier trinken Sie?**	*What kind of beer are you drinking?*
Plural	**Was für Geschäfte sind hier im Ort?** (no article needed)	*What kinds of shops are (there) in this town?*	**Was für Geschäfte verkaufen Bierkrüge?**	*What kinds of shops sell beer steins?*

In the following exercise, you're spending some time in Munich. You're curious about everything around you, so you ask a lot of questions. Write the questions in German using the cues in English. Table 6-3 can help you decide the case and gender endings; the noun and its gender are given in German in parentheses.

Q. What kind of ticket is the "Streifenkarte"? (German has two words for *transport ticket:* **die Fahrkarte** and **der Fahrschein.** You also see the word **das Ticket** in German usage.)

A. **Was für eine Fahrkarte/ein Fahrschein ist die "Streifenkarte"?** (*What kind of ticket is the "Streifenkarte"?*) **Die Streifenkarte** is a strip ticket, and it's your best choice when you want to take a few rides over a period of a couple of days. Nominative case here; the verb **sein** (*to be*) uses nominative.

30. What kind of a museum is that? (the museum = **das Museum**)

_____

31. What kind of a salad are you eating? (the salad = **der Salat**)

_____

32. What kind of a beverage is that? (the beverage = **das Getränk**)

_____

33. What kind of a store is that? (the store = **das Geschäft**)

_____

34. What kind of music does this pub/bar have? (the music = **die Musik**)

_____

Using the Imperative: Do It!

When you want to give someone orders to do something, you can use the *imperative* form, also called the *command* form. However, you can also use the imperative form in other situations, such as giving instructions, offering encouragement, making suggestions, and persuading people. This section gives the lowdown on the imperative.

Giving orders

When telling someone to do something, you use the imperative. You want to ensure you use the correct verb form and punctuation so the person you're talking to understands. (However, that still doesn't mean he or she will do what you say.) Keep reading to see how to use the imperative correctly.

Verb forms

English has one verb form for the imperative (*stop* here please, *get* me a pen please, *go* home, *watch* out!). You may be talking to one person, several people, a bus driver, a friend, or your neighbor's dog. On the other hand, German has three forms, depending on whom you're addressing. They correspond to the three German pronouns that represent *you* — **Sie, ihr,** and **du.** Table 6-4 shows examples of these three imperative forms and explains how to form the verbs. I mention the few exceptions right after the table.

Table 6-4		The Three German Imperative Forms of *You*		
German Pronoun	**Translation**	**German Example Sentence**	**Translation**	**How to Form the Verb**
Sie	*you* (formal, singular or plural)	**Zeigen Sie mir, bitte! (zeigen)**	*Please show me.*	Same as present-tense **Sie** form
ihr	*you* (informal, plural)	**Öffnet bitte die Fenster! (öffnen)**	*Please open the windows.*	Same as present-tense **ihr** form
du	*you* (informal, singular)	**Fahre vorsichtig! (fahren)**	*Drive carefully.*	Stem of a verb + **-e**

Normally, the **du** imperative form is straightforward: verb stem + **-e** (for example, **geh** + **-e** = **gehe** [*go*]). Here are the three **du** imperative exceptions:

✔ In informal German, the **-e** is often dropped: **pass auf** (*watch out*)

✔ In verbs with a stem ending in **-d** or **-t,** you often *don't* drop the **-e: arbeite** (*work*)

✔ If the verb has a stem vowel change, the imperative has this vowel change and does *not* have **-e** at the end of the verb: **essen = iss** (*eat*). (See Chapter 4 for verbs with stem vowel changes.)

The verb **sein** (*to be*) is irregular (of course!) in the imperative:

✔ **Sie** form: **seien Sie**

✔ **ihr** form: **seid**

✔ **du** form: **sei**

Punctuation

When you write a command in German, put an exclamation mark at the end of the phrase. It isn't intended to make the command sound like a do-or-die situation; it's simply a grammatical element of the imperative form, just as a question mark belongs at the end of a question.

The liberal use of exclamation marks on German signage as a means of signaling warning can be a bit overwhelming at first. **Rasen nicht betreten!** (*Don't walk on the grass*) may seem threatening, but don't let it give you the impression that you'll go straight to jail if you dare to place even one toe on the grass. The exclamation mark is meant to draw your attention to the sign so you recognize it as a directive that you need to adhere to. Grammatically speaking, the format of **Rasen nicht betreten!** is an imperative, but it's the infinitive form of the verb that you see more often on signs, and it often takes the form of a prohibition with **nicht** preceding the infinitive. **Nicht hinauslehnen!** (*Don't lean out!*) is an example of a sign posted on a train window. The exclamation mark adds strength to the message.

Requests and suggestions: Looking at question-command hybrids

In some cases, the imperative walks the fine line between asking and telling someone to do something. Both have inverted word order with the verb first, followed by the subject. Look at the question **Können Sie das bitte machen?** (*Could you do that, please?*). You're asking someone to do something, so you generally formulate your request more politely using a helping verb such as **können** (*could*). In addition, you end the request in a rising voice, and you use a question mark. By contrast, when you want to tell someone to do something in more direct but polite language, you make a request such as **Machen Sie das, bitte** (*Please do that*). Your voice falls at the end, and you use a period.

> **Können Sie mir bitte helfen?** (*Could you help me, please?*) The question form, **können,** and **bitte** indicate a request that you're asking someone (politely) to do something. When you say it, your voice rises at the end.

> **Helfen Sie mir, bitte.** (*Please help me/Give me a hand, please.*) The imperative form is a request in more direct language, but **bitte** makes it sound polite. This is probably something you'd say, not write.

Another use of the imperative is for making suggestions. When referring to **wir** (*we*) as the people who may follow the suggestion, the German looks like this: **Fahren wir Fahrrad** (*Let's go bicycling*). It's the **wir** verb form with inverted word order.

For each infinitive, provide the imperative verb forms for **Sie, ihr,** and **du.** Use all the preceding information to help you form the three different imperative forms. Because these are commands, they all need the exclamation mark.

Q. schneller arbeiten (*to work faster*)

A. Sie: **Arbeiten Sie schneller!**   ihr: **Arbeitet schneller!**   du: **Arbeite schneller!**

35. langsam essen (*to eat slowly*)

  Sie: _____ ihr: _____ du: _____

36. vorsichtig fahren (*to drive carefully*)

  Sie: _____ ihr: _____ du: _____

37. nicht gehen (*to not walk*)

  Sie: _____ ihr: _____ du: _____

38. lesen (*to read*)

  Sie: _____ ihr: _____ du: _____

39. machen (*to make, do*)

  Sie: _____ ihr: _____ du: _____

Answer Key

1 B: **Ja. Fahren Sie innerhalb Deutschlands?** (*Yes. Are you traveling within Germany?*)

R: Ja. Ich möchte nach Berlin fahren. (*Yes. I'd like to go to Berlin.*)

2 B: **Wollen Sie ein Ticket 1. Klasse oder 2. Klasse nehmen?** (*Do you want a first- or second-class ticket?*)

3 R: Ich weiß nicht. **Ist das Ticket 1. Klasse sehr teuer?** (*I don't know. Is the first class ticket very expensive?*)

4 B: Nein, es kostet nur 45€ mehr. **Reisen Sie nach Berlin hin und zurück?** (*No, it's only 45€ more. Are you going round trip to Berlin?*)

R: Ja, genau. (*Yes, exactly.*)

5 B: **Haben Sie viel Gepäck dabei?** (*Do you have much luggage with you?*) For an extra fee, you may have your luggage picked up at your home and delivered to your destination.

6 R: Nein, nur eine Tasche. **Kann ich aber ein Fahrrad mitnehmen?** (*No, only one bag. But can I take a bicycle with me?*)

B: Sicher, kein Problem. (*Of course. No problem.*) You can also rent bicycles from many train stations.

7 R: **Ist der Transport für das Fahrrad sehr teuer?** (*Is it expensive to transport the bicycle?*)

B: Nun, Sie müssen 20€ für das Rad bezahlen. (*Well, you have to pay 20€ for the bicycle.*)

8 R: **Fährt ein Zug am Nachmittag?** (*Is there a train leaving in the afternoon?*)

B: Ja, Sie können um 13.30 Uhr oder um 15.15 Uhr abfahren. (*Yes. You can leave at 1:30 p.m. or 3:15 p.m.*) The 24-hour clock time system is easily calculated by adding 12 to p.m. times.

9 R: Gut, dann nehme ich den Zug um 13.30 Uhr. **Gibt es ein gutes Hotel am Bahnhof in Berlin?** (*Good, then I'll take the train at 1:30 p.m. Is there a good hotel at the train station in Berlin?*)

B: Ja, es gibt mehrere Hotels. (*Yes, there are several hotels.*)

R: Sehr freundlich, vielen Dank für Ihre Auskunft. (*That's very kind of you. Thank you for your information.*)

10 A: Interface Sprachenschule, guten Morgen! (*Interface Language School. Good morning.*)

J: Guten Morgen, Julian Stromberger von der Firma Nordstern. (*Good morning. This is Julian Stromberger from Nordstern Company.*) **Note:** In German business situations, and even with private telephone calls, people answer the phone and identify themselves with their last name, but there is a trend to give the whole name.

A: Kann ich Ihnen helfen? (*Can I help you?*)

J: Ja, wir möchten einen Sprachkurs für Spanisch machen. (*Yes. We'd like to do a Spanish language course.*)

A: Kein Problem, sehr gerne. (*No problem. That's fine.*)

J: **Wie viel** kostet so ein Sprachkurs? (*How much does such a language course cost?*)

11   A: **Wie viele** Personen machen den Kurs? (*How many people are taking the course?*)

J: Wir sind vier Personen. (*There are four of us.* Literally: *We are four people.*)

A: Dann kostet der Kurs 500€ pro Person. (*Then it costs 500€ per person.*)

12   J: **Wie viele** Stunden sind es? (*How many hours is it?*)

A: Es sind 40 Stunden. (*It's 40 hours.*)

13   J: **Warum** ist es so teuer? (*Why is it so expensive?*)

A: Weil es nur vier Personen sind. (*Because there are only four people.*) The conjunction **weil** requires that the verb be placed at the end of the phrase.

14   J: **Wo** ist der Unterricht? (*Where is the class?*)

A: Der Unterricht kann in Ihrer Firma sein. (*The class can take place in your company.*)

J: Oh, in Ordnung, einverstanden. (*Oh, all right. That's agreed.*) Another alternative translation for **einverstanden** is *very well*.

15   A: **Wohin** soll die Lehrerin fahren? (*Where should the teacher go?*)

J: Sie muß nach Starnberg fahren. (*She'll need to go to Starnberg.*) **Müssen** means *must,* but it carries a stronger connotation in English than in German.

A: Einverstanden. (*Very well.*) Another alternative translation for **einverstanden** is *agreed* or *that's agreed.*

16   J: **Wer** macht den Unterricht? (*Who is teaching the class?*)

A: Eine junge Lehrerin. (*A young teacher.*)

17   J: **Wie** heißt die Lehrerin? (*What is the teacher's name?*) The fixed expression you use to ask someone's name, **wie heißen Sie?** literally means *how are you called?*

A: Sie heißt Cristina. (*Her name is Cristina.*)

18   J: **Woher** kommt sie? (*Where is she from?*)

A: Sie kommt aus Santiago de Chile. (*She's from Santiago de Chile.*)

19   J: **Wann** können wir anfangen? (*When can we begin?*)

A: Sie können nächste Woche am Montag anfangen. (*You can start on Monday next week.*)

J: Ah, gut, vielen Dank. Auf Wiederhören. (*Oh, great, thank you very much. Goodbye.*) In telephone language, you say, literally speaking, *hear you later.*

A: Danke für Ihren Anruf. Auf Wiederhören. (*Thank you for you call. Goodbye.*)

20   Der Mann da drüben heißt Herr Storch, **nicht**? (*The man over there is Herr Storch, isn't he?*) This sounds like a business situation, or at least formal situation, because the man is described with his last name, so definitely you should use the "official" tags.

21   Wir haben noch eine Stunde Zeit, **nicht wahr**? (*We have another hour, don't we?*) If you're talking with a good friend, you can use **gell** or **oder**.

22   Hier regnet es oft im Frühling, **nicht wahr**? (*It often rains here, doesn't it?*) If you're talking with a good friend, you can use **gell** or **oder**.

23 Sie sind morgen im Büro, **nicht?** (*You'll be in the office tomorrow, won't you?*) Stick to the **nicht/nicht wahr** — it's a formal situation.

24 Sie hat uns alle wichtigen Informationen gegeben, **nicht wahr?** (*She gave us all the important information, didn't she?*) If you're talking with a good friend, you can use **gell** or **oder**.

25 **Worauf** wartest du? (*What are you waiting for?*) Ich warte auf meine Freundin. (***I'm waiting for my [girl] friend.***) The fixed expression is **auf etwas warten.** The preposition **auf** takes the accusative.

26 **Wofür** ist er? (*What is he for?*) Er ist für mehr Freiheit. (***He's for more freedom.***) The opposite of **für** is **gegen** (*against*): **Er ist gegen die Freiheit.** (*He's against freedom.*)

27 **Worum** bitten Sie? (*What are you asking for?*) Ich bitte um einen Stift. (***I'm asking for a pencil.***) **Um etwas bitten** is the fixed expression. **Um** takes the accusative.

28 **Wodurch** werden Sie krank? (*What can you get sick from?*) Durch schlechten Fisch werde ich krank. (***I get sick from bad fish.***) The preposition **durch** changes meaning when used in the expression, but its original meaning *through* helps you to get the gist of the expression **durch etwas krank werden.**

29 **Woran** halten Sie sich? (*What do you adhere to/observe?*) Ich halte mich an die Gesetze. (***I adhere to/observe the laws.***) The literal translation of **sich an etwas halten** (*to hold oneself to*) makes enough sense to help you understand the question.

30 Was für **ein Museum** ist das? Nominative case here; the verb **sein** (*to be*) uses the nominative.

31 Was für **einen Salat** essen Sie? Accusative case here; **einen Salat** is the direct object, and the subject is **Sie.**

32 Was für **ein Getränk** ist das? Nominative case here; the verb **sein** (*to be*) uses the nominative. The plural of **Getränk** is **Getränke.**

33 Was für **ein Geschäft** ist das? Nominative case here; the verb **sein** (*to be*) uses the nominative.

34 Was für **eine Musik** hat dieses Lokal/diese Bar? Accusative case here; **eine Musik** is the direct object. **Lokal/Bar** is the subject. **Das Lokal** is a popular word to describe an eatery that tends to have a more casual atmosphere — and music — than **ein Restaurant.**

35 Sie: **Essen Sie langsam!**   ihr: **Esst langsam!**   du: **Iss langsam!** (stem vowel-change verb in **du** and **er/sie/es** present tense)

36 Sie: **Fahren Sie vorsichtig!**   ihr: **Fahrt vorsichtig!**   du: **Fahr vorsichtig!**

37 Sie: **Gehen Sie nicht!**   ihr: **Geht nicht!**   du: **Geh nicht!**

38 Sie: **Lesen Sie!**   ihr: **Lest!**   du: **Lies!** (stem vowel-change verb in **du** and **er/sie/es** present tense)

39 Sie: **Machen Sie!**   ihr: **Macht!**   du: **Mach!**

Chapter 7

Answering Intelligently with Yes, No, and Maybe

In This Chapter

▶ Responding with yes or no

▶ Understanding **kein** and **nicht**

▶ Getting into **da-** compounds

▶ Being diplomatic: Agreeing and disagreeing

*Y*ou're listening as your aunt talks on the phone in the room next to you, and you know the conversation can't be very interesting, because all you hear is *yes, yes, no, yeah, yes, yeah, no, no, yes.* Your aunt is probably employing most of those yeses and nos for more than answering a question; she's likely signaling that she's still listening or is simply being polite. If she were in the same room as the person she's talking to, she likely wouldn't even need to talk — it'd suffice for her to bob her head around, nodding in agreement or shaking it to express disagreement.

You have to agree that knowing how to say *yes* and *no* in German is essential, but one-word answers to questions can be as off-putting as the wrong answer. You certainly need to use **ja** (*yes*) and **nein** (*no*) in many different situations when answering questions, responding to information, or agreeing and disagreeing with others. Yet even with an answer that's a complete sentence, you can get in trouble if you don't express it clearly enough. The humor in *yes, we have no bananas* isn't an issue of poor grammar but rather the confusion of *yes* and *no* in one sentence. In this chapter, I present various ways to clearly express yes and no and the shades in between for situations when you don't want to commit yourself to a definite answer because you'd rather bide your time, or **vielleicht** (*maybe*) you'd like to suggest an alternative.

Knowing a range of positive and negative responses to show agreement and disagreement is another section in this chapter. I also take you through the steps you need to know in order to choose between **kein** and **nicht,** which are the two ways of negating information in German. This chapter also describes the ins and outs of **da-** compounds: how to form them and when and how you use the range of these handy prepositional combinations. (Chapter 6 deals with the kissing cousins of **da-** compounds, the **wo-** compounds, which are used in questions.)

Getting to Yes: Variations on Ja

When you want to show someone that you understand, that you're listening, and so on, you use **ja** (*yes*) and its extended family: **Ja, das ist richtig** (*Yes, that's right*). In these instances, all you need to do is add **ja** to what you want to say. Use **ja** the way you do in English: To answer a question in the affirmative, or to say that you agree to something. It can stand alone, or if **ja** is in a sentence, it generally comes at the beginning of an affirmative sentence, just as it does in English.

When you get bored with saying **ja** all the time, try a few variations that render the same meaning with slightly different emphasis. Table 7-1 contains nine alternatives for good old **ja.** The example sentences put these common substitutes into a context, and the English explanations describe the implications behind these expressions.

Table 7-1	Alternatives for Ja		
Ja Equivalent	*Explanation*	*Example Sentence*	*Translation*
genau	*exactly, precisely* — the English translation sounds stilted, but not so to the German ear	**Genau, mein Familienname ist Schranner.**	*Exactly, my family name is Schranner.*
gewiss	*of course, sure enough* — somewhat formal sounding in German	**Gewiss. Sie werden um 7.00 Uhr geweckt.**	*Of course. You'll be woken up at 7 a.m.*
ja, ja	*yes, yes* — can express enthusiasm or skepticism	**Ja, ja, das weiß ich schon.**	*Yes, yes, I already know that.*
jawohl	*exactly* — has a somewhat formal ring	**Jawohl, meine Frau kommt aus Sydney.**	*Exactly, my wife is from Sydney.*
klar	*of course* (Literally: *clear* or *clearly*) — somewhat casual, colloquial tone	**Klar kann ich segeln.**	*Of course I know how to sail.*
natürlich	*naturally* — neutral, neither formal nor colloquial	**Natürlich helfen wir Ihnen.**	*Naturally, we'll help you.*
richtig	*right* — neutral, neither formal nor colloquial	**Richtig. Er mietet ein Auto.**	*Right. He's renting a car.*
selbstverständlich	*certainly* — good choice for business, formal situations	**Selbstverständlich lade ich Sie zum Mittagessen ein.**	*Certainly, I'm inviting you to lunch.*
sicher	*certainly, sure*	**Sicher mache ich das Licht aus.**	*Sure, I'll turn off the light.*

Notice in the example sentences, when the **ja** substitute is followed by a comma or a period, you start the next phrase in the usual German word order of subject followed by the verb in second position. (In the example sentences, the comma and period are interchangeable.) When the **ja** replacement word functions as the first element in the sentence (no comma or period), the verb follows in second position.

When you want to add more emphasis to show that you really understand or agree with someone, you can add **ja** or **aber** (*but*) to the preceding expressions. Take a look:

Ja, klar! (*Yes, of course!*)

Aber natürlich! (*Certainly!*)

Aber selbstverständlich! (*Why, certainly!*)

Ja, sicher! (*Yes, sure!*)

The preceding examples place the **ja** words at the beginning of the sentence. However, when you want to express understanding or agreement within a sentence, you can construct sentences that use these words in more or less fixed expressions like **genau richtig** or **es ist (mir) klar**. In addition, **genau, gewiss, klar, natürlich, richtig, selbstverständlich,** and **sicher** can work as adjectives or in some cases as adverbs, and they have similar meanings. (See Chapter 12 for more on adjectives.)

Das wird selbstverständlich gemacht. (*That will certainly be done.*)

Es ist mir klar, daß ich abnehmen soll. (*I realize that I should lose weight.* Literally: *It's clear to me that I should lose weight.*)

Die Straßen waren gewiss sehr gefährlich nach dem Sturm. (*The streets were certainly very dangerous after the storm.*)

Sie haben es genau richtig geraten. (*You guessed it exactly right.*)

In the following exercise, insert one of the alternatives for **ja** in each space provided. In all cases, several solutions are possible. (**Hint:** The choices have something to do with comma and period usage.) Use Table 7-1 to decide which words to use.

0. _____ können wir zu Fuß zum Bahnhof gehen.

A. **Klar** können wir zu Fuß zum Bahnhof gehen. (*Of course we can walk to the train station.*) Other alternatives are **natürlich, selbstvertändlich,** and **sicher** because these expressions don't need to be separated by a comma or a period, which means that the next word is the verb.

1. _____, ich komme morgen.

2. _____ können wir mit dem Zug nach Köln fahren.

3. _____, das ist in Ordnung.

4. _____ geht die ganze Familie in Urlaub.

5. _____, wir fliegen am Dienstag nach Genf.

6. _____. Mein Chef kann bis morgen warten.

7. _____, das ist überhaupt kein Problem.

8. _____ helfe ich Ihnen.

9. _____. Ich bin Herr Gravenstein.

Responding with No: The Difference between Kein and Nicht

Saying *no* in German is plain and simple: **nein.** However, when you want to negate an action, or an object or person, you have two ways to express *not* (or *not any*): **kein** and **nicht.** Getting them straight is a matter of knowing what they negate in a sentence. The word order of these negations is important to know, as is how to form the endings of **kein** (**nicht** doesn't change). In this section, I take you through the steps of when and how to use **nicht** and **kein.**

Negating with nicht

The nuts and bolts of **nicht** are straightforward as far as its form is concerned. **Nicht** is all you need to know (unlike **kein,** which has case and gender endings — see the next section). **Nicht** generally negates a verb: **nicht einladen** (*not to invite*), **nicht fahren** (*not to drive, travel*), **nicht feiern** (*not to celebrate*). It can also negate an adjective, as in **nicht interessant** (*not interesting*), or an adverb, as in **nicht pünktlich** (*not on time*). What you do need to figure out is how to position **nicht** in a sentence. Because **nicht** is an adverb, it negates the action of the verb or modifies an adjective or an adverb, and it's generally next to these parts of speech. For example:

Sie fliegen nicht nach London. (*They're not flying to London.*) **Nicht** directly follows the verb in this sentence, negating the idea that they're flying.

Martin spricht nicht gut Deutsch. (*Martin doesn't speak good German.*) In this sentence, **nicht** tells you that Martin's ability to speak German is not good, so **nicht** immediately follows the verb.

Gestern kamen wir nicht pünktlich zum Termin. (*Yesterday we didn't get to our appointment on time.*) **Nicht** links with the adverb **pünktlich** (*on time*), and you place it before **pünktlich.**

Das Buch ist nicht interessant. (*The book isn't interesting.*) The negation connects the verb **ist** (*is*) and the adjective **interessant** (*interesting*); **nicht** modifies **interessant,** so you place it in front of the adjective.

Placement is the more complex part of **nicht,** but most of the time, if you're not perfect with word order, you'll still be understandable in spoken or written German. Table 7-2 explains some guidelines when using **nicht,** which should help you to sort out where to put this valuable chess piece.

Table 7-2	Guidelines for Positioning Nicht	
Position of Nicht	**Example Sentence**	**Translation**
Follows		
A conjugated verb	Maria fährt **nicht** nach Kiel.	*Maria isn't driving to Kiel.*
A conjugated verb and precedes a separable prefix	Felix und Gretl sehen **nicht** fern. (Fernsehen is a separable-prefix verb.)	*Felix and Gretl aren't watching TV.*
Most specific adverbs of time	Ich war gestern **nicht** zu Hause. (Gestern is the specific adverb of time.)	*I wasn't at home yesterday.*
Comes at the end of		
Yes/no questions	Essen Sie den Apfel **nicht?**	*Aren't you going to eat the apple?*
A sentence or question with a direct object	Ich kenne diesen Mann **nicht.** (Diesen Mann is the direct object.)	*I don't know that man.*
Precedes		
Most adjectives	Das Hotel ist **nicht** gemütlich. (Gemütlich is the adjective.)	*The hotel isn't cozy.*
Most adverbs, except for specific adverbs of time	Ihr lauft **nicht** schnell. (Schnell is the adverb.)	*You don't run fast.*
Infinitives connected to a verb	Ich gehe **nicht** einkaufen. (Einkaufen is the infinitive.)	*I'm not going shopping.*
Most prepositional phrases	Dieser Käse kommt **nicht** aus Frankreich. (Aus Frankreich is the prepositional phrase.)	*This cheese isn't from France.*
The combinations of parts in a sentence (usually)	Matthias geht **nicht** sehr oft in die Bibliothek. (Two parts are here — sehr oft and in die Bibliothek.)	*Matthias doesn't go to the library very often.*

In this exercise, your task is to figure out the word order of the reply to the question. Read the question, and then write the reply in the correct word order using Table 7-2 to show you where to place **nicht** in the sentence. The replies in this exercise all begin with **nein,** followed by a comma. When all else fails, sneak a look at the answer key to help you get started.

Q. Gehst du heute Abend ins Kino?

Nein,/ich/Kino/gehe/heute/nicht/ins/Abend

A. Gehst du heute Abend ins Kino? (*Are you going to the cinema this evening?*)

Nein, ich gehe heute Abend **nicht** ins Kino. (*No, I'm not going to the cinema this evening.*)

10. Ist das dein Haus?

Nein,/Haus/das/mein/nicht/ist _____

11. Kommen Sie am Mittwoch zu uns?

Nein,/nicht/wir/am Mittwoch/zu/kommen/Ihnen. _____

12. Gehen Sie jetzt Golf spielen?

Nein,/ich/spielen/Golf/nicht/gehe. _____

13. Trinken Sie den Orangensaft nicht?

Nein,/ihn/nicht/trinke/ich. _____

14. Liegt Duisburg in einer schönen Gegend?

Nein,/liegt/schönen/nicht/einer/in/Gegend/Duisburg.

_____

15. Geht ihr heute Nachmittag schwimmen?

Nein,/heute/nicht/Nachmittag/gehen/schwimmen/wir.

_____

Negating with kein

Using **kein** (*no, not, not any*) is almost as easy as using **nicht** (see the preceding section). **Kein** functions as an adjective; it describes nouns by expressing negation such as **keiner Polizist** (*no policeman*), **keine Jeans** (*no jeans*), **kein Brot** (*no bread*), and so on. However, before you can jump in and start adding **kein** into your sentences, you need to know the gender and case of the noun you're negating. Look at the following sentence: **Keiner Polizist hat einen leichten Job** (*no policeman has an easy job*). **Keiner Polizist** is the subject of the sentence, so it's in nominative case. **Polizist** is masculine (**der**), so you add **-er** to **kein** = **keiner Polizist. Keiner** is the singular masculine form of **kein** in nominative case. (See Chapter 2 for more on gender and case.)

When you look at **kein,** you can see the indefinite article **ein** (*a, an*). Good news again on the grammar front: The indefinite article **ein** and other very commonly used words are often referred to as **ein-** words because they follow the same pattern in case and gender endings. In the nominative case, **ein** and **kein** are the masculine and neuter forms, and **eine** and **keine** are the feminine and plural forms.

You need to remember only one set of endings for the following words:

- **ein** (*a, an*), the indefinite article

- **kein** (*no, not, not any*), the adjective that negates a noun

- **mein, dein, sein, ihr, unser, eurer, ihr, Ihr** (*my, your, his, her, our, your, their, your*), the possessive adjectives

Table 7-3 shows how to remember the endings for **kein,** with the case and gender endings in bold. (Chapter 2 provides background information on case and gender.) Masculine and neuter are grouped together, and feminine and plural are in one column. This table is also valid for **ein-** words except for **ein** itself, which has no plural form.

Table 7-3	Endings of Kein	
Case	*Masculine / Neuter*	*Feminine / Plural*
Nominative	kein	kein**e**
Accusative	kein**en** (masc.), kein (n.)	kein**e**
Dative	kein**em**	kein**er** (fem.), kein**en** (pl.)
Genitive	kein**es**	kein**er**

Notice that masculine and neuter endings are almost all the same for **kein** and **ein-** words; the accusative is the only one that differs. You can also remember feminine and plural together, keeping in mind that the dative is the only one that isn't the same for the two genders. Look at the example sentences with **kein** in the four cases, followed by the English equivalent and the grammar note explaining the gender:

- Nominative case: **Keine Menschen leben auf der Insel.** (*No people live on the island.*) **Menschen** (plural) is the subject of the sentence, so **keine Menschen** is nominative plural**.**

- Accusative case: **Nach dem grossen Abendessen hatte ich keinen Hunger.** (*I wasn't hungry after the big dinner.*) Literally, **ich hatte keinen Hunger** means *I had no hunger.* **Der Hunger** (masculine) changes to the accusative singular **keinen Hunger** because it's the object of the sentence.

- Dative case: **In keinem alten Auto gibt es GPS.** (*There's no GPS in any old car[s].*) Literally, **in keinem alten Auto gibt es GPS** means *in no old car is there GPS.* The prepositional phrase **in keinem alten Auto** is in dative case; therefore, **das Auto** becomes **keinem (alten) Auto.**

- Genitive case: **Während keiner Nacht in der letzten Woche habe ich gut geschlafen.** (*I didn't sleep well [during] any night last week.*) Literally, **während keiner Nacht in der letzten Woche habe ich gut geschlafen** means *during no night in the past week did I sleep well.* **Während** (*during*) is a genitive preposition, and **die Nacht** is feminine singular. (Chapter 15 shows you details of prepositions.) You need the genitive case ending **-er** for **kein.**

When you're reading German, use the examples you see to understand the grammar involved. Train yourself to take a step back and think carefully about which word endings you're dealing with in a sentence. The pieces of the grammar puzzle begin to fit into place when you recognize which gender and case you're looking at.

The purpose of the next exercise is to put the correct ending on **kein.** You need to know the gender of the noun, and when a preposition is involved, you need to know which case the preposition takes. Here's the situation: Daniel is writing a good riddance letter to Susanne, who has run off with Jonas.

14/3/08

Liebe Susanne,

dieser Brief ist (16)_____ typischer Brief von mir. Ich

habe (17)_____ guten Worte für dich, und

(18)_____ Zeit, sehr lange zu schreiben. Du bist

(19)_____ Frau für mich, weil du (20)_____

Interesse mehr an mir hast. Warum bist du so? Ich habe mit

(21)_____ anderen Frau geflirtet.

Du hast (22)_____ Grund, mit Jonas zu flirten. Er schenkt

dir (23)_____ Blumen wie ich es immer tue, er hat (24)

_____ Auto, und noch schlimmer, er hat (25)_____

Arbeit. Ich sage dir, Jonas ist (26)_____ Mann für dich.

Veilleicht magst du mich nicht, weil ich (27)_____

Haare habe und auch (28) _____ Muskeln. Was kann ich

dazu sagen? Du bist auch (29) _____ Schönheit. Leb wohl.

Daniel

Avoiding blunt negative replies

You don't want to sound overly negative when answering yes/no-type questions with a straight **nein.** You can politely answer some questions negatively by adding a few words to cushion the impact.

How can you avoid being blunt in polite conversation? You can make a positive impression on German speakers when giving positive and even negative replies by using *idiomatic expressions* — fixed phrases — that help you avoid sounding overly negative. Keep a handful stored in the corner of your brain marked **Deutscher Wortschatz** (*German vocabulary*). Literally speaking, **Wortschatz** means *word treasures*, which is a great way to regard vocabulary! Consider this exchange:

Haben Sie Kleingeld für 2€? (*Do you have change for 2€?*)

Nein, es tut mir leid. (*No, I'm sorry. I don't.*)

In the response, you soften the blow of **nein** by adding the apology **es tut mir leid** (*I'm sorry*). You can also give an excuse (hopefully a plausible one) such as **nein, da mein Portmonnaie zu Hause ist** (*No, because my wallet is at home*).

Table 7-4 provides a sampling of expressions that help you avoid sounding too strongly negative.

Table 7-4	Avoiding Bluntness with Negative Answers	
Phrase	**English Equivalent**	**Comments**
Es tut mir leid	*I'm sorry*	The apology **Es tut mir leid** prefaces the rest of the information.
fast keine (Zeit)	*hardly any (time)*	**Fast keine Zeit** (*hardly any time*) is the same as **kaum Zeit.**
praktisch kein	*practically no*	You can also use **praktisch** in the positive sense: Sie ist **praktisch** fertig (*She's practically/virtually ready*).
Im Grunde genommen	*basically*	The signal of a refusal — **Im Grunde genommen** — comes at the beginning of the sentence, softening the negative.
nicht hundertprozentig/ nicht ganz	*not 100%/ not completely*	You don't need to admit that you understand only 70%. Chances are, the speaker will repeat him/herself. Stating **nein** flatly may not get you anywhere.
nicht nur (. . . sondern auch)	*not only (. . . but also)*	**nicht nur** (*not only*) can be linked like this: **Nicht nur** mein Vater, **sondern auch** mein Großvater kam aus Irland. (*Not only my father but also my grandfather came from Ireland.*)
Ich habe nicht die leiseste Ahnung	*I haven't the faintest idea*	This is a fixed expression that can also be stated like this: Ich **habe keine Ahnung** (*I have no idea*).

The following points show these expressions embedded in dialogue. For each example, a question is followed by an answer with a softener that avoids the bluntness of **kein** and **nicht.** The modifying words are set in bold:

✔ Können wir noch einen Kaffee trinken? (*Can we have another cup of coffee?*)

   Es tut mir leid, aber wir haben **fast keine** Zeit. (*I'm sorry, but we have hardly any time.*)

✔ Interessieren Sie sich für diese Musik? (*Are you interested in this music?*)

   Ich habe **praktisch kein** Interesse für solche Musik. (*I have practically no interest in such music.*)

✔ Können Sie in diesem Fall eine Ausnahme machen? (*Can you make an exception in this case?*)

   Im Grunde genommen, dürfen wir keine Ausnahmen machen. (*Basically, we can't make any exceptions.*)

   Note: You can also use **nicht** with a verb: **Im Grunde genommen,** geht das **nicht.** (*Basically, that won't work*).

✔ Verstehen Sie, was ich meine? (*Do you understand what I mean?*)

Nicht hundertprozentig/Nicht ganz. (*Not one hundred percent/Not completely.*)

✔ Sie Sind Engländer, nicht wahr? (*You're English, aren't you?*)

Nicht nur Engländer, da mein Vater aus Irland kam. (*Not only English, because my father came from Ireland.*)

✔ Ändert sich das Klima heutzutage? (*Is the climate changing nowadays?*)

Ich **habe nicht die leiseste Ahnung.** (*I haven't the faintest idea.*)

Explaining Answers Using Da- Compounds

You're probably aware of German's propensity for combining words or word fragments into one humongous word that's as long as its definition (if you're not, check out Chapter 4). **Da-** compounds are far simpler because they combine only two parts: **da-** and a preposition. These compounds are handy for replacing the object of the preposition; **da-** can be translated as *it* or *that,* and in the case of plural nouns, *them.* You don't need to repeat the prepositional phrase, making you sound intelligent as well as fluent in German.

Use combinations of **da-** + preposition when you want to refer to the prepositional phrase (**mit meinem neuen Computer** [*with my new computer*]) without repeating it — for example, in a reply or to make reference to a prepositional phrase that someone has already mentioned before — just as you say something like *I like to work with it* (**Ich arbeite gern damit**) in English. **Damit** is a combination of **da-** + **mit** (literally *it* + *with*), and it can stand in for **mit meinem neuen Computer**.

Look at this example question with two different replies. Clearly, the second reply is much less redundant than the first one, and you sound much more like you know what you're talking about — even though you say that you **verstehe nichts davon** (*understand nothing about it*)!

✔ **Verstehen Sie etwas von dieser Grammatik?** (*Do you know/understand anything about this grammar?*)

✔ **Nein, ich verstehe nichts von dieser Grammatik.** (*No, I don't know/understand anything about this grammar.*)

Nein, ich verstehe nichts davon. (*No, I know/understand nothing about it.*)

Notice how **davon** translates in the second reply: *about it.* You can also translate **davon** as *about that,* though in Table 7-5, **von** has two translations, *from* and *by.* That's because the meaning of the preposition can change when it's plunked into a prepositional phrase or (especially) a verbal phrase that includes a preposition (a verbal phrase is a more or less fixed expression that has a verb in it). The verbal phrase in the example is **etwas von etwas verstehen,** which is what you'd see in a dictionary entry under the headword **verstehen,** translated as *to know sth about sth* (*sth* is a standard abbreviation for *something*).

To form these compounds with **da-,** study Table 7-5 and then find the appropriate compound for the practice exercise that follows. The table shows the most common compounds formed by adding **da-** to the prepositions. The English equivalents help you to get a feel for the preposition, but keep in mind that they can alter their meaning according to the context of the sentence. When the preposition begins with a vowel, the letter **r** is inserted between the two elements of the word (as in **da + r + über = darüber**)

Table 7-5	**Answering with Da- Compounds**	
German Preposition	*Translation*	*Da- Compound (Preposition + it, that, them)*
an	*on, at, to*	**daran**
auf	*on top of, to*	**darauf**
aus	*out of, from*	**daraus**
bei	*at, with*	**dabei**
durch	*through, by*	**dadurch**
für	*for*	**dafür**
gegen	*against*	**dagegen**
in	*in, inside of*	**darin**
hinter	*behind, after*	**dahinter**
mit	*with, by*	**damit**
nach	*after, to*	**danach**
neben	*next to*	**daneben**
über	*over, above*	**darüber**
um	*around*	**darum**
unter	*under*	**darunter**
von	*from, by*	**davon**
vor	*in front of, before*	**davor**
zu	*to, at*	**dazu**
zwischen	*between*	**dazwischen**

In this exercise, read the question and the answer. Decide which **da-** compound to place in the spaces, and cut and paste the appropriate compound into the answer that follows the question. Then try your hand at translating the complete answer (not the question) into English.

Q. Haben Sie etwas gegen diesen Vorschlag?

Nein, ich habe nichts _____.

A. Haben Sie etwas gegen diesen Vorschlag? (*Do you have anything against this suggestion?*)

Nein, ich habe nichts **dagegen. (*No, I have nothing against it.*)**

30. Denken Sie an die Besprechung?

Ja, ich denke _____.

English: _____

31. Warten Sie noch auf Ihre Bestellung?

Ja, ich warte noch _____.

English: _____

32. Schreibst du mit dem Laptop?

Nein, ich schreibe nicht _____.

English: _____

33. Arbeitet er für 8€ in der Stunde?

Nein, _____ arbeitet er nicht.

English: _____

34. Steht der Stuhl vor dem Fenster oder hinter dem Tisch?

Der Stuhl steht nicht _____ und nicht _____; er steht in einem anderen Zimmer.

English: _____

Sounding Diplomatic: Using Maybe, Suggesting, and Refusing Politely

Ever feel like blurting out a resounding *No!* in the middle of a meeting when you totally disagree with the proposal being discussed? Ever wanted to shake someone who's always negative into saying an unequivocal *Yes* to something you suggest? If so, you likely used a bit more tact when you actually did speak up. Even if you haven't had such experiences, you do need to practice diplomacy in a great deal of situations, and it's even more crucial to know how to couch your agreement or disagreement in diplomatic words when you speak another language. Although German may — acoustically speaking — sound direct and even harsh at times, you can sound more diplomatic and polite simply by adding a few measures of *maybes* and *wells* to replies that may otherwise sound too blunt.

Add words such as **vielleicht** (*maybe*) or **nun** (*well*) where you would in English, namely at the beginning of the idea that you intend to disagree with or answer with a negative reply. Longer expressions are generally at the beginning of the sentence you're expressiong doubts about; these need to be memorized as fixed expressions.

Es kann sein, dass der Bericht einige Fehler hat. (*It could be that the report has some mistakes.*) The expression **es kann sein** is a fixed expression connected to the rest of the sentence by the conjunction **dass.** (For more on conjunctions, see Chapter 14.)

Um ehrlich zu sein, das wäre schwierig. (*To be honest, that would be difficult.*) The expression **um ehrlich zu sein** is a fixed expression. Following it is the information that you're being honest about.

North Americans — and possibly even more so, the British — enjoy a great reputation for using a broad range of polite language when expressing indecision, agreement, and disagreement with others. The German language isn't quite as famous for sounding reserved. Why? The language itself has a stronger ring to the ears than English because of the **Tonfall** (*inflection* or *tone*) and the fact that it bunches more consonants together. Speakers of German don't deliberately try to be blunt; rather, the effect comes from the sound of the language.

Table 7-6 walks you through a wider range of ways you can respond diplomatically when you want to signal your reservations. Each German expression is followed by an example phrase and its English equivalent. Some of the expressions are one-word introductory signals that you use to preface your opinion; others are longer phrases that you use in German to sound diplomatic, to qualify your standpoint, or to negotiate acceptance of your suggestion.

Another bonus for using such expressions is that you gain time while you decide whether you really want to agree or disagree with the person you're conversing with. That's a thankful bonus when you're speaking a language that isn't your own and you want to sound intelligent — and intelligible — in what you say.

Table 7-6	Diplomatic Answering Gambits	
German Expression	*Example Phrase*	*English Equivalent*
Expressing maybe/perhaps		
Vielleicht . . .	**Vielleicht kommt er . . .**	*Maybe he'll come . . .*
Eventuell . . .	**Eventuell kann man . . .**	*You could possibly . . .*
Möglicherweise . . .	**Möglicherweise regnet es nicht . . .**	*Perhaps it won't rain . . .*
Introducing doubt		
Nun . . .	**Nun, wenn es so ist . . .**	*Well, if it's like that . . .*
Eigentlich . . .	**Eigentlich dachte ich . . .**	*Actually, I thought . . .*
. . . aber . . .	**Ich verstehe, aber . . .**	*I understand, but . . .*
Mit allem Respekt . . .	**Mit allem Respekt muss ich dazu sagen . . .**	*With all due respect, I must say . . .*
Suggesting		
Machen wir so, . . .	**Machen wir so, wir schieben . . .**	*Let's do it like this: We'll delay . . .*
Wir könnten . . .	**Wir könnten morgen mit einander treffen . . .**	*We could meet tomorrow . . .*

(continued)

Table 7-6 *(continued)*

German Expression	Example Phrase	English Equivalent
Wie wäre es . . .	Wie wäre es wenn wir versuchen würden . . .	How would it be if we tried . . .

(The introduction to the sentence **wie wäre es** implies that it will continue in the subjunctive because you're imagining something.)

German Expression	Example Phrase	English Equivalent
Was halten Sie davon, wenn . . .	Was halten Sie davon, wenn wir abwarten . . .	What do you think about waiting . . .
Modifying negation		
. . . kaum . . .	Das ist kaum möglich . . .	That's hardly possible . . .
. . . fast nicht . . .	Das ist fast nicht machbar . . .	That's just about impossible to do . . .
Ich habe einige Bedenken . . .	Ich habe einige Bedenken dazu . . .	I have a few doubts about that . . .
. . . etwas zu . . .	Der Preis ist etwas zu hoch . . .	The price is somewhat too high . . .
. . . ein bißchen . . .	Wir brauchen ein bißchen mehr Zeit . . .	We need a bit more time . . .
Refusing diplomatically		
Leider . . .	Leider kann ich nicht mitkommen . . .	Unfortunately, I can't come along . . .
Es tut mir leid . . .	Es tut mir leid, aber das geht nicht . . .	I'm sorry, but that won't work . . .
Entschuldigung, aber . . .	Entschuldigung, aber ich habe wenig Zeit . . .	Sorry, but I have little time . . .
Ist das nicht . . .	Ist das nicht etwas früh?	Isn't that a bit early?

In this exercise, you're overseas conducting business with an Austrian ski manufacturer who wants you to buy their products, which are very good but overpriced. You have the opportunity to express your doubt, make a counter suggestion, refuse diplomatically, or say maybe. Use the phrases in Table 7-6 to practice straddling the fence politely without sounding like you're too rough at refusing or too wishy-washy about decision making. There may be two or three solutions for each reply.

Q. Ich möchte Sie morgen zum Abendessen einladen.

_____.

A. Ich möchte Sie morgen zum Abendessen einladen. (*I'd like to invite you to dinner tomorrow.*)

Leider kann ich nicht. (*Unfortunately, I can't.*)

35. Die Preise unserer Skier sind ganz in Ordnung.

_____, Ihre Preise sind uns zu hoch.

36. Sie müssen sich jetzt entscheiden.

Ist das nicht _____ früh?

37. Ich denke, Sie finden keine besseren Preise.

_____ ich finde Ihre Preise zu hoch.

38. Es gibt eine billigere Alternative zu diesem Produkt.

_____ können Sie sie uns zeigen.

39. Möchten Sie eine Woche skifahren - auf unseren Kosten?

Da habe ich _____.

Answer Key

1 **Genau,** ich komme morgen. (*Exactly. I'll come tomorrow.*) All other alternatives are possible; with a comma (or a period) separating the two sentence parts, you start the next part with a subject.

2 **Natürlich** können wir mit dem Zug nach Köln fahren. (*Naturally, we can take the train to Cologne.*) Other alternatives are **klar, selbstvertändlich,** and **sicher** because these expressions don't need to be separated by a comma or a period, which means that the next word is the verb.

3 **Ja, ja,** das ist in Ordnung. (*Yes, that's fine.*) All other alternatives are possible; with a comma (or a period) separating the two sentence parts, you start the next part with a subject.

4 **Klar** geht die ganze Familie in Urlaub. (*Of course the whole family is going on vacation.*) Other alternatives are **natürlich, selbstvertändlich,** and **sicher** because these expressions don't need to be separated by a comma or a period, which means that the next word is the verb.

5 **Sicher**, wir fliegen am Dienstag nach Genf. (*Sure, we're flying to Geneva on Tuesday.*) All other alternatives are possible; with a comma (or a period) separating the two sentence parts, you start the next part with a subject.

6 **Gewiss.** Mein Chef kann bis morgen warten. (*Of course. My boss can wait until tomorrow.*) All other alternatives are possible; with a period (or a comma) separating the two sentence parts, you start the next part with a subject.

7 **Jawohl,** das ist überhaupt kein Problem. (*Yes, that's no problem at all.*) All other alternatives are possible; with a comma (or a period) separating the two sentence parts, you start the next part with a subject.

8 **Selbstverständlich**helfe ich Ihnen. (*Certainly, I'll help you.*) Other alternatives are **klar, natürlich,** and **sicher** because these expressions don't need to be separated by a comma or a period, which means that the next word is the verb.

9 **Richtig.** Ich bin Herr Gravenstein. (*Right. I'm Herr Gravenstein.*) All other alternatives are possible; with a period (or a comma) separating the two sentence parts, you start the next part with a subject.

10 Ist das dein Haus? (*Is that your house?*)

Nein, das ist **nicht** mein Haus. (*No, it isn't my house.*) **Nicht** follows the verb.

11 Kommen Sie am Mittwoch zu uns? (*Are you coming to see us on Wednesday?*)

Nein, am Mittwoch kommen wir **nicht** zu Ihnen. (*No, we're not coming on Wednesday to see you.*) **Nicht** precedes the prepositional phrase **zu Ihnen.**

12 Gehen Sie jetzt Golf spielen? (*Are you going to play golf now?*)

Nein, ich gehe **nicht** Golf spielen. (*No, I'm not going to play golf.*) **Nicht** precedes the infinitive expression **Golf spielen.**

13 Trinken Sie den Orangensaft nicht? (*Aren't you going to drink the orange juice?*)

Nein, ich trinke ihn **nicht.** (*No, I'm not going to drink it.*) Nicht follows the direct object **ihn.**

14 Liegt Duisburg in einer schönen Gegend? (*Is Duisburg in a pretty area?*)

Nein, Duisburg liegt **nicht** in einer schönen Gegend. (*No, Duisburg isn't in a pretty area.*) **Nicht** precedes the prepositional phrase **in einer schönen Gegend.**

15 Geht ihr heute Nachmittag schwimmen? (*Are you going swimming this afternoon?*)

Nein, wir gehen heute Nachmittag **nicht** schwimmen. (*No we're not going swimming this afternoon.*) **Nicht** precedes the infinitive **schwimmen.**

In the following letter, the reason for the endings on **kein** are shown in parentheses at the end of each negation.

16 – **29**

Liebe Susanne,

dieser Brief ist (16) **kein** typischer Brief (der Brief is nominative) von mir. Ich habe (17) **keine** guten Worte (die Worte is plural, accusative.) für dich, und (18) **keine** Zeit, (die Zeit is accusative) sehr lange zu schreiben. Du bist (19) **keine** Frau (die Frau is nominative) für mich, weil du (20) **kein** Interesse (das Interesse is accusative) mehr an mir hast. Warum bist du so? Ich habe mit (21) **keiner** anderen Frau (die Frau is dative because mit is a dative preposition) geflirtet.

Du hast (22) **keinen** Grund, (der Grund is accusative) mit Jonas zu flirten. Er schenkt dir (23) **keine** Blumen (die Blumen is plural, accusative) wie ich es immer tue, er hat (24) **kein** Auto, (das Ato is accusative) und noch schlimmer, er hat (25) **keine** Arbeit (die Arbeit is accusative). Ich sag' dir, Jonas ist (26) **kein** Mann (der Mann is nominative) für dich.

Vielleicht magst du mich nicht, weil ich (27) **keine** Haare (die Haare is plural, accusative) habe und auch (28) **keine** Muskeln (die Muskeln is plural, accusative). Was kann ich dazu sagen? Du bist auch (29) **keine** Schonheit (die Schönheit is nominative). Leb wohl.

Daniel

Dear Susanne,

This letter is no typical letter from me. I don't have any good words for you, and no time to write a long letter. You're not the woman for me because you have no more interest in me. Why are you like that? I didn't flirt with any woman.

You have no reason to flirt with Jonas. He doesn't give you flowers like I always do, he doesn't have a car, and even worse, he has no work. I'm telling you, Jonas is not the man for you.

Perhaps you don't like me because I don't have any hair or muscles. What can I say? You're no beauty queen yourself. Farewell.

Daniel

30 Denken Sie an die Besprechung? (*Will you remember/ think about the meeting?*)

Ja, ich denke **daran.** (***Yes, I'll remember it.***)

31 Warten Sie noch auf Ihre Bestellung? (*Are you waiting for your order?*)

Ja, ich warte noch **darauf.** (***Yes, I'm still waiting for it.***)

32 Schreibst du mit dem Laptop? (*Are you writing with the laptop?*)

Nein, ich schreibe nicht **damit.** (***No, I'm not writing with it.***)

33 Arbeitet er für 8€ in der Stunde? (*Does he work for 8€ an hour?*)

Nein, **dafür** arbeitet er nicht. (***No, he doesn't/won't work for that.***)

34 Steht der Stuhl vor dem Fenster oder hinter dem Tisch? (*Is the chair in front of the window or behind the table?*)

Der Stuhl steht nicht **davor** und nicht **dahinter**; er steht in einem anderen Zimmer. (***The chair isn't in front of or behind it; it's in another room.***)

35 Die Preise unserer Skier sind ganz in Ordnung. (*The prices of our skis are completely right.*)

Mit allem Respekt, Ihre Preise sind uns zu hoch. (*With all due respect, your prices are too high for us.*)

36 Sie müssen sich jetzt entscheiden. (*You need to make a decision now.*)

Ist das nicht **etwas zu** früh? (*Isn't that a bit too early?*) An alternative is **ein bißchen.**

37 Ich denke, Sie finden keine besseren Preise. (*I think you won't find any better prices.*)

Entschuldigung, aber ich finde Ihre Preise zu hoch. (*Excuse me, but I think your prices are too high.*)

38 Es gibt eine billigere Alternative zu diesem Produkt. (*There's a more inexpensive alternative to this product.*)

Vielleicht können Sie sie uns zeigen. (*Perhaps you could show them to us.*) Alternatives are **eventuell** or **möglicherweise.**

39 Möchten Sie eine Woche skifahren — auf unseren Kosten? (*Would you like to ski for a week — at our expense?*)

Da habe ich **einige Bedenken.** (*I have a few doubts about that.*)

Chapter 8

Describing Your Mood: Summing Up the Subjunctive

Most English and German speakers who aren't used to analyzing their language — and that probably includes zillions of otherwise perfectly normal people — would be seriously challenged if they had to explain the ins and outs of the subjunctive. Although the word *subjunctive* may conjure up thoughts of doctors discussing an unpleasant eye infection, it's actually an innocuous description for the way verbs tell events that are contrary to fact. Consider the subjunctive as an umbrella term for describing all sorts of unreal situations: hypothetical, unlikely, uncertain, potential, probable, or doubtful events.

In German, the subjunctive gets extra mileage because you also use it to describe polite requests. This chapter deals with how to construct the various forms of the subjunctive and how to use them in German. You also find out the differences between the subjunctive and conditional in German and English. To get you off and running, the next section explains the terminology surrounding the subjunctive.

Terms and Conditions: Unraveling Subjunctive Terminology

Discussing the subjunctive is pretty tough if you're not familiar with the lingo. The following sections help you keep the terms straight so you can better understand the subjunctive and how to use it.

Getting in the mood

If someone asks you what your mood is today, you're unlikely to answer, "Oh, I'm in a real indicative mood today, but yesterday I was kind of subjunctive." But if sentences could speak about themselves, that's exactly what they'd say. See, a *mood* in language terms (as opposed to emotional terms) is the manner in which the speaker perceives an action. Take a look:

- ✔ **Indicative mood:** The indicative mood states a fact or deals with a real situation, usually in the form of a statement or a question, such as *I live in Waterford* or *Where are you from originally?*

- ✔ **Imperative mood:** This mood is the command form (which I discuss in Chapter 6), such as *Get out of here!*

- ✔ **Subjunctive mood:** The subjunctive mood expresses non-factual, hypothetical, or similar "unreal" actions and thoughts as a statement or a question. In German, you'd use the subjunctive form in these example sentences:

    I'd like 200 grams of that cheese, please.

    Would you marry someone 25 years younger than you?

Comparing subjunctive types and the conditional

In English grammar terms, the *conditional* can refer to a clause or a sentence that describes circumstances in varying stages of "reality." A typical example of a conditional sentence in English is the if-type question: *What would you do if you were to win a million in the lottery?* The verb in the main clause *what would you do* is in the conditional.

In German, you use verbs in the subjunctive form in if-type conditional sentences that express a condition contrary to fact. But that's not the only use of the subjunctive — you find two subjunctive groups in German. Here's how they compare:

- ✔ **Subjunctive I:** People use Subjunctive I in indirect discourse (indirect speech), most often in the printed media to report what someone says. For this reason, when you do come across this subjunctive form, try to recognize what the verbs mean; you'll probably never need to use Subjunctive I yourself.

- ✔ **Subjunctive II:** In terms of importance to you, Subjunctive I takes a back seat to Subjunctive II. You use Subjunctive II for expressing imagined things, describing information contrary to fact, or making wishes and requests.

(*Note:* Both Subjunctive I and Subjunctive II forms can refer to events in the present, past, and future.)

The common denominator of subjunctives in both English and German is that they express a specific mood, namely — you'll never believe it! — the subjunctive mood. Beyond that, in everyday German, the Subjunctive II form is very much alive and kicking, but in English, it's relegated to a dusty corner in terms of how often you use it.

Both groups, the German Subjunctive I and Subjunctive II, have definite differences in form and function from each other and from verbs in the indicative mood. In contrast, very few English verbs even have a special subjunctive form, so you may be using it without realizing it. One example of the subjunctive in English is *If I were you.* In a sentence without *if,* you'd say *I was,* but with *if* (the element that adds unreality to the action), you use the subjunctive: *If I were you.*

In the following sections, I first map out what you need to know about the present and past Subjunctive II forms so that you can recognize them, form them, and use them in everyday spoken and written German. After that, I discuss the present and past forms of the not-so-common Subjunctive I.

Selecting the Present Subjunctive II: How and When to Use It

When you pack your suitcase to travel to a German-speaking region, remember to include the Subjunctive II form. That way, you can order in a café: **Ich möchte eine Tasse Kaffee bitte** (*I'd like a cup of coffee*) or agree with the tour guide's suggestion to visit the king's private quarters: **Ich hätte schon Interesse daran** (*I'd be really interested in that*). With a few more subjunctive expressions in your bag, you can express actions that are contrary to fact and more.

Even though the subjunctive is used a lot more frequently in German than in English, the average German speaker would probably get tangled up trying to explain the Subjunctive II, let alone listing all its uses. It's so embedded in the language that its use isn't obvious to the native speaker. So relax, take a deep breath, and read on.

In this section, I show you two ways to form the present Subjunctive II to make hypothetical statements, request something, and express wishes. The most frequent form of present Subjunctive II is the construction of **würde** + infinitive. Look at this example: **Ich würde gern nach Hamburg fahren** (*I'd like to go to Hamburg*). Most verbs use this two-part construction.

The other means of forming the present Subjunctive II that I show you in this section is common for only a small but important group of verbs. You form this subjunctive by putting the main verb itself into the subjunctive form. All verbs have subjunctive forms, but in formal written German, you find only a few — and an even smaller number is in everyday written and spoken German. The verbs that do commonly use the present Subjunctive II in the main verb are the modal verbs (see Chapter 9 for modal verbs), the auxiliaries **haben** (*to have*) and **sein** (*to be*) (see Chapter 5 for more on **haben** and **sein**), and a few others. I describe this present subjunctive form in the section "Forming the Subjunctive II of haben, sein, and modal verbs." After that, I go over how to use these two forms of the Subjunctive II. Read on.

Creating the present Subjunctive II with würde

The present Subjunctive II form using **würde** + infinitive has many uses. To make a request, you need to sound polite, especially when you're asking someone to do (or not do) something; therefore, you use this form — for example, **Würden Sie mir bitte helfen?** (*Would you help me please?*). In this section, I show you how to form the **würde** construction to make hypothetical statements, request something, and express wishes.

The common form of present subjunctive, using the **würde** construction, is easy to remember. It uses the simple past form of the infinitive **werden** (which translates to *will* in this context) plus an umlaut: **Wurde** changes to **würde,** the subjunctive of **werden,** and becomes equivalent to *would* in English. (In other words, it uses the present subjunctive form of **werden** like a modal verb — see Chapter 9 for more on modal verbs.) Add the infinitive form of the main verb you want to express in a subjunctive mood, and presto!

Look at the conjugation of **werden** in the verb table. It builds the **würde** subjunctive construction in the present. You use the subjunctive form of **werden** plus the main verb in the infinitive. In the verb table, **arbeiten** (*to work*) is the main verb.

würde arbeiten (subjunctive: *would work*)	
ich **würde** arbeiten	wir **würden** arbeiten
du **würdest** arbeiten	ihr **würdet** arbeiten
er/sie/es **würde** arbeiten	sie **würden** arbeiten
Sie **würden** arbeiten	
Ich **würde** gerne in Wien **arbeiten.** (*I'd [really] like to work in Vienna.*)	

Look at some examples:

> **Würden Sie mir bitte mit meinem Koffer helfen?** (*Would you help me with my suitcase, please?*) The speaker is making a polite request.
>
> **Ich würde gerne nach Salzburg reisen.** (*I'd love to travel to Salzburg.*) The speaker is wishfully thinking of traveling to Salzburg.
>
> **An deiner Stelle würde ich lieber den Kilimanjaro anschauen.** (*If I were you, I'd rather see Kilimanjaro.*) The speaker is making a hypothetical statement with the condition *if I were you.*

The modal verbs **dürfen, können, mögen, müssen, sollen,** and **wollen,** as well as the auxiliaries **haben** and **sein,** don't generally use the subjunctive construction using **würde.** See the next section for details.

Complete the sentences, putting the correct form of **würden** into the spaces. The people I mention are imagining they've made a windfall profit in the stock market (no harm in imagining, right?). The sentences all answer the question **Was würden sie tun?** (*What would they do?*).

0. Mein Bruder _____ uns das Geld geben.

A. Mein Bruder **würde** uns das Geld geben. (*My brother would give us the money.*)

1. Die Großeltern _____ nach Florida umziehen.

2. Ich _____ eine lange Reise machen.

3. Helga _____ ein kleines Segelboot kaufen.

4. Du _____ das Geld auf die Bank bringen.

5. Ihr _____ ein neues Auto kaufen.

6. Johannes weiß nicht, was er machen _____.

7. Marianne und Michael _____ den ganzen Tag singen.

8. Ich _____ nicht alles ausgeben.

9. Der Nachbar _____ eine gigantische Party organisieren.

10. Und was _____ du tun?

Forming the Subjunctive II of haben, sein, and modal verbs

German speakers often use **haben** (*to have*) and **sein** (*to be*) in the present subjunctive form to express wishes, hypothetical situations, and things contrary to fact, such as **ich hätte mehr Zeit** (*I would have more time*) or **es wäre einfacher** (*it would be easier*). The modal auxiliary verbs use the present subjunctive for expressing wishes and other situations by combining with another verb in the infinitive form — for example, **Sie sollten vorsichtig fahren** (*You/they should drive carefully*). All these verbs — plus a few strong verbs — take the same subjunctive endings.

Haben and sein

To form the subjunctive with **haben** (*to have*), start with **hatte** (the simple past tense), remove the **-e**, and add an umlaut plus the appropriate subjunctive ending: **-e, -est, -e, -en, -et, -en,** and **-en.**

hätte (subjunctive: *would have*)	
ich hätt**e**	wir hätt**en**
du hätt**est**	ihr hätt**et**
er/sie/es hätt**e**	sie hätt**en**
Sie hätt**en**	
Ich **hätte** lieber ein umweltfreundliches Auto. (*I'd rather have an environmentally friendly car.*)	

As for **sein** (*to be*), to form the present subjunctive, start with **war** (the simple past tense) and add an umlaut and the appropriate subjunctive ending: **-e, -est, -e, -en, -et, -en,** and **-en.**

wäre (subjunctive: *would be*)	
ich wär**e**	wir wär**en**
du wär**est**	ihr wär**et**
er/sie/es wär**e**	sie wär**en**
Sie wär**en**	
Wir **wären** sicher reich. (*We'd certainly be rich.*)	

Modal verbs and other special verbs

German uses the present Subjunctive II with modal verbs (**dürfen, können, mögen, müssen, sollen,** and **wollen**) quite frequently, and forming the present subjunctive with these verbs isn't that difficult. Just take the simple past form of the verb, add an umlaut if there's one in the infinitive, and add the appropriate subjunctive endings: **-e, -est, -e, -en, -et, -en,** and **-en.** Only two modals — **sollen** and **wollen** — have no umlaut in the infinitive. (For information on simple past tense of modals, see Chapter 17.)

könnte (subjunctive: *could, would be able to*)	
ich könn**te**	wir könn**ten**
du könn**test**	ihr könn**tet**
er/sie/es könn**te**	sie könn**ten**
Sie könn**ten**	
Sie **könnte** uns helfen. (*She could/would be able to help us.*)	

As you see in the three preceding verb tables, the meaning in the subjunctive is differ-ent from the present-tense indicative form. You see *would* in the English translation of the subjunctive verb. *Have* changes to *would have*, and *be* changes to *would be*. In the case of **können,** both of its meanings undergo a transformation: *Able to* changes to *would be able to*, and *can* changes to *could*.

Note: Although all verbs have subjunctive forms of the main verb, only a few are common in informal written and spoken German. These verbs use the subjunctive form of the main verb instead of the **würde** + infinitive construction. The verbs you are most likely to come across include **gehen** (*to go*), **heißen** (*to be called*), **tun** (*to do*), **werden** (*to become*), and **wissen** (*to know [a fact]*). These verbs form the subjunctive as follows:

- For strong verbs, as with modal verbs, the present subjunctive is based on the simple past form of the verb + umlaut (when applicable) + subjunctive endings -**e,** -**est, -e, en, -et, -en,** and -**en** — for example, **gehen** (*to go*) becomes **ginge** (*would go*).

- For weak verbs, the present subjunctive is the same as the simple past tense (you use the same simple-past endings) — for example, **kaufen** (*to buy*) becomes **kaufte** (*would buy*).

See Chapter 16 and Appendix A for more on strong and weak verbs.

Using the present Subjunctive II

This section breaks down the ways you can use the present Subjunctive II. In every-day German, you can use this multi-tasker to express a variety of contrary-to-fact situ-ations. In addition, you can express wishes and make polite requests. For example, imagine you're planning what do to during your three-day stay in **Wien** (*Vienna*). You say, **Wir könnten die Spanische Reitschule sehen** (*We could see the Spanish Riding School*). In the example, **könnten** is the subjunctive form (in the present) of the verb **können** (*can*). Look at the most important uses of the present Subjunctive II.

Describing a hypothetical situation or a wish

When you want to express a hypothetical situation or a wish that can or can't be ful-filled, you often imagine a scenario. German uses the subjunctive in such situations:

Wenn ich nur etwas mehr Zeit hätte! (*If only I had a little more time!*) You don't have more time, so you're wishing you did. **Hätte** (*had*) is the subjunctive form of **haben** (*to have*).

Ich wollte, ich hätte mehr Geschwister. (*I wish I had more siblings*.) This sentence contains two subjunctives, **wollte** and **hätte**. If you want to get technical, **ich wollte** actually means *I would wish*.

Describing a condition

You use the subjunctive to talk about a condition that's contrary to fact — for example, when you're considering what you would (or wouldn't) do if something that isn't true now were true. (See the earlier section "Terms and Conditions: Unraveling Subjunctive Terminology" for more on conditional sentences with *if*.) Look at the examples:

Wenn du kein Affe wärest, würde ich dich heiraten. (*If you weren't a monkey, I'd marry you.*) The verbs **wärest** (*were*) and **würde** (*would*) + infinitive **heiraten** (*to marry*) are both subjunctive forms. In English, the verb in the main clause (*I'd marry you*) is a conditional; technically speaking, the if-clause uses the subjunctive mood, expressed by *weren't*.

Hätte ich die Zeit, so würde ich den Roman lesen. (*If I had time, I'd read that novel.*) Both verbs **hätte** (*had*) and **würde** (*would*) + infinitive **lesen** (*to read*) are subjunctives; in English, the verb in the main clause (*I'd read novels*) is a conditional; the if-clause uses the subjunctive mood, expressed by *had*.

Politely making a request

You use the subjunctive to make a polite request — for example, when you're hungry and you'd like to have something:

Könnte ich noch ein Stück Fleisch nehmen? (*Could I take another piece of meat?*) **Könnte** (*could*) is the subjunctive form of **können** (*can, to be able to*), and using it makes your request sound polite. **Kann ich . . . ?** (*Can I . . . ?*), where the verb is in the indicative mood, is direct; it lacks the politeness of the subjunctive **Könnte ich . . . ?**

Ich möchte die Speisekarte, bitte. (*I'd like the menu, please.*) The subjunctive **Ich möchte** (*I'd like*) is the polite way of ordering food, selecting an item in a store, and so on.

Expressing your feelings and/or opinion

When you state your feelings or express your opinion on something, you often use the subjunctive in German:

Das wäre prima! (*That would be fantastic!*) Your enthusiastic reply to someone's suggestion about going to hear your favorite band includes the subjunctive **wäre** (*would be*).

Wir sollten diese Wurst probieren. (*We should try this sausage.*) You think something would be a good idea, so you use the subjunctive. Here, the subjunctive is **sollten** (*should*) + infinitive **probieren** (*try*).

Some employees are planning a party for Peter, a colleague who is relocating to India. It's supposed to be **eine Überraschung** (*a surprise*). Complete the sentences by filling in the forms of the subjunctive verbs using the infinitive verbs in parentheses.

Q. Walbie _____ (sollen) das Wohnzimmer dekorieren.

A. Walbie **sollte** das Wohnzimmer dekorieren. (*Walbie should decorate the living room.*)

11. Hartmut und Richard _____ (sein) bereit, das Essen zu machen.

12. Wir _____ (dürfen) unsere Familien nicht einladen.

13. Es _____ (können) bis Mitternacht dauern . . .

14. . . . aber leider_____ (müssen) Peter früher nach Hause gehen.

15. Ich _____ (mögen) die Musik organisieren.

Forming and Using the Past Subjunctive II

When you want to express events that might have taken place in the past, you use the past Subjunctive II. Perhaps you wish you'd accomplished something, but you never got around to it. You may regret having done something — or the other way around. You use the past Subjunctive II for such situations.

Imagine you want to describe something that you would (or wouldn't) have done in a certain situation in the past; you say, **Ich hätte das nicht gemacht** (*I wouldn't have done that*). You form the past Subjunctive II with the present subjunctive form of either **haben** or **sein** + the past participle of the main verb that you want to express in the subjunctive. In the preceding example, the past subjunctive is **hätte** (*would have*) + **gemacht** (*done*).

This section runs through the details of forming and using the past Subjunctive II.

Forming the past Subjunctive II

The past subjunctive deals with past actions and events that might have happened in the past. At first glance, the past subjunctive seems to be a clone of the past perfect (see Chapter 17 for past perfect). Indeed, it's the same, with the exception of an umlaut in **hätte** and **wäre**. You can simply remember that the past subjunctive is formed like this:

- Present subjunctive of **haben** = **hätte** + past participle (**geholfen**) = **hätte** (**geholfen**)
- Present subjunctive of **sein** = **wäre** + past participle (**gegangen**) = **wäre** (**gegangen**)

The endings for the present subjunctive are always the same (in this case, you add them to **hätt-** and **wär-**): **-e, -est, -e, -en, -et, -en, -en.**

Using the past Subjunctive II

Do you reflect on situations? Time slips by, and events, relationships, and memories drop off into oblivion. Before that happens, though, you may catch yourself saying, "I wouldn't have jumped into marriage so quickly," or "I might have dyed my hair green." The past subjunctive lets you do this type of reminiscing in German, describing scenarios that may or may not have happened. And even if you aren't the type to dwell on the past, you'll be able to understand what other people are talking about when they say **ich hätte sie angerufen** (*I would have called her*).

You can use three past-tense verb forms in the indicative, but you need only one form of the past subjunctive. Look at the examples:

- **Er hätte uns geholfen.** (*He would have helped us.*) This past Subjunctive II form stands in for three indicative sentences in the past:

    Er hat uns geholfen. (*He helped/has helped us.*)

    Er half uns. (*He helped us.*)

    Er hatte uns geholfen. (*He had helped us.*)

- **Sie wäre gegangen.** (*She would have gone.*) This past Subjunctive II form stands in for three indicative sentences in the past:

    Sie ist gegangen. (*She went/has gone.*)

    Sie ging. (*She went.*)

    Sie war gegangen. (*She had gone.*)

In order to get the hang of putting your ideas into the past Subjunctive II, try changing past actions from fact into a hypothetical situation; in other words, start with a sentence that describes something that did or didn't happen (that's the indicative mood). Write it down in German — for example, **Ich habe eine Katze gehabt.** (*I had a cat.*). Now imagine you didn't have a cat, but you *would've had* one if your parents hadn't had allergies. Change the verb as a fact (*had*) into past subjunctive (*would have had*) by changing **habe** to **hätte**. Now you have **Ich hätte eine Katze gehabt** (*I would have had a cat*).

In the following exercise, you see sentences written in the indicative mood. They describe some event that has happened. Change them into the past subjunctive mood to indicate that these events could have happened in the past (but didn't). Before you start, review the verb tables for the subjunctive of **haben** and **sein,** and check out the information in the bulleted list showing how the three types of indicative past forms change into the past subjunctive. The example sentence leads the way.

Q. Sascha hat einen Job gefunden.

A. Sascha **hätte** einen Job gefunden. (*Sascha would have found a job.*)

16. Liselotte und Heinz haben ein Haus in Ludwigshafen gekauft.

_____

17. Ich ging mit euch ins Theater.

_____

18. Sie hatten uns im Sommer besucht.

_____

19. Du hast die Reise besser geplant.

_____

20. Er wanderte den ganzen Tag in den Bergen.

_____

Two-timing the past subjunctive: Using double infinitives

If only more wishful thinking using the subjunctive were coming your way . . . oh, it is! This time, the infinitive verb comes in a double pack, and one of the verbs is a modal verb — **dürfen, können, mögen, müssen, sollen,** or **wollen.** The purpose of adding the modal verb to another verb is to express what you _might have been allowed to do_ (**hätte machen dürfen**), _could have done_ (**hätte machen können**), and so on.

The construction consists of the present Subjunctive II, **hätte.** (**Wäre** doesn't combine with the modal verbs.) The two infinitive verbs are together at the end of the phrase, with the modal in the second position. Look at the two example sentences:

> **Ich hätte eine längere Reise machen können.** (_I could have made/could have been able to make a longer trip._) The word order follows the standard procedure, with the active verb **hätte** in second position in the sentence. The verb **machen** precedes the modal verb **können** at the end of the phrase.

> **Er hätte früher nach Hause fahren sollen.** (_He should have driven home earlier._) The word order follows the standard procedure with the active verb **hätte** in second position in the sentence. The main verb **fahren** and the modal **sollen** go to the very end of the sentence.

Subjunctive 1: Used in Indirect Discourse

Another way to describe _indirect discourse_ is _indirect speech_. It's the kind of information you read in print when someone writes something that someone else said, but it's not in quotation marks. Journalists use this form of writing to avoid quoting someone directly. Indirect speech frees the writer from taking responsibility for the statement's accuracy. As far as your needs go, you can leave its usage to the media pundits. Just get the hang of what this subjunctive looks like by understanding how you form the Subjunctive I, knowing where you run across it, and what it means, and you're all set.

Note: In English and German, you encounter this subjunctive form almost exclusively in the third-person singular — **er** (_he_), **sie** (_she_), **es** (_it_) — or the plural **sie** (_they_). In English, the present Subjunctive I is the infinitive form of the verb. In its rare appearances in English, it may be be a (somewhat obsolete) statement such as _so be it_, or it may invoke a higher power: _May the spirit of the holiday season be with you._

Recognizing the present Subjunctive 1

As you read a German newspaper or magazine, you encounter the present Subjunctive I when the writer wants to report someone else's original statement. The information — an indirect quotation — may be a opinion, a fact, a plan, and so on, as in **Sie meinte, sie habe nicht genug Zeit** (*She thought [that] she didn't have enough time*). You always use a comma to separate the indirect statement from the person who's telling the information.

You form the present Subjunctive I by taking the infinitive stem of the verb and adding the subjunctive verb endings: **-e, -est, -e, -en, -et, -en,** and **-en.** All verbs follow this pattern with one exception: **sein** (*to be*). Look at the verb table showing **gehen** (*to go, walk*), paying special attention to the commonly used third-person forms. The infinitive stem is **geh-.** The endings are indicated in bold.

gehe (present Subjunctive I: *go/walk*)	
ich geh**e**	wir geh**en**
du geh**est**	ihr geh**et**
er/sie/es geh**e**	sie geh**en**
Sie geh**en**	
Er sagte, er **gehe** nicht. (*He said he wasn't going.*)	

Look at the only irregular exception for present Subjunctive I, the verb **sein:**

sei (present Subjunctive I: *am/is/are/was/were*)	
ich **sei**	wir **seien**
du **seist**	ihr **seiet**
er/sie/es **sei**	sie **seien**
Sie **seien**	
Sie sagte, es **sei** zu früh. (*She said it was too early.*)	

Note: In indirect speech in English, journalists often use the past tense to describe events that may still be occurring (to reflect that the original statement referred to events as they were at the time of speech). Thus, I use the past tense in the English translations.

Look at the examples of present Subjunctive I:

> **Er sagte, er habe eine neue Freundin.** (*He said he had a new girlfriend.*) **Habe** is the present Subjunctive I form of **haben.** Although you say *He said he had . . .* , the information (usually) has present meaning.

> **Der Bundeskanzler sagte, er werde das Problem lösen.** (*The German Chancellor said he would solve the problem.*) **Werde** is the present Subjunctive I form of **werden.** This statement expresses a future event using **werde + lösen.**

Recognizing the Past Subjunctive 1

The past Subjunctive I is the subjunctive you find in the press to describe actions that are what someone else has said about an event in the past. German uses the past subjunctive to describe three past tenses: simple past (see Chapter 17), present perfect (Chapter 16), and past perfect (Chapter 17).

You form the past Subjunctive I by using the appropriate conjugated form of the present subjunctive of **haben** (*to have*) or **sein** (*to be*) and adding the past participle (for information on the past participle, see Chapter 16). All verbs follow this pattern. Look at the past Subjunctive I conjugation of the verb **wohnen** (*to live, reside*), which uses the auxiliary verb **haben.**

habe gewohnt (past Subjunctive I: *had lived*)	
ich **habe gewohnt**	wir **haben gewohnt**
du **habest gewohnt**	ihr **habet gewohnt**
er/sie/es **habe gewohnt**	sie **haben gewohnt**
Sie **haben gewohnt**	
Sie sagte, sie **habe** in einer kleinen Wohnung **gewohnt.** (*She said she had lived in a small apartment.*)	

Look at the past Subjunctive I conjugation of **gehen,** which uses the auxiliary verb **sein.**

sei gegangen (past Subjunctive I: *had gone*)	
ich **sei gegangen**	wir **seien gegangen**
du **seist gegangen**	ihr **seiet gegangen**
er/sie/es **sei gegangen**	sie **seien gegangen**
Sie **seien gegangen**	
Er sagte, er **sei** in die Stadt **gegangen.** (*He said he had gone into the city.*)	

Look at the examples of past Subjunctive I. The most common use for indirect discourse (indirect speech) is to report what someone said.

Er sagte, er habe letzte Woche Golf gespielt. (*He said he had played golf last week.*) To form the past Subjunctive I, you combine **habe,** the present Subjunctive I form of **haben,** with the past participle of **spielen: habe gespielt.**

Die Bundeskanzlerin sagte, sie sei nicht mit dem Verteidigungsminister geflogen. (*The German Chancellor said she hadn't flown with the Defense Secretary.*) To form the past Subjunctive I, you combine **sei,** the present Subjunctive I form of **sein,** with the past participle of **fliegen: sei geflogen.**

Answer Key

1 Die Großeltern **würden** nach Florida umziehen. (*The grandparents would move to Florida.*)

2 Ich **würde** eine lange Reise machen. (*I'd take a long trip.*)

3 Helga **würde** ein kleines Segelboot kaufen. (*Helga would buy a small sailboat.*)

4 Du **würdest** das Geld auf die Bank bringen. (*You'd take the money to the bank.*)

5 Ihr **würdet** ein neues Auto kaufen. (*You'd buy a new car.*)

6 Johannes weiß nicht, was er machen **würde.** (*Johannes doesn't know what he'd do.*) The verb (**würde**) is at the end of subordinate clauses.

7 Marianne und Michael **würden** den ganzen Tag singen. (*Marianne and Michael would sing all day long.*)

8 Ich **würde** nicht alles ausgeben. (*I wouldn't spend all of it.*) The verb **ausgeben** literally means *to give out.*

9 Der Nachbar **würde** eine gigantische Party organisieren. (*The neighbor would organize a gigantic party.*)

10 Und was **würdest** du tun? (*And what would you do?*)

11 Hartmut und Richard **wären** bereit, das Essen zu machen. (*Hartmut and Richard would be willing to make the food.*)

12 Wir **dürften** unsere Familien nicht einladen. (*We wouldn't be allowed to invite our families.*)

13 Es **könnte** bis Mitternacht dauern . . . (*It could last until midnight . . .*)

14 . . . aber leider **müsste** Peter früher nach Hause gehen. (. . . *but unfortunately Peter would have to go home earlier.*) Word order in German is time (**früher**) before place (**nach Hause**).

15 Ich **möchte** die Musik organisieren. (*I'd like to organize the music.*)

16 Liselotte und Heinz **hätten** ein Haus in Ludwigshafen gekauft. (*Liselotte and Heinz would have bought a house in Ludwigshafen.*)

17 Ich **wäre** mit euch ins Theater gegangen. (*I would have gone to the theater with you.*) **Gehen** (*to go*) is the infinitive, and its helping verb is **sein.** Be careful: The simple past **ging** has only one verb, but the past subjunctive has two parts, **wäre** and **gegangen.**

18 Sie **hätten** uns im Sommer besucht. (*They/you would have visited us in the summer.*)

19 Du **hättest** die Reise besser geplant. (*You would have planned the trip better.*)

20 Jonas **hätte** gestern in einem teuren Restaurant gegessen. (*Jonas would have eaten in an expensive restaurant yesterday.*)

Chapter 9

In the Mood: Combining Verbs with Modal Auxiliaries

I hope you're in a good mood as you start on this chapter about modal auxiliary verbs. I'm talking about attitude with a capital *A* in the next few pages. In grammar mumbo jumbo, *modals* are auxiliary (helping) verbs that indicate an attitude about the main verb, even though they don't directly alter the main verb's action.

This motley band of modal verbs helps set the mood of the sentence. They can, at times, be quite influential in their mood-altering abilities — and all without illegal substances. *Mood* is grammarspeak for how something is expressed in a sentence: The mood of a verb indicates a wide range of, yes, *moods* such as probability, impossibility, certainty, doubt, or even just plain old facts, without all the **Schnickschnack** (*bells and whistles*).

If you're asking yourself whether you can get by without using modals, the answer is plain and simple: No way, José — not unless you're willing to put up with being misunderstood in daily situations in which the modals should make your intended thought clear to the listener. In this chapter, you find out what the seven modal verbs are, together with their equivalents in English, and you discover the importance of modal verbs in everyday situations. You get the present-tense conjugation of these verbs and the particulars on important characteristics of these verbs. Then you put the information all together and try your hand at the exercises at the end of each verb section.

The 4-1-1 on Modal Verbs

Modal verbs modify the main verb in the sentence. Here's how they work: You take a plain old verb or phrase like *eat, sleep, walk, plant a garden, play tennis, learn how to play chess,* or *do nothing.* Then you think about your attitude toward these activities, and you decide you want to say *I like to eat, I must sleep more, I would like to walk every day, I should plant a garden, I can play tennis well, I want to learn how to play chess,* or *I may do nothing.* The underlined modal verbs offer you a wide range of ways to express your attitude toward actions such as *eat, sleep, play,* and *learn.*

You find modals working their magic in sentences in the *indicative mood*. This type of mood is for stating facts. Modal verbs also crop up in sentences expressed in the *subjunctive mood*. That's what you use when you want to sound polite when requesting or suggesting something or when you want to make hypothetical statements. (Chapter 8 is where you find out about the subjunctive.) This section gives you a quick overview of what modal verbs are and how they work. The rest of this chapter focuses on the seven specific modal verbs.

Identifying modals: Assistants with attitude

Modals are your ticket to conveying your attitude or how you feel about an action. They usually accompany another verb and appear in the second position of a sentence. The verb they assist generally appears at the end of the clause.

Table 9-1 shows the German modal verbs in infinitive form and the English translation, followed by a statement using the modal verb. Look at the various ways of modifying the statement **Ich lerne Deutsch** (*I learn German*) with the modal verbs. Notice that the modal verb is in second position in the sentence, and the main verb gets booted to the end.

Table 9-1		German Modal Verbs	
German Modal Verb	*Translation*	*Example*	*English Equivalent*
dürfen	*may, to be allowed to*	Ich **darf** Deutsch lernen.	*I may/am allowed to learn German.*
können	*can, to be able to*	Ich **kann** Deutsch lernen.	*I can/am able to learn German.*
mögen	*to like to*	Ich **mag** Deutsch lernen.	*I like to learn German.*
möchten	*would like to*	Ich **möchte** Deutsch lernen.	*I would like to learn German.*
müssen	*must, to have to*	Ich **muss** Deutsch lernen.	*I must/have to learn German.*
sollen	*should, to be supposed to*	Ich **soll** Deutsch lernen.	*I'm supposed to learn German/I should learn German.*
wollen	*to want to*	Ich **will** Deutsch lernen.	*I want to learn German.*

These verbs all have regular verb endings in their plural forms (**wir, ihr, sie,** and **Sie**). Most of them also have irregular verb changes, some of which you can see in the examples in Table 9-1. As you go through **Die Glorreichen Sieben** (*The Magnificent Seven* — modal verbs, that is) in this chapter, you see the irregular verb endings of these verbs in the present tense.

In English, you typically have two verbs in a sentence that has a modal verb; the second one is described as the *main verb*. In German, however, the modal verb may be the only verb. The one true rogue is the verb **mögen,** which frequently stands alone, and to a lesser extent, its sidekick **möchten.** (Check out the sections "I Like That: Mögen, the Likeable Verb" and "What Would You Like? Möchten, the Preference Verb" for more information on these two.)

Understanding word order and modals

In terms of word order for modals, German uses pretty much the same order as for other verbs that require an auxiliary verb to complete the meaning of the main verb. The present perfect and the future tenses also use a secondary, auxiliary verb to complete the main verb's meaning. With these verb types (and tenses), you conjugate the auxiliary verb, put it in second position in the sentence, and generally put the main verb at the end of the clause or phrase. (See Chapter 16 for present perfect verbs and Chapter 18 for future tense verbs and their word order.)

Look at the examples in Table 9-1. The conjugated, active verb is in second position in the sentence. It directly follows the subject or other elements, such as a reference to time or a prepositional phrase. When you need more than one verb, the others go to the very end of the sentence.

Questions follow a slightly different word order (inverted word order) if they're the type of question that can be answered with *yes, no,* or *maybe.* See Chapter 6 for more on forming questions.

May I? Dürfen, the Permission Verb

Some people feel rules and customs crimp their personal style, but such guidelines give people an idea of what they can expect from each other. The rules of the road allow you to do something (or not) — you may proceed with caution at a yield sign, but you're not allowed to cross the double yellow line. And being polite by asking permission — May I use your bathroom? May I have another cookie? — is certainly not limited to little boys and girls. Adults in all parts of the world know that asking for and granting permission is part of the code of polite interaction.

You use the modal verb **dürfen** to ask for and grant permission. Look at the conjugation of **dürfen.** It's irregular in the singular forms: **ich, du,** and **er/sie/es.** In the table, the irregular forms are bold, and the regular forms show the endings in bold.

dürfen *(may, to be allowed to, to be permitted to)*	
ich **darf**	wir dürf**en**
du **darfst**	ihr dürf**t**
er/sie/es **darf**	sie dürf**en**
Sie dürf**en**	
Sie **dürfen** dort nicht parken. (*You're not allowed to park there.*)	

German uses **dürfen** in a wide variety of everyday situations. Table 9-2 lists four commonly used idiomatic expressions with **dürfen,** followed by an example sentence in German and the English equivalent. You frequently hear these expressions in polite exchanges between people who don't know each other well.

Table 9-2	Uses of Dürfen In Polite Conversation	
Situation	*Example*	*English Equivalent*
to ask whether a customer needs assistance	Was **darf** es sein?	*May I help you?*
to signal someone to do a favor such as opening the door	**Darf** ich Sie bitten?	*May I trouble you?*
to say that you'd like to introduce two people to each other	**Darf** ich Ihnen Frau Feuerstein vorstellen?	*May I introduce you to Mrs. Feuerstein?*
to explain that something is not allowed	Das Obst **dürfen** Sie nicht anfassen.	*You may not/must not touch the fruit.*

Generally speaking, German and English use **dürfen** (*may, to be allowed to, to be permitted to*) in very similar ways: to ask for permission, to grant permission, and to state that something is (or is not) permitted or allowed.

German sometimes uses the impersonal form **man** (*it, one, you*) with **dürfen;** in English, you use the passive construction (*parking/passing/stopping isn't allowed here*), or you simply say *no parking/passing/stopping (allowed here).*

English uses *may* to express possibility, whereas **dürfen** doesn't have this meaning. Instead, you'd use **vielleicht** (*maybe/perhaps*) to express possibility or chance. For instance, you can translate **Vielleicht komme ich spät nach Hause** as *I may come home late.* However, *Perhaps I'll come home late* is closer to the word-for-word translation, even though German doesn't use the future tense in the example sentence. (For more information on the present tense, see Chapter 5.)

Watch out for false friends (which I discuss in Chapter 4). The modal verb **müssen** looks somewhat similar to the English *must*, which is the correct meaning in English; however, you express *must not* in German with **nicht dürfen: Sie dürfen hier nicht rauchen** (*You must not/are not allowed to smoke here*).

You Can Do It! Können, the Ability Verb

Can you run a marathon barefoot? Do you know how to play chess (and win) against a computer? Are you able to make a five-course dinner for 12 guests without batting an eye? No matter what your hidden talents may be, if you have a healthy ego, then chances are you enjoy talking about yourself. Know-how, ability, and can-do attitude — all are expressed with the verb **können.**

As one of the seven players in the modal verb dugout, **können** (*can, to be able to, to know how to*) is a true champ. In general, German and English use **können** in similar ways. The verb goes up to bat whenever you need to express that

✔ You *can* or *can't* do something: **Kannst du Tennis/Tischtennis/Volleyball/ Schach/Poker spielen?** (*Can you play tennis/table tennis/volleyball/chess/ poker?*)

✔ You *know* or *don't know how to* do something: **Er kann Geige/Klavier/ Keyboards/Gitarre/Klarinette/Saxophon spielen.** (*He knows how to play the violin/piano/keyboards/guitar/clarinet/saxophone.*) In German, you don't use the definite article **der, die, das** [*the*] to talk about playing an instrument.

✔ You *are able to* do something: **Ich kann bis Mittag schlafen.** (*I'm able to/can sleep until noon.*)

✔ You want to request or offer help in a polite but direct way: **Können Sie mir sagen, wo der Bahnhof/die Straßenbahnhaltestelle/das Hotel Blaue Gans/ das Kunstmuseum ist?** (*Can you tell me where the train station/the streetcar stop/the Hotel Blaue Gans/the art museum is?*)

Note: Notice the comma after the first clause. In German, you need this comma to separate the subordinate clause (**. . . wo der Bahnhof ist?**) from the main clause (**Können Sie mir sagen, . . .**). Subordinate clauses often begin with words like **wo** (*where*), **was** (*what*), **wie viel** (*how much*), **wer** (*who*), and **warum** (*why*). The conjugated verb in the subordinate clause, **ist** (*is*), gets the boot and lands at the end of the sentence. (For more on subordinate clauses, see Chapter 14.)

Look at the conjugation of **können.** It's irregular in the singular forms: **ich, du,** and **er/sie/es.** The irregular forms are bold, and the regular forms show the endings in bold.

können (*can, to be able to, to know how to*)	
ich **kann**	wir könn**en**
du **kannst**	ihr könn**t**
er/sie/es **kann**	sie könn**en**
Sie könn**en**	
Ich **kann** Ihnen mit ihrem Gepäck helfen. (*I can help you with your luggage.*)	

One striking difference between English and German is that German sometimes describes what can or can't be done using **können** but no main verb. Typically, you hear the following expressions in spoken, casual conversation. Table 9-3 lists the situation, an example sentence in German, and its equivalent in English.

Table 9-3	Uses of Können without a Main Verb	
Situation	*Example*	*English Equivalent*
to say someone can speak a language	Meine Frau **kann** sehr gut Französisch.	*My wife can speak French very well.*
to say that you give up trying	Ich **kann nicht** weiter. Es ist zu schwer.	*I can't go on. It's too difficult.*
to explain that you can't help doing	Ich **kann nichts** dafür. Es schmeckt so gut!	*I can't help it. It tastes so good!* (excusing yourself for taking a third piece of chocolate cake)
to interject that you can do something	Das **kann** ich wohl!	*Of course I can do that!*

A number of common **können** expressions are reflexive (they use a reflexive pronoun [*me, you, us,* and so on] with the verb) in German but not in English. German uses the reflexive much more frequently than English. (For more information on reflexive verbs, check out Chapter 11.) Table 9-4 lists these common expressions, an example sentence in German, and the English translation.

Table 9-4	Uses of Können with a Reflexive Verb	
Situation	*Example*	*English Equivalent*
to say you can('t) decide	Ich **kann mich** nicht entscheiden.	*I can't decide.*
to express that you can get away with something	Wie **kannst** du **dir** so etwas erlauben?	*How can you get away with something like that?*
to be able (or unable) to afford something	Wir **können uns** kein teueres Auto leisten.	*We can't afford an expensive car.*
to give assurance that someone/ something can be trusted	Sie **können sich** auf mich verlassen.	*You can depend on me.*

Decide whether the word order for the following expressions is correct. If not, make the necessary correction in word order. Remember that when there are two verbs, the main verb (the one that's in infinitive form) gets kicked to the end of the sentence. (Harsh treatment for some decent, upstanding verbs, but it's true!)

Q. Sie kann spielen Klarinette.

A. **Sie kann Klarinette spielen.** (*She can play the clarinet.*) The word order needs to have the conjugated verb **kann** in second position and the main verb **spielen** (in the infinitive form) at the end of the sentence.

1. Können Sie helfen mir?

_____

2. Wir können uns kein neues Auto leisten.

_____

3. Könnt ihr gut Tennis spielen?

_____

4. Ich kann Englisch, Deutsch, und Spanisch.

_____

5. Ich kann spielen Fußball.

_____

I Like That: Mögen, the Likeable Verb

Want to talk about likes and dislikes? **Mögen** is the verb for you. Consider these sentences: **Magst du kaltes Wetter?** (_Do you like cold weather?_) **Nein, ich mag den Winter überhaupt nicht.** (_No, I don't like the winter at all._) Want to express your feelings toward someone? Try **ich mag dich** (_I like you_).

The main definition of **mögen** is that of liking or disliking someone or something. When talking about such preferences, you usually don't need an additional verb:

> **Magst du diese Sängerin?** (_Do you like this female singer?_)

> **Er mag kein Starkbier.** (_He doesn't like strong beer._)

The modal verb **mögen** comes as a double dipper. Why? Because **mögen** (_to like, to care for_) is so likeable that it has a sidekick, **möchten** (_would like, would like to do_), which is similar in meaning to **mögen.** (Check out the next section for more on **möchten.**)

This verb table shows you the conjugation of **mögen.** It follows the typical pattern of modal verbs: the singular verb forms are the irregular ones — **ich mag, du magst, er/sie/es mag.** The irregular forms are shown in bold, and the regular forms show the endings in bold.

mögen (_to like, to care for_)	
ich **mag**	wir mög**en**
du **magst**	ihr mög**t**
er/sie/es **mag**	sie mög**en**
Sie mög**en**	
Ich **mag** klassische Musik. (_I like classical music._)	

When you want to express dislike for someone or something, you put **nicht** at the end of the sentence when no other verb is along for the ride:

> **Ihr mögt diese Farbe nicht.** (*You don't like this color.*)

> **Mögen sie Schokoladeneis nicht?** (*Don't they like chocolate ice cream?*)

To add some oomph to **mögen,** you can use a number of expressions with **gern** (**gern** is similar to *a lot* when you add it to other words). I arranged the list in order of most positive to most negative:

- ✔ **mögen . . . besonders gern** (*to especially like*): **Ich mag Bratkartoffeln besonders gern.** (*I especially like roast potatoes.*) They're similar to home fries.

- ✔ **mögen . . . (sehr) gern** (*to like [very much]*): **Ich mag Kartoffelklöße (sehr) gern.** (*I like potato dumplings very much.*) In southern Germany and Austria, **Klöße** are referred to as **Knödel,** both of which are *dumplings*.

- ✔ **mögen . . . nicht gern** (*not to like very much*): **Ich mag Pommes frites nicht gern.** (*I don't like French fries very much.*)

- ✔ **mögen . . . überhaupt nicht gern** (*not to like at all*): **Ich mag Salzkartoffeln überhaupt nicht gern.** (*I don't like boiled potatoes at all.*)

A few idiomatic expressions use **mögen:**

- ✔ **Das mag sein.** (*That could be true.*)

- ✔ **Ich mag ihn leiden.** (*I care for him.*) You can also leave off **leiden** without changing the meaning much, but **leiden** stresses the emotion of caring.

- ✔ **Darin mögen Sie Recht haben.** (*You have a point there.*)

Take a crack at these exercises. Put the correct form of **mögen** into the sentence. The example gets you started.

0. Meine Eltern _____ die Oper sehr gern.

A. Meine Eltern **mögen** die Oper sehr gern.

6. _____ du den Salat?

7. Nein, ich _____ ihn überhaupt nicht.

8. Er _____ Horrorfilme.

9. _____ ihr Klaviermusik nicht?

10. Ja, aber wir _____ alle Musikarten gern.

What Would You Like? Möchten, the Preference Verb

Life is full of choices, and you're likely to have some opinions on what you like best. When the **Kellner/Kellnerin** (*waiter/waitress*) in a German restaurant asks me **"Was möchten Sie?"** (*What would you like?*), I make sure I order something to drink first — **"Ich möchte eine Apfelsaftschorle"** (*I'd like an apple juice/mineral water drink*). That way, I have time to peruse the eight-page menu and order the meal later.

To say you'd like to do something in German, you use the modal verb **möchten.** Although **möchten** (*would like [to do]*) is often lumped together with **mögen** (*to like, care for*) (see the preceding section for more info), it's definitely important enough to get top billing in the modal verb lineup. Look at the conjugation of **möchten.** The verb endings are in bold.

möchten (*would like [to]*)	
ich möcht**e**	wir möcht**en**
du möcht**est**	ihr möcht**et**
er/sie/es möcht**e**	sie möcht**en**
Sie möcht**en**	
Ich **möchte** am Wochenende Rad fahren. (*I'd like to go bicycling on the weekend.*)	

The important similarity that **möchten** and **mögen** share, aside from their meanings, is that neither modal verb needs a main verb to express something clearly. For instance, when ordering in a restaurant, the context can typically indicate what you'd like to have. Using **möchten** as the modal verb, you can omit the following main verbs:

- **essen** (*to eat*)
- **trinken** (*to drink*)
- **haben** (*to have*)
- **fahren** (*to drive*)
- **gehen** (*to go, walk*)

Look at the two example sentences, one with and one without the main verb. Assuming you know they're spoken in a restaurant, the meaning of the first sentence, which has no main verb, is clear:

> **Ich möchte ein Glas Rotwein, bitte.** (*I'd like a glass of red wine, please.*)

> **Ich möchte ein Glas Rotwein trinken, bitte.** (*I'd like to drink a glass of red wine, please.*) Or you can use **haben** (*to have*) instead of **trinken,** and you'd still get a glass of red wine.

German often expresses a preference by using **möchten** in combination with **lieber** (*rather*). The example dialogue shows **haben** in parentheses to indicate that it's not necessary in the context of the situation:

> **Möchten Sie einen Fensterplatz (haben)?** (*Would you like a window seat?*)

> **Nein, ich möchte lieber einen Gangplatz (haben).** (*No, I'd rather have an aisle seat.*)

It's your turn to see how polite you sound in German and how good you are at expressing things people would like to do. Write the sentences or questions in German, using the English cues. To help you, I've indicated some difficult elements in bold.

Q. I'd like a cup of coffee.

A. **Ich möchte eine Tasse Kaffee.**

11. I'd like a pizza, please.

_____

12. We'd like to learn German.

_____

13. I'd like to stay here. (**hier bleiben** means *to stay here*)

_____

14. She'd like to dance with Andreas.

_____

15. Would you like a glass of water? (s., fam.)

_____

Do I Have To? Müssen, the Verb of Necessity

As a child, you may have heard something along the lines of "No, you don't have to finish your broccoli au gratin, but you have to try at least three bites." So now that you've grown up — or at least other people think you have — far more serious obligations haunt you, such as paying taxes, mowing the lawn, and having the first local strawberries of the season before anyone else.

Müssen bears a vague resemblance to *must*, making it easier to get down to the nitty-gritty of how this modal works, when you *need* it, when you *have to* use it, when it's a *must*, and when you *don't have to* deal with it. What about *must not?* Oddly enough, *must not* is **darf nicht** in German, with the modal verb **dürfen** (*to be allowed to*). (Check out the earlier section on **dürfen** if you're a bit foggy on the difference between the two verbs.)

Necessity and obligation are the core meanings of **müssen** in both English and German, although in the English-speaking world and among North Americans in particular, there's a tendency to downplay the use of *must* because it sounds so strong to the ear. *Do I have to?* works just fine at getting the obligation message across (especially when uttered by whining 10-year-olds after you've told them to turn off the TV and go to bed).

Take a look at the conjugation of **müssen.** Like most of its fellow modal verbs, it's irregular in the singular forms: **ich, du,** and **er/sie/es.** The irregular forms are in bold, and the regular forms show the endings in bold.

müssen (*must, to have to, need to*)	
ich **muss**	wir müss**en**
du **musst**	ihr müss**t**
er/sie/es **muss**	sie müss**en**
Sie müss**en**	
Er **muss** morgen früh aufstehen. (*He has to get up early tomorrow.*)	

Don't get lulled into thinking that **muss nicht** is equivalent to *must not.* When you turn **müssen** into a negative expression, the similarities between German an English go down the drain. German has two expressions for indicating whether something is forbidden or simply not necessary:

✔ **nicht dürfen** (*not allowed, must not, not permitted*): A no-no; strong prohibition, such as **Du darfst das nicht trinken** (You *mustn't* drink that).

✔ **nicht müssen** (*not necessary, don't need to*): An absence of necessity or obligation, such as **Du musst das nicht trinken** (You *don't need to* drink that).

Should I or Shouldn't I? Sollen, the Duty Verb

There are things in life that you have to do and things you're supposed to do. I prefer the latter because they're easier to put off. But wasting valuable vacation time to accomplish everything on your checklist is something you really shouldn't do. So the to-do list just gets longer and longer until the day it fortuitously gets lost in the trash.

When you want to describe an action you *should* or *shouldn't do* or that you're *supposed to* or *not supposed to do*, **sollen** is the verb to use. Look at the conjugation of this modal verb in the table that follows. **Sollen** is irregular only in two places — the **ich** and **er/sie/es** forms. The irregular forms are in bold, and the regular forms show the endings in bold.

sollen (*should, to be supposed to*)	
ich **soll**	wir soll**en**
du soll**st**	ihr soll**t**
er/sie/es **soll**	sie soll**en**
Sie soll**en**	
Du **sollst** die Katze füttern. (*You should feed the cat.*)	

You, the non-native speaker of German, should be careful not to sound too forceful when it isn't necessary. **Sollen,** the modal duty verb, is the verb you use for giving advice or expressing a duty that's an expected, right-kind-of-thing-to-do action. The negative version, **nicht sollen,** expresses what you shouldn't do. The cousin **müssen** is the modal verb of necessity and strong directives — see the earlier section on **müssen.**

How's your sense of duty in German? Finish the sentences with the right conjugated form of **sollen** or **nicht sollen.** The second sentence of these exercises has a clue to help you decide which one is logical. The sample exercise shows how to proceed.

0. Ich _____ etwas trinken. Ich habe Durst.

A. Ich **soll** etwas trinken. Ich habe Durst. (*I should drink something. I'm thirsty.*)

16. Wir _____ unsere Schuhe putzen. Sie sind schmutzig.

17. Du _____ spät ins Bett gehen. Du siehst sehr müde aus.

18. Ich _____ den neuen Film sehen. Er ist super.

19. Maria _____ ein kleineres Auto kaufen. Das Benzin ist sehr teuer.

20. Du _____ zum Konzert gehen. Die Gruppe ist wirklich schlecht.

I Want to Be Famous: Wollen, the Intention Verb

When you were little, did you want to travel around the world in a hot air balloon? Chances are, by now you've scaled back such grand intentions: You wish you could just remember the names of three famous movie stars. However, you do intend to travel more — to your son's soccer games. No matter how grandiose or mundane your wants and desires may be, you can express them all with **wollen,** the intention verb.

Expressing your wants (as well as intentions, desires, and a secret wish or two) in German is simple when you know how to use **wollen.** Like some others in the band of modal verbs, it's irregular in the following forms: **ich, du,** and **er/sie/es** — the singular forms. The irregular forms are in bold, and the regular forms show the endings in bold. Look at the verb conjugation.

wollen (*to want to, intend to, wish*)	
ich **will**	wir woll**en**
du **willst**	ihr woll**t**
er/sie/es **will**	sie woll**en**
Sie woll**en**	
Ich **will** jetzt nach Hause fahren. (*I want to drive home now.*)	

When you're expressing something you *want to do* or *intend to do,* you can substitute **möchten** for **wollen** and come up with virtually the same results (see the earlier section "What Would You Like? Möchten, the Preference Verb"). Look at the following examples. The difference between them is minimal in both languages. The speaker could be talking to someone or doing some wishful thinking:

> **Ich will ein neues Auto kaufen.** (*I want to buy a new car.*)

> **Ich möchte ein neues Auto kaufen.** (*I would like to buy a new car.*)

When you want something from someone else, the two verbs are not interchangeable. **Wollen** is direct: You *want* something. **Möchten** does express a *want* in the form of *would like to,* but it carries the ring of politeness. Compare the two example sentences that follow. The speaker is a dinner guest in someone's living room.

> **Ich will fernsehen.** (*I want to watch TV.*) The guest is simply stating what he or she wants or intends to do. There's no hint, direct or indirect, of a request.

> **Ich möchte fernsehen.** (*I would like to watch TV.*) The guest sounds polite by using **möchte.** A request is likely to follow up the stated intention with a question, such as **Haben Sie etwas dagegen?** (*Do you mind?*).

The expressions using **wollen** in the following sentences show how its meaning can bend slightly in conjunction with another word or words:

- ✔ **wollen . . . gern + infinitive:** Stresses desire. (*Note:* Look at the section in this chapter on **mögen** for more ways to use **gern.**) For example, **Er will gern Musik hören** (*He feels like listening to music*).

- ✔ **wollen . . . unbedingt:** Underscores that you absolutely want something, without fail, such as **Ich will unbedingt nach Australien reisen** (*I'm dying to travel to Australia*).

- ✔ **wie + subject + wollen:** Notes that a decision is up to somebody else, such as **Wie Sie wollen** (*It's up to you*). The German title of Shakespeare's *As You Like It* is *Wie Ihr Wollt.*

- ✔ **wollen . . . nicht + past participle + haben/sein:** Expresses that someone doesn't want to admit having done something (see Chapter 16 for more on past participles), such as **Sie wollen den Unfall nicht gesehen haben** (*They claim not to have seen the accident*). In other words, they don't want to admit to having seen the accident.

- ✔ **wollen nichts damit zu tun haben:** Notes that the subject doesn't want to be involved with something, such as **Ich will nichts damit zu tun haben** (*I want no part of that* or *I don't want anything to do with it*).

Check that you know how to use the modal verb **wollen** in the following exercise. What do these people want to do? Change the German sentence by adding the correct form of the modal verb **wollen.** Word order is important here: Remember to replace the main verb with the conjugated form of **wollen;** then throw the main verb to the back (of the sentence, that is), changing it in midair into the infinitive form. Look at the example to get you going.

0. Du **machst** einen Salat.

A. Du **willst** einen Salat **machen.** (*You want to make a salad.*) **Machst** changes to **machen** before it lands at the end of the sentence.

21. Ich **spiele** morgen um 17.00 Uhr Tennis. _____

22. Wir **trinken** Orangensaft. _____

23. Ihr **geht** in die Stadt. _____

24. Heidi und Thomas **gehen** heute Abend ins Restaurant.

    _____

25. Sophie **isst** ein Stück Apfelkuchen. _____

Answer Key

1 **Können Sie mir helfen?** (*Can you help me?*) **Können** is the conjugated verb, and in a yes/no question, it's first; the verb **helfen** needs to be at the end.

2 **Wir können uns kein neues Auto leisten.** (*We can't afford a new car.*) The word order is correct.

3 **Könnt ihr gut Tennis spielen?** (*Can you play tennis well?*) The word order is correct.

4 **Ich kann Englisch, Deutsch, und Spanisch.** (*I can speak English, German, and Spanish.*) The sentence is correct. **Können** needs no other verb here. However, you can add **sprechen** (*to speak*) at the end of the sentence, especially if you want to go on and say something different about another language: **Ich kann Französisch verstehen, aber nicht sprechen.** (*I can understand French but not speak it.*)

5 **Ich kann Fußball spielen.** (*I can play soccer.*) The word order is incorrect; in the correct order, the conjugated modal verb **kann** is in second position, and the main verb **spielen** (in infinitive form) is at the end of the sentence.

6 **Magst** du den Salat? (*Do you like the salad?*)

7 Nein, ich **mag** ihn überhaupt nicht. (*No, I don't like it at all.*) The strong negative is expressed with **überhaupt nicht. Ihn** is the accusative case pronoun that replaces the accusative, masculine noun **den Salat.**

8 Er **mag** Horrorfilme. (*He likes horror movies.*)

9 **Mögt** ihr Klaviermusik nicht? (*Don't you like piano music?*) Notice that **nicht** is at the end of the sentence.

10 Ja, aber wir **mögen** alle Musikarten gern. (*Yes, but we fancy/really like all kinds of music.*)

11 **Ich möchte eine Pizza, bitte.**

12 **Wir möchten Deutsch lernen.**

13 **Ich möchte hier bleiben.**

14 **Sie möchte mit Andreas tanzen.**

15 **Möchtest du ein Glas Wasser?**

16 Wir **sollen** unsere Schuhe putzen. Sie sind schmutzig. (*We should clean our shoes. They're dirty.*)

17 Du **sollst nicht** spät ins Bett gehen. Du siehst sehr müde aus. (*You shouldn't go to bed late. You look very tired.*)

18 Ich **soll** den neuen Film sehen. Er ist super. (*I should see the new movie. It's super.*)

19 Maria **soll** ein kleineres Auto kaufen. Das Benzin ist sehr teuer. (*Maria should buy a smaller car. Gas is very expensive.*)

20 Du **sollst nicht** zum Konzert gehen. Die Gruppe ist wirklich schlecht. (*You shouldn't go to the concert. The group is really bad.*)

21 Ich **will** morgen um 17.00 Uhr Tennis **spielen.** (*I want to play tennis tomorrow at 5 p.m.*)

22 Wir **wollen** Orangensaft (**trinken**). (*We want to drink* [*some*] *orange juice.*)

23 Ihr **wollt** in die Stadt **gehen.** (*You want to go into the city.*) **In die Stadt gehen** usually means *to the city center,* which typically has a pleasant pedestrian area with stores and cafés.

24 Heidi und Thomas **wollen** heute Abend ins Restaurant **gehen.** (*Heidi and Thomas want to go to a/the restaurant this evening.*)

25 Sophie **will** ein Stück Apfelkuchen **essen.** (*Sophie wants to eat a piece of apple cake.*) German **Apfelkuchen** is **hervorragend** (*excellent*).

Chapter 10

Sorting Out Separable- and Inseparable-Prefix Verbs

In This Chapter

▶ Juggling separable-prefix verbs

▶ Keeping it together with inseparable-prefix verbs

▶ Rounding up dual-prefix verbs

*A*ll you couch potatoes: Use it or lose it! *Get up* off the couch, *put* your shoes *on,* *breathe* some air *in,* and get ready to *work out!* Why the exercise hype in a chapter on separable- and inseparable-prefix verbs? Wouldn't it be more appropriate as a pep talk in a health magazine? Actually, the verbs I deal with in this chapter are the types you see in italics here. In English, they're called *two-part* or *phrasal verbs,* and their German counterparts are called *separable-* or *inseparable-prefix verbs. Separable prefixes* can separate from the verb itself, depending on the verb tense you use, and the *inseparable prefixes* never separate from the verb. These verb types are equally common in German and English.

This chapter deals with three categories of verbs: separable-prefix verbs, inseparable-prefix verbs, and dual-prefix verbs, which I dub the double-crossers because the prefixes can be separable or inseparable.

Looking at the Prefix

The German *prefix* (which corresponds to the second part of a two-part verb in English) may stand for a preposition like *up* or an adverb like *away.* In both English and German, the prefix alters the meaning of the original verb, sometimes only slightly, sometimes radically.

To remember whether these verbs are separable- or inseparable-prefix verbs, practice pronouncing them aloud. The separable-prefix verbs stress the prefix in spoken German, but the inseparable-prefix verbs don't stress the prefix. For instance, **umsteigen** (*to change [trains, planes, and so on]*) is separable, so when you say it, stress the prefix **um-** like this: **UM-steig-en. Unterbrechen** (*to interrupt*) is inseparable, so you don't stress the prefix, but you do stress the first syllable of the verb **brechen** like this: **un-ter-BRECH-en.**

Two-part verbs in English are generally exactly that, in two parts: *get* + *up* = *get up*. They're a dime a dozen: *turn away, put on, take off* — you get the picture. The German equivalent is different because it has the prefix attached directly to the infinitive (the base verb form). For example, **aufstehen** (*to get up*) has the prefix **auf-**. (Literally, **auf-** + **stehen** is *up* + *stand*.) Such German verbs are extremely common.

You can remember verbs with prefixes using two approaches. First, find out the meanings of the prefixes, and second, know what the prefix and verb mean together. By using the prefix/verb lists in this chapter, you have the opportunity to try both methods at the same time. (Refer to Chapter 15 for more on prepositions.) Although this may sound complicated, a great deal of these verbs (sans prefix) are garden-variety types you encounter often in German. By the time you finish the exercises, you should have a good foundation of these verbs and know how to form and use them.

Simplifying Separable-Prefix Verbs

With separable-prefix verbs, the verb and the prefix can — drum roll please — split up (surprise, surprise). Of the three groups of verbs that I discuss in this chapter, this group is the largest because it has the largest number of prefixes as well as the largest number of verbs that connect with these prefixes. Knowing the meaning of the verb without the prefix can help, but make sure you know the separable-prefix verb and its English meaning. Take a look at the following example. **Aufstehen** (*to get up*) is a separable-prefix verb. Its prefix, **auf-**, means *up* in this context. The verb **stehen** means *to stand* or *stay*. Notice that the prefix **auf-**, appears at the end of the sentence: **Ich stehe meistens um sechs Uhr auf** (*I usually get up at six a.m.*).

You get your money's worth with the prefixes in this section. They're a great help when you're expanding your vocabulary. Why? Not only do they combine with verbs, but some also combine with nouns and adjectives. Most verb prefixes have more than one specific meaning, and as you become familiar with them, you start seeing a pattern in the way a prefix alters the meaning of the verbs it combines with. When you come across a new German verb with the same prefix, you can make an educated guess about its meaning. These itty bitty sound bites are very influential, so start your own collection right away.

Table 10-1 shows separable prefixes, their English meanings, and some verbs that use the prefix. Although this prefix list is fairly complete, the number of separable-prefix verbs is huge. This sample list contains high-frequency verbs.

Table 10-1	Separable Prefixes and Verb Combinations		
Prefix	*English Definition*	*Example Verb*	*English Equivalent*
ab-	*from*	**abbrechen**	*to break away, stop*
		abnehmen	*to pick up, reduce, take off*
		abschaffen	*to do away with*
an-	*at, to, on*	**anfangen**	*to begin, start*
		anhaben	*to have on, wear*
		anrufen	*to phone*

Prefix	English Definition	Example Verb	English Equivalent
auf-	on, out, up	aufbauen aufgeben aufstehen	to put up, build up to give up, check (bags) to get up, stand up
aus-	from, out	ausbilden ausfallen aussehen	to train, educate to cancel, fall out (hair) to look (like), appear
bei-	with, along	beilegen beitreten	to insert (in a document) to join, enter into (a pact)
da-	there	dableiben	to stay behind
dabei-	there	dabeibleiben	to stay with, stick with (it)
daran-	on	daranmachen	to get down to (it)
ein-	in, into, down	einkaufen einladen einschlafen	to go shopping, to buy to invite to go to sleep
entgegen-	against, toward	entgegenkommen	to approach, accommodate
fehl-	wrong	fehlschlagen	to go wrong
fest-	fixed	festhalten	to hold on, keep hold of
fort-	onward, away	fortbilden fortführen fortpflanzen	to continue education to carry on, continue to reproduce, propagate
gegenüber-	across from	gegenüberstehen	to be opposite, face
gleich-	equal	gleichstellen	to treat as equal
her-	from, here	herstellen	to manufacture, establish
heraus-	from, out of	herausfinden herausreden herausfordern	to find out to talk one's way out of to challenge
hin-	to, towards, there	hinfahren	to drive there, go there
hinzu-	in addition	hinzufügen	to add (details), enclose
kennen-	know	kennenlernen	to get to know, meet
los-	start, away	losbrechen losfahren loslassen	to break off to drive off to let go of
mit-	along, with (similar to English prefix *co-*)	mitarbeiten mitmachen mitteilen	to collaborate to go along with, join in to inform (someone)
nach-	after, copy (similar to English prefix *re-*)	nachahmen nachfragen nachgeben	to imitate to ask, inquire to give way, give in

(continued)

Table 10-1 *(continued)*

Prefix	English Definition	Example Verb	English Equivalent
statt-	no equivalent	stattfinden	to take place (event)
vor-	before (similar to English prefixes pre- and pro-)	vorbereiten vorführen vorlesen vormachen	to prepare to present, perform to read aloud to show someone how to do something, fool someone
weg-	away, off	wegbleiben	to stay away
zu-	shut, to, upon	zulassen zusichern zusteigen	to authorize, license to assure someone to get on, board
zurück-	back	zurückkommen zurücktreten zurückzahlen	to return, come back to step back, resign to pay back
zusammen-	together	zusammenarbeiten zusammenfassen zusammenwachsen	to work together to summarize to grow together
zwischen-	between	zwischenlanden	to stop over (flight)

This section shows you how to use separable-prefix verbs in the present, the past, and the present perfect. I break it down by these three tenses; for each verb tense, you find out whether to do separation work or not, details on how to form the verb tense, and where to place the two verb parts in the sentence.

Using verbs in the present tense

When you write an e-mail to your friend in Berlin or speak to your German boss, you'll probably end up using separable-prefix verbs in the present tense. When doing so, word order is a really big deal. Why? If you mix up word order, the reader or listener may not get your intended message. Also, keep in mind that the prefix alters the basic verb's meaning, so if you leave it out, you're likely to cause confusion. (For more on word order in present tense, see Chapter 5.)

With separable-prefix verbs in the present tense, keep the following two points in mind:

✔ The prefix — such as **fest-** in **festhalten** (*to hold* on) — goes to the end of the sentence. In spoken German, you stress the prefix.

✔ The verb itself, which is the part you conjugate, is generally in second position in the sentence, as in **Ich halte mich fest** (*I'm holding on tight*). **Halte,** the conjugated part of the verb, is in second position.

Here are some guidelines for word order, depending on the type of sentence:

- ✔ **Statements, both positive and negative:** The verb is generally in second position, such as in **Wir haben viel vor** (*We're planning to do a lot [of activities]*). The verb is **vorhaben** (*to plan*). The verb **haben** is in second position, and the prefix **vor-** is at the end of the sentence. The same sentence expressed negatively would look like this: **Wir haben nicht viel vor** (*We're not planning to do much*).

- ✔ **Yes/no questions and commands:** The verb and subject are inverted, meaning that the verb is first, followed by the subject, such as with **Kommst du am Sonntag vom Urlaub zurück?** (*Are you coming back from vacation on Sunday?*). The verb is **zurückkommen** (*to come back*). **Kommst,** the conjugated part of the verb **zurückkommen,** is in first position in a yes/no question, and the prefix **zurück** is at the end of the question.

- ✔ **Sentences or questions with a modal verb (such as dürfen or möchten) in addition to the separable-prefix verb:** Conjugate the modal verb, put it (usually) in second position, and place the separable-prefix verb in the infinitive form at the end of the phrase, such as with **Alle Gäste dürfen mitmachen** (*All the guests may join in*). The verb is **mitmachen** (*to join in*). The modal verb **dürfen** (*may, to be allowed to*) is in second position, and **mitmachen,** the infinitive form of the separable-prefix verb, goes to the end of the sentence. (See Chapter 9 for info on modal verbs.)

For sentences that have more than one clause, the guidelines follow those for two-part sentences, (see Chapter 14).

Use the verb list in Table 10-1 and the preceding guidelines to rewrite the statements, questions, or commands in the present tense, making sure you use the correct word order. The separable-prefix verb is in parentheses in the infinitive form. Be careful: The verb may be in one part only.

Q. du schnell? (einschlafen)

A. **Schläfst** du schnell **ein?** (*Do you go to sleep quickly?*)

1. wir viele Gäste zum Fest (einladen). _____

2. diese Firma viele Produkte im Ausland (herstellen). _____

3. die besten Pläne oft (fehlschlagen). _____

4. können Sie mir die Details? (mitteilen) _____

Using verbs in the simple past

The simple past (also referred to as the narrative past) is used mainly by speakers in the north and east of Germany and in the written language of the media, especially for narrating a sequence of events in the past. (For information on how to form the simple past, see Chapter 17.) When you use separable-prefix verbs in the simple past, word order is just as important as with the present (and present perfect as well). The guidelines for using the simple past are the same as those for present. Refer to the information in the preceding section, "Using verbs in the present tense."

The following examples are the same as those in the present tense section except they're in the simple past. Note that the command form doesn't exist in simple past.

> **Wir hatten viel vor.** (*We were planning/planned to do a lot [of activities].*)
>
> **Kamst du am Sonntag vom Urlaub zurück?** (*Did you come back from vacation on Sunday?*)
>
> **Alle Gäste durften mitmachen.** (*All the guests were allowed join in.*)

The verbs in this exercise are all in simple past. Write the parts of the sentence in the correct word order. For help with word order, refer to the examples and the guidelines for present. You can find the separable-prefix verbs in Table 10-1.

Q. ein / Helena / Kleid / an / hatte / schwarzes

A. Helena **hatte** ein schwarzes Kleid **an.** (*Helena was wearing/wore a black dress.*)

5. fuhr / Nach einer Pause / fort / der Redner _____

6. ab / Arbeit / Markus und Jonathan / Brachen / ihre? _____

7. sahen / Im Herbst / aus / sehr / die Bäume / schön _____

8. vor / die Geschichte / Regina / las _____

9. der Bus / los / Fuhr / Johanna / ohne ? _____

Using verbs in present perfect tense

To make a sentence in present perfect using a separable-prefix verb, you need to know how to form this tense and where to place the two verb parts. Word order is the name of the game. (For more on how to form the present perfect tense and the past participle, go to Chapter 16.)

With separable-prefix verbs in the present perfect tense in general, keep the following points in mind:

✔ The past participle is at the end of the sentence. For example, the past participle of **hinfahren** (*to drive there, go there*) is **hingefahren** (*driven there*). Here's how you get it:

   • Split the prefix (**hin-**) from the main part of the verb (**fahren**).

   • Form the past participle with **ge-** by squeezing the **ge-** into the middle of the past participle: **hin- + ge- + fahren.**

✔ The auxiliary verb, either **haben** or **sein,** is conjugated in present tense, and it's generally in second position in the sentence. Exceptions are yes/no questions, which have inverted order: The auxiliary verb is placed first, and the subject is second.

✔ In spoken German, you stress the prefix in the verb. For example:

> **Meine Schwester hat mich angerufen.** (*My sister called me.*) The verb is **anrufen** (*to call, phone*). The auxiliary verb **hat** is in second position. The past participle is formed with **an-** + **ge-** + **rufen**: **Ge-** is squeezed in the middle of **an-** and **-rufen.**

> **Der Präsident ist zurückgetreten.** (*The president resigned.*) The verb is **zurücktreten** (*to step down, resign*). The auxiliary verb **ist** is in second position. The past participle is formed with **zurück-** + **ge-** + **treten**: **Ge-** is squeezed in the middle of **zurück-** and **-treten.**

> **Ist noch jemand zugestiegen?** (*Has anyone gotten on [the train?]*) Ticket collectors say this to ask new passengers to show their tickets. The verb is **zusteigen** (*to get on, board*). The auxiliary verb **ist** is in first position because the sentence is a question. The past participle is formed with **zu-** + **ge-** + **stiegen**: **Ge-** is squeezed in the middle of **zu-** and **-stiegen.**

Referring to the verb list in Table 10-1, complete the sentences using the past participle of the verb in parentheses. To get the correct form of the past participle, keep in mind that some of these verbs are weak, and others are strong (see Chapter 16 for more on strong versus weak verbs). Verbs that use the auxiliary verb **sein** have that indicated in parentheses.

Q. Ich _____ an diesem Projekt _____. (mitmachen)

A. Ich **habe** an diesem Projekt **mitgemacht.** (*I worked on this project.*)

10. Wir _____ viel Käse _____. (einkaufen)

11. Das Flugzeug _____ in Bangkok _____. (zwischenlanden) (auxiliary verb **sein**)

12. Das Rockkonzert _____ im Olympiastadion _____. (stattfinden)

13. _____ ihr das Gepäck schon _____? (aufgeben)

14. Um wie viel Uhr_____ der Film _____? (anfangen)

Investigating Inseparable-Prefix Verbs

Although the number of inseparable-prefix verbs isn't as large as that of separable-prefix verbs, you still need to be aware of these verbs so you can include them in your writing and speech. The good news is that many of these inseparable-prefix verbs are common German verbs. In addition, some equivalent verbs in English have the same prefix. For these reasons, recognizing many of these inseparable-prefix verbs is fairly simple.

The following points define *inseparable-prefix verbs:*

✔ You don't stress the prefix in spoken German.

✔ The prefix alters the original meaning of the verb.

✔ The prefix sticks with the verb stem in all tenses. For instance, consider the verb **vollenden** (*to finish, complete*). The prefix is **voll-** (*full*), and the verb is **enden** (*to finish*). In the third-person singular, the present tense is **vollendet** (*finish*), the simple past is **vollendete** (*finished*), and the present perfect is **hat . . . vollendet** (*has finished*).

✔ Word order in these tenses follow the same rules as verbs that have no prefix. (See Chapters 5, 16, and 17 for details on word order in present, present perfect, and simple past tenses.)

✔ The past participle doesn't have the prefix **ge-**.

✔ The ending of the past participle may be

- **Weak (formed with -t):** For instance, the past participle of **entdecken** (*to discover*) is **entdeckt** (*discovered*).

- **Strong (formed with -en):** For instance, the past participle of **empfehlen** (*to recommend*) is **empfohlen** (*recommended*).

Wer entdeckte Nordamerika? (*Who discovered North America?*) **Entdecken** (*to discover*) is an inseparable-prefix verb. Its prefix, **ent-**, means *away from*, and it corresponds to the English prefix *de-* or *dis-*. The verb **decken** means *to cover*.

Ich verspreche dir einen Rosengarten. (*I promise you a rose garden.*) The verb is **versprechen** (*to promise*).

Verfahren sich viele Touristen in der Stadt? (*Do many tourists get lost in the city?*) The verb **verfahren** means *to get lost*. In yes/no questions, the verb is at the beginning of the question.

Table 10-2 lists inseparable prefixes, their English meanings, and some verbs that use the prefix. A number of the prefixes have direct comparable usages in English, and many of the verbs are frequently used. **Erkennen Sie einige Verben?** (*Do you recognize some verbs?*)

Table 10-2	Inseparable Prefixes and Verb Combinations		
Prefix	**English Definition**	**Example Verb**	**English Equivalent**
be-	similar to English prefix *be-*	**sich befinden** (reflexive) **befreunden** **bekommen** **bemerken**	*to be located* *to befriend* *to get* *to notice*
emp-	no equivalent	**empfehlen** **empfinden**	*to recommend* *to feel*
ent-	similar to English prefixes *de-* and *dis-*	**entbehren** **entdecken** **entkommen** **entstehen**	*to do without* *to discover* *to escape* *to originate*

Prefix	English Definition	Example Verb	English Equivalent
er-	sometimes no equivalent, sometimes similar to the English prefix *re-* or the meaning of *fatal*	**erhängen** **erkennen** **erklären** **erschiessen** **ertrinken** **erzählen**	*to hang (execute)* *to recognize* *to explain, declare* *to shoot dead* *to drown* *to tell*
ge-	no equivalent	**gebrauchen** **gefallen** **gehören** **gestalten**	*to use, make use of* *to like* *to belong to* *to form, shape*
miss-	similar to English prefix *mis-*	**missbrauchen** **misstrauen** **missverstehen**	*to misuse, abuse* *to mistrust* *to misunderstand*
ver-	similar to English prefix *for-*	**verbieten** **vergeben** **vergessen**	*to forbid* *to forgive* *to forget*
ver-	*(go) awry*	**sich verfahren** (reflexive) **verkommen**	*to get lost* *to go to ruin*
ver-	*away, lose*	**verlassen** **verlieren**	*to leave, abandon* *to lose*
ver-	no equivalent	**vergrößern** **verfhaften** **versprechen**	*to enlarge* *to arrest* *to promise*
voll-	*complete*	**vollenden** **vollführen**	*to complete, come to an end* *to execute, perform*
zer-	*completely (ruin)*	**zerbrechen** **zerstören**	*to shatter* *to destroy*

You were about to read the synopsis of a German movie, but your puppy ripped it to shreds. Piece it back together by putting the sentences in the correct order. (Use the corresponding letters instead of rewriting the entire sentence.) After that, write a brief English summary of the story. **Hint:** It's a lowbrow love story with a tragic ending. **Viel Spaß!** (*Have fun!*) Look at the list of inseparable-prefix verbs in Table 10-2 to help you.

A. Der Film beginnt mit Leo der Lugner (*Leo the Liar*) als er aus einem Gefängnis (*prison*) **entkommt.**

B. Nach zwei Monaten zusammen, **verkommt** das Verhältnis (*relationship*) der beiden.

C. Am Anfang (*In the beginning*) **misstraut** er diese Frau in schwarz, . . .

D. Das Gefängnis **befindet sich** in der Nähe von der Lüneburger Heide im Norddeutschland.

E. Plötzlich (*Suddenly*) **bemerkt** er eine schöne Frau in einem schwarzen Kleid.

F. Bald kommt die Polizei und **verhaftet** Leo Lügner.

G. Eines Nachts (*One night*) **zerbricht** Leo eine Flasche (*bottle*) Bier über Silkes Kopf.

H. Dann **erschiesst** er die schöne Silke.

I. Leo Lügner **entdeckt** ein altes Fahrrad, in der Heide und fährt damit los.

J. . . . ich **werde** (*will*) dich nie (*never*) **verlassen.**î

K. Die beiden (*The two of them*) sprechen über das Leben im Gefangnis, und **vergessen** ihre schreckliche Situation.

L. Schreckliche Silke sagt, "Ich **verspreche** dir . . .

M. . . . aber sie sagt, "Mein Name ist Schreckliche Silke (*Horrible Silke*), und ich bin aus dem Gefangnis **entkommen.**"

N. Bald (*Soon*) **verfährt** er sich in der Heide.

Q. _____

A. **A.** Der Film beginnt mit Leo der Lügner (*Leo the Liar*) als er aus einem Gefängnis (*prison*) **entkommt.**

15. _____

16. _____

17. _____

18. _____ ***Hint:*** Plötzlich . . .

19. _____

20. _____

21. _____ ***Hint:*** Die beiden . . .

22. _____

23. _____

24. _____

25. _____

26. _____

27. _____

Summary of the movie in English:

Dealing with Dual-Prefix Verbs: To Separate or Not to Separate?

The *dual-prefix verbs,* the ones I call the *double-crossers,* are characterized by having a prefix that can combine to make both separable-prefix verbs and inseparable-prefix verbs. This means that with some main verbs, the prefix is separable, and with other main verbs, the same prefix is inseparable. For example, you can use the prefix **unter-** (*down*) to form the verb **unterzeichnen** (*to sign [a document]*), which is an inseparable-prefix verb. You can also combine **unter-** with **bringen** (*to bring*) to form **unterbringen** (*to accommodate*), a separable-prefix verb. The list of these prefixes is short. Without the prefix, many of the verbs are high-frequency types that you may already be familiar with.

Follow these guidelines to help you remember dual-prefix verbs:

- ✔ Some dual prefixes are mainly separable, and others are mainly inseparable.

  - **Um-** is a prefix that is mainly separable. **Umziehen** (*to move*), with the prefix **um-** (*around*), is an example of a separable-prefix verb: **Wann ziehst du um?** (*When are you moving?*).

  - **Über-** is a prefix that is mainly inseparable. **Übernachten** (*to sleep*), with the prefix **über-** (*over, across*), is an inseparable-prefix verb: **Im Sommer übernachten wir oft im Zelt** (*We often sleep in a tent in the summer*).

- ✔ Some dual-prefix verbs are both separable and inseparable. The verb in its literal meaning has a separable prefix, such as with **Die Fähre setzt uns ans andere Ufer über** (*The ferry is taking us across to the other bank [side]*). **Übersetzen** (*to ferry across*) is a separable-prefix verb. The prefix **über-** (*over, across*) is at the end of the sentence. The literal meaning involves physical movement from one place to another: to *cross over, travel across, go across*.

  The verb in its figurative meaning has an inseparable prefix, such as with **Sie übersetzt sehr schnell** (*She translates very quickly*). **Übersetzen** (*to translate*), with the prefix **über-** (*over, across*), is an inseparable-prefix verb. The figurative meaning involves changing over: *to translate from one language to another*.

Dual-prefix verbs follow the guidelines for formation, usage, and word order according to whether the prefix is separable or inseparable. (Use the guidelines in the earlier two sections for separable and inseparable prefix verbs.)

Table 10-3 is a list of dual prefixes and their English definitions, a sampling of dual-prefix verbs indicating whether they're separable- or inseparable-prefix verbs, and the English verb equivalents. Five verb pairs have both separable (sep.) and inseparable (insep.) prefixes. Notice that the last two prefixes, **wider-** and **wieder-**, have two separate meanings and spellings.

Table 10-3	Dual Prefixes and Verb Combinations		
Prefix	*English Definition*	*Example Verb*	*English Equivalent*
durch- (usually sep.)	*through*	**durchbringen** (sep.)	*to get through*
		durchfahren (sep.)	*to drive through*
		durchkommen (sep.)	*to come through*
hinter-	*behind*	**hinterlassen** (sep.)	*to let someone go behind*
		hinterlassen (insep.)	*to leave, bequeath*
über- (usually insep.)	*over, across*	**überfahren** (sep.)	*to ferry across, cross [over]*
		überfahren (insep.)	*to run over*
		überfallen (insep.)	*to attack, hold up (a bank and so on)*
		übernachten (insep.)	*to sleep (in a hotel and such)*
		übersetzen (insep.)	*to translate*
		übersetzen (sep.)	*to ferry across*

Prefix	English Definition	Example Verb	English Equivalent
um- (usually sep.)	*around*	**umbauen** (sep.) **umbauen** (insep.) **umsteigen** (sep.) **umziehen** (sep.)	*to renovate* *to enclose, build around* *to change (trains)* *to move (to a new home), change (clothes)*
unter-	*down, under*	**unterbrechen** (insep.) **untergehen** (sep.) **unterkommen** (sep.) **unternehmen** (insep.)	*to interrupt, disconnect* *to sink, go down* *to find accommodation* *to do, undertake*
wider- (usually insep.)	*against* (similar to English prefix *re-*)	**widerrufen** (insep.) **widersprechen** (insep.) **widerstehen** (insep.)	*to recall (product), withdraw* *to contradict* *to resist, withstand*
wieder-	*again*	**wiedergeben** (sep.) **wiederholen** (insep.) **wiederholen** (sep.) **wiedersehen** (sep.)	*to give back, play back, restore* *to repeat* *to get back* *to see again, meet again*

This exercise is multiple choice. First, read the sentence, decide which verb in parentheses is correct, and write it in the space(s) provided. Second, translate the sentence. Refer to Table 10-3 for these verbs.

0. Ich _____ im nächsten Bahnhof _____. (steige . . . um / ziehe . . . um)

A. Ich **steige** im nächsten Bahnhof **um.** (*I'm changing [trains] in the station.*)

28. _____ Sie bitte ihre Telefonnummer. (widersprechen / wiederholen)

_____

29. Hilfe! Das Schiff _____ ! (setzt . . . über / geht . . . unter)

_____

30. Die Firma _____ alle defekten Produkte. (unternimmt / widerruft)

_____

31. Mein Freund _____ sein altes Haus _____. (hat . . . umgebaut / hat . . . umbaut)

_____

32. Das Auto _____ einen Waschbär. (durchfuhr / überfuhr)

_____

Answer Key

1 Wir **laden** viele Gäste zum Fest **ein**. (*We're inviting many guests to the party.*)

2 Diese Firma **stellt** viele Produkte im Ausland **her**. (*This company produces many products in foreign countries.*)

3 Die besten Pläne **schlagen** oft **fehl**. (*The best plans often go wrong.*)

4 Können Sie mir die Details **mitteilen?** (*Can you inform me of the details?*) This is a question, and it has a modal verb. Put the conjugated modal verb in first position and the verb in its infinitive form at the end.

5 Nach einer Pause **fuhr** der Redner **fort**. (*After a break, the speaker continued.*)

6 **Brachen** Markus und Jonathan ihre Arbeit **ab?** (*Did Markus and Jonathan stop their work?*)

7 Im Herbst **sahen** die Bäume sehr schön **aus**. (*The trees looked pretty in the fall.*)

8 Regina **las** die Geschichte **vor**. (*Regina read the story aloud.*)

9 **Fuhr** der Bus ohne Johanna **los?** (*Did the bus leave without Johanna?*)

10 Wir **haben** viel Käse **eingekauft**. (einkaufen) (*We bought a lot of cheese.*)

11 Das Flugzeug **ist** in Bangkok **zwischengelandet**. (zwischenlanden) (*The plane stopped over in Bangkok.*)

12 Das Rockkonzert **hat** im Olympiastadion **stattgefunden**. (stattfinden) (*The rock concert took place in the Olympic Stadium.*)

13 **Habt** ihr das Gepäck schon **aufgegeben?** (aufgeben) (*Have you checked your bags yet?*)

14 Um wie viel Uhr **hat** der Film **angefangen?** (*At what time did the movie start?*)

15 **D.** Das Gefängnis **befindet sich** in der Nähe von der Lüneburger Heide im Norddeutschland.

16 **I.** Leo Lügner **entdeckt** ein altes Fahrrad, in der Heide und fährt damit los.

17 **N.** Bald (*Soon*) **verfährt** er sich in der Heide.

18 **E.** Plötzlich (*Suddenly*) **bemerkt** er eine schöne Frau in einem schwarzen Kleid.

19 **C.** Am Anfang (*In the beginning*) **misstraut** er diese Frau in schwarz, . . .

20 **M.** . . . aber sie sagt, "Mein Name ist Schreckliche Silke (*Horrible Silke*), und ich **bin** aus dem Gefängnis **entkommen**."

21 **K.** Die beiden (*The two of them*) sprechen über das Leben im Gefängnis, und **vergessen** ihre schreckliche Situation.

22 **L.** Schreckliche Silke sagt, "Ich **verspreche** dir . . .

23 **J.** . . . ich **werde** (*will*) dich nie (*never*) **verlassen.**"

24 **B.** Nach zwei Monaten zusammen, **verkommt** das Verhältnis (*relationship*) der beiden.

25 **G.** Eines Nachts (*One night*) **zerbricht** Leo eine Flasche (*bottle*) Bier über Silkes Kopf.

26 **H.** Dann **erschiesst** er die schöne Silke.

27 **F.** Bald kommt die Polizei und **verhaftet** Leo Lügner.

Leo Lügner escapes from a prison near the Lüneburger Heide, where he discovers a bicycle that he uses to escape. He soon gets lost in the heath but all of a sudden, he notices a beautiful woman in a black dress; he's suspicious of her at first. However, when Leo discovers that this woman named Schreckliche Silke is also an escaped convict, they begin talking about life in prison and forget the terrible situation they're in. Schreckliche Silke promises Leo Lügner that she'll never leave him, but after two months together, their relationship falls apart. One night, Leo breaks a beer bottle over Silke's head and shoots her dead; soon, the police come and arrest Leo Lügner.

28 **Wiederholen** Sie bitte ihre Telefonnummer. (widersprechen / wiederholen) (***Please repeat your phone number.***)

29 Hilfe! Das Schiff **geht unter!** (setzt . . . über / geht . . . unter) (***Help! The ship is sinking!***) German present continuous doesn't exist, but when you translate, it makes a lot more sense to say the ship's sinking, not that the ship sinks!

30 Die Firma **widerruft** alle defekten Produkte. (unternimmt / widerruft) (***The company is recalling all of the defective products.***) German present continuous doesn't exist, so when you translate, you can use it in English for this type of sentence; if you write *the company recalls all . . .* , you're stressing that the company issues recalls as a general fact, not that it's happening at the moment.

31 Mein Freund **hat** sein altes Haus **umgebaut.** (hat . . . umgebaut / hat . . . umbaut) (***My friend renovated his old house.***)

32 Das Auto **überfuhr** einen Waschbär. (durchfuhr / überfuhr) (***The car ran over a raccoon.***) Great picture language here: Raccoons do wash their hands often, and they look a little bit like a bear, don't they?

Part III
Fine Tuning Your Writing with Flair

The 5th Wave   By Rich Tennant

"It says children are forbidden from running, touching objects, or appearing bored during the tour of the castle."

In this part . . .

In Chapter 11, you discover how to use reflexive verbs to talk about the things you do to yourself. You also add a little style to your German by using expressions to discuss your interests, likes and dislikes, and more.

Want to add even more panache to your writing and speech? Imagine you're about to plant a beautiful garden with small but fragrant pansies; sunflowers standing tall, proudly facing the sun; and maybe a couple of cherry tomato plants. The descriptive words for this garden are the kinds of adjectives you find tucked into Chapter 12. I also ask you to look at how adjectives use case endings to fit into a sentence. Chapter 13 is where you work out how to make comparisons like *fast, faster, fastest* or *good, better, best*. In Chapter 14, you discover the key role of connecting-words (conjunctions) such as *but, and, because,* and *that*. Wrapping up this part is Chapter 15's primer on prepositions, those little guys you need to describe all the things you can watch 6-year-old Brendan doing on the playground: climb *up* the ladder, go *down* the slide *on* his belly, jam his face *into* the sand, and wipe the sand *out of* his mouth.

Chapter 11

Sounding More Like a Native with Verb Combinations

. . . .

In This Chapter
▶ Reflecting on reflexive verb combos
▶ Verbalizing with verb/preposition combos

. . . .

*W*hat, exactly, marks the difference between the dabbler in German who is struggling to order a cup of coffee and the customer in a three-star restaurant who has the wait staff surrounding the table, offering yet another sample from the chef's newest concoction? The customer's sway over the servers may have to do with his or her command of native German expressions. You can notice how well a person has mastered German — or any language — by observing the timely use of idiomatic language, which is the ability to insert fixed expressions into spoken and written language with ease. This chapter takes a closer look at idiomatic expressions that involve verbs. By using these expressions in your writing and speech, you can take your German to the next level and come across sounding like a native speaker.

Set in Their Ways: Grasping Idiomatic Verb Expressions

Idiomatic language involves stringing words together into a fixed expression that's more than the sum of its parts. One group of fixed expressions is the vast family of *idiomatic verb expressions:* combinations of verbs and other words to form a slightly different meaning. For example, left to its own devices, the preposition **um** generally means *around:* **Wir haben einen Zaun um das ganze Haus** (*We have a fence around the whole house*). But in the expression **Er bittet um Hilfe** (*He's asking for help*), the preposition **um** takes on a special meaning in combination with **bitten.**

Idiomatic German flows easily from the mouths of native speakers, who know when and how much to season their language with verb expressions. You can add some flair to your German speech and writing by using one of the following major types of idiomatic verb expressions:

> ✔ **Reflexive verbs:** Verbs are reflexive when you use them with reflexive pronouns, which include words such as *myself, themselves,* and *himself* in English. Look at the following example: **Ich erinnere mich an unserem ersten Tanz** (*I remember our first dance.* Literally: *I recall to myself at our first dance*). German expresses a

great deal of actions using reflexive pronouns linked to the verb, an area in which English makes minimal use.

- ✔ **Verbs associated with certain prepositions:** In this chapter, you find out about idiomatic expressions that pair the verb with a particular preposition in either the dative or accusative case. For instance, the preposition **vor** usually means *in front of;* but in the example **Ich habe Angst vor Schlangen** (*I'm afraid of snakes*), the fixed expression combines the verb **haben** (*to have*) with **Angst** (*fear*) and the dative preposition **vor.**

- ✔ **Verbs with separable or inseparable prefixes:** A *separable verb* is a verb with a prefix that detaches from the verb when it's conjugated. The confusion comes about because more often that not, these prefixes are nothing more than prepositions in disguise. (For more on verbs with separable and inseparable prefixes, see Chapter 10.)

To add more factors to this equation, you find combos of combos; some verb/preposition combos are actually separable or inseparable verb combos at the same time. In the following verb/preposition expression, the verb **ankommen** (*to arrive*) is a case in point because it has a separable verb prefix **an-.** When you add the preposition **auf** (*on*) to the expression, the meaning changes. Look at the example: **Es kommt darauf an** (*It depends*). The prefix **an-** is separated from **-kommen,** the word **darauf** (Literally: *on it*) accompanies the verb, and the sum of its parts is no longer *arrive* but *depend on.* The preposition **auf** (*on*) in the word **darauf** is a combination of **da-** + **(r)** + **auf.** (See Chapter 7 for more on expressions using **da-.**)

In the following sections, I show you various ways of using verb combinations to talk about yourself, others, and things. These three groups of idiomatic expressions combine a verb with another word (or words), such as a reflexive pronoun or a preposition, to form expressions.

In the Looking Glass: Reflecting on Reflexive Verbs

Look at yourself in the mirror and smile. What do you see (besides a stunningly beautiful or handsome person)? You are, grammatically speaking, *reflecting on yourself.* *Reflexive verbs* have a subject that carries out an action directed at itself. Typically, the verb combines with a reflexive pronoun to describe an action. The reflexive pronoun refers back to the subject of the sentence, which is carrying out the action indicated by the verb.

German and English both have reflexive verbs, but German uses them much more liberally. To make a long story short, your German can benefit from flexing (yourself) at the reflexive verb gym. This section helps you understand reflexive verbs and how you can use them correctly in your writing and speech.

Self-ish concerns: Meeting the reflexive pronouns

A reflexive verb has two elements: the verb and the reflexive pronoun. In English, a reflexive pronoun has the ending *-self* (*myself, yourself*) for singular forms and

-selves for plural forms (*ourselves, yourselves*). Both English and German have two cases of reflexive pronouns: the accusative and the dative case. The two cases are identical in English; in German, there are only two variations between the two cases, namely in the first- and second-person singular forms.

Table 11-1 shows the reflexive pronouns together with their translations. As a guide, I list the corresponding nominative pronouns in the left-hand column. Notice how frequently **sich** steps up to bat. Here's the key to the abbreviations: s. = singular, pl. = plural, inf. = informal, and form. = formal.

Table 11-1	Reflexive Pronouns: Accusative and Dative Case	
Nominative (nom.) Pronouns for Reference	**Accusative (acc.)**	**Dative (dat.)**
ich (*I*)	**mich** (*myself*)	**mir** (*myself*)
du (*you*) (s., inf.)	**dich** (*yourself*)	**dir** (*yourself*)
er/sie/es (*he/she/it*)	**sich** (*himself/herself/itself*)	**sich** (*himself/herself/itself*)
wir (*we*)	**uns** (*ourselves*)	**uns** (*ourselves*)
ihr (*you*) (pl., inf.)	**euch** (*yourselves*)	**euch** (*yourselves*)
sie (*they*)	**sich** (*themselves*)	**sich** (*themselves*)
Sie (*you*) (s. or pl., form.)	**sich** (*yourself* or *yourselves*)	**sich** (*yourself* or *yourselves*)

On the case! Choosing the right form of reflexive pronoun

Reflexive pronouns are either in the accusative case or the dative case. The case you use depends on how the pronoun functions in the sentence. It may be the direct object (accusative case) or the indirect object (dative case). Case shows the relationship of words to each other in a sentence — for instance, who's doing what (where the reflexive pronoun is in the accusative case) or who's doing what to what/whom (where the reflexive pronoun is in the dative case). Look at the example **Ich putze mir die Zähne** (*I brush my teeth*). It explains *who's doing what to what*, so German expresses this activity with a reflexive pronoun in dative case, **mir. Die Zähne** is the direct object, the receiver of the action, and it's in the accusative case. (See Chapter 2 for more on cases.) Check out the examples:

> **Ich fühle mich viel besser.** (*I feel/I'm feeling much better.*) **Mich** (*myself*) is the accusative form of the reflexive pronoun; it's the direct object that refers back to the subject performing the action of the verb **fühlen.** (The information answers the question *who's doing what?* Therefore, the reflexive pronoun is in the accusative case.)

> **Ich ziehe mir eine Jeans an.** (*I put on/I'm putting on a pair of jeans.*) **Mir** is the dative form of the reflexive pronoun; **eine Jeans** is the direct object (accusative case) in the sentence. (The information answers the question *who's doing what to what/whom?* Therefore, the reflexive pronoun is in the dative case.)

The verbs using the dative reflexive pronoun are those in sentences that have a separate direct object; the verbs using an accusative reflexive pronoun have no separate direct object in the sentence.

The reflexive pronoun can also be a part of a *verb + preposition* expression, and certain prepositions can require either the accusative or the dative case, as with **Wir freuen uns auf den Feiertag nächste Woche** (*We're happy about the holiday next week*). The preposition **auf** (*about*) requires the accusative case, as do time expressions. (I talk more about verb/preposition idioms in the upcoming section "Combining Verbs with Prepositions: Making Cool Combos").

Placing your pronoun

Word order plays an important role in sentence construction with reflexive pronouns. Check out the following important points to remember with word order and reflexive pronouns:

- ✔ In a statement, the reflexive pronoun immediately follows the conjugated verb; **sich** comes right after **haben** in this example: **Die Touristen haben sich die schöne Umgebung angesehen** (*The tourists looked at the beautiful surroundings*).

- ✔ In a question, if the subject is a pronoun (**ihr** [*you*]), then you place the reflexive pronoun (**euch** [*you*]) directly after it. For example, **Habt ihr euch beide schon wieder erkältet?** (*Have you both caught a cold again?*).

- ✔ In the present tense, you push the prefix of a separable-prefix verb to the end of the sentence. In the following example, the verb **anziehen** (*to get dressed*) is a separable-prefix verb; the reflexive pronoun **mich** comes after the conjugated verb **ziehe** and before the prefix **an-** (refer to Chapter 10): **Ich ziehe mich an** (*I get/I'm getting dressed*).

Identifying which verbs need to be reflexive

Many German verbs require a reflexive pronoun such as **mich** (*myself*), **dich** (*yourself*), or **uns** (*ourselves*) in situations when you don't use a reflexive pronoun in English, such as with **Beeilen Sie sich!** (*Hurry up!*).

In German, you frequently find the reflexive in references to parts of the body. These verbs often describe what you do to yourself when you're in the bathroom. For example, shaving (**sich rasieren** [*to shave oneself*]) is a reflexive verb. In English, you can say that the *man shaved himself* or that *he shaved,* period. The first version is expressed reflexively using *himself.* The second statement, *he shaved,* is just as understandable, and it isn't reflexive in structure. But German has only one, reflexive way of expressing this action: **Er rasiert sich** (*He shaves himself*).

To further add to the mix, some German verbs can go either way: with or without the reflexive pronoun. With such verbs, the reflexive format is different from the verb without the reflexive pronoun. The next three examples show you **waschen** (*to wash*) expressed with a reflexive pronoun in the accusative case, then in the dative case, and finally without a reflexive pronoun:

Ich wasche mich am Abend. (*I wash myself in the evening.*) **Mich,** the reflexive pronoun in accusative case, refers back to the subject of the sentence, **ich.** And **ich** (*I*) is carrying out the action on **mich** (*myself*).

Waschbären waschen sich oft die Hände. (*Raccoons often wash their hands.*) Notice that German speakers express *their hands* with **die Hände** (*the hands*), so if you want to say *I wash my hands* in German, it looks like this: **Ich wasche mir die Hände. Mir** is the dative case reflexive pronoun *myself*, and **die Hände** is the accusative case (direct object) *the hands.*

Christian wäscht sein Auto jeden Samstag. (*Christian washes his car every Saturday.*) In both the English and the German sentences, the verb **wäscht** (*washes*) is followed by a direct object that refers to another living being or thing.

Table 11-2 lists some of the more common reflexive verbs, many of which have to do with daily routine, especially personal hygiene. In German, you express the verbs on this list with a reflexive pronoun. The helpful grammar details give you clues about case and whether you have a separable-prefix verb.

Table 11-2	Reflexive Verbs: The Daily Routine	
German Expression	*English Equivalent*	*Helpful Grammar Details*
sich abschminken (acc.)	*to take off one's makeup*	Separable-prefix verb; accusative reflexive pronoun
sich abtrocknen (acc.) **sich (die Hände) abtrocknen** (dat.)	*to dry oneself off* *to dry (one's hands)*	Separable-prefix verb; accusative or dative reflexive pronoun
sich anziehen (acc.) **sich (das Hemd) anziehen** (dat.)	*to get dressed* *to put on (one's shirt)*	Separable-prefix verb; accusative or dative reflexive pronoun
sich ausziehen (acc.) **sich (die Stiefel) ausziehen** (dat.)	*to get undressed* *to take off (one's boots)*	Separable-prefix verb; accusative or dative reflexive pronoun
sich beeilen (acc.)	*to hurry (up)*	Accusative reflexive pronoun
sich duschen (acc.)	*to take a shower*	Accusative reflexive pronoun
sich freuen auf den Tag (acc.)	*to look forward to the day*	Accusative reflexive pronoun
sich freuen auf das Frühstück (acc.)	*to look forward to (having) breakfast*	Accusative reflexive pronoun
sich kämmen (acc.) **sich (die Haare) kämmen** (dat.)	*to comb oneself* *to comb (one's hair)*	Accusative or dative reflexive pronoun
sich die Zähne putzen (dat.)	*to brush/clean one's teeth*	Dative reflexive pronoun
sich rasieren (acc.) **sich (das Gesicht) rasieren** (dat.)	*to shave oneself* *to shave (one's face)*	Accusative or dative reflexive pronoun
sich schminken (acc.)	*to put on one's makeup*	Accusative reflexive pronoun
sich waschen (acc.) **sich das Gesicht waschen** (dat.) **sich die Haare waschen** (dat.) **sich die Hände waschen** (dat.)	*to wash oneself* *to wash (one's face)* *to wash (one's hair)* *to wash (one's hands)*	Accusative or dative reflexive pronoun

Write about your daily routine using the German expressions provided in Table 11-2. Remember that with separable-prefix verbs, you place the prefix at the end of the sentence. Make sure you pay attention to whether the reflexive pronoun is expressed in the accusative case (for example, **mich** [*myself*]) or dative case (**mir** [*myself*]).

0. sich das Gesicht rasieren _____

A. **Ich rasiere mir das Gesicht.** (*I shave my face.*)

1. sich das Gesicht waschen _____

2. sich die Zähne putzen _____

3. sich duschen _____

4. sich die Haare waschen _____

5. sich abtrocknen _____

Combining Verbs with Prepositions

Prepositions are short, cute words that can have a great influence on other parts of a sentence. Some German cuties and their English counterparts look similar at times: **in** (*in*), **an** (*on*), or **für** (*for*).

Having said that, however, I need to add that they can be sly little creatures that change their tune when they hook up with different verbs, changing the verb's meaning. No matter how you cut the cake, certain prepositions that work together with certain verbs make for powerful, effective means of expression in German and English. You may refer to them as *idioms, idiomatic expressions,* or the bare bones term: *verb/preposition combos.* I prefer the latter. When you want to sound like your mother tongue is German, you need to acquire as many of these combos as you can fit in your repertoire. (To find out about dative and accusative terminology, go to Chapter 2.)

Verb/preposition combinations are more than the sum of their parts. Why? These prepositions are slick: When combined with a verb to form a fixed expression, they can alter the meaning of the verb they appear with. That's why mastering the verb/preposition combos as a unit is important. You can't predict which preposition partners with which verb, and you can't know ahead what the whole shebang means, even if you know the meaning of the verb alone, without a preposition.

Table 11-3 lists some of the most frequently used German prepositions that change their meaning in combination with a verb. Notice that the English equivalents aren't always the same as in the expression. The third column gives an example of a verb/preposition combo, and the fourth column shows an example sentence with its English translation. For the prepositions that can be both accusative and dative, I give only one example sentence. As you look through the example sentences and their English equivalents, notice that the preposition generally changes its original meaning. Look at the key to understand the abbreviations used in the table: acc. = accusative, dat. = dative.

Table 11-3		Prepositions Used in Idiomatic Verb Expressions	
Preposition	*Usual English Equivalent*	*Example Verbal Expression/ English Translation*	*Example Sentence*
an (acc./dat.)	*on, at, to*	**denken an** (acc.) (*to think of/about*)	**Er denkt oft an seinen Eltern.** (acc.) (*He often thinks of his parents.*)
auf (acc./dat.)	*on top of, to*	**warten auf** (acc.) (*to wait for*)	**Sie warten auf den Zug.** (acc.) (*They're waiting for the train.*)
aus (dat.)	*out of, from*	**bestehen aus** (dat.) (*to consist of*)	**Die Uhr besteht aus vielen kleinen Teilen.** (*The clock consists of many small parts.*)
für (acc.)	*for*	**halten für** (acc.) (*to take someone for/consider*)	**Ich halte ihn für einen engen Freund.** (*I consider him a close friend.*)
in (acc./dat.)	*in, inside of*	**sich verlieben in** (acc.) (*to fall in love with*)	**Sie hat sich in ihn verliebt.** (acc.) (*She fell in love with him.*)
mit (dat.)	*with*	**fahren mit** (dat.) (*to go with*)	**Ich fahre gern mit der U-Bahn.** (*I like to take the subway.*)
über (acc.)	*over, above*	**reden über** (acc.) (*to talk about*)	**Wir reden über dich.** (*We're talking about you.*)
um (acc.)	*around*	**bitten um** (acc.) (*to ask for*)	**Er bittet um Hilfe.** (*He's asking for help.*)
von (dat.)	*from, of*	**sprechen von** (dat.) (*to speak about/of*)	**Wir sprechen von dem/vom Präsidenten. (von + dem = vom)** (*We're talking about the president.*)
vor (dat.)	*in front of*	**Angst haben vor** (dat.) (*to be afraid of*)	**Hast du Angst vor Spinnen?** (*Are you afraid of spiders?*)

German prepositions all use case to indicate the relationship they have to other parts of the sentence, namely the object of the preposition. Some of the prepositions use the accusative case; others use the dative case. Another group, the switch hitters, can work in the accusative or dative case. (This is true of some other prepositions as well, including those that don't partner with verbs to form idiomatic expressions.) The following sections delve deeper into these three situations to help you understand the differences. (Check out Chapter 15 for more information on prepositions.)

1D-ing common combos in the accusative case

In this section, I show you an important group of verb/preposition combos you can use to add real German sparkle to your written and spoken language. Verbs that combine with prepositions using the accusative case make up this useful group. These common verb/preposition combos are fixed expressions for which you need to remember which preposition partners with which verb, which case the preposition takes (accusative for this list), and what the expression means.

Table 11-4 lists the commonly used verb/preposition combos with prepositions in the accusative case. Used alone, these prepositions may be switch hitters, the kind that can work in both the accusative and dative case, but in combination with these verbs, they go to up to bat as accusatives. The expressions are listed alphabetically by verb.

Table 11-4   Idiomatic Verb Expressions with Accusative Prepositions

Verbal Expression	Example Sentence	English Equivalent
ankommen auf (*to depend on*) **Note:** Ankommen has a separable prefix **an-**	**Es kommt auf das Wetter an.**	*It depends on the weather.*
bitten um (*to ask for*)	**Wir bitten um Ihre Unterstützung.**	*We're asking for your support.*
denken an (*to think of/about*)	**Denkst du oft an deine Kindheit?**	*Do you often think about your childhood?*
glauben an (*to believe in*)	**Sie glauben nicht an Gott.**	*They don't believe in God.*
halten für (*to take someone for/consider*)	**Hältst du ihn für einen Dieb?**	*Do you take him for a thief?*
reden über (*to talk about*)	**Sie redet über diverse Themen.**	*She talks about different topics.*
schreiben an (*to write to*)	**Ich schreibe an die Zeitung.**	*I'm writing to the newspaper.*
schreiben über (*to write about*)	**Schreibst du über mich?**	*Are you writing about me?*
sorgen für (*to take care of*)	**Wir sorgen für unsere Oma.**	*We're taking care of our grandma.*
sich verlieben in (*to fall in love with*)	**Ich habe mich in ihn verliebt.**	*I fell in love with him.*
verzichten auf (*to do without*)	**Ich kann auf meinen Urlaub verzichten.**	*I can do without my vacation.*
warten auf (*to wait for*)	**Wartest du auf uns?**	*Are you waiting for us?*

Read the following text, and fill in the two spaces (one for the verb, one for the preposition) with the missing parts of the verb/preposition combos you find in Table 11-4. The missing expression is written in parentheses in English. To make your task easier, read through first, checking out the context of each blank space. The paragraph is a love letter written by a completely unknown writer of romantic fiction. **Viel Vergnügung!** (*Have a good time!*)

Mein Liebling,

Q. Ich _____ diesen Brief _____ (to write to) dich, weil ich dich liebe.

A. Ich **schreibe** diesen Brief **an** dich, weil ich dich liebe. (*I'm writing you this letter because I love you.*)

Ich weiß, du (6) _____ oft _____ (to think about) mich, und ich

(7) _____ oft _____ (to think about) dich. Jeden Tag

(8) _____ ich _____ (to wait for) deinen Telefonanruf. Ich kann nicht

(9) _____ deine täglichen Anrufe _____ (to do without). In der Arbeit

(10) _____ ich immer _____ (to talk about) dich. Meine Kollegen

(11) _____ mich _____ (to take me for/consider) eine Idiotin, aber

das ist nicht wichtig. Wichtig ist nur eins: ich (12) _____ mich _____

dich verliebt (to fall in love with). Ich (13) _____ _____ (to ask for)

einen Anruf von dir heute Abend.

Deine Sarah

Eyeing common combos in the dative case

Verbs that combine with prepositions using the dative case are a commonly used group of verb/preposition combos. When you're able to plunk these expressions into your written and spoken German, you're well on the way to sounding like you're originally from a German-speaking country. These frequently used combos are fixed expressions for which you need to remember which preposition combines with which verb, which case the preposition takes (dative for this list), and what the expression means.

Table 11-5 lists some commonly used expressions with prepositions in the dative case. Used alone, these prepositions may be accusative or dative, but in these expressions, they require the dative. I list the expressions alphabetically by verb.

Table 11-5 Idiomatic Verb Expressions with Dative Prepositions

Verbal Expression	*Example Sentence*	*English Equivalent*
abhängen von (*to depend on*) *Note:* Abhängen has a separable prefix **ab-**	**Es hängt von dem Wetter ab.**	*It depends on the weather.*
Angst haben vor (*to be afraid of*)	**Hast du Angst vor Grizzlybären?**	*Are you afraid of grizzly bears?*
arbeiten an (*to work on*)	**Ich arbeite sehr fleißig an dem Projekt.**	*I'm working very diligently on the project.*

(continued)

Table 11-5 *(continued)*

Verbal Expression	Example Sentence	English Equivalent
bestehen aus (*to consist of*)	**Die Schweiz besteht aus vier Sprachregionen.**	*Switzerland consists of four language regions.*
erzählen von (*to talk about*)	**Er erzählt oft von seinen Reisen.**	*He often talks about his trips.*
fahren mit (*to go/ride with*)	**Ich fahre mit dir.**	*I'll go (or ride) with you.*
gehören zu (*to belong to*)	**Sie gehören zu unserer Mannschaft.**	*They belong to our team.*
halten von (*to think of, have an opinion about*)	**Sie hält nicht viel von der neuen Regierung.**	*She doesn't think much of the new government.*
rechnen mit (*to count on*)	**Sie rechnen mit einer langen Nacht.**	*They're counting on a long night.*
sprechen von (*to talk about*)	**Ich spreche nicht von dir.**	*I'm not talking about you.*
studieren an (*to study at*)	**Viele Studenten studieren an technischen Universitäten.**	*Many students study at technical universities. (Usually: engineering schools)*
verstehen von (*to understand about*)	**Verstehst du etwas von Motorrädern?**	*Do you know something about motorcycles?*

Q. _____ Sie etwas _____ (*to know something about*) Reisen?

A. **Verstehen** Sie etwas **von** Reisen? (*Do you know something about traveling?*)

Was (14) _____ Sie _____ (*to think of*) einer Traumreise? Na, ja. Ich (15) _____ jetzt _____ (*to talk about*) meiner speziellen Reise. Sie (16) _____ _____ (*to consist of*) einem Besuch auf drei Inseln: Banga, Tanga, und Zanga. Zuerst (17) _____ wir _____ (*to go by* [*means of*]) einem Ruderboot (*rowboat*) von Banga nach Tanga. Dort (18) _____ Sie Haifische (*sharks*) _____ (*to study at*) der Tanga Universität. Dann (19) _____ ich zusammen mit Ihnen _____ (*to work on*) einem Segelboot (*sailboat*) - wir bauen das Boot! (20) _____ Sie Angst _____ (*to be afraid of*) dem Segeln? Dann (21) _____ Sie _____ (*to belong to*) der Gruppe, die ein Haus auf Zanga baut. . . .

Answer Key

1 **Ich wasche mir das Gesicht**. (*I wash my face.*) The reflexive pronoun **mir** is in the dative case, and the direct object **das Gesicht** is in accusative case.

2 **Ich putze mir die Zähne.** (*I brush my teeth.*) The reflexive pronoun **mir** is in the dative case, and the direct object **die Zähne** is in accusative case.

3 **Ich dusche mich.** (*I take a shower.*) The reflexive pronoun **mich** is in the accusative case. It refers back to the action of the subject **ich.**

4 **Ich wasche mir die Haare.** (*I wash my hair.*) The reflexive pronoun **mir** is in the dative case, and the direct object **die Haare** is in accusative case.

5 **Ich trockne mich ab**. (*I dry myself.*) The reflexive pronoun **mich** is in the accusative case. It refers back to the action of the subject **ich.** The separable prefix verb requires the prefix **ab** at the end of the sentence.

Mein Liebling,

Ich weiß, du (6) **denkst** oft **an** mich, und ich (7) **denke** oft **an** dich. Jeden Tag (8) **warte** ich **auf** deinen Telefonanruf. Ich kann nicht (9) **auf** deine täglichen Anrufe **verzichten.** In der Arbeit (10) **rede** ich immer **über** dich. Meine Kollegen (11) **halten** mich **für** eine Idiotin, aber das ist nicht wichtig. Wichtig ist nur eins: ich (12) **habe** mich in dich **verliebt.** Ich (13) **bitte um** einen Anruf von dir heute Abend.

Deine Sarah

My darling,

I know you often think about me, and I often think about you. Every day I wait for your telephone call. I canít do without your daily calls. At work I always talk about you. My colleagues take me for an idiot, but that's not important. Only one thing is important: I've fallen in love with you. I'm asking for a call from you this evening.

Your Sarah

Was (14) **halten** Sie **von** einer Traumreise? Na, ja. Ich (15) **erzähle** jetzt **von** meiner speziel-len Reise. Sie (16) **besteht aus** einem Besuch auf drei Inseln: Banga, Tanga, and Zanga. Zuerst (17) **fahren** wir **mit** einem Ruderboot von Banga nach Tanga. Dort (18) **studieren** Sie Haifische **an** der Tanga Universität. Dann (19) **arbeite** ich zusammen mit Ihnen **an** einem Segelboot — wir bauen das Boot! (20) **Haben** Sie Angst **vor** dem Segeln? Dann (21) **gehören** Sie **zu** der (or **zur:** **zu** + **der** = **zur**) Gruppe, die ein Haus auf Zanga baut. . . .

What do you think of a dream trip? Good. I'll talk about my special trip. It consists of a visit to three islands: Banga, Tanga, and Zanga. First we travel by rowboat from Banga to Tanga. There we study sharks at Tanga University. Then I'll work together with you on a sailboat — we'll build the boat! Are you afraid of sailing? Then you'll be a part of the group that builds a house on Zanga. . . .

What do you think of a dream trip? Good. I'll talk about my special trip. It consists of a visit to three islands: Banga, Tanga, and Zanga. First we travel by rowboat from Banga to Tanga. There we study sharks at Tanga University. Then I'll work together with you on a sailboat — we'll build the boat! Are you afraid of sailing? Then you'll be a part of the group that builds a house on Zanga. . . .

Chapter 12

Adding Adjectives for Description

In This Chapter

▶ Categorizing adjectives for easy reference

▶ Forming adjectives with endings

▶ Using possessive adjectives

Adjectives add spice, distinctive flavor, and creativity to a sentence. They dress up nouns for a vigorous winter workout in Arlberg. What's in it for you? Why not be content with the basics? Cross out *vigorous* from *vigorous winter workout,* and you still get the picture. But the listener doesn't perk up and become involved. Adjectives add depth and character to the power of a noun. Besides, they're **interessant** (*interesting*), **lustig** (*funny*), **unglaublich** (*incredible*), **ruhig** (*quiet*), and **praktisch** (*practical*).

I have good news and not-so-good news. First the good news: There are a large number of cognates among German adjectives. In the first paragraph, you probably recognize **interessant,** and you may get the meaning of **praktisch** if you know that the ending **-isch** often stands in for English adjective endings like *-ic* and *-ical.* The not-so-good news is that you have to address grammar — gender, number, and case — when handling adjectives. Depending on where you place the adjective in the sentence, you may or may not need to put the adjective in synch with the noun it modifies. How? By adding the appropriate endings to indicate agreement with the noun.

Keine Sorge. (*Not to worry.*) This chapter explains how to categorize types of adjectives in German for easy reference, form case endings of adjectives, and use possessive adjectives. You discover how to wade through these adjective pitfalls so you can comfortably and safely use them in your writing and speech.

Organizing Adjectives: Opposites, Cognates, and Collocations

Adjectives are so numerous that it's essential to find a system for categorizing them as a means of easy reference. When you encounter a new adjective, try to find a hook to hang it on. You may be able to group them three different ways:

✔ **Opposites:** Some adjective types lend themselves to pairing up with an adjective of the opposite meaning.

✔ **Cognates:** Cognates, which are similar words in English and German, are instantly recognizable; after you check that the meaning is the same in both languages, you only need to know how to form their endings in sentences.

✔ **Collocations:** *Collocations* are semi-fixed, frequently used word combinations, so look for adjective + noun phrases.

Get into the habit of recognizing collocations that adjectives occur in. It takes a bit more work than figuring out what an adjective alone means, but in the end, it saves time. Add them to your range of expression, and you're on the path to successful, idiomatic German.

This section helps you place adjectives in these three different groupings. By doing so, you can more easily remember these descriptors, and then you can use them when you want to discuss appearance, personal traits, weather, and more.

Letting opposites attract

You can master many groups of descriptive adjectives as opposite pairs. Two common groups I deal with in this section are the adjectives that describe people's appearance and personal traits and adjectives that describe the weather.

Describing appearance and personal traits

When you want to say what people are like, you use descriptive adjectives to describe them; for example, **sie ist groß** (*she's tall*) or **er ist freundlich** (*he's friendly*). In Table 12-1, you see such adjectives grouped as opposites; looking at them this way saves you time when you're remembering them.

Table 12-1	Adjectives of Personal Appearance and Traits		
German	*English*	*German Opposite*	*English Opposite*
attraktiv	attractive	**unattraktiv**	unattractive
freundlich	friendly	**unfreundlich**	unfriendly
glücklich	happy	**traurig/unglücklich**	sad, unhappy
heiter	cheerful	**ernst**	serious
interessant	interesting	**uninteressant/langweilig**	uninteresting/boring
jung	young	**alt**	old
klein	short	**groß**	tall
neu	new	**alt**	old
ruhig	quiet	**laut**	loud
schlank	thin/slim	**mollig**	plump/chubby
stark	strong	**schwach**	weak
sportlich	athletic	**unsportlich**	unathletic
sympathisch	likable, friendly	**unsympathisch**	unpleasant, disagreeable
tolerant	tolerant	**intolerant**	intolerant
zuverlässig	reliable	**unzuverlässig**	unreliable

Refer to Table 12-1 and match the adjective with its opposite. The adjectives describe appearance and personal traits of Paula and Philip, twins who couldn't be more opposite from one another.

0. Philip ist zuverlässig, aber Paula ist _____.

A. Philip ist zuverlässig, aber Paula ist **unzuverlässig.** (*Philip is reliable, but Paula is unreliable.*) Notice that German also uses the prefix *un-* to mean *not.*

1. Paula ist klein, aber Philip ist _____.

2. Paula ist attraktiv, aber Philip ist _____.

3. Philip ist sympathisch, aber Paula ist _____.

4. Philip ist stark, aber Paula ist _____.

5. Paula ist sportlich, aber Philip ist _____.

6. Philip ist laut, aber Paula ist _____.

Describing the weather

No matter where you are, talking about **das Wetter** (*the weather*) is the perfect ice-breaker. It also provides you with ammunition to make your friends jealous when you're writing them **Ansichtskarten** (*postcards*) while you're **im Urlaub** (*on vacation*). Look at the weather vocabulary in Table 12-2. Great news: Most of the adjectives have near opposites, so it's economical to remember them in pairs.

Table 12-2	Adjectives of Weather		
German	*English*	*German Opposite*	*English Opposite*
gut, schön	*good, nice*	**schlecht**	*bad*
sonnig	*sunny*	**wolkig, bewölkt**	*cloudy*
wunderschön	*delightful, lovely*	**furchtbar**	*awful*
warm	*warm*	**kühl**	*cool*
heiß	*hot*	**kalt**	*cold*
trocken	*dry*	**nass**	*wet*

More weather-related adjectives include **frostig** (*chilly*), **schön warm** (*nice and warm*), **neb(e)lig** (*foggy*), **regnerisch** (*rainy*), **schwül** (*humid*), and **stürmisch** (*gusty, blustery*).

You're on vacation. Finish the postcard, describing the weather and someone you met there. Fill in the blanks using some adjectives describing weather and people. ***Note:*** The first word in a letter isn't capitalized unless it's a noun.

Q. Hier ist es sehr _____.

A. Hier ist es sehr **heiß.** (*It's very hot here.*)

Postcard

18/2/08

Liebe Christine,

wie geht es dir? Ist das Wetter zu Hause
(7)_____? Heute ist es
(8)_____, aber gestern war es
(9)_____ und (10)_____.
Ich bin sehr (11)_____!
Im Hotel gibt es einen Mann, der sehr
(12)_____ ist. Er ist auch
(13)_____. Wenn das Wetter
morgen (14)_____ ist, machen wir
eine Bergtour.

Alles Gute, Siggi

Christine Schroeder

Holtstr. 95

10472 Berlin Deutschland

A family resemblance: Describing with cognates

Although German does have some incredibly foreign sounding words, the number of cognates is surprisingly large. You can put them in several categories for easy access. Some example categories are based on the adjective's ending. See Table 12-3.

Table 12-3	Common Endings on German Adjectives	
German Ending	*Usual English Ending*	*Examples*
-al	same	**diagonal, digital, emotional, formal, ideal, integral, interkontinental, international, irrational, kollegial, liberal, national, normal, optimal, original, sentimental, sozial, total, universal**
-ant or **-ent**	same	**elegant, exzellent, intelligent, interessant, intolerant, kompetent, tolerant, uninteressant**
-ell	*-al*	**generell, individuell, informell, konventionell, kriminell, offiziell, partiell, rationell, sensationell, visuell**

German Ending	Usual English Ending	Examples
-isch	-ic or -ical	allergisch, alphabetisch, analytisch, charakteristisch, chemisch, dynamisch, egoistisch, elastisch, elektrisch, elektronisch, ethisch, exotisch, exzentrisch, fanatisch, fantastisch, klassisch, harmonisch, hygienisch, identisch, idiomatisch, idyllisch, ironisch, logisch, lyrisch, melodisch, militärisch, musikalisch, mythisch, patriotisch, philosophisch, politisch, praktisch, romantisch, sarkastisch, sporadisch, symmetrisch, systematisch, tropisch
-iv	-ive	aktiv, alternativ, exklusiv, explosiv, intensiv, interaktiv, kreativ, massiv, passiv
-lich or -ig	-y, -ly, or -ally	freundlich, frostig, hungrig, persönlich, sportlich, sonnig, unfreundlich, unpersönlich, unsportlich, windig

Some cognates — such as **bitter, blind, blond, fair, golden, human, illegal, legal, liberal, mild, modern, neutral, parallel, solid, uniform, warm,** and **wild** — have the same meaning and the same spelling. Others have a few spelling changes from English to German, such as

- ✔ *c* → **k: direct, exakt, intakt, komplex, konstant, korrekt, nuklear**
- ✔ *c* → **k;** *ve* → **v: aktiv, effektiv, exklusiv, kreativ**
- ✔ *le* → **el: flexibel, kompatibel, miserabel, variabel**
- ✔ *d* → **t: hart, laut** (*loud*)
- ✔ *y* → **ig: frostig, hungrig, sonnig, windig**

Get in the habit of remembering cognates in groups. Repeat them out loud, alphabetically and rhythmically. They'll stick with you and serve you well when you need them.

Traveling companions: Describing with collocations

Acquiring word chunks is far more economical than studying isolated words. *Collocations* are chunks of words that are very predictable, some so predictable that they nearly always stick together. By some definitions, collocations include idioms and other fixed expressions. Collocations are made up of all kinds of word combinations: adjective + noun, noun + noun, adverb + adjective, and so on. In this section, I deal with adjective combos.

Some collocations translate well: **Starke Nerven** is the same as *strong nerves*. Other expressions aren't as close: **Das ist ein starkes Stück** in literal English means *that's a strong piece*. Yet in German, it's like saying *that's a bit too much*, as in *that's over the top*. Take a look at some example collocations:

Unsere Produkte werden nur in umweltfreundlichen Verpackungen verkauft.
(*Our products are sold only in environmentally friendly packaging.*) The collocation
is the combination of **umweltfreundlich(en) + Verpackung(en)** (*environmentally
friendly + packaging*). Notice the fixed combination *environmentally friendly* is an
adverb + adjective in English; in German, it's a noun + adjective: **die Umwelt** (*the
environment*) + **freundlich** (*friendly*).

Ich ärgere mich grün und blau. (*I'm hopping mad.* Literally, it's something like,
I'm annoyed green and blue.) You can also describe this expression as an idiom.
Whatever the terminology, if you were to ask a German speaker to finish the sen-
tence **ich ärgere mich . . . und . . .,** he wouldn't hesitate to add the right colors.

Use only German collocations you're sure about using correctly. Although you know a
collocation in English, it may very well translate into German as nonsense. For example, take the German adjective **stark.** Put the English collocation *stark raving mad* into
German word-for-word, and you get gibberish. Why? The whole three-word chunk is
the German collocation **total verrückt** (*totally crazy*). When you know that **stark**
means *strong* in German, not *harsh* as in English, you're halfway on the road to using it
correctly.

Read and listen actively to German. Make it your goal to recognize chunks of language, not only single words. Knowing a stack of collocations with adjectives offers
you great opportunities for expressing yourself clearly and succinctly.

Brighten up your language with colorful collocations. Look at the expressions using
colors. Match the English equivalents and write them next to the German expression.

0. Sie treffen ins Schwarze.

A. ***They hit the bull's eye.***

~~They hit the bull's eye.~~	They're drunk.	They're working illegally, not paying taxes.
They're not at work/school, pretending to be sick.	They're blushing.	They're riding (the train) without a ticket.
They're hopping mad.	They're outdoors.	They're getting tan.

15. Sie sind blau. _____

16. Sie fahren schwarz. _____

17. Sie sind im Grünen. _____

18. Sie werden rot. _____

19. Sie arbeiten schwarz. _____

20. Sie werden braun. _____

21. Sie ärgern sich grün und blau. _____

22. Sie machen blau. _____

Helping Adjectives Meet a Satisfying End

Expanding your adjective arsenal is the first step; knowing how to form and use adjectives correctly in a sentence is the goal for any intermediate language learner. This section entails deciding whether the adjectives need endings and, if so, how to form these endings.

English uses adjectives as is, straight up, no changes needed to plunk them into a combination with a noun. German is quite different. Before a German adjective can sidle up to a noun, it quite often needs an ending that reflects the gender and case of the noun it modifies. As in English, a German adjective usually comes right before the noun it describes: **meine schwarze Handschuhe** (*my black gloves*).

However, not all adjectives in all sentences need special attention as far as necessary ending changes are concerned. An adjective has no ending when it follows the verbs **sein** (*to* be), **werden** (*to become*), or **bleiben** (*to remain*) and modifies the subject. See the two examples:

> **Das Wetter bleibt warm.** (*The weather remains warm.*)
>
> **Die Berge in Bayern sind wunderschön.** (*The mountains in Bavaria are gorgeous.*)

Work at recognizing the case and gender of nouns in the sentence and knowing how to add the correct endings. In this section, you need to know the difference between endings when an adjective stands alone in front of the noun — for example, **frisches Obst** (*fresh fruit*) — and when an adjective has a word such as **der, ein,** or **dieser** at the beginning of the phrase — for example, **das frische Obst** (*the fresh fruit*).

Forming endings on adjectives not preceded by der- or ein- words

When you describe something in general such as food prices, you simply say something like *fresh pineapples are expensive.* You don't need to add *the, those,* or *our.* It's the same in German, except you have the added factor of case endings for adjectives. In other words, when you say **frische Ananas sind teuer** (*fresh pineapples are expensive*), you need to know that the ending for **frisch** is **-e.** *Note:* In phrases that do have an article or modifier like *the, those,* or *our* (as in *those fresh pineapples*), the adjective endings are different. Check out the following section, "Preceded adjectives: Forming the endings," for details.

This section deals with endings for an adjective that modifies and precedes a noun, but the adjective isn't preceded by an article (such as **der/die/das** or **ein/eine**) or other modifiers (**der-** words, such as **dieser** and **solcher,** and **ein-** words, such as **mein** and **kein**).

Here are the characteristics that define adjectives without **der-** or **ein-** words preceding them:

- ✔ Because no article or other modifier precedes the noun, the adjective must indicate gender and case of the noun; it has a double duty of adjective and article.

- ✔ These adjectives have mostly the same endings as **der-** words, with the exception of the masculine and neuter genitive, where the ending is **-en.**

To form these adjective endings, you need to know the gender, case, and number of the noun that the adjective modifies. For example, take the adjective **gut** (*good*). In order to say **guter Käse ist teuer** (*good cheese is expensive*), you need to know that **Käse** is masculine singular (**der Käse**) and that in this sentence, it's in the nominative case (subject). You add that nominative masculine ending **-er** onto **gut,** so you have **gut + -er = guter Käse.**

The four adjectives in Table 12-4 deal with food: **gut** (*good*), **schmackhaft** (*tasty*), **lecker** (*delicious, mouth-watering, scrumptious*), and **köstlich** (*delicious, luscious, exquisite*). The endings that agree in case, number, and gender with the noun they modify are in bold. For easy reference, I also list the adjective ending separately in bold with each example. Add these endings to adjectives that are not preceded by **der-** or **ein-** words.

Table 12-4   Adjective Endings Not Preceded by Der- or Ein- Words

Case	Masculine	Feminine	Neuter	Plural
Nominative (subject)	**-er** gut**er** Käse (*good cheese*)	**-e** schmackhaft**e** Wurst (*tasty sausage*)	**-es** lecker**es** Brot (*delicious bread*)	**-e** köstlich**e** Kuchen (*delicious cakes*)
Accusative (direct object)	**-en** gut**en** Käse	**-e** schmackhaft**e** Wurst	**-es** lecker**es** Brot	**-e** köstlich**e** Kuchen
Dative (indirect object)	**-em** gut**em** Käse	**-er** schmackhaft**er** Wurst	**-em** lecker**em** Brot	**-en** köstlich**en** Kuchen
Genitive (possessive)	**-en** gut**en** Käses	**-er** schmackhaft**er** Wurst	**-en** lecker**en** Brotes	**-er** köstlich**er** Kuchen

Check out some examples:

> **Leckeres Brot findet man überall in deutschen Bäckereien.** (*You can find delicious bread everywhere in German bakeries.*) The adjective **lecker + -es** (*delicious*) describes the noun **(das) Brot** (*bread*); **leckeres Brot** is in the accusative case because it's the direct object. The neuter singular accusative ending for unpreceded adjectives is **-es.**

> **Es gibt köstliche Kuchen in österreichischen Cafés.** (*There are luscious cakes in Austrian cafés.*) The adjective **köstlich + -e** describes the noun **(der) Kuchen,** in plural form. **Köstliche Kuchen** is in the accusative case because it's the direct object. The plural accusative ending for unpreceded adjectives is **-e.**

Add the correct ending to the adjectives in parentheses. Write the adjective in the space provided. Use Table 12-4 for reference.

Q. Im Winter trinken wir gern _____ Tee. (heiß)

A. Im Winter trinken wir gern **heißen** Tee. (*We like to drink hot tea in the winter.*) **Tee** is masculine. **Heißen Tee** is in accusative case; it's the direct object of the sentence.

23. Im Sommer schmeckt mir _____ Bier vom Faß. (erfrischend)

24. Ich trinke auch gern _____ Getränke. (alkoholfrei)

25. Mögen Sie _____ Wein? (deutsch)

26. Ja, _____ Weißweine gefallen mir. (trocken)

Preceded adjectives: Forming the endings

When you want to be specific about something, you use articles and modifiers like *the, those,* or *a* to say something like *the modern painting, those violent movies,* or *a fantastic restaurant.* In English, you simply add the adjective of your choice, and you're all set. Not so in German. Both the article/modifier and the adjective need to reflect the gender, number, and case of the noun they modify.

This section deals with endings for an adjective that modifies and precedes a noun that's preceded by an article (such as **der/die/das** or **ein/eine**) or other modifiers (**der-** words such as **dieser** and **solcher,** and **ein-** words such as **mein** and **kein**). (See Chapters 1 and 2 for information on articles and **der-** and **ein-** words.) Preceded adjectives appear in phrases with an article or other modifier, an adjective, and a noun.

Take the example **ein lockeres Hemd ist bequem** (*a loose shirt is comfortable*). **Hemd** is singular, neuter, and in the nominative case because it's the subject of the sentence, so the article **ein** and the adjective **lockeres** reflect the neuter gender, number, and case of **Hemd.** Check out Table 12-5.

Table 12-5		Preceded Adjective Endings		
Case	*Masculine*	*Feminine*	*Neuter*	*Plural*
Nominative (subject)	**der** lustige Manne **ein** lustig**er** Mann	**die** glückliche Frau **eine** glückliche Frau	**das** brave Kind **ein** brav**es** Kind	**die** braven Kinder **keine** braven Kinder
Accusative (direct object)	**den** lustig**en** Mann **einen** lustig**en** Mann	**die** glückliche Frau **eine** glückliche Frau	**das** brave Kind **ein** brav**es** Kind	**die** braven Kinder **keine** braven Kinder
Dative (indirect object)	**dem** lustig**en** Mann **einem** lustig**en** Mann	**der** glücklich**en** Frau **einer** glücklich**en** Frau	**dem** brav**en** Kind **einem** brav**en** Kind	**den** brav**en** Kindern **keinen** brav**en** Kindern
Genitive (possessive)	**des** lustig**en** Mann**es** **eines** lustig**en** Mann**es**	**der** glücklich**en** Frau **einer** glücklich**en** Frau	**des** brav**en** Kind**es** **eines** brav**en** Kind**es**	**der** braven Kinder **keiner** braven Kinder

You're on vacation on the island of **Rügen, in der Ostsee** (*Rügen, in the Baltic Sea*). Write a letter describing some activities you're doing there. Fill in the blanks using the adjectives in parentheses. Look at Table 12-4 for the adjective endings needed. *Note:* The first word in a letter isn't capitalized unless it's a noun.

Q. Die Insel Rügen hat eine _____ (herrlich) Küste.

A. Die Insel Rügen hat eine **herrliche** Küste. (*The island of Rügen has a wonderful coastline.*) **Eine herrliche Küste** is singular accusative; it's the object of the sentence. **Eine** is the hint that **Küste** is feminine; you indicate the agreement with **-e** tacked onto **herrlich**.

Hallo Margit und Thomas,

was macht ihr mit den (27) _____ (klein) Kindern zu Hause? Hier auf

der Insel Rügen gibt es leider keine (28) _____ (exotisch) Blumen,

aber gestern haben wir die (29) _____ (spektakular) (30) _____

(weiß) Felsen gesehen. Kennst du die Bilder von dem (31) _____

(bekannt) Maler Caspar David Friedrich? Diese (32) _____ (herrlich)

Landschaft hat er oft gemalt. Wir geniessen die (33) _____ (gesund)

Luft, und morgen machen wir einem (34) _____ (lang) Spaziergang

bei Binz. Heute Abend essen wir mit einem (35) _____ (interessant)

Ehepaar aus Ostdeutchland. Sie sagen, diese (36) _____

(wunderschön) Insel ist ihr Urlaubziel seit vielen Jahren. Am Donnerstag

fahren wir zu einer (37) _____ (klein) Insel mit einem (38) _____

(komisch) Namen - Hiddensee. Dort gibt es einen (39) _____ (lang)

Strand und einen (40) _____ (schön) Leuchtturm.

Machts gut, Liesl und Hansi

Using Possessive Adjectives: My Place or Your Place?

Possessive adjectives are the words describing ownership, possession, or relationship, such as *my, your, his, her,* and so on. They're also referred to as *possessive pronouns.* (That's because technically speaking, a possessive adjective is a pronoun that's used as an adjective to show who "owns" the noun following it.) Identifying possessive adjectives is easy because they're grouped together with the **ein-** words (they have the same endings, even if they don't rhyme with **ein**). The **ein-** words include **ein, kein,** and all the possessive adjectives.

The singular possessive adjectives are **mein** (*my*), **dein** (*your*), **sein** (*his*), **ihr** (*her*), and **sein** (*its*). The plural possessive adjectives are **unser** (*our*), **euer** (*your*), **ihr** (*their*), and **Ihr** (*your* — formal, singular and plural).

Table 12-6 shows possessive adjective endings in all cases and genders. This is the same pattern for **ein-** and **kein-** in Table 12-5. The following table shows **mein** and **unser** together. All other possessive adjectives use these same endings. The endings are shown separately in bold.

Table 12-6 Possessive Adjective Endings and First-Person Examples

Case	Masculine	Feminine	Neuter	Plural
Nominative (subject)	- mein, unser	-**e** mein**e**, unser**e**	- mein, unser	-**e** mein**e**, unser**e**
Accusative (direct object)	-**en** mein**en**, unser**en**	-**e** mein**e**, unser**e**	- mein, unser	-**e** mein**e**, unser**e**
Dative (indirect object)	-**em** mein**em**, unser**em** unser**em**	-**er** mein**er**, unser**er**	-**em** mein**em**, unser**em**	-**en** mein**en**, unser**en**
Genitive (possessive)	-**es** mein**es**, unser**es**	-**er** mein**er**, unser**er**	-**es** mein**es**, unser**es**	-**er** mein**er**, unser**er**

Using Table 12-6, complete the sentences in the exercise. Put the adjectives in parentheses into the sentences, being mindful of the endings.

Q. Ich kann _____ Schlüssel (plural) nicht finden. (mein)

A. Ich kann **meine** Schlüssel nicht finden. (*I can't find my keys.*) **Meine** is plural accusative.

41. _____ Schlüssel liegen auf dem Tisch. (dein)

42. Und ist _____ Gepäck schon fertig? (unser)

43. Nein. Uli hat _____ Koffer noch nicht gepackt. (sein)

44. Na ja, _____ Urlaub fängt schon mit vielen Problemen an. (unser)

Answer Key

1 Paula ist klein, aber Philip ist **groß.** (*Paula is short, but Philip is tall.*)

2 Paula ist attraktiv, aber Philip ist **unattraktiv.** (*Paula is attractive, but Philip is unattractive.*)

3 Philip ist sympathisch, aber Paula ist **unsympathisch.** (*Philip is likable, but Paula is disagreeable.*)

4 Philip ist stark, aber Paula ist **schwach.** (*Philip is strong, but Paula is weak.*)

5 Paula ist unsportlich, aber Philip ist **sportlich.** (*Paula is unalthletic, but Philip is athletic.*)

6 Philip ist laut, aber Paula ist **ruhig.** (*Philip is loud, but Paula is quiet.*)

Postcard

18/2/08

Liebe Christine,

wie geht es dir? Ist das Wetter zu Hause (7) **kalt**? Heute ist es (8) **wunderschön**, aber gestern war es (9) **kühl** und (10) **windig**. Ich bin sehr (11) **glücklich!** Im Hotel gibt es einen Mann, der sehr (12) **sympathisch** ist. Er ist auch (13) **sportlich**. Wenn das Wetter morgen (14) **schön warm** ist, machen wir eine Bergtour.

Alles Gute, Siggi

Christine Schroeder

Holtstr. 95

10472 Berlin Deutschland

DEUTSCHE POST WORLD NET 50

Dear Christine,

How are you? Is the weather cold at home? Today it's lovely, but yesterday it was cool and windy. I'm really happy! There's a man in the hotel who is very friendly. He's also athletic. If the weather's nice and warm tomorrow, we're going climbing.

All the best, Siggi

15 *They're drunk.*

16 *They're riding [the train] without a ticket.*

17 *They're outdoors.*

18 *They're blushing.*

19 *They're working illegally, not paying taxes.*

20 *They're getting tan.*

21 *They're hopping mad.*

22 *They're not at work/school, pretending to be sick.*

23 Im Sommer schmeckt mir **erfrischendes** Bier vom Faß. (*I enjoy refreshing draft beer in the summer.*) **Bier** is neuter, and it's the subject, so it's in the nominative case. The adjective takes the neuter nominative ending **-es.**

24 Ich trinke auch gern **alkoholfreie** Getränke. (*I also like to drink non-alcoholic beverages.*) **Getränke** is plural, and it's a direct object, so it's in the accusative case. The adjective takes the plural accusative ending **-e.**

25 Mögen Sie **deutschen** Wein? (*Do you like German wine?*) **Wein** is masculine, and it's a direct object, so it's in the accusative case. The adjective takes the masculine accusative ending **-en.**

26 Ja, **trockene** Weißweine gefallen mir. (*Yes, I like dry white wines.*) **Weißweine** is plural, and it's the subject, so it's in the nominative case. The adjective takes the plural nominative ending **-e.**

	Hallo Margit und Thomas,
	was macht ihr mit den (27) **kleinen** Kindern zu Hause? Hier auf der Insel
	Rugen gibt es leider keine (28) **exotischen** Blumen, aber gestern haben
	wir die (29) **spektakularen** (30) **weißen** Felsen gesehen. Kennst du die Bilder
	von dem (31) **bekannten** Maler Caspar David Friedrich? Diese (32) **herrliche**
	Landschaft hat er oft gemalt. Wir geniessen die (33) **gesunde** Luft, und
	morgen machen wir einem (34) **langen** Spaziergang bei Binz. Heute Abend
	essen wir mit einem (35) **interessanten** Ehepaar aus Ostdeutchland. Sie
	sagen, diese (36) **wunderschöne** Insel ist ihr Urlaubziel seit vielen Jahren.
	Am Donnerstag fahren wir zu einer (37) **kleinen** Insel mit einem (38) **komischen**
	Namen - Hiddensee. Dort gibt es einen (39) **langen** Strand und einen
	(40) **schönen** Leuchtturm.
	Machts gut, Liesl und Hansi

Hi Margit and Thomas,

What are you doing with the little children at home? Here on the island of Rügen, there aren't any exotic flowers, but yesterday we saw the spectacular white cliffs. Do you know the paintings by the famous painter Caspar David Friedrich? He often painted this wonderful landscape. We're enjoying the healthy air, and tomorrow we're going on a long walk near Binz. This evening we're having dinner with an interesting couple from eastern Germany. They say this beautiful island is where they've been spending their vacations for many years. On Thursday we're going to a small island with a funny name — Hiddensee. There's a long beach there and a nice lighthouse.

See you soon, Liesl and Hansi

41 **Deine** Schlüssel liegen auf dem Tisch. (*Your keys are on the table.*) **Deine Schlüssel** is plural nominative.

42 Und ist **unser** Gepäck schon fertig? (*And is our luggage ready?*) **Unser Gepäck** is singular, neuter nominative.

43 Nein. Uli hat **seinen** Koffer noch nicht gepackt. (*No. Uli hasn't packed his suitcase yet.*) **Seinen Koffer** is singular, masculine accusative.

44 Na ja, **unser** Urlaub fängt schon mit vielen Problemen an. (*Oh well. Our vacation is already starting with a lot of problems.*) **Unser Urlaub** is singular, masculine nominative.

Chapter 13

Comparing with Adjectives and Adverbs

In This Chapter

▶ Understanding regular adjective and adverb comparative forms

▶ Grasping irregular adjective and adverb comparative forms

▶ Comparing equals/unequals

*Y*ou may be wondering why I mix adjectives and adverbs in the same chapter, especially after Chapter 12 deals with adjectives. I have some very good reasons. Both have the power to make comparisons. What's even better is that German adjectives and adverbs are one and the same word in most cases. Take, for instance, the adjective *good* and its adverbial counterpart *well*. The German equivalents are exactly the same for both adjective and adverb: **gut.** Best of all, using comparative and superlative forms of adjectives and adverbs offers great opportunities for making your language more precise, more useful, and more interesting.

In this chapter, you make comparisons using adjectives and adverbs — for example, **freundlich, freundlicher, am freundlichsten** (*friendly, friendlier, friendliest*). Many adjectives and adverbs follow a regular pattern for making words of comparison. Some forms are irregular; they need more attention to master. Grammar comes into play with comparative adjectives that precede a noun. (See Chapter 12 for preceded adjectives.) Some types of adjectives and adverbs have a unique grammatical structure; I explain these word groups in this chapter. These groups include adjectives that omit the noun, participles (verb forms like *loving* or *loved*) that function as adjectives or adverbs, and adverbs that modify adjectives. The last section in this chapter deals with comparing equals/unequals — for example, **(nicht) so teuer wie** (*[not]* as *expensive as*).

Comparing Regular Adjectives and Adverbs: Fast, Faster, Fastest

Adjectives modify or describe nouns; *adverbs* modify or describe verbs, other adverbs, or adjectives. (The verb **sein** [*to be*] is an exception: Adverbs can't modify the verb **sein.**) When you're using comparative and superlative forms, German makes adjectives and adverbs in similar ways. *Comparative* means that you compare two objects, people, activities, ideas, and so on (for example, *longer* is the comparative form of *long*); *superlative* means that you compare three or more objects, people, activities, ideas, and so on (*longest* is the superlative form).

Forming the comparative and superlative forms of adjectives and adverbs from the basic form isn't difficult when you see the similarities to English. The endings that vary from the most-frequent pattern mostly have to do with facilitating pronunciation. The following guidelines show how to add **-er** and **-(e)st** endings as well as the endings for adjectives that come before nouns (see Chapter 12 for details on adjective agreement).

Comparing two things

For both adjectives and adverbs, when you want to compare two things, people, and so on, take the base form (the adjective or adverb as you see it in the dictionary) and form the comparative by adding **-er** to the base form — for instance, **witzig → witziger** (*witty → witti*er). To express *than* in a comparison, the German equivalent is **als.**

> **Mein Onkel Richard ist nett, aber meine Tante Christel ist netter als Onkel Richard.** (*My uncle Richard is nice, but my aunt Christel is nicer than uncle Richard.*) The adjective **nett** is the base form; **netter als** (*nicer than*) is the comparative form.

> **Onkel Richard fährt schnell, aber Tante Christel fährt schneller als Onkel Richard.** (*Uncle Richard drives fast, but aunt Christel drives faster than uncle Richard.*) The adverb **schnell** is the base form; **schneller als** (*faster than*) is the comparative form. *Note:* **Schnell** is both an adjective and an adverb, just as *fast* is in English.

Adjectives ending in **-el** and **-er** leave the last **-e** off the base form and then add **-er** to make the comparative: **dunkel → dunkler** (*dark → darker*), **teuer → teurer** (*expensive → more expensive*).

When you want to use a comparative adjective that precedes the noun, you follow the same guidelines as with other adjectives that precede the noun. Look at the following examples to show you three different scenarios for preceded adjective endings:

> **Du hast ein neueres Auto als ich.** (*You have a newer car than I do.*) The direct object, **ein neueres Auto,** is in accusative case, and it's singular. The indefinite article **ein** (*a*) has no ending in accusative singular case: It's neuter to reflect the neuter noun **(das) Auto.** The base form of the adjective **neu** (*new*) has the comparative ending **-er** + the neuter, singular ending **-es** to form **neueres (neu + -er + -es).**

> **Ich habe den kleineren Wagen.** (*I have the smaller car.*) The direct object, **den kleineren Wagen,** is in accusative case, and it's singular. The definite article **den** (*the*) has the accusative masculine ending: It's masculine to reflect the masculine noun **(der) Wagen.** The base form of the adjective **klein** (*small*) has the comparative ending **-er** + the masculine, singular, accusative ending **-en** to form **kleineren (klein + -er + -en).**

> **Köstlicheres Brot ist kaum zu finden.** (*It's hard to find more delicious bread.*) The subject of the sentence, **köstlicheres Brot,** is in nominative case, and it's singular. The base form of the adjective **köstlich** (*delicious*) has the comparative ending **-er** + the neuter, singular ending **-es** to reflect the neuter noun **(das) Brot.** The comparative **köstlicheres** is formed like this: **köstlich + -er + -es = köstlicheres.**

German doesn't use **mehr** (*more*) together with the **-er** ending. In English, the comparative adjective form can look like this: *more intelligent* or *more interesting*. German uses only the **-er** ending: **intelligenter** or **interessanter.**

Absolutely the most! Discussing superlatives

The superlative form for adverbs as well as for adjectives that follow a noun in a sentence is the following: **am** + adjective/adverb + **-sten:**

> **Dieser Supermarkt ist am billigsten.** (*This supermarket is the cheapest/most inexpensive.*) **Billig** is the base form of the adjective, and **am billigsten** is the superlative.

> **Tante Gisela kocht am besten.** (*Aunt Gisela cooks the best.*) **Gut** is the base form of the adverb; **am besten** is the superlative form.

A superlative adjective often precedes the noun it modifies, which means it needs to reflect the noun's gender, number, and case. You get the superlative form of such adjectives by adding **-st** to the base form and then adding the adjective ending (see Chapter 12): **höflich** → **höflichst-** + adjective ending (*polite* → *most polite*).

> **Manuela ist die höflichste Kollegin im Büro.** (*Manuela is the most polite colleague in the office.*) **Höflich** is the base form of the adjective; **die höflichst-** + **-e (Kollegin)** is feminine, singular, nominative case.

> **Onkel Kalle hat das schönste Haus.** (*Uncle Kalle has the nicest house.*) **Schön** is the base form of the adjective; **das schönst-** + **-e (Haus)** is the superlative form that reflects the neuter, singular accusative noun **das Haus.** *Note:* Here's the alternative form, which uses an adjective that follows the noun: **Sein Haus ist am schönsten** (*His house is the nicest*).

You make the superlative form for adjectives ending in **-t** or **-z** (and a few others) by adding **-e** + **-st** = **-est** for ease of pronunciation: **elegantest-** (*most elegant*). For example, **Du findest die elegantesten Schuhe bei Salamander** (*You find the most elegant shoes at Salamander [a well-known shoe store]*). **Elegant** is the base form of the adjective; **die elegant-** + **est-** + **-en** is the superlative form that reflects the accusative plural noun **Schuhe.**

Considering common comparisons

Table 13-1 contains a list of some adjectives and adverbs that are frequently used for making comparisons of people and things. The fourth column shows any differences in spelling, as in **nett** → **netter** → **am nettesten,** where you add the **-e** in front of **-st.** The superlative form for all words is shown at first as **am** + **(e)sten.** You use this form when the adjective follows the noun and for adverbs. The form shown in parentheses is the form that you use when a superlative adjective precedes the noun. You add the adjective endings to this form. *Remember:* All adjectives that precede the noun take adjective endings that reflect the noun's gender, number, and case.

Table 13-1		Regular Comparison Forms		
English	*Base*	*Comparative*	*Superlative*	*Spelling Changes*
modest	bescheiden	bescheidener	am bescheidensten (bescheidenst-)	
cheap, inexpensive	billig	billiger	am billigsten (billigst-)	
dark	dunkel	dunkler	am dunkelsten (dunkelst-)	drop the last -e in the comparative
elegant	elegant	eleganter	am elegantesten (elegantest-)	add -e + st in the superlative
fit, in shape	fit	fitter	am fittesten (fittest-)	double the t; add -e + st in the superlative
hard working, industrious	fleißig	fleißiger	am fleißigsten (fleißigst-)	
flexible	flexibel	flexibler	am flexibelsten (flexibelst-)	drop the last -e in the comparative
friendly	freundlich	freundlicher	am freundlichsten (freundlichst-)	
generous	großzügig	großzügiger	am großzügigsten (großzügigst-)	
ugly	hässlich	hässlicher	am hässlichsten (hässlichst-)	
polite	höflich	höflicher	am höflichsten (höflichst-)	
pretty	hübsch	hübscher	am hübschesten (hübschest-)	add -e + st in the superlative
intelligent	intelligent	intelligenter	am intelligentesten (intellegentest-)	add -e + st in the superlative
musical	musikalisch	musikalischer	am musikalischsten (musikalischst-)	
brave	mutig	mutiger	am mutigsten (mutigst-)	
nice	nett	netter	am nettesten (nettest-)	add -e + st in the superlative
neat	ordentlich	ordentlicher	am ordentlichsten (ordentlichst-)	
chic, stylish	schick	schicker	am schicksten (schickst-)	
pretty, beautiful	schön	schöner	am schönsten (schönst-)	

English	Base	Comparative	Superlative	Spelling Changes
athletic	**sportlich**	**sportlicher**	**am sportlichsten** (**sportlichst-**)	
expensive	**teuer**	**teurer**	**am teuersten** (**teuerst-**)	drop the last **-e** in the comparative
sensible	**vernünftig**	**vernünftiger**	**am vernünftigsten** (**vernünftigst-**)	
witty	**witzig**	**witziger**	**am witzigsten** (**witzigst-**)	

When making a sentence, remember to add the appropriate endings to adjectives of comparison when needed. Adjectives following a noun don't need to reflect the gender, number, and case of the noun, but adjectives that precede the noun do need agreement. (See Chapter 12 for more on adjectives.)

Complete the sentences using the comparative or superlative form of the word in parentheses. The context of the sentence gives clues as to whether you need the comparative or superlative form. Then translate the sentences into English.

0. Im Frühling gibt es die _____ Blumen. (pretty)

_____

A. Im Frühling gibt es die **schönsten/hübschesten** Blumen. (***The prettiest flowers are in spring.***) The adjective **(die) schönsten/hübschesten** is in the accusative plural form to reflect number and case of **(die) Blumen.**

1. Claudia fährt am _____. (sensible)

_____

2. Mein Bruder ist _____ als ich. (witty)

_____

3. Wir waren vorher _____ als jetzt. (brave)

_____

4. Siegbert machte den _____ Eindruck. (nice)

_____

5. Ich bin _____ als du. (fit)

_____

6. Am _____ bin ich mit meiner Familie. (happy)

_____

7. Wiebke hat jetzt _____ Haar als früher. (dark)

_____

Adding the umlaut in regular comparisons

German wouldn't be the same without its three interesting-looking letters that have umlauts (not to mention that cool **ess-tset,** the letter **ß**). When forming the comparative and superlative forms of some adjectives and adverbs, be careful to add the umlaut when you need it.

The general guideline for adding umlauts in comparisons is simple to remember:

✔ Many adjectives and adverbs with one syllable and with an **-a, -o,** or **-u** in the base form add an umlaut in the comparative and superlative forms: **alt** → **älter** → **ältest-** (*old* → *older* → *oldest*).

✔ Some common one-syllable words with an **-a, -o** or **-u** in the base form don't have an umlaut: **blond** (*blond[e]*), **bunt** (*colorful*), **falsch** (*wrong*), **froh** (*glad*), **klar** (*clear*), **toll** (*amazing, great*), **wahr** (*true*), and **laut** (*loud, noisy*). ***Note:*** **Laut** has **-au** in the base form, unlike the others in this list. I include it here because it doesn't add an umlaut in the comparative and superlative forms.

Herr Diefenbacher ist alt, aber Frau Kolbe ist noch älter. (*Herr Diefenbacher is old, but Frau Kolbe is even older.*) The adjective **alt** (base form) changes to **älter,** with an umlaut in the comparative form.

Die ärmsten Länder brauchen sehr viel Unterstützung. (*The poorest countries need a lot of aid.*) The adjective **ärmsten** is the superlative form; **die ärmsten Länder** is the subject (nominative case), and it's plural. **Ärmsten** precedes the noun, so it needs the adjective ending to reflect **Länder.** You form it like this: **arm-** (base form) changes to **ärm-** (add the umlaut) + **-est** (superlative ending) + **en** (nominative plural ending).

Complete the following with the forms of the adjectives and adverbs that are missing. Remember to include the umlaut and **-e** with **-st** if needed. Some exercises have all three words missing; these are cognates.

English	Base	Comparative	Superlative
O. *old*	alt	_____	_____
A. *old*	alt	**älter**	**am ältesten**
8. *poor*	_____	_____	am ärmsten
9. *stupid*	_____	dümmer	_____
10. *crude, coarse*	_____	gröber	_____
11. *large, big, tall*	groß	_____	_____
12. *hard, tough*	hart	_____	_____
13. *young*	_____	_____	_____
14. *cold*	_____	_____	_____

Using Irregular Comparison Forms

German has some wayward characters among adjectives and adverbs, but luckily, a few of these irregular types have parallels to English odd ducks. The classic example is **gut → besser → am besten,** which is easily recognizable in English as *good → better → best*. These words are high frequency, and there are only a small number of them, so getting them into your active vocabulary should be a snap. All you need to do is memorize this list of commonly used irregular comparison forms. Look at Table 13-2 for the list of irregular adjectives and adverbs.

Table 13-2	Irregular Comparison Forms		
English Equivalent	*Base*	*Comparative*	*Superlative*
soon, sooner, soonest	**bald**	**eher**	**am ehesten**
like/enjoy (doing something), prefer, like most of all	**gern**	**lieber**	**am liebsten**
good, better, best	**gut**	**besser**	**am besten**
high, higher, highest	**hoch**	**höher**	**am höchsten**
near, nearer, nearest	**nah**	**näher**	**am nächsten**
much, more, most	**viel**	**mehr**	**am meisten**

The use of **gern** (the base form of the word meaning *to like, enjoy* [*doing something*]) is easiest to remember in the context of some common expressions:

✔ **Ich spiele gern Klavier/Ich tanze gern/Ich esse gern Fisch.** (*I like to play the piano/I like to dance/I like to eat fish.*) You use this construction to express that you like an activity, sport, game, food, and so on. Also: **Ich spiele lieber Tennis/ich trinke am liebsten Wasser.** (*I prefer playing tennis/I like drinking water most of all.*) The base form of these sentences are **Ich spiele gern Tennis** and **Ich trinke gern Wasser** (*I like to play tennis* and *I like to drink water*).

✔ **Ich möchte gern wissen, ob . . .** (*I wonder if . . .*)

✔ **Was möchtest du lieber . . . ?** (*Which would you rather . . . ?*)

✔ **Am liebsten möchte ich . . .** (*Most of all, I'd like to . . .*) Use this expression to talk about an activity/food/place that you like or would like to do/eat/go to/and so on.

These exercises are grouped in three sentences with the base form, comparative form, and the superlative form. Complete the three unfinished sentences in each exercise using the irregular comparison forms in Table 13-2. The question heading each group of three questions indicates the English equivalent of the German word to use.

Which mountain is higher?

0. Die Zugspitze ist _____.

Der Großglockner ist _____.

Der Mont Blanc ist _____.

A. Die Zugspitze ist **hoch.** (*The Zugspitze is high.*) Zugspitze is Germany's highest mountain.

Der Großglockner ist **höher.** (*Großglockner is higher.*) Großglockner is Austria's highest mountain.

Der Mont Blanc ist **am höchsten.** (*Mont Blanc is the highest.*) Mont Blanc is the highest mountain in the Alps, located at the border between France and Italy.

Which dinner is more expensive?

15. Ein Abendessen im Restaurant Bei Mario kostet _____.

16. Ein Abendessen im Restaurant Chez Philippe kostet _____.

17. Ein Abendessen im Restaurant Zur Goldenen Gans kostet _____.

Who's coming home sooner?

18. Monika kommt _____ nach Hause.

19. Jennifer kommt _____ nach Hause.

20. Sarah kommt _____ nach Hause.

Which sport do you like better?

21. Ich fahre _____ Fahrrad.

22. Ich fahre _____ Wasserski.

23. Ich fahre _____ Ski.

Comparing Equals and Nonequals

When you were a kid, you probably boasted about yourself, saying that you were better than the rest. After you grow up, you have to consider a lot more factors. You may want to sound more diplomatic and leave the boasting to the playground mentality. Using the expressions in this section, you can sound smooth enough to impress almost anyone. Use the following structures for expressing equality and inequality of items, places, people, what have you. They do wonders for increasing your range of expression.

Table 13-3 shows the list of commonly used expressions that describe equality or inequality between things, people, or ideas. The example sentences show how these expressions fit into sentences. Notice the word order of the information in each example sentence; with the exception of **je . . . desto** (*the . . . -er, the . . . -er*), you use the same word order in German and English to make comparisons using these expressions. The adjective or adverb that you're using as a comparison is in the middle of the two parts of the expression. For example, if you use the adverb **schnell** (*fast*) to say *just as fast as . . .* , you say **genauso schnell wie . . .** in German.

Table 13-3		Comparison Forms of Equals/Nonequals	
Comparison of Equals/Nonequals	**English Equivalent**	**Example Sentence**	**English Equivalent**
genauso . . . wie	*just as . . . as . . .*	Mein Auto fährt **genauso** schnell **wie** sein Motorrad.	*My car goes just as fast as his motorcycle.*
halb so . . . wie . . .	*half as . . . as . . .*	Das Ergebnis war nur **halb so** schlimm **wie** wir erwarteten.	*The result was only half as bad as we expected.*
nicht so . . . wie . . .	*not as . . . as . . .*	Ich bin **nicht so** stark **wie** ich dachte.	*I'm not as strong as I thought.*
so . . . wie . . .	*as . . . as . . .*	Unsere Produkte sind **so** zuverlässig **wie** importierte Produkte.	*Our products are as reliable as imported products.*
je . . . , desto . . . (comparative words follow **je . . . , desto . . .**)	*the . . . -er, the . . . -er* (adjectives or adverbs in comparative form)	**Je mehr** Sie lesen, **desto besser** informiert werden Sie. (***Note:*** The word order is different in English)	*The more you read, the better informed you'll be.*

In the following exercise, put the words into the correct word order. The example shows how to complete the sentence. Then translate the sentence into English.

0. verdient / so viel / Pilot / wie / ein / Ein Polizist / nicht

A. Ein Polizist verdient **nicht so viel wie** ein Pilot. (***A policeman doesn't earn as much as a pilot.***)

24. so viel wie/BMW/Mercedes/kostet/ein/Ein neuer/neuer

_____

25. halb so viel/wie/Fußballspieler/Ein/ein/läuft/Baseballspieler

_____

26. er/er/Poker/spielt/desto reicher/wird/Je mehr

_____

27. viel/ nicht so/Die neuen/benutzen/Benzin/wie die/alten Modelle/Autos

_____

28. Farbfilme/Schwarz-Weiß-Filme/sind/wie/genauso spannend

_____

29. desto mehr/Je qualifizierter/ist/verdient/man/man

_____

30. wie/in/in/Deutschland/ist/Das Wetter/Neuengland/so schön/das Wetter

Identifying Unique Adjective and Adverb Groups

The structure and usage of some adjectives and adverbs is unique. These types include adjectives that are used as nouns, participles used as adjectives or adverbs, and adverbs that modify adjectives. Most are fairly easy to remember because they have parallel meanings and structures in English.

You need to know these groups because they're high frequency words and expressions that you come across in everyday language, and they help you express yourself more clearly. They're easy to remember if you understand how to use these structures in sentences. This section includes the following three unique groups:

- ✔ Naturally, adjectives used as nouns are the type that stand in for the noun; they omit the noun — for example, **das Richtige** (*the right thing/decision/choice*).

- ✔ The second group includes participles that function as adjectives or adverbs, such as **am motiviertesten** (*the most motivated*). The present participle of **motivieren** (*to motivate*) is **motivierend** (*motivating*), and the past participle of is **motiviert** (*motivated*).

- ✔ The third group I deal with in this section is made up of adverbs that modify adjectives. The combination serves to make the adjective more descriptive; for example, in the expression **wirklich interessant,** you use the word **wirklich** (*really, absolutely*) to modify **interessant** (*interesting*).

Adjectives that act as nouns

Sometimes adjectives replace a noun to represent an abstract idea, a person, an object, and so on. The noun that the adjective replaces may be singular or plural, and it may be the subject or the object of a sentence; in short, it functions the same as a noun. The same structure exists in English and German for adjectives that take over as nouns; for example, *the poor, the brave, the lonely one, the new ones.* The only difference is that in German, nouns are capitalized and the spelling reflects gender, number, and case. In addition, there's no equivalent for *one/ones* in English; the German adjective stands alone to represent the noun.

To understand how such adjectives work, imagine you're discussing with your friend which cat you want to take home from the animal shelter. You talk about **die Große, die Braune,** and **die Ruhige** (*the little one, the brown one, the quiet one*). You're replacing the word **Katze** (*cat*) by describing a characteristic of each cat and using that adjective to represent that cat. You use the feminine article **die** because **Katze** is a feminine noun. If you're talking about taking home a dog, **der Hund,** you refer to each one as **der Große, der Braune,** and **der Ruhige.** When you make your decision, you may say something like **Ich nehme den Braunen** (*I'll take the brown one [dog]*). The adjective has the accusative masculine singular case ending **-en** to reflect the noun it's replacing.

Don't make the mistake of thinking that adjectives like **das Gute** (*the good thing*) are in the superlative. Adjectives that describe something abstract are neuter nouns; **das** signifies the neuter noun in this case, not the superlative form. (See the earlier section "Comparing Regular Adjectives and Adverbs: Fast, Faster, Fastest" for more on superlatives.) Compare the following sentences:

> **Ich wünsche euch das Beste.** (*I wish you the best.*) This has a superlative meaning, but **das Beste** is a noun. By contrast, **die beste Idee** (*the best idea*) is a combination of the superlative adjective **die beste** and the noun **Idee.**

> **Kennst du die Kleine da drüben?** (*Do you know the small [woman] over there?*) The article **die** combines with **Kleine** to stand in for the noun *woman* (**die Frau**).

Note: **Die Kleine** doesn't necessarily have to refer to a small woman. However, if it's used to refer to a woman, it's colloquial, a bit like saying *that babe.*

Participles that function as adjectives or adverbs

In German, as in English, present and past participles can function as adjectives or adverbs. If the adjectives precede a noun, they agree in gender, number, and case with the noun they modify. A *present participle* is the infinitive (for instance, *fly, tumble,* or *seethe*) with the ending *-ing.* When you use it in English as an adjective, you combine it with the noun you want to modify; for example, *the flying squirrels, the tumbling acrobats,* or *the seething volcano.*

To create the present participle in German, start with a verb, such as **laufen** (*to run*). Verbs form the present participle by dropping the infinitive ending **-en** and adding **-end** to the infinitive form (**lauf-** + **-end** = **laufend**). The present participle of **laufen** is **laufend** (the closest thing to the English word *running*). Look at an example:

> **Er erzählte Witze am laufenden Band.** (*He told an endless stream of jokes. Literally: He told jokes on a running band/belt.*)

A *past participle* of a regular verb is the infinitive of a verb with *-ed* or *-d* added. For an irregular verb, it's the form such as *eaten, hidden,* or *seen* that you use to form the present perfect tense and other compound verb tenses. (An example of the present perfect tense is *Scruffy has already eaten,* where you combine the past participle *eaten* with the auxiliary verb *have.*) You can use the past participle as a descriptive word; for example, *the drenched cat, sunken treasure,* or *forbidden fruit.*

Verbs form past participles differently, depending on the verb type (see Chapter 16); for instance, the past participle of **pflegen** is **gepflegt** (*groomed, taken care of*). The phrases **gepflegtes Essen** (*first-rate food*) and **gepflegte Weine** (*quality wines*) are typical descriptions that restaurants use to impress their clientele. Literally speaking, these expressions mean *groomed food/wines* in the sense that the restaurant has a carefully selected menu or wine list.

Some German verbs, namely the verbs ending in **-ieren,** have the same meanings in English, making them easily recognizable. The past participle form of these verbs is formed with **-iert** at the end; the ending is the same, regardless of whether you're using the past participle as an adjective or adverb.

Many of these common adjectives have comparative and superlative forms: Some common adjectives with this structure are **dekoriert** (*decorated*), **diszipliniert** (*disciplined*), **fasziniert** (*fascinated*), **frustriert** (*dissastified, frustrated*), **interessiert** (*interested*), **motiviert** (*motivated*), **organisiert** (*organized*), and **talentiert** (*talented*). They can all form comparative and superlative adjectives (and possibly adverbs):

> **Der Gefreite Schwarz war der diszplinierteste Soldat in seiner Kompanie.** (*Private Schwarz was the most disciplined soldier in his company.*) **Diszipliniertest-** is a superlative adjective.

> **In der Schule war ich motivierter als meine Schwester.** (*I was more motivated than my sister when I was in school.*) **Motivierter** is a comparative adjective.

> **Wir schauten die Olympische Spiele fasziniert zu.** (*We watched the Olympic Games with fascination.*) **Fasziniert** is an adverb describing how (we) watched.

Some frequently used adjectives derived from past participles don't have comparative forms. Among the more common are **ausprobiert** (*tested*), **diskutiert** (*discussed*), **fotografiert** (*photographed*), and **probiert** (*tried/tested*). See the earlier section titled "Comparing Regular Adjectives and Adverbs: Fast, Faster, Fastest" for more on comparatives.

Adverbs that modify adjectives

Adverbs modify verbs, but they can also modify adjectives. In order to express that something or someone is *quite good, especially interesting,* or *really motivated,* you use adverbs to modify the adjective. Those adverbs frequently used in German are **besonders** (*especially*), **etwas** (*somewhat*), **relativ** (*relatively*), **sehr** (*very*), **viel** (*much, a lot*), **wirklich** (*absolutely, really*), and **ziemlich** (*quite*). Good news here is that they don't have any changes in the endings.

To use an adverb to modify an adjective, just place the adverb in front of the adjective it's modifying, and voilà! To show you how this works, imagine you're talking about the hotels you stayed at on your last trip to Europe. One hotel was especially luxurious. To express this in German, you place the adverb **wirklich** (*really*) in front of **luxuriös** (*luxurious*), and if the adjective precedes the noun that it modifies, add the appropriate adjective ending; for example, **Wir haben zwei Nächte in einem wirklich luxuriösen Hotel übernachtet** (*We spent two nights in a really luxurious hotel*). Check out these examples:

> **Der Sommer war etwas wärmer als in vergangenen Jahren**. (*The summer was somewhat warmer than in previous years.*) The adverb **etwas** modifies the adjective **wärmer,** which is in the comparative form. The adjective **wärmer** needs no ending because it doesn't precede the noun that it modifies, **der Sommer.**

> **Letztes Jahr hatten wir einen ziemlich langen Winter.** (*Last year we had quite a long winter.*) The adverb **ziemlich** modifies the adjective **lang: einen ziemlich langen.** *Winter* is the direct object of the sentence, so the other modifiers — **einen** and **langen** — have masculine, singular, accusative endings to reflect **(der) Winter.**

Answer Key

1   Claudia fährt **am vernünftigsten.** (*Claudia drives the most sensibly.*)

2   Mein Bruder ist **witziger als** ich. (*My brother is wittier than I.*)

3   Wir waren vorher **mutiger** als jetzt. (*We were braver then than now.*)

4   Siegbert machte den **nettesten** Eindruck. (*Siegbert made the nicest impression.*)

5   Ich bin **fitter** als du. (*I'm in better shape than you.*)

6   Am **glücklichsten** bin ich mit meiner Familie. (*I'm happiest [when I'm] with my family.*)

7   Wiebke hat jetzt **dunkleres** Haar als früher. (*Wiebke now has darker hair than before.*)

8	poor	**arm**	**ärmer**	am ärmsten
9	stupid	**dumm**	dümmer	**am dümmsten**
10	crude, coarse	**grob**	gröber	**am gröbsten**
11	large, big, tall	groß	**größer**	**am größten**
12	hard, tough	hart	**härter**	**am härtesten**
13	young	**jung**	**jünger**	**am jüngsten**
14	cold	**kalt**	**kälter**	**am kältesten**

15   Ein Abendessen im Restaurant Bei Mario kostet **viel.** (*A dinner in Mario's restaurant is expensive.*)

16   Ein Abendessen im Restaurant Chez Philippe kostet **mehr.** (*A dinner in Philippe's restaurant is more expensive.*)

17   Ein Abendessen im Restaurant Zur Goldenen Gans kostet **am meisten.** (*A dinner in the Goldenen Gans restaurant is the most expensive.*)

18   Monika kommt **bald** nach Hause. (*Monika is coming home soon.*)

19   Jennifer kommt **eher** nach Hause. (*Jennifer is coming home sooner.*)

20   Sarah kommt am **ehesten** nach Hause. (*Sarah is coming home the soonest.*)

21   Ich fahre **gern** Fahrrad. (*I like bicycling.*)

22   Ich fahre **lieber** Wasserski. (*I like waterskiing better.*)

23   Ich fahre **am liebsten** Ski. (*I like skiing the most.*)

24   Ein neuer BMW kostet **so viel wie** ein neuer Mercedes. (**A new BMW costs as much as a new Mercedes.**) Or vice versa.

25 Ein Baseballspieler läuft **halb so viel wie** ein Fußballspieler. (*A baseball player runs half as much as a soccer player.*) Baseball is definitely the slower game!

26 **Je mehr** er Poker spielt, **desto reicher** wird er. (*The more he plays poker, the richer he becomes.*) This one has tricky word order. Did you remember the comma, too? You need it to separate the two phrases, just as you do in English. (Check out Table 13-3.)

27 Die neuen Autos benutzen **nicht so viel Benzin wie** die alten Modelle. (*The new cars don't use as much gas as the old models.*) Or vice versa.

28 Schwarz-Weiß-Filme sind **genauso spannend wie** Farbfilme. (*Black and white movies are just as exciting as movies in Technicolor.*) Or vice versa.

29 **Je qualifizierter** man ist, **desto mehr** verdient man. (*The more qualified one is, the more one earns.*) This statement doesn't make sense the other way. This one has tricky word order. Did you remember the comma, too? You need it to separate the two phrases.

30 Das Wetter in Deutschland ist **so schön wie** das Wetter in Neuengland. (*The weather in Germany is as nice as the weather in New England.*) Or vice versa.

Chapter 14

Connecting with Conjunctions

· ·

· ·

Conjunctions are the glue that connects parts of a sentence, such as clauses, phrases, or words. In order to reach beyond basic sentence structure in German, you need these small yet important words to form more sophisticated sentences. German uses two types of conjunctions: *coordinating conjunctions,* such as **oder** (*or*), and *subordinating conjunctions,* such as **weil** (*because*). Your choice between them is based on the structure of the clauses, phrases, or words that you're joining together. In the first section of this chapter, I clarify the difference between these two types of conjunctions, and in the rest of this chapter, I explain how to use the most common German conjunctions to express your ideas clearly and intelligently.

Conjunctions and Clauses: Terminating Terminology Tangles

To get a good grasp on conjunctions and how to use them, you first need to understand and keep track of the basic grammatical vocab. You're probably already familiar with many of the following terms, but here's a quick recap of the differences among phrases, clauses, and sentences:

✔ **Phrase:** A group of connected words that have neither subject nor verb, such as **nach Zürich** (*to Zürich*)

✔ **Clause:** A group of related words that have a subject and a verb, such as **Ich fliege** (*I'm flying*)

• **Main clause (independent clause):** A clause that can stand on its own; it has a sentence structure, as in **der Nachrichtensprecher war enttäuscht** (*the newscaster was disappointed*). This is just about the same as a sentence, except it doesn't have a proper beginning (capitalized **D** in **der**) or a punctuation mark at the end (a period in this example).

- **Subordinate clause (dependent clause):** This clause has a sentence structure with a subject and a verb, but it can't stand on its own; it needs some help from its friends, the independent clause and the conjunction. If you see such a clause alone without a main clause — for example, **weil er seine Stimme verloren hat** (*because he lost his voice*) — you're left waiting to find out more information.

✔ **Sentence:** A group of words that has it all: subject, verb, and an ending like a period, exclamation point, or question mark — the whole shebang, as in **Ich fliege nächste Woche nach Zürich** (*I'm flying to Zürich next week*).

Conjunctions are the connectors, the cement, the orangutan glue that you use to combine sentence parts. Here are the two types of conjunctions:

✔ **Coordinating:** A coordinating conjunction joins main clauses, phrases, or words.

> **Der Nachrichtensprecher hat seine Stimme verloren, und er musste zu Hause bleiben.** (*The newscaster lost his voice, and he had to stay home.*) The coordinating conjunction **und** (*and*) combines the two main clauses; a comma placed before **und** separates the two clauses.

> **Martin ging nach Hause und machte sich ein Käsebrot zum Abendessen.** (*Martin went home and made [himself] a cheese sandwich for supper.*) **Und** (*and*) is a coordinating conjunction; it combines two actions (verbs) that Martin did.

✔ **Subordinating:** This conjunction introduces a subordinate clause and relates it to another clause in the sentence.

> **Der Nachrichtensprecher war enttäuscht, weil er seine Stimme verloren hat.** (*The newscaster was disappointed because he lost his voice.*) **Weil** (*because*) is the subordinating conjunction. The subordinate clause **weil er seine Stimme verloren hat** (*because he lost his voice*) has complete meaning when it's connected to **der Nachrichtensprecher war enttäuscht** (*the newscaster was disappointed*).

> **Martin ging nach Hause, obwohl er sehr einsam war.** (*Martin went home, although he was very lonely.*) The subordinating conjunction **obwohl** (*although*) introduces the subordinate clause that follows it and connects the two parts of the sentence, **Martin ging nach Hause** and **er sehr einsam war.**

In English, conjunctions such as *and, because, but, or,* and *when* are simple to use in a sentence; the word order comes naturally for fluent speakers. German conjunctions, however, require a conscious effort to keep in mind which type of conjunction you're dealing with and how to get the word order straight. You also need to remember the comma. Keep reading for how to correctly use these two types of conjunctions.

Connecting with Coordinating Conjunctions

The *coordinating conjunctions,* the ones that join main clauses, phrases, or words, are the easier of the two types to master. The number of German coordinating conjunctions is small, and they correspond well to their English counterparts in meaning and usage — except for a few easy-to-understand differences.

Table 14-1 shows the common coordinating conjunctions, together with their English equivalents and comments relating to the conjunction in a clause.

Table 14-1	Common Coordinating Conjunctions		
German	*English Equivalent*	*Comma Separates Joined Sentence Parts?*	*Comment*
aber	*but*	yes	Used the same way in English
denn	*for, because*	yes	**Denn** is also used as a flavoring particle, often to interest the listener; **weil**, a subordinating conjunction, also means *because*, but it has a different word order.
oder	*or*	no (unless the writer chooses a comma for clarity)	Used the same way in English
sondern	*but*	yes	Used to express *on the contrary, rather,* or *instead;* it's preceded by a clause that makes a negative statement
und	*and*	no (unless the writer chooses a comma for clarity)	Used the same way in English

Note: In German, you don't use a comma in front of **und** in a series (or list of words), although this practice is common in English. Example: **Wir haben Kartoffelbrei, Spinat und Kabeljau gegessen.** (*We ate mashed potatoes, spinach, and cod.*)

Working on word order: Coordinating conjunctions

When you form German sentences with coordinating conjunctions, the separate sentence parts maintain their word order. Keep in mind that in standard German word order, the active, conjugated verb is placed in second position. The standard word order is the same for English and German: Take the subject + the verb + the other information, like an object or a prepositional phrase, and add the conjunction to combine the other sentence part. Now you have two parts combined into one sentence:

Luca geht ins Kaufhaus, aber sein Hund bleibt zu Hause. (*Luca goes to the department store, but his dog stays home.*) **Aber** (*but*) is the coordinating conjunction.

Although the preceding word order is exactly the same in English and German, I can't let you go away without pointing out other German sentences using a coordinating conjunction that have a different word order from the standard subject + verb + other information structure. (Go to Chapter 1 for more on word order.)

Time expressions (descriptions of time such as *this morning, in the eighteenth century, at five o'clock,* and so on) can take the place of the subject. The verb is still in second position, but the subject goes behind the verb. This point is important because it distinguishes coordinating conjuctions from their cousins, the subordinating conjunctions. I explain the differences between these two conjunction types in the "Using subordinating conjunctions" section of this chapter. The example shows you how this word order change looks:

> **Wir fahren heute mit dem Zug nach Hamburg, denn morgen in der Früh möchten wir zum Fischmarkt gehen.** (*We're taking the train to Hamburg today because tomorrow morning we'd like to go to the fish market.*) The time expression **morgen in der Früh** immediately follows the coordinating conjunction **denn.**

When forming a German sentence, remember *time, manner, place.* It's the mantra for positioning information describing when, how, and where. The standard word order is

1. Time (tells when)

2. Manner (tells how)

3. Place (tells where)

For example, in the sentence, **wir fahren heute mit dem Zug nach Hamburg, heute** = time, **mit dem Zug** = manner, and **nach Hamburg** = place. In the second clause, **denn morgen in der Früh möchten wir zum Fischmarkt gehen, morgen in der Früh** = time and **zum Fischmarkt** = place.

The following sentence elements are in the wrong word order. Rewrite the sentences in the correct word order. Remember to use the comma if appropriate. The first word is in the correct position.

Q. Ich / das Wasser / möchte / zu kalt / aber / schwimmen / ist

A. **Ich möchte schwimmen, aber das Wasser ist zu kalt**. (*I'd like to go swimming, but the water is too cold.*)

1. Kai / zwei / drei / und / Stefanie / Brüder / hat / hat Schwestern (four alternatives)

_____

2. Sven / aber / sehr intelligent / er / nicht amüsant / ist / ist (two alternatives)

_____

3. Heike / sie / sind / wohnen / Haus / aber / in einem / sehr kleinen / und Georg / glücklich darin

_____

4. Heute / denn / ich / nicht / ich / eine / Erkältung / arbeite / habe

---

Using coordinating conjunctions

Incorporating coordinating conjunctions into your writing and speech shouldn't be too difficult. The coordinating conjunctions are straightforward in usage and meaning. You just combine two sentence parts by using the coordinating conjunction that fits what you intend to say about the relationship between them.

The common coordinating conjunctions are as follows:

- **aber** (*but*)
- **denn** (*for, because*)
- **oder** (*or*)
- **sondern** (*but*)
- **und** (*and*)

When writing in German, **oder** and **und** don't need a comma preceding them, although using a comma sometimes improves clarity. **Aber, sondern,** and **denn** do need a preceding comma to connect clauses, phrases, and words. **Denn,** however, connects clauses only; it has the same function as *because* in English. Otherwise, word order follows the guidelines as described in the preceding section for coordinating conjunctions.

> **Ich gehe zur Bank, denn ich brauche Geld.** (*I'm going to the bank because I need some money.*)

> **Heute esse ich ein saftiges Steak im Restaurant, oder ich mache Spaghetti zu Hause.** (*Today I'll have a juicy steak in a restaurant, or I'll make spaghetti at home.*)

Sondern and **aber** both mean *but;* however, their uses differ. You use **sondern** to express *but, but rather* in cases where the preceding clause has a negative expression (is negated) and where the two ideas cancel each other; for example, **Ich wohne nicht in der Stadtmitte, sondern am Stadtrand** (*I live not downtown but [rather] on the outskirts of the city*). The main clause in the beginning (**Ich wohne nicht in der Stadtmitte**) contains a negative, **nicht,** and the two ideas are mutually exclusive. **Sondern** links the prepositional phrase **am Stadtrand** to the rest of the sentence. You use **aber** in the same manner as in English — to connect two ideas that aren't mutually exclusive.

Connect the two sentence parts together using the coordinating conjunction that makes the most sense.

Q. Karsten bleibt im Bett, _____ er ist krank.

A. Karsten bleibt im Bett, **denn** er ist krank. (*Karsten is staying in bed because he's ill.*) The conjunction **denn** is by far the best choice; **denn er ist krank** (*because he's ill*) explains the reason Karsten is staying in bed.

5. Ich möchte gern ins Theater gehen, _____ ich habe kein Geld.

6. Ich fliege nicht am Samstag, _____ am Sonntag.

7. Gudrun spielt sehr gut Squash, _____ ihr Mann spielt auch sehr gut.

8. Essen wir heute Abend bei dir _____ bei mir?

9. Der Film hatte nicht nur gute Schauspieler, _____ auch hervorragende Musik.

Connecting with Subordinating Conjunctions

The trick with subordinating conjunctions is remembering three things: the correct word order, where to put the comma, and of course, the meaning of the subordinating conjunction. A *subordinate clause* (dependent clause) has a simple structure with a subject and a verb, but it can't stand on its own without help from a main clause and a subordinating conjunction. A *subordinating conjunction* introduces a subordinate clause and relates that clause to the main clause in the sentence.

Table 14-2 presents a list of commonly used German subordinating conjunctions with their English equivalents and comments on their usage.

Table 14-2	Common Subordinating Conjunctions	
German	*English Equivalent*	*Comment*
als	*as, when*	Describes an event in the past. Example: **Als ich elf Jahre alt war** . . . (*When I was eleven* . . .)
bevor	*before*	Used the same way in English
da	*since (inasmuch as)*	Not to be confused with the preposition **seit** (*since* + a point in time) or **da** (*there*)
damit	*so that*	Used to express *in order that* . . .; not to be confused with **damit**, a compound of **da + mit** to express *with that/it/them*
dass	*that*	Rarely begins a sentence; in English, you can leave out the conjunction *that*, but you can't in German. Example: **Ich wusste, dass er** . . . (*I knew [that] he* . . .)
falls	*in case*	Used to describe *in the situation/event that* . . .
ob	*if, whether*	Not interchangeable with **wenn; ob** can be used to begin an indirect yes/no question
obwohl	*although*	Used the same way in English
weil	*because*	Same meaning as **denn** (coordinating conjunction) but with a different word order in the subordinate clause
wenn	*if, when, whenever*	Not interchangeable with **ob; wenn** starts a clause that stipulates the condition of something possibly happening or not, such as *if A, then B*

Using subordinating conjunctions

Subordinating conjunctions have some similarities to their cousins, the coordinating conjunctions: Both types of conjunctions link ideas together, both introduce one of the ideas, and both generally use commas to separate the two ideas. The distinguishing characteristics of subordinating conjunctions are as follows:

- ✔ A subordinating conjunction begins a subordinate clause: **Ich hoffe, dass du kommst** (*I hope that you come*). **Dass** is the subordinating conjunction, and the subordinate clause is **dass du kommst.**

- ✔ A comma always separates the main clause from the subordinate clause: **Ich hoffe** (main clause) + , (comma) + **dass . . .** (subordinate clause).

- ✔ Subordinating conjunctions affect word order of verbs: They push the conjugated (main) verb to the end of the subordinate clause.

Two subordinating conjunctions, **als** and **wenn,** have similar meanings; both can mean *when.* However, **als** describes an event (a single event) in the past, and **wenn** functions the way it does in English; you can use it for an action that's repeated in any verb tense.

> **Als ich in der Stadt lebte, hatte ich kein Auto.** (*When I lived in the city, I didn't have a car.*) You don't live in the city anymore; that event is over.

> **Wenn ich nicht mehr arbeite, möchte ich noch fit bleiben.** (*When I'm no longer working, I'd like to stay in shape.*) This sentence is in present tense; it describes an imagined scenario in the future.

Ob and **wenn** are similar because they can both mean *if.* However, **ob** can begin an indirect yes/no question, and **wenn** starts a clause that stipulates the condition of something possibly happening or not. **Falls** and **wenn** are also similar. **Falls** can be used in such situations when you want to express *in case* or *in the case that.*

> **Ich weiß nicht, ob das richtig ist.** (*I don't know if that's right.*) You're posing a question to yourself that would have a yes/no answer.

> **Wenn/Falls es morgen regnet, bleiben wir zu Hause.** (*If/In case it rains tomorrow, we'll stay home.*)

Look at the following examples of how you use **da, bevor,** and **damit** in German sentences. In the next section, you find example sentences with **dass, obwohl,** and **weil.**

> **Da ich wenig Geld habe, hoffe ich einen reichen Partner zu finden.** (*Since I have little money, I hope to find a rich partner.*) You can also use **weil** in place of **da** in this sentence when you want to express *because.*

> **Bevor ich den richtigen Mann finde, werde ich meine Freiheit genießen.** (*Before I find the right man, I'll enjoy my freedom.*)

> **Ich brauche viel Geld, damit ich Luxusartikeln kaufen kann.** (*I need a lot of money so I can buy luxury goods.*)

Using the correct word order

Clarity is the name of the game, and to properly use subordinating conjunctions, you need to make sure you put everything in its proper order:

✔ The conjugated verb is thrown (ruthlessly!) to the end of the end of the subordinate clause: **Ich hoffe, dass sie das Basketballspiel gewinnen** (*I hope [that] they win the basketball game*). The verb **gewinnen** (*win*) is at the end of the subordinate clause, which begins with the word **dass. Dass** very rarely begins a sentence.

✔ When a subordinate clause begins a sentence, the word directly following the clause is the conjugated verb of the main clause. Why? Because the whole subordinate clause counts as one sentence element (one unit), so the verb in the main clause is in its usual second position: **Wenn ich zu spät aufstehe, verpasse ich den Zug** (*When I get up too late, I miss the train*). The verb **verpasse** (*miss,* as in *to miss an opportunity*) directly follows the subordinate clause.

Look at the annotated examples of three sentences using subordinating conjunctions:

Ich hoffe, dass sie das Basketballspiel gewinnen. (*I hope [that] they win the basketball game.*) The main clause comes first, followed by the subordinate clause.

1. **Ich hoffe** (*I hope*) = main clause
2. **dass** (*that*) = subordinating conjunction introducing the subordinate clause
3. **sie** (*they*) = subject
4. **das Basketballspiel** (*the basketball game*) = direct object, in accusative case
5. **gewinnen** (*win*) = verb at the end of the subordinate clause

Obwohl ich oft zu spät aufstehe, erreiche ich den Zug. (*Although I often get up too late, I catch the train.*) The subordinate clause comes first, followed by the main clause.

1. **Obwohl** (*although*) = subordinating conjunction introducing the sentence
2. **ich oft zu spät** (*I often too late*) = subject and other information
3. **aufstehe** (*get up*) = verb at the end of the subordinate clause
4. **erreiche** (*catch*) = verb at the beginning of the independent clause (counts as second position in the sentence)
5. **ich den Zug** (*I the train*) = subject and direct object in accusative case

Weil ich viel zu spät aufgestanden bin, habe ich den Zug verpasst. (*Because I [have gotten] got up much too late, I [have] missed the train.*) The subordinate clause comes first, with the main clause in second position; both clauses use the present perfect verb tense (see Chapter 16 for more on the present perfect). In the subordinate clause, the two verb parts are at the end of the clause, with the past participle (**aufgestanden**) preceding the conjugated verb (**bin**). In the main clause (**habe ich den Zug verpasst**), the word order of the verbs follows that of present perfect in a sentence with only one clause: The conjugated verb is in second position (**habe**), and the past participle is at the end of the clause/sentence. Remember that the whole subordinate clause functions as a subject, or as one unit of information, with a comma separating the two clauses. The conjugated verb is, grammatically speaking, in second position.

1. **Weil** (*because*) = subordinating conjunction introducing the sentence

2. **ich zu spät** (*I too late*) = subject and other information

3. **aufgestanden** (*got up*) = past participle of **aufstehen** (*to get up*)

4. **bin** (*have; Literally: am*) = conjugated verb thrown to the end of the subordinate clause so it follows the past participle **aufgestanden** (*got up*)

5. **habe** (*have*) = conjugated verb at the beginning of the main clause

6. **ich den Zug** (*I the train*) = subject and direct object, accusative case

7. **verpasst** (*missed*) = past participle of **verpassen** (*to miss*)

In the following exercises, the independent clause begins the sentence. This part of the sentence has the correct word order. Decide whether the word order of the subordinate clause is correct. If not, rewrite the sentence in the correct word order.

0. Ich weiss, dass Sie sprechen gut Deutsch.

A. Ich weiss, **dass Sie gut Deutsch sprechen.** (*I know that you speak good German.*) The word order is incorrect; the verb must go to the end of the subordinate clause.

10. Ich möchte, dass du morgen mit mir kommst.

_____

11. Es ist gut, dass am Freitag er hat Zeit.

_____

12. Wir möchten, dass sie den Vertrag unterschreiben.

_____

13. Es ist nicht gut, dass Norbert ist allein.

_____

Answer Key

1 **Kai hat zwei/drei Brüder und Stefanie hat zwei/drei Schwestern.** (*Kai has two/three brothers/sisters, and Stefanie has two/three sisters/brothers.*) It doesn't matter who has how many brothers or sisters, so the order of the numbers is up to you, as is who has brothers and who has sisters.

2 **Sven ist nicht amüsant/sehr intelligent, aber er ist nicht amüsant/sehr intelligent.** (*Sven is not amusing/very intelligent but he is not amusing/very intelligent.*) Either placement of the descriptions **nicht amüsant** or **sehr intelligent** is possible.

3 **Heike und Georg wohnen in einem sehr kleinen Haus, aber sie sind glücklich darin.** (*Heike and Georg live in a very small house, but they're happy in it.*) The phrase following **aber** has a reference to Heike and Georg (**sie**), as well as to the house (**darin**), so this phrase logically follows the phrase **Heike und Georg wohnen in einem sehr kleinen Haus. In einem + sehr kleinen + Haus** is a prepositional phrase; **in** takes the dative case, and the case endings of **einem** and **kleinen** reflect this.

4 **Heute arbeite ich nicht, denn ich habe eine Erkältung.** (*I'm not working today because I have a cold.*) The expression of time, **heute,** is in first position.

5 **Ich möchte gern ins Theater gehen, aber ich habe kein Geld.** (*I'd really like to go to the theater, but I don't have any money.*)

6 **Ich fliege nicht am Samstag, sondern am Sonntag.** (*I'm flying not on Saturday but rather on Sunday.*) The hint is the negative **nicht** in the independent clause and that the relationship between the two days is logically not Saturday but rather Sunday because they're mutually exclusive.

7 **Gudrun spielt sehr gut Squash, und ihr Mann spielt auch sehr gut.** (*Gudrun plays squash very well, and her husband also plays very well.*) The hint is in the second phrase, **auch sehr gut —** the information in the two sentence parts is equal.

8 **Esssen wir heute Abend bei dir oder bei mir?** (*Are we having dinner at your place or my place tonight?*) If you're ravenous and want two dinners, use **und.**

9 **Der Film hatte nicht nur gute Schauspieler, sondern auch hervorragende Musik.** (*The movie had not only good actors but also excellent music.*)

10 **Ich möchte, dass du morgen mit mir kommst.** (*I'd like you to come with me tomorrow.*) The word order is correct.

11 **Es ist gut, dass er am Freitag Zeit hat.** (*It's good that he has time on Friday.*) The subject **er** comes after the conjunction **dass,** and the verb **hat** must go to the end of the clause.

12 **Wir möchten, dass sie den Vertrag unterschreiben.** (*We want them to sign the contract.*) The sentence is correct as it stands.

13 **Es ist nicht gut, dass Norbert allein ist.** (*It's not good that Norbert's alone.*) Put the verb at the end of the sentence.

Chapter 15

Your Preposition Primer

What's in a preposition? **Zwischen** (*between*) by any other name would sound as strange. A *preposition* is a small word that shows the relationship between its object (a noun) and another word or words in the sentence. It's part of a *prepositional phrase,* which starts with a preposition and has an article, noun, and other words.

You find out how crucially important these little guys are in expressing such things as

✔ Place/where something is located, as with **in** (*in*): **es gibt eine Fliege in meiner Suppe** (*there's a fly in my soup*).

✔ Movement/the direction where something is going, as with **unter** (*under*): **eine Maus läuft unter meinen Stuhl** (*a mouse is running under my chair*).

✔ Information showing relationships, as with **trotz** (*in spite of*): **trotz dieser Überraschungen, schmeckt mir das Essen** (*in spite of these surprises, the food tastes good*).

In this chapter, I break down German prepositions into four groups: accusative, dative, genitive, and accusative/dative prepositions. The latter group are what I call the *two-timers* because they can be either accusative or dative. I give an easy and logical explanation for these wise guys in the section pertaining to them. One more section of this chapter deals with preposition combinations, the fixed expressions like **zu Hause** (*at home*) and **nach Hause** (*to home [going home]*).

Prepping for Prepositions: Basic Guidelines

Prepositions, such as *around, before,* and *with,* combine with other words to form prepositional phrases that provide information on where (*around the corner*), when (*before noon*), who (*with you*), and much more. Prepositions perform incredible tasks when they combine with other words, notably nouns and verbs, to create a diverse range of expressions. But all those possibilities come at a price. Prepositions are finicky little critters, much more so in German than in English. They abide by grammar rules. So how in the world do you get to feel even remotely comfortable with understanding, let alone using, German prepositions with the right case? For a start, look at these guidelines.

Getting the importance of case

In German, case is one key to perfecting the fine art of prepositioning. Both English and German have many prepositions, and both languages use prepositions in similar ways. However, English doesn't have much truck with cases and case endings. In fact, if you bring up the subject of case in English grammar, some people may tell you to go home, lie down for a while, and forget all about it. But case is hugely important to getting a grip on using German prepositions correctly in a prepositional phrase.

As with other German words like nouns, adjectives, and verbs, prepositions need to be understood together with the other trappings of language. A lowly two-letter preposition like **in** (*in, into, to*) has so much power that it forces the rest of the prepositional phrase — the noun and other words following the preposition — to take the same case endings. The preposition doesn't change; it "tells" the others to conform — in other words, to follow the case of that preposition. The result is that the case endings in the prepositional phrase help you to a) recognize the links between the preposition and the words in the phrase, and b) understand the prepositional phrase in context of the whole sentence.

The three cases that prepositions identify with are accusative, dative, and genitive. Some prepositions are two-timers: They may use accusative or dative case, depending on meaning. The following examples show all four groups of prepositions. (Chapter 2 deals with the basics of case.)

- Accusative preposition **durch: Mein Hund Bello läuft gern durch den Wald.** (*My dog Bello likes to run through the woods.*) The prepositional phrase is **durch den Wald** (*through the woods*). **Der Wald** in accusative case is **den Wald.**

- Dative preposition **mit: Ich laufe gern mit ihm (Bello).** (*I like to run with him.*) The phrase is **mit ihm** (*with him*). **Ihm** is the dative case form of the personal pronoun **er.**

- Genitive preposition **während: Während des Winters bleiben Bello und ich oft zu Hause.** (*During the winter, Bello and I often stay at home.*) The phrase is **während des Winters** (*during the winter*). Because **während** is a genitive preposition, **der Winter** in nominative case changes to **des Winters** in genitive case.

- Accusative/dative preposition **auf: Meistens liege ich allein auf der Couch, aber manchmal springt Bello auf die Couch.** (*I usually lie on the couch alone, but sometimes he jumps onto the couch.*) **Auf der Couch** (*on the couch*) is dative case; **auf die Couch** (*onto the couch*) is accusative case. The first denotes place, and the second describes movement.

Check out the section "Accusative, Dative, and Genitive Cases: How the Rest of the Phrase Shapes Up" for a complete discussion of case and why case is important when using prepositions.

Understanding what it all means

Meaning is another key to success with German prepositions. Know that the rules of mathematics don't apply here — the prepositions and their English counterparts aren't always equal. The preposition **in** looks like the English preposition *in*. Indeed, you can use it the same way in both languages: **Wie viele Fernseher haben Sie in Ihrem Haus?** (*How many TVs do you have in your house?*). However, it can also mean *into* or *to*. Another preposition, **bei,** sounds like *by* but has a variety of meanings, including *at, near,* and *with*: **Bei mir gibt es keine Flimmerkisten** (*There aren't any idiot boxes at my place*).

Prepositions crop up in places you'd never suspect, and they take on new meaning in combinations with other words that can be surprising. It may be easy to assume there's a parallel in meaning between some German prepositions that resemble English prepositions, either in spelling, pronunciation, or both. You need to be very careful because one preposition may have several different meanings. Often, these meanings don't parallel the way the preposition is used in English.

Know one or two common phrases or words that combine with each preposition to get a feeling for the various meanings a preposition may have. The trick to taming these beasties is remembering them in commonly used phrases, fixed idioms, or standard prepositional phrases — not all alone and naked.

When you come across an unfamiliar expression that includes a preposition, look at (or listen to) the context of the phrase. You can often make an accurate guess of the meaning by checking whether the literal meaning or the figurative meaning makes more sense. Your experience in your own language can help you make the leap of faith to understanding figurative meaning.

Accusative, Dative, and Genitive Cases: How the Rest of the Phrase Shapes Up

When you use prepositions in your German writing and speech, you want to use them correctly, right? If so (and I hope you said *yes*), this section is key. It explains the role that cases play in using prepositions. So what exactly is case? *Case* is like a marker, a tag, or an ID for a word; it shows the word's role in relationship to other words in the sentence. There are three groups of prepositions, organized by the case that they need to form phrases. These three cases are accusative, dative, and genitive. Having said that, by far the most frequently used group of prepositions is yet another group, namely those that use both accusative and dative cases (fondly called the two-way prepositions). For that reason, I deal with them in a separate section later in this chapter.

As you go through this section, keep in mind that prepositions pop up everywhere in German (and English for that matter). It's definitely worth your while to be patient and master the cases one by one. In addition, keep in mind that the context of the phrase influences the meaning of the preposition: **nach** can mean three different things in English: *after, past,* or *to*. Yet **nach dem Weg fragen** (*to ask for directions*) doesn't even translate using one of those three prepositions.

No finger pointing: Accusative prepositions

Accusative prepositions express movement, opposition to something, and acts of excluding or receiving. The small band of accusative prepositions includes **bis, durch, für, gegen, ohne,** and **um.** These are strictly linked to the accusative case. Look in Table 15-1 for a list of these prepositions, their English equivalents, and a sample phrase.

Table 15-1		Accusative Prepositions	
Preposition	*English Equivalent(s)*	*Sample Phrases*	*English Equivalent*
bis	*till, until* (also: conjunction *until*)	**bis nächsten Sonntag**	*until next Sunday*
durch	*through, by*	**durch die Stadt** (jemanden) durch einen Freund kennenlernen	*through the city* *meet (someone)* *through a friend*
für	*for*	**für Sie** **für meine Freunde**	*for you* *for my friends*
gegen	*against, for*	**gegen die Regeln** **etwas gegen Kopfschmerzen nehmen**	*against the rules* *take something for a headache*
ohne	*without*	**ohne mich** **ohne Herrn Adler**	*without me* *without Herr Adler*
um	*around, for, at*	**um das Haus** **Ich bewerbe mich um die Stelle.**	*around the house* *I'm applying for the job.*

To form phrases with accusative prepositions, start with the preposition and add the information that the preposition is linking to the rest of the sentence — the preposition's object (noun) and any modifiers. If necessary, change the endings of any articles, pronouns, adjectives, and nouns following the preposition to the accusative case. The following outlines what needs to change:

✔ Some definite articles change. The definite articles are easy because the only change is **der → den. Die** (feminine and plural) and **das** don't change. (See Chapter 2 for definite articles.)

✔ The accusative prepositions build some contractions:

- **durch + das = durchs**

- **für + das = fürs**

- **um + das = ums**

In spoken, colloquial German, these contractions are very common.

✔ Most of the pronouns change. The personal pronouns in accusative (direct object) case are **mich** (*me*), **dich** (*you*), **ihn/sie/es** (*him/her/it*), **uns** (*us*), **euch** (*you*), **sie** (*them*), and **Sie** (*you*).

✔ Adjectives may or may not undergo an ending change. (See Chapter 12 for adjectives.)

✔ A few nouns undergo an ending change. (See Chapter 2 for more on nouns.)

Sammy das Stinktier sitzt ganz allein, ohne seine Freunde. (*Sammy the skunk is sitting all alone without his friends.*) The preposition **ohne** is followed by **seine Freunde**; both words have accusative plural endings.

Dann läuft er durch den Garten der Familie Finkenhuber. (*Then he runs through the Finkenhuber's garden.*) The preposition **durch** (*through* in this context) indicates movement. **Den Garten** is the masculine singular form of **der Garten** in the accusative case.

Sammy läuft um den Hund Bello und . . . psst! (*Sammy runs around Bello the dog and . . . psst!*) The preposition **um** (*around*) indicates movement. **Den Hund** is the masculine singular form of **der Hund** in the accusative case.

In this exercise, use Table 15-1 to help you write the phrases in German. Some vocabulary is indicated in parentheses. Remember to change the articles, pronouns, adjectives, and nouns following the prepositions — if necessary.

0. for you (singular, familiar) _____

A. **für dich**

1. around the garage (die Garage) _____

2. through the woods (der Wald) _____

3. for him _____

4. until tomorrow _____

5. against the law (das Gesetz) _____

6. for my boss (der Chef) _____

7. without me _____

Dative prepositions

Dative prepositions include some heavy hitters. Most dative prepositions express relationships of time (when), motion (where to), and location (where). Some have surprising variations in meaning. Nine are on the hit list: **aus, außer, bei, gegenüber, mit, nach, seit, von,** and **zu.** These particular prepositions have an exclusivity clause with the dative case. Table 15-2 shows the nine dative prepositions, their English equivalents, and some sample phrases for each.

Table 15-2		Dative Prepositions	
Preposition	*English Equivalent(s)*	*Sample Phrases*	*English Equivalent*
aus	*from, out of*	**aus den USA** **aus der Arbeit**	*from the U.S.A.* *from/out of work*
außer	*besides, except for*	**außer uns** **außer den Kindern**	*besides/except for us* *except for the children*
bei	*at* (a home of, a place of business), *near, with*	**bei Katharina** **bei der Straße** **Es ist anders bei mir.**	*at Katherina's* (place) *near the street* *It's different with me.*
mit	*with, by* (means of transportation)	**mit dem Hund** **mit dem Zug**	*with the dog* *by train*
nach	*after, past, to*	**nach einer Stunde** **Es ist fünf nach vier.** **nach Moskau** (no article for cities and countries in German)	*after an hour* *It's five past four.* *to Moscow*
seit	*for, since*	**seit zwanzig Jahren** **seit dem Krieg**	*for 20 years* *since the war*
von	*by, from, of*	**von einem deutschen Maler** **ein Geschenk von dir** **am Ende vom Film**	*by a German artist* (created by someone) *a present from you* *at the end of the movie*
zu	*to* (with people and certain places)	**zur Universität** **Was gibt's zum Abendessen?**	*to the university* *What's for dinner?*

To form phrases with dative prepositions, start with the preposition and add the information that the preposition connects to the rest of the sentence (the object of the preposition and any articles or adverbs that modify it). Change the endings of any articles, pronouns, adjectives, and nouns following the prepositions — if necessary — to the dative case. The following list outlines what needs to change:

✔ The definite articles change like this (see Chapter 2 for definite articles):

  • **der** → **dem**

  • **die** → **der** (feminine)

  • **das** → **dem**

  • **die** → **den** (plural)

Note: Not all prepositional phrases need an article (**dem, einen,** and so on) with the noun; these are generally fixed expressions such as clock times: **es ist Viertel nach acht** (*it's quarter past eight*) or other types: **zu Hause** (*at home*).

✔ The contractions that dative prepositions build are

- **bei + dem = beim**

- **von + dem = vom**

- **zu + dem = zum**

- **zu + der = zur**

In spoken, colloquial German, these contractions are very common.

✔ All the pronouns change. The personal pronouns in dative case are **mir** (*me*), **dir** (*you*), **ihm/ihr/ihm** (*him/her/it*), **uns** (*us*), **euch** (*you*), **ihnen** (*them*), and **Ihnen** (*you*). (See Chapter 2 for pronouns.)

✔ Adjectives may or may not undergo an ending change. (See Chapter 12 for adjectives.)

✔ A few nouns undergo an ending change. (See Chapter 2 for more on nouns.)

Essen wir heute Abend bei dir? (*Shall we have dinner at your place tonight?*) **Bei** is a true chameleon as far as variations in meanings goes. Here, take **bei,** add the dative pronoun **dir,** and presto! — **bei dir** = *at your place.*

Nein, ich möchte lieber zum Restaurant um die Ecke gehen. (*No, I'd rather go to the restaurant around the corner .*) The contraction of **zu + dem = zum.**

Luigis? Es ist seit einem Monat geschlossen. (*Luigi's? It's been closed for a month.*)

Wichtig ist nur, ich esse mit dir. (*It's only important that I eat with you.*)

This exercise is multiple choice. Decide which of the three prepositions fits into the phrase or sentence, write it in the space, and then translate the sentence into English. Use Table 15-2 to help you.

0. Was machen wir _____ diesem perfekten Tag?   a) seit   b) nach   c) zu

A. **b) nach.** Was machen wir nach diesem perfekten Tag? (***What shall we do after this perfect day?***)

8. Ich möchte allein _____ Strand gehen.   a) mit   b) bis   c) zu

_____

9. Ich möchte _____ dir sein.   a) zu   b) bei   c) aus

_____

10. _____ drei Jahren sagst du das.   a) mit   b) außer   c) seit

_____

11. Und _____ mir hast du noch eine Freundin.   a) außer   b) bei   c) zu

_____

12. Nein, _____ Lisa habe ich keine Beziehung.   a) zu   b) nach   c) mit

_____

Genitive prepositions

The list of genitive prepositions is small, but these types are used almost as frequently as the others in this chapter. The *genitive prepositions* describe duration of time, reasons for something, or opposition to something. Most of these expressions are equivalent to English expressions that include *of: instead of, because of,* and *inside* or *outside of*. These prepositions include **anstatt/statt, außerhalb, innerhalb, trotz, während,** and **wegen.** A few other genitive prepositions exist, but they're used less frequently.

Especially in spoken German, but also in written German, it's common to use the dative personal pronouns with genitive prepositions; for example, **wegen mir** (*because of me*) or **statt dir** (*instead of you*). Look at Table 15-3. This list of genitive-type prepositions is short but powerful in expression and variations of usage. The table shows the six most common genitive prepositions, their English equivalents, and sample phrases.

Table 15-3		Genitive Prepositions	
Preposition	*English Equivalent(s)*	*Sample Phrases*	*English Equivalent*
(an)statt (no difference between **anstatt** and **statt**)	*instead of*	**(an)statt meines Autos**	*instead of my car*
außerhalb	*outside of*	**außerhalb des Hauses**	*outside of the house*
innerhalb	*inside of*	**innerhalb der Firma**	*within the company*
trotz	*in spite of, despite*	**trotz des Wetters** **trotz des Lärms**	*despite the weather in spite of the noise*
während	*during*	**während des Tages**	*during the day*
wegen	*because of, on account of*	**wegen der Kosten** **wegen mir**	*on account of the costs because of me*

To form genitive prepositional phrases, begin with the preposition and then add the information that the preposition links to the rest of the sentence. You need to change the endings of any articles, pronouns, adjectives, and nouns following the prepositions — if necessary — so that they're also in the genitive case. (See Chapter 2 for cases.)

Wegen der Hitze gehen wir nicht spazieren. (*We're not going for a walk because of the heat.*) **Die Hitze** in nominative case becomes **der Hitze** in genitive case.

Während des Winters bleiben wir meistens zu Hause. (*We usually stay at home during the winter.*) **Der Winter** in nominative case becomes **des Winters** in genitive case.

Note: In spoken German, some genitive prepositions — **anstatt/statt, trotz, wegen,** and **während** — are typically used with the dative case. This is especially true in the south and southwest German-speaking regions: **Bayern, Österreich, und die Schweiz**

(*Bavaria, Austria, and Switzerland*). **Während** uses dative case less frequently in colloquial German than the other three. The meaning of these prepositions doesn't change
when you use dative case.

In this exercise, fill in the spaces using the prepositions in Table 15-3. Two tourists
staying at a Salzburger **Pension** (*bed and breakfast*) are talking **während des
Frühstücks** (*during breakfast*).

Q. _____ des Lärms ist diese Pension wunderbar, oder?

A. **Trotz** des Lärms ist diese Pension wunderbar, oder? (*Despite the noise, this pension is
wonderful, isn't it?*)

13. Ja, _____ der Nacht habe ich sehr gut geschlafen.

14. Ich bin _____ fünf Minuten eingeschlafen.

15. Mmm. Heute trinke ich Kaffee _____ Tee.

16. Ich auch, aber _____ des Koffeins soll ich nur eine Tasse trinken.

17. Fahren wir heute _____ der Stadt? Ich möchte die Berge sehen.

Tackling Two-Way Prepositions: Accusative/Dative

The nine prepositions in this section are the types that can use either accusative or
dative case, depending on meaning. The preposition in the accusative case describes
movement, whereas the dative case describes position. Another way to tell them
apart is by knowing that the preposition uses the accusative case to show a change of
location, and it answers the question **wohin?** (*where to?*). The same preposition uses
the dative case to refer to a location; the dative preposition answers the question **wo?**
(*where?*).

English sometimes has two different prepositions that do the work of one German
two-way preposition. Take *in* and *into*: *In* expresses where something is, and *into*
refers to the movement from one place *into* the other. The German preposition **in** can
use either accusative or dative case, depending on whether it expresses position
(location) or movement (from one location to another).

To determine whether you need to use the preposition in accusative or dative case, visu-
alize what you want to say. These prepositions indicate concrete spatial relationships,
not intangible concepts, which makes it simple to imagine the difference between a cat
lying *on* the table — **eine Katze liegt auf dem Tisch** (location = dative case) — and a
cat jumping *onto* the table — **eine Katz springt auf den Tisch** (movement = accusative
case).

Table 15-4 shows the two-way prepositions, their English equivalents, and a sample
phrase for each with the English translation. Remember — there's no present continuous in German, so the present tense (*the mouse runs*), present continuous (*the mouse
is running*), or both may be logical translations.

Table 15-4		Two-Way Prepositions	
Preposition	**English Equivalent(s)**	**Accusative Example**	**Dative Example**
an	*at, on, to*	**Die Katze geht ans (an + das) Fenster.** (*The cat walks to the window.*)	**Die Katze sitzt am Fenster.** (*The cat is sitting at the window.*)
auf	*on, onto, to*	**Die Katze springt auf den Tisch.** (*The cat jumps onto the table.*)	**Die Katze steht auf dem Tisch.** (*The cat is standing on the table.*)
hinter	*behind, to the back of*	**Die Katze geht hinter die Couch.** (*The cat is going behind the couch.*)	**Die Katze sitzt hinter der Couch.** (*The cat is sitting behind the couch.*)
in	*in, into, to*	**Die Katze läuft in die Küche.** (*The cat is running into the kitchen.*)	**Die Katze ist in der Küche.** (*The cat is in the kitchen.*)
neben	*beside, next to*	**Der Hund legt sich neben die Katze hin.** (*The dog lays itself down next to the cat.*)	**Die Katze liegt neben dem Hund.** (*The cat is lying next to the dog.*)
über	*above, over*	**Eine Maus läuft über den Teppich.** (*A mouse is running over the carpet.*)	**Eine Lampe hängt über dem Tisch.** (*A lamp is hanging over the table.*)
unter	*under, underneath*	**Die Maus läuft unter den Teppich.** (*The mouse runs under the carpet.*)	**Der Teppich liegt unter dem Tisch.** (*The carpet is lying under the table.*)
vor	*in front of*	**Die Maus läuft vor die Katze.** (*The mouse is running in front of the cat.*)	**Der Hund sitzt vor dem Fernseher.** (*The dog is sitting in front of the TV.*)
zwischen	*between*	**Die Katze legt sich zwischen die Pfoten des Hundes.** (*The cat lies down between the dog's paws.*)	**Der Hund steht zwischen der Maus und der Katze.** (*The dog is standing between the mouse and the cat.*)

To form phrases with accusative/dative prepositions, follow the guidelines I describe in the previous two sections for accusative prepositions and dative prepositions. Some two-way prepositions combine with articles to make contractions. These are mostly used in spoken, colloquial German:

- ✔ **an + das = ans**
- ✔ **an + dem = am**
- ✔ **auf + das = aufs**
- ✔ **in + das = ins**
- ✔ **in + dem = im**

Other contractions that aren't as frequently used as contractions with **das** and **dem** include **hinters, hinterm, übers, überm, unters, unterm, vors,** and **vorm.**

The following examples clarify how to form and use these prepositions correctly.

> **Die Kinder sind im Bett.** (*The children are in bed.*) The preposition **in** (here it means *in*) uses dative case here to express location. Where are the children? In bed.

> **Die Kinder gehen ins Bett.** (*The children are going to bed.*) The preposition **in** (here it means *into*) uses accusative case to express movement. Where are the children going? To bed.

> **Ich wohne über einer Buchhandlung.** (*I live above a bookstore.*) The preposition **über** (*over*) describes where it is. *Where* describes location; it takes the dative case.

> **Der Zeppelin fliegt über die Stadt.** (*The zeppelin [blimp] is flying over the city.*) The preposition **über** (*over*) describes movement; it's in the accusative case.

In this exercise, decide whether to insert the accusative or the dative prepositional phrase and write it in the space provided.

Q. Ich schwimme gern _____. (im Meer / ins Meer)

A. Ich schwimme gern **im Meer.** (*I like to swim in the ocean.*) You swim in the water when you're already in it, so you need the dative prepositional phrase here.

18. Marco sitzt _____. (ans Fenster / am Fenster)

19. Alexandra arbeitet _____. (auf der Bank / auf die Bank)

20. Gehen wir _____? (ins Restaurant / im Restaurant)

21. Die Autos fahren schnell _____. (über der Brücke / über die Brücke)

22. Stellen Sie bitte ihre Schuhe _____. (unter den Sessel / unter dem Sessel)

Understanding Quirky Combinations

German has several quirky yet important prepositional phrases that you encounter on a regular basis. You can easily grasp and incorporate these phrases into your written and spoken German, so you need to be aware of what they look like and how to use them. These prepositional phrases are easiest to remember in verb/preposition combinations. *Verb/preposition combinations* are high-frequency expressions that combine verbs with prepositions. Try to remember these examples as complete sentences so that you can use them later. (Refer to Chapter 11 for details on verb/preposition combinations.) To understand what sets these prepositional phrases apart from the others in this chapter, look at the descriptions of these prepositions followed by examples:

✔ **Zu Hause** and **nach Hause** are two prepositional phrases that are often confused. **Zu Hause** means *at home*. It indicates location. **Nach Hause** means *going home*. It implies movement, motion in the direction of home.

> **Wo ist Birgit? Sie ist zu Hause.** (*Where's Birgit? She's at home.*)
>
> **Wohin geht Lars? Er geht nach Hause.** (*Where is Lars going? He's going home.*)

✔ **Bis** (*till, until*) is an accusative preposition. What makes it different is the fact that it's used most often in combination with other prepositions, not as a stand-alone. Look at the following expressions:

> **von 8.30 Uhr bis 19.00 Uhr** (*from 8:30 a.m. till 7 p.m.*): This expression represents a sign on a store posting opening hours; clock time expressions don't need an article.
>
> **bis zum bitteren Ende** (*until the bitter end*): **Zu** takes dative case: **zu + dem = zum.**
>
> **bis ins kleinste Detail** (*in[to] the smallest detail*): **Ins = in + das,** the accusative case.
>
> **bis in den Abend hinein** (*on into the evening*): The phrase is in accusative case.

✔ **Entlang** (*along, down*) is the preposition that works the case crowd. It actually has three case combinations: accusative, dative, and genitive. In addition, **entlang** often follows the information it modifies. (And it also functions as an adverb!) Look at the three examples of **entlang** using the three cases:

> **Gehen Sie den Weg entlang.** (*Walk along the path.*) **Den Weg** is accusative case. You use the accusative case here because you're describing the motion of walking along.
>
> **Die Grenze verläuft entlang dem Fluß.** (*The border follows the river.*) **Dem Fluß** is dative case. You use dative here because you're describing the place, the location where the border is.
>
> **Entlang des Ufers gibt es viele Schwäne.** (*There are a lot of swans along the shore.*) **Des Ufers** is genitive case. Usage of **entlang** in genitive case is typical in southern Germany and Austria.

✔ **Gegenüber** (*across from, opposite*) is another oddity among prepositions. A true multitasker, **gegenüber** is not only a dative preposition but also an adjective, adverb, and even a noun — **das Gegenüber** is *the opponent,* or *the person opposite you.* It also combines with verbs as a separable-prefix verb (**gegenüberstehen: er steht mir gegenüber** [*he's standing opposite me*]). As a preposition, it can be in front of or after its object; it makes no difference in meaning

> **Wir wohnen gegenüber dem Park.** (*We live across from a park.*) The object, **dem Park,** follows **gegenüber.**
>
> **Der Präsident stand mir gegenüber.** (*The president was standing opposite me.*) The object, **mir,** precedes **gegenüber.** Technically speaking, prepositions that combine with verbs belong in a separate group called *prefix verbs.* (See Chapter 10 for separable- and inseparable-prefix verbs.)

Answer Key

1 **um die Garage.** No change necessary here. Only **der** changes to **den** in accusative.

2 **durch den Wald. Der** changes to **den; der Wald** is singular.

3 **für ihn**

4 **bis morgen**

5 **gegan das Gesetz**

6 **für meinen Chef**

7 **ohne mich**

8 **c) zu.** Ich möchte allein **zum** Strand gehen. **(*I'd like to go to the beach alone.*)** The contraction **zum** is a combination of **zu + dem.**

9 **b) bei.** Ich möchte **bei** dir sein. **(*I'd like to be with you/at your place.*)** **Bei dir sein** indicates where; it's the location. With **zu dir,** you'd need **gehen** (*go to your place*).

10 **c) seit. Seit** drei Jahren sagst du das. **(*You've been saying that for three years.*)** In German, the present tense is used with **seit.**

11 **a) außer.** Und **außer** mir hast du noch eine Freundin. **(*And besides me, you have another girlfriend.*)** Notice the word order. The verb **hast** is in second position after **außer mir;** the subject **du** (*you*) follows the verb.

12 **c) mit.** Nein, **mit** Lisa habe ich keine Beziehung. **(*No, I don't have a relationship with Lisa.*)**

13 Ja, **während** der Nacht habe ich sehr gut geschlafen. (*Yes, I slept very well during the night.*) The genitive case of **die (Nacht)** is **der.**

14 Ich bin **innerhalb** fünf Minuten eingeschlafen. (*I fell asleep within five minutes.*) No article is necessary with this clock time expression.

15 Mmm. Heute trinke ich Kaffee **statt** Tee. (*Mmm. Today I'll have coffee instead of tea.*) No article needed here with **Tee.**

16 Ich auch, aber **wegen** des Koffeins soll ich nur eine Tasse trinken. (*Me too, but because of the caffeine, I should drink only one cup.*) Salzburg is world famous for its "Kaffee Kultur," as is Vienna.

17 Fahren wir heute **außerhalb** der Stadt? Ich möchte die Berge sehen. (*Shall we drive outside of the city today? I'd like to see the mountains.*)

18 Marco sitzt **am Fenster.** (*Marco is sitting at the window.*) **Wo?** Where's Marco? At the window. Dative case here.

19 Alexandra arbeitet nicht mehr **auf der Bank.** (*Alexandra doesn't work at the bank anymore.*) The fixed expression for place-of-work is in dative case.

20 Gehen wir **ins Restaurant?** (*Shall we go to a restaurant?*) **Wohin?** Movement indicates accusative case.

21 Die Autos fahren schnell **über die Brücke.** (*The cars are driving fast over/across the bridge.*) **Wohin?** The cars are moving, so you need accusative case.

22 Stellen Sie bitte ihre Schuhe **unter den Sessel.** (*Put your shoes under the armchair.*) **Wohin?** Moving your shoes means you need the accusative.

Part IV
Looking Back and Ahead: Writing in the Past and the Future

The 5th Wave   By Rich Tennant

"Mona's trying to form endings to German adjectives. This from a woman who can't form an ending to a conversation."

In this part . . .

*E*ver wanted to travel in a time machine? Then this part
is for you. In Chapter 16, you take a ride to the past
and stop off at the *conversational past* (officially called the
present perfect). As the name implies, the conversational
past is what you use to talk about your last trip, business
or pleasure; it's how you describe the first time you ate
an artichoke and other exciting events in your life up
to now. Climb back into the time machine and proceed
to Chapter 17, which covers the simple past, the stuff
of fairy tales and serious newspaper reporters; it's
largely reserved for written narratives about the past.
In Chapter 18, you leap into the future, delving into the
realm of expressing what will or won't happen. You don't
need a crystal ball for this; the helping verb **werden** (*will*)
works just fine.

Chapter 16

Conversing about the Past: Perfecting the Present Perfect

. . . .

In This Chapter

▶ Forming the present perfect

▶ Contrasting English and German usage

▶ Expressing yourself informally

. . . .

*P*resent perfect in German is commonly described as the *conversational past* because — naturally — you use it in conversation. You also typically see present perfect in informal writing such as personal letters and e-mails. German uses the present perfect to talk about all actions or states in the past, finished or unfinished. English, on the other hand, tends to use the present perfect for actions that began in the past but have a link to the present.

The present perfect in German has two elements:

✔ An auxiliary verb, also known as a *helping verb* (English present perfect uses *have*)

✔ A past participle (English examples are *gone, been,* and *known*)

The two auxiliary verbs are **haben** (*to have*) and **sein** (*to be*). First you conjugate the auxiliary in the present tense, and then you add the past participle of the verb (**gelebt** [*lived*]; **gewesen** [*been*]; **geschwommen** [*swum*]).

This chapter shows you how to form and use the present perfect in German and explains how the present perfect differs between German and English. You also get ample opportunities to practice the present perfect in German.

Forming the Present Perfect with Haben

The majority of verbs form the present perfect with the auxiliary verb **haben** (*to have*) plus the past participle of the verb you want to use. There are two main categories of verbs, classified by the way the past participle is formed. They're called *weak* and *strong* verbs. (Don't worry — you don't have to go to the gym to find the strong verbs!) Check out the next three sections for more information on weak and strong verbs.

To conjugate a verb in the present perfect with **haben,** you choose the simple present-tense form of **haben: ich habe, du hast, er/sie/es hat, wir haben, ihr habt, sie haben,** or **Sie haben.** You then add the past participle of the verb. Check out the following example of **wohnen** (*to live, reside*) in the present perfect.

wohnen (*to live*)	
ich **habe gewohnt**	wir **haben gewohnt**
du **hast gewohnt**	ihr **habt gewohnt**
er/sie/es **hat gewohnt**	sie **haben gewohnt**
Sie **haben gewohnt**	
Ich **habe** ein Jahr in Paris **gewohnt**. (*I have lived/lived in Paris for a year.*)	

German word order follows specific rules. When you form a sentence with two verbs, the conjugated verb, (**haben** [*to have*], **sein** [*to be*], **werden** [*will*], **möchten** [*would like*], and so on) takes second position in the sentence, and you push the past participle to the end of the sentence. (See Chapter 1 for more info on word order.)

Forming the present perfect with regular weak verbs

Regular weak verbs are the largest group of verbs. To form the past participle, take the unchanged present-tense stem and add the **ge-** prefix and the ending **-t** or **-et.** You need the **-et** ending in the following cases:

- ✔ For verbs whose stem ends in **-d** or **-t** — for example, **heiraten** (*to marry*) becomes **geheiratet** (*married*)
- ✔ For some verbs whose stem ends in **-m** or **-n** — **regnen** (*to rain*) becomes **geregnet** (*rained*)
- ✔ For verbs recently taken over from English — such as **flirten** (*to flirt*) changes to **geflirtet** (*flirted*)

However, the verbs ending in **-ieren** — such as, **interpretieren** (*to interpret*), which changes to **interpretiert** (*interpreted*) — don't add the prefix **ge-.** (You find the lowdown on these verbs that have no **ge-** prefix later in this chapter in "Outing the Oddball Verbs.")

So with the verb **arbeiten** (*to work*), you conjugate **haben** in the appropriate person and then add the past participle. To create the past participle, you chop off the ending **-en,** take the stem **arbeit,** and add **ge-** and **-et** like this: **ge-** + **arbeit** + **-et** = **gearbeitet.**

arbeiten (*to work*)	
ich **habe gearbeitet**	wir **haben gearbeitet**
du **hast gearbeitet**	ihr **habt gearbeitet**
er/sie/es **hat gearbeitet**	sie **haben gearbeitet**
Sie **haben gearbeitet**	
Sie **hat** im Herbst bei der Filmgesellschaft **gearbeitet**. (*She worked at the film company in the fall.*)	

Table 16-1 shows some regular weak verbs with the German and English infinitives, followed by the German and English past participles.

Table 16-1	Past Participles of Regular Weak Verbs		
Infinitive	**Past Participle**	**Infinitive**	**Past Participle**
arbeiten (*to work*)	**gearbeitet** (*worked*)	**lieben** (*to love*)	**geliebt** (*loved*)
drucken (*to print*)	**gedruckt** (*printed*)	**lernen** (*to learn*)	**gelernt** (*learned*)
führen (*to lead*)	**geführt** (*led*)	**machen** (*to make*)	**gemacht** (*made*)
hören (*to hear*)	**gehört** (*heard*)	**passen** (*to fit*)	**gepasst** (*fit*)
hoffen (*to hope*)	**gehofft** (*hoped*)	**regnen** (*to rain*)	**geregnet** (*rained*)
kaufen (*to buy*)	**gekauft** (*bought*)	**sagen** (*to say*)	**gesagt** (*said*)
kosten (*to cost*)	**gekostet** (*cost*)	**schenken** (*to give [a present]*)	**geschenkt** (*given*)
kriegen (*to get*)	**gekriegt** (*gotten/got*)	**spielen** (*to play*)	**gespielt** (*played*)
lächeln (*to smile*)	**gelächelt** (*smiled*)	**surfen** (*to surf*)	**gesurft** (*surfed*)
leben (*to live*)	**gelebt** (*lived*)	**tanzen** (*to dance*)	**getanzt** (*danced*)

Got the hang of creating the past participle? Fill in the blank with the corresponding correct answer. The first word is the infinitive. Next is the past participle.

Infinitive/Meaning   **Past Participle/Meaning**

0. **fragen** (*to ask*)   _____ (_____)

A. fragen (*to ask*)   **gefragt** (*asked*)

1. **brauchen** (*to need*)   _____ (_____)

2. **chatten** (*to chat*)   _____ (_____)

3. _____ (_____)   **gefeiert** (*celebrated*)

4. **glauben** (*to believe*) _____ (_____)

5. **jobben** (*to do odd jobs*) _____ (_____)

6. _____ (_____) **gekocht** (*cooked*)

7. **schmecken** (*to taste*) _____ (_____)

8. _____ (_____) **geschneit** (*snowed*)

9. **suchen** (*to look for, search*) _____ (_____)

10. _____ (_____) **getötet** (*killed*)

11. **wohnen** (*to live*) _____ (_____)

12. _____ (_____) **gezahlt** (*paid*)

Forming the present perfect with irregular weak verbs

A very small number of weak verbs is irregular. What makes them irregular? They do have the prefix **ge-** and the ending **-t,** but they don't follow the same pattern as the regular weak verbs. The present-tense stem changes when you put it in the past participle. The good news is there aren't many of these rebels. The bad news: The only way to really identify them is to memorize these past participles because they don't follow any recognizable pattern.

To form these irregular weak verbs in the present perfect, conjugate **haben** in the present tense and then add the past participle. Check out the following example with the verb **denken** (*to think*).

denken (*to think*)	
ich **habe gedacht**	wir **haben gedacht**
du **hast gedacht**	ihr **habt gedacht**
er/sie/es **hat gedacht**	sie **haben gedacht**
Sie **haben gedacht**	
Luka **hat** oft an seine Frau **gedacht.** (*Luka often thought about his wife.*)	

Table 16-2 shows irregular weak verbs with the German and English infinitives, followed by the German and English past participles.

Table 16-2	Past Participles of Irregular Weak Verbs
Infinitive	*Past Participle*
brennen (*to burn*)	**gebrannt** (*burned*)
bringen (*to bring*)	**gebracht** (*brought*)
denken (*to think*)	**gedacht** (*thought*)
kennen (*to know a person*)	**gekannt** (*known a person*)
nennen (*to name, call*)	**genannt** (*named, called*)
wissen (*to know information*)	**gewusst** (*known information*)

You can remember the past participles of the irregular weak verbs you use frequently by writing your own example sentences; then refer to them as needed.

Change the following sentences into the present perfect tense. Conjugate **haben** accordingly and add the appropriate past participle.

0. Franz kennt ein sehr gutes Restaurant in Berlin.

A. Franz **hat** ein sehr gutes Restaurant in Berlin **gekannt.** (*Franz knew a very good restaurant in Berlin.*)

13. Das Haus brennt sehr schnell.

_____

14. Wir bringen unsere Wanderschuhe.

_____

15. Ich weiß deine Emailadresse nicht.

_____

16. Der Verkäufer kennt die Produkte sehr gut.

_____

17. Die Kunden denken nur an den Preis.

_____

Forming the present perfect with strong verbs

Identifying a *strong verb* is fairly easy. Its past participle ends in **-en.** (The one exception is the verb **tun** [*to do*]; its past participle is **getan** [*done*].) In most strong verbs, the past participle begins with **ge-.** Many of these past participles can seem pesky at first. Why? They often have vowels and consonants that differ from those in the infinitive. I have good news, though: A lot of these verbs whose past participles go through such spelling contortions are high-frequency verbs. To form the present perfect with strong verbs, you conjugate **haben** in the appropriate person and then add the past participle.

trinken (*to drink*)	
ich **habe getrunken**	wir **haben getrunken**
du **hast getrunken**	ihr **habt getrunken**
er/sie/es **hat getrunken**	sie **haben getrunken**
Sie **haben getrunken**	
Wir **haben** gestern viel Mineralwasser **getrunken.** (*We drank a lot of water yesterday.*)	

Table 16-3 shows some other strong verbs. I list the German verb with the English infinitive followed by the German past participle and its English translation.

Table 16-3	Past Participles of Strong Verbs		
Infinitive	*Past Participle*	*Infinitive*	*Past Participle*
backen (*to bake*)	**gebacken** (*baked*)	**schreiben** (*to write*)	**geschrieben** (*written*)
beginnen (*to begin*)	**begonnen** (*begun*)	**singen** (*to sing*)	**gesungen** (*sung*)
essen (*to eat*)	**gegessen** (*eaten*)	**sitzen** (*to sit*)	**gesessen** (*sat*)
finden (*to find*)	**gefunden** (*found*)	**sprechen** (*to speak, talk*)	**gesprochen** (*spoken, talked*)
geben (*to give*)	**gegeben** (*given*)	**stehen** (*to stand*)	**gestanden** (*stood*)
halten (*to hold*)	**gehalten** (*held*)	**tragen** (*to wear*)	**getragen** (*worn*)
heißen (*to be called*)	**geheißen** (*been called*)	**treffen** (*to meet*)	**getroffen** (*met*)
helfen (*to help*)	**geholfen** (*helped*)	**trinken** (*to drink*)	**getrunken** (*drunk*)
lassen (*to leave, let*)	**gelassen** (*left, let*)	**tun** (*to do*)	**getan** (*done*)
lesen (*to read*)	**gelesen** (*read*)	**verlassen** (*to leave*)	**verlassen** (*leave*)
liegen (*to lie, be located*)	**gelegen** (*lain, been located*)	**verlieren** (*to lose*)	**verloren** (*lost*)
nehmen (*to take*)	**genommen** (*taken*)	**verstehen** (*to understand*)	**verstanden** (*understood*)
rufen (*to call*)	**gerufen** (*called*)	**waschen** (*to wash*)	**gewaschen** (*washed*)
schlafen (*to sleep*)	**geschlafen** (*slept*)	**ziehen** (*to pull*)	**gezogen** (*pulled*)

You can easily remember the meanings of many strong verbs because they're reasonably similar to the English verbs. Another plus: You can even find similar patterns to the English past participle forms. Take a look at these examples: **beginnen, begonnen** (*begin, begun*); **singen, gesungen** (*sing, sung*); and **trinken, getrunken** (*drink, drunk*).

Go ahead and complete these sentences. Put the following verbs into the present perfect tense. You can find these verbs in Table 16-3.

Q. Wir _____ viele Freunde auf dem Fest _____. (treffen)

A. Wir **haben** viele Freunde auf dem Fest **getroffen.** (*We met a lot of friends at the party.*)

18. Der Fahrgast _____ die Fahrkarte aus dem Automat _____.
(nehmen)

19. _____ du das Buch schon _____? (lesen)

20. Letztes Jahr _____ ich meine Kollegen in München _____. (treffen)

21. _____ du schon alle Emails _____? (schreiben)

22. Um wie viel Uhr _____ der Zug den Bahnhof _____? (verlassen)

Forming the Present Perfect with Sein

Some verbs form the present perfect with the auxiliary verb **sein** (*to be*) plus the past participle of the verb you want to use. All these verbs that use **sein** have two similarities:

- ✔ They don't have a direct object, which means they're *intransitive.* For example, the verb **laufen** (*to run*) is intransitive: **Wir sind schnell gelaufen** (*We ran fast*). An example of a transitive verb (with a direct object) is **trinken** (*to drink*), and it looks like this: **Ich habe eine Tasse Tee getrunken** (*I drank a cup of tea*).

- ✔ They show a change in some condition — as with **werden** (*to become*) — or some motion to or from a place: **kommen** (*to come*).

Generally, you form the past participle with **ge-** + the stem from the infinitive + the ending **-en:** For example, **kommen** (*to come*) becomes **gekommen** (come). However, you also have the types of past participles that have gone through some spelling changes from the original infinitive form: **Gehen** (*to go, walk*) changes to **gegangen** (*gone, walked*).

But of course, there are some rogues. The verbs **bleiben** (*to stay*) and **sein** (*to be*) don't meet the second criterion, but they still need **sein** to form the present perfect. And then you have yet another rogue: **rennen** (*to run, race*), which changes to **gerannt** (*run, raced*). It has a **-t** ending in the past participle.

To form the present perfect with **sein,** you first conjugate the present tense of the verb **sein** and then add the right past participle.

fahren (*to drive*)	
ich **bin gefahren**	wir **sind gefahren**
du **bist gefahren**	ihr **seid gefahren**
er/sie/es **ist gefahren**	sie **sind gefahren**
Sie **sind gefahren**	
Bist du die ganze Nacht **gefahren?** (*Did you drive all night?*)	

Even in conversation, it's a lot more common to use the simple past of **sein** than the present perfect; for example, **Wie war der Flug von Zürich nach San Francisco?** (*How was the flight from Zürich to San Francisco?*). (For more information on how to form and use the simple past, check out Chapter 17.)

Look at Table 16-4, which shows a list of verbs that use **sein** in the present perfect. Some past participles have no stem change; others go through contortions to form the past participle, so you need to memorize them.

Table 16-4	Verbs Conjugated with Sein in the Present Perfect		
Infinitive	*Sein + Past Participle*	*Infinitive*	*Sein + Past Participle*
bleiben (*to stay, remain*)	**ist geblieben** (*stayed, remained*)	**reiten** (*to ride [horseback]*)	**ist geritten** (*ridden*)
fahren (*to drive*)	**ist gefahren** (*driven*)	**schwimmen** (*to swim*)	**ist geschwommen** (*swum*)
fallen (*to fall*)	**ist gefallen** (*fallen*)	**sein** (*to be*)	**ist gewesen** (*been*)
fliegen (*to fly*)	**ist geflogen** (*flown*)	**steigen** (*to climb*)	**ist gestiegen** (*climbed*)
fließen (*to flow, run*)	**ist geflossen** (*flowed, run*)	**sterben** (*to die*)	**ist gestorben** (*died*)
gehen (*to go, walk*)	**ist gegangen** (*gone, walked*)	**wachsen** (*to grow*)	**ist gewachsen** (*grown*)
kommen (*to come*)	**ist gekommen** (*come*)	**werden** (*to become*)	**ist geworden** (*become*)
laufen (*to run, walk*)	**ist gelaufen** (*run, walked*)		

Now it's your turn. Put the verbs into the present perfect tense in the following dialogues. Refer to the example for the conjugation of **sein** with the past participle of the verb **fahren.** You find the past participles you need in Table 16-4.

0. Maria: Uwe, _____ du nach Hawaii _____? (fliegen)

A. Maria: Uwe, **bist** du nach Hawaii **geflogen**? (*Uwe, did you fly to Hawaii?*)

23. Christian: _____ du heute Morgen _____? (reiten)

24. Barbara: Nein, ich _____ im Park _____. (laufen)

25. Udo: _____ er vom Dach _____? (fallen)

26. Franz: Ja, und zwei Tage später _____ er _____. (sterben)

27. Helena: _____ ihr im Winter in die Schweiz _____? (fahren)

28. Ulla: Nein wir _____ zu Hause _____. (bleiben)

29. Hannes: Wann _____ du zum Fest _____? (gehen)

30. Janina: Ich weiß nicht. Ich glaube, ich _____ sehr spät nach Hause
_____. (kommen)

31. Michaela: _____ deine Kinder gestern im Park _____? (sein)

32. Jan: Nein, sie _____ im See_____. (schwimmen)

Eyeing the Present Perfect: German versus English

In the present perfect, German and English have some similarities and some differences. In both languages, you use the present perfect to talk about past activities, and both are used in conversation. Also, the construction looks similar, at least when you use the auxiliary verb **haben;** for example, **Ich habe einen Kojoten gesehen** (*I have seen a coyote*).

The differences in the present perfect come about when you want to add a time element, such as **gestern** (*yesterday*): **Gestern habe ich einen Kojoten gesehen** (*Yesterday I saw a coyote*). You use the present perfect in German, but in English, you use *saw* (the simple past). On the other hand, when you want to describe a past action that's still going on, you say something like **Seit einigen Jahren sehe ich Kojoten** (*I've been seeing coyotes for a few years*). Here, German uses the simple present, yet English uses the present perfect continuous. In this section, I provide you with variations of these differences in verb tense usage.

One for all: Representing three English tenses

Both English and German use the present perfect in conversation. The distinction here is that in German, you actually use it a lot more frequently in conversation and informal written language. Look at this example, which uses present perfect in German but simple past in English because *last night* is finished:

> **Was hast du gestern Abend im Fernsehen gesehen?** (*What did you see on TV last night?*)

German has only the one verb tense, the present perfect, to represent three tenses in English. Depending on what you want to say in German, the following forms are possible. Here are three acceptable translations of **Sie haben in Wien gelebt:**

- **Present perfect:** *They have lived in Vienna* (expresses that they may still live there)

- **Simple past:** *They lived in Vienna* (says they no longer live there)

- **Past continuous:** *They were living in Vienna* (talks about a relationship between two completed past actions — usually one is longer than the other; the other past action may be described in a previous or subsequent sentence or in the same sentence)

Look at the sentence *They were living in Vienna.* Because you don't even have past continuous in German (or any other continuous forms for that matter), you use the present perfect as the pinch hitter like this: **Während des kalten Krieges haben sie in Wien gelebt** (*During the Cold War, they were living in Vienna*).

As soon as you understand how to form the present perfect, you'll find yourself using it very frequently to describe a great deal of situations in the past. In fact, unless you intend to pursue a career in German journalism, you won't have much use for the simple past or other past-tense verb forms.

Opting for the German present

Now look at two more German sentences and their literal and real English translations. You may be surprised (and relieved) that in German, you get by with the simple present in some situations where you have to use the present perfect in English. And one more economizing step: You express both *since* and *for* with **seit** in German. For example,

> **Seit wie lange warten Sie auf die U-Bahn?** (*How long have you been waiting for the subway?* Literally: *Since how long wait you for the subway?*)

> **Wir stehen hier seit zehn Minuten.** (*We've been standing here for ten minutes.* Literally: *We stand here for ten minutes.*)

Outing the Oddball Verbs

You need to do a bit of juggling with some German verbs that have prefixes when you form the present perfect. I describe three types of oddball verbs:

✔ **Separable-prefix verbs:** These verbs are recognizable by a prefix, such as **-auf-,** that separates from the main verb in some verb tenses. It's added to a main verb, one that can usually stand alone, like **geben** (*to give*) to form **aufgeben** (*to give up, to check* [*luggage*]). These verbs may have either strong or weak endings in present perfect, but they have the **ge-** prefix: **aufgegeben.**

✔ **Inseparable-prefix verbs:** These verbs are identified by a prefix, such as **be-,** that doesn't separate from a main verb, like **kommen** (*to come*): **bekommen** (*to get*). These verbs may have either strong or weak endings in present perfect, but they lack the **ge-** prefix: **bekommen.**

✔ **Verbs ending in -ieren:** These verbs are easy to spot because they generally have the same meaning in English if you take off the **-ieren** and substitute an English ending such as *-ify:* **spezifizieren** (*to specify*). You form the past participle without **ge-** but with **-t: spezifiziert.**

In this section, you identify these verbs and find out how to form the present perfect, and then you practice writing sentences in the present perfect. (For more background on verbs with prefixes, separable or inseparable, go to Chapter 10.)

Separable-prefix verbs

With separable-prefix verbs, you leave the prefix at the front of the verb, squish **ge-** in the middle, and follow up with the rest of the participle. Most of the commonly used verbs in this group resemble strong verbs (past participle ending in **-en**); others resemble weak verbs (past participle ending in **-t** or **-et**). And just to put more into the mix, a few verbs use the auxiliary verb **sein.** (See Chapter 10 for more on separable-prefix verbs.)

You put together the present perfect of these verbs by conjugating **haben** or **sein** in the present tense and adding the past participle. So if the infinitive is **anrufen** (*to call [on the phone]*), you get the past participle **angerufen** (*called*), which has the three elements **an** + **ge** + **rufen**. Take a look at the conjugation of **fernsehen** (*to watch TV*).

fernsehen (*to watch TV*)	
ich **habe ferngesehen**	wir **haben ferngesehen**
du **hast ferngesehen**	ihr **habt ferngesehen**
er/sie/es **hat ferngesehen**	sie **haben ferngesehen**
Sie **haben ferngesehen**	
Habt ihr am Wochenende **ferngesehen?** (*Did you watch TV on the weekend?*)	

You pronounce the separable-prefix verbs with the stress on the first syllable, which is the prefix.

Table 16-5 shows you what the past participle looks like. I've included **ist** before the past participles that need the infinitive **sein**.

Table 16-5	Verbs with Separable Prefixes		
Infinitive	*Past Participle*	*Infinitive*	*Past Participle*
anfangen (*to begin, start*)	**angefangen** (*begun, started*)	**mitbringen** (*to bring along*)	**mitgebracht** (*brought along*)
ankommen (*to arrive*)	**ist angekommen** (*arrived*)	**mitmachen** (*to join in*)	**mitgemacht** (*joined in*)
anrufen (*to call*)	**angerufen** (*called*)	**stattfinden** (*to take place*)	**stattgefunden** (*taken place*)
aufgeben (*to give up, check [luggage]*)	**aufgegeben** (*given up, checked [luggage]*)	**vorhaben** (*to plan*)	**vorgehabt** (*planned*)
aussehen (*to look [like]*)	**ausgesehen** (*looked [like]*)	**zurückgehen** (*to decline, go back*)	**ist zurückgegangen** (*declined, gone back*)
einkaufen (*to go shopping*)	**eingekauft** (*gone shopping*)	**zusammenfassen** (*to summarize*)	**zusammengefasst** (*summarized*)
einladen (*to invite*)	**eingeladen** (*invited*)	**zusammenkommen** (*to meet*)	**ist zusammengekommen** (*met*)
fernsehen (*to watch TV*)	**ferngesehen** (*watched TV*)		

Now try your hand at forming the present perfect tense with these verbs. Take the helping verb **haben** (or in some cases, **sein**), conjugate it in the present tense, and then assemble the past participle to create the present perfect tense.

Q. Die Nachbarn _____ uns zum Essen _____. (einladen)

A. Die Nachbarn **haben** uns zum Essen **eingeladen.** (*The neighbors invited us to dinner.*)

33. Nach dem Regen _____ die Pflanzen viel besser _____. (aussehen)

34. _____ Sie ihr Gepäck schon _____? (aufgeben)

35. Das Konzert _____ mit einer Stunde Verspätung _____. (anfangen)

36. Wo _____ die Handelsmesse _____? (stattfinden)

37. Unser Zug _____ um 20.45 Uhr in Stuttgart _____. (ankommen)

Inseparable-prefix verbs

With inseparable-prefix verbs, the past participle can have a strong verb ending (**-en**) or a weak verb ending (**-t** or **-et**), but the rest is relatively easy. To help you distinguish how these verbs differ from separable-prefix verbs, just look at these three characteristics for the past participle of inseparable-prefix verbs:

- The prefix always sticks to the rest of the verb, including the past participle.

- You don't add the prefix **ge-** to the past participle.

- You don't stress the prefix. Look at the infinitive **erken'nen** (*to recognize*) and its past participle **erkannt'** (*recognized*).

You put together the present perfect of these verbs by conjugating **haben** in the present tense and adding the past participle. Check out the conjugation of **bekommen** (*to get, receive*).

bekommen (*to get, receive*)	
ich **habe bekommen**	wir **haben bekommen**
du **hast bekommen**	ihr **habt bekommen**
er/sie/es **hat bekommen**	sie **haben bekommen**
Sie **haben bekommen**	
Warum **hast** du die Zeitung heute nicht **bekommen?** (*Why didn't you get the newspaper today?*)	

Table 16-6 is a list of some more inseparable-prefix verbs with their past participles. Notice how similar the two forms of the verbs are — a few are exactly the same.

Table 16-6		Verbs with Inseparable Prefixes	
Infinitive	*Past Participle*	*Infinitive*	*Past Participle*
beantworten (*to answer*)	**beantwortet** (*answered*)	**gebrauchen** (*to use, make use of*)	**gebraucht** (*used, made use of*)
bekommen (*to get, receive*)	**bekommen** (*gotten, received*)	**gefallen** (*to like*)	**gefallen** (*liked*)
besuchen (*to visit*)	**besucht** (*visited*)	**gehören** (*to belong to*)	**gehört** (*belonged to*)
bezahlen (*to pay*)	**bezahlt** (*paid*)	**gewinnen** (*to win*)	**gewonnen** (*won*)
erkennen (*to recognize*)	**erkannt** (*recognized*)	**missverstehen** (*to misunderstand*)	**missverstanden** (*misunderstood*)
erklären (*to explain*)	**erklärt** (*explained*)	**vergessen** (*to forget*)	**vergessen** (*forgotten*)
erzählen (*to tell*)	**erzählt** (*told*)	**verlieren** (*to lose*)	**verloren** (*lost*)

Now it's your turn. Put the verbs into the present perfect tense in the following sentences. Refer to the example for the conjugation of **haben** with the past participle of the verb **bekommen.** You find the past participles you need in Table 16-6.

Q. Sie _____ uns viele lustige Witze _____. (erzählen)

A. Sie **haben** uns viele lustige Witze **erzählt.** (*They told us a lot of funny jokes.*)

38. Moritz _____ meinen Namen _____. (vergessen)

39. _____ du die Fahrkarten schon _____? (bekommen)

40. Ich _____ sie an der Kasse _____. (bezahlen)

41. Wir _____ unsere Regenschirme oft _____. (gebrauchen)

42. Entschuldigung, ich _____ Sie _____. (missverstehen)

Verbs ending in -ieren

I save an easy-to-remember group of verbs for last. The **-ieren** verbs are oddball verbs for several reasons. First, they end in **-ieren,** unlike mainstream verbs, which end in **-en.** In addition, they form the past participle without **ge-** but with **-t** at the end.

You can usually recognize the meanings of these verbs, and the English equivalent of the infinitive often ends in *-ify* (**verifizieren** = *to verify*) or *-ate* (**vibrieren** = *to vibrate*). When forming the present perfect with **-ieren** verbs, all you need to know is the following:

   ✔ You form the past participle without **ge-**.

   ✔ You always form the past participle with **-t.**

Look at how easily you can use these verbs:

   ✔ **fotografieren** (*to photograph*): Der Journalist **hat** die Demonstration **fotografiert.** (*The journalist photographed the demonstration.*)

   ✔ **dekorieren** (*to decorate*): Vor dem Neujahrsfest **haben** wir das Wohnzimmer **dekoriert.** (*Before the New Year's Eve party, we decorated the living room.*)

   ✔ **probieren** (*to try, sample*): **Hast** du die Torte schon **probiert?** Sie ist lecker! (*Have you tried the torte [cake] yet? It's delicious!*)

This time, you need to fill in only the past participle. The cognates you see in this exercise end in **-ieren** in German. Sometimes these words end in *-ate* or *-ify* in English, but they're nearly always easy to guess. **Das ist aber einfach!** (*That's really easy!*)

0. dekorieren (*to decorate*) → _____

A. **dekoriert** (*decorated*)

43. denunzieren (*to denounce*) → _____

44. finanzieren (*to finance*) → _____

45. fixieren (*to fixate*) → _____

46. fotografieren (*to photograph*) → _____

47. frustrieren (*to frustrate*) → _____

48. klassifizieren (*to classify*) → _____

49. organisieren (*to organize*) → _____

Answer Key

1. gebraucht (*needed*)

2. gechattet (*chatted*)

3. feiern (*to celebrate*)

4. geglaubt (*believed*)

5. gejobbt (*done odd jobs*)

6. kochen (*to cook*)

7. geschmeckt (*tasted*)

8. schneien (*to snow*)

9. gesucht (*looked for, searched*)

10. töten (*to kill*)

11. gewohnt (*lived*)

12. zahlen (*to pay*)

13. Das Haus **hat** sehr schnell **gebrannt.** (*The house burned very fast.*)

14. Wir **haben** unsere Wanderschuhe **gebracht.** (*We have brought/brought our hiking boots.*)

15. Ich **habe** deine Emailadresse nicht **gewusst.** (*I didn't know your e-mail address.*)

16. Der Verkäufer **hat** die Produkte sehr gut **gekannt.** (*The salesperson knew the products very well.*)

17. Die Kunden **haben** nur an den Preis **gedacht.** (*The customers thought only about the price.*)

18. Der Fahrgast **hat** die Fahrkarte aus dem Automaten **genommen.** (*The passenger took the ticket out of the machine.*)

19. **Hast** du das Buch schon **gelesen?** (*Have you read the book yet?*)

20. Letztes Jahr **habe** ich meine Kollegen in München **getroffen.** (*Last year I met my colleagues in Munich.*)

21. **Hast** du schon alle Emails **geschrieben?** (*Have you already written all the e-mails?*)

22. Um wie viel Uhr **hat** der Zug den Bahnhof **verlassen?** (*When did the train leave the station?*)

23. Christian: **Bist** du heute Morgen **geritten?** (*Did you go riding this morning?*)

24. Barbara: Nein, ich **bin** im Park **gelaufen.** (*No, I ran in the park.*)

25. Udo: **Ist** er vom Dach **gefallen?** (*Did he fall off the roof?*)

26 Franz: Ja, und zwei Tage später **ist** er **gestorben.** (*Yes, and two days later he died.*)

27 Helena: **Seid** ihr im Winter in die Schweiz **gefahren?** (*Did you go to Switzerland in the winter?*)

28 Ulla: Nein wir **sind** zu Hause **geblieben.** (*No, we stayed home.*)

29 Hannes: Wann **bist** du zum Fest **gegangen?** (*When did you go to the party?*)

30 Janina: Ich weiß nicht. Ich glaube, ich **bin** sehr spät nach Hause **gekommen.** (*I don't know. I think I came home very late.*)

31 Michaela: **Sind** deine Kinder gestern im Park **gewesen?** (*Were your children in the park yesterday?*)

32 Jan: Nein, sie **sind** im See **geschwommen.** (*No, they went swimming in the lake.*)

33 Nach dem Regen **haben** die Pflanzen viel besser **ausgesehen.** (*After the rain, the plants looked much better.*)

34 **Haben** Sie ihr Gepäck schon **aufgegeben?** (*Have you already checked your luggage?*)

35 Das Konzert **hat** mit einer Stunde Verspätung **angefangen.** (*The concert began after a one-hour delay.*)

36 Wo **hat** die Handelsmesse **stattgefunden?** (*Where did the trade fair take place?*)

37 Unser Zug **ist** um 20.45 Uhr in Stuttgart **angekommen.** (*Our train arrived in Stuttgart at 8:45 p.m.*)

38 Moritz **hat** meinen Namen **vergessen.** (*Moritz forgot my name.*)

39 **Hast** du die Fahrkarten schon **bekommen?** (*Have you already gotten the tickets?*)

40 Ich **habe** sie an der Kasse **bezahlt.** (*I paid for them at the cashier.*)

41 Wir **haben** unsere Regenschirme oft **gebraucht.** (*We often used our umbrellas.*)

42 Entschuldigung, ich **habe** Sie **missverstanden.** (*Excuse me, I misunderstood you.*)

43 **denunziert** (*denounced*)

44 **finanziert** (*financed*)

45 **fixiert** (*fixated*)

46 **fotografiert** (*photographed*)

47 **frustriert** (*frustrated*)

48 **klassifiziert** (*classified*)

49 **organisiert** (*organized*)

Chapter 17

Narrating the (Simple) Past: Fact and Fiction

Master storytellers and journalists both have an incredible knack for drawing their audience into a narrative. Storytellers lend a façade of reality to the wildest tales as they twist and turn, fold and unfold in front of rapt listeners (or readers), and well-written news reports of violence, natural disasters, and human prowess can also rivet the readers' attention. What these two types of narrators have in common is they have a command of the *simple past tense,* also referred to as the *imperfect* or the *narrative past.*

To describe any events or stories, you need verbs — and lots of them. In German, the verb tense of choice when narrating fact or fiction is the simple past tense — for example, **er ging** (*he went*), **wir mussten** (*we had to*), or **ich sprach** (*I spoke*). This chapter compares the simple past tense to the other past tenses and helps improve your German writing by focusing on forming and using the simple past tense.

To remember the difference in usage between the simple past and the present perfect in German, think of the simple past as the narrative past; you run across it more frequently in written German. Think of the present perfect as the conversational past, the one that you hear in offices, cafés, and on the streets. (Check out Chapter 16 for more on the present perfect.)

Conjugating the Simple Past

To write or talk formally about something that happened, you need to know how to correctly conjugate verbs in the simple past tense. However, before I discuss conjugations, I brief you on how the simple past relates to English.

Although you may know that the simple past in German is translated as the simple past in English, you may not be aware of other ways to render it. In some respects, the simple past is a gold mine for expressing various verb tenses in English. Table 17-1 shows the English equivalents for the same German phrase, along with the context for these differences in English translation.

Table 17-1	English Equivalents for the German Simple Past		
German Phrase in the Simple Past	**English Equivalent**	**English Verb Tense**	**Context/Intended Idea**
Fritz **spielte** sehr gut Gitarre.	Fritz *played* the guitar very well.	Simple past	Commenting about Fritz; he played very well last night
Fritz **spielte** sehr gut Gitarre.	Fritz *was playing* the guitar very well.	Past continuous (this verb tense doesn't exist in German)	Fritz was playing very well, when all of a sudden lightning struck the amplifiers
Fritz **spielte** sehr gut Gitarre.	Fritz *used to play* the guitar very well.	*Used to* + verb to describe habitual actions that no longer apply (the *used to* + *verb* isn't described verbally in German; instead, you use **damals** [*then*])	Telling about Fritz's former talents; he's 78 years old now, and he's lost his edge
Fritz **spielte** sehr gut Gitarre.	Fritz *did play* the guitar very well.	Simple past, emphatic form (the emphatic form is described with **doch** [*indeed/really*] in German)	Fritz did indeed play well; he was working up a storm on Saturday night

The simple past verb form isn't too difficult to master. You just need to know that there are several types of endings according to which category the verb falls into:

- ✔ Regular verbs, also called *weak verbs*
- ✔ Irregular verbs, also known as *strong verbs*
- ✔ Other irregular verbs like **sein, haben,** and the modal verbs, also called *auxiliary* or *helping verbs*

Note: A fourth category of verbs, the separable-prefix verbs, includes verbs that have a prefix like **ab-** or a preposition like **mit-** in front of the verb; these verbs may be regular or irregular. The prefix is separated when you conjugate the verb, and it's generally placed at the end of the phrase. Two examples are **abfahren** (*to leave*) and **mitkommen** (*to come along*). Chapter 10 deals with separable- and inseparable-prefix verbs.

The applications of the simple past are quite different when you compare German and English. The single most important aspect of the simple past in English is that it describes an action that's completed in the past, often with a reference to the past: *last month, in 2006,* or *when I was 13.* English uses the simple past in a great number of situations: to describe past events of both formal and informal (casual) nature, as well as for spoken and written language. German, on the other hand, tends to use the simple past in written language, especially newspapers, books, written texts, narrated stories, and even fairy tales. In German, the simple past is also a means of describing past events not connected to the present.

This section shows you how to conjugate different German verbs, including regular (weak) and irregular (strong), **haben** and **sein,** and modals. After you read this section, you can write about the past with eloquence and style.

Forming regular (weak) verbs in simple past

Regular verbs are the ones that don't have a stem change between the present tense and the simple past tense. For example, the present tense stem of **wohnen** is **wohn-**, and the simple past stem is also **wohn-**. The endings are what makes the difference between the two tenses.

Here's how to form the simple past of regular verbs:

1. Take the **-en** off the infinitive.
2. Add **-te,** which I refer to as the *-te tense marker*.
3. Add the additional endings (with the exception of the **ich** and **er/sie/es** forms, which have no ending other than **-te**). The endings are as follows: nothing, **-st**, nothing, **-n, -t, -n,** and **-n**.

Compare the present and the simple past of the verb **wohnen** (*to live*). The present form is in parentheses after the simple past.

wohnen (*to live*) — Simple Past (Present)	
ich wohn**te** (wohn**e**)	wir wohn**ten** (wohn**en**)
du wohn**test** (wohn**st**)	ihr wohn**tet** (wohn**t**)
er/sie/es wohn**te** (wohn**t**)	sie wir wohn**ten** (wohn**en**)
Sie wohn**ten** (wohn**en**)	
Ich **wohnte** in Dortmund. (*I lived in Dortmund.*)	

A second group of regular verbs are those with a stem ending in **-d** or **-t**. A small number of verbs with the stem ending in **-fn** or **-gn** also fall into this category. With these verbs, for the purpose of making them easier to pronounce, you put an additional **e** in front of the **-te** tense marker. Taking **arbeiten** (*to work*) as an example, you form the simple past like this: **ich arbeit + e + te = ich arbeitete.** Compare the present and the simple past.

arbeiten (*to work*) — Simple Past (Present)	
ich arbeit**ete** (arbeit**e**)	wir arbeit**eten** (arbeit**en**)
du arbeit**etest** (arbeit**est**)	ihr arbeit**etet** (arbeit**et**)
er/sie/es arbeit**ete** (arbeit**et**)	sie arbeit**eten** (arbeit**en**)
Sie arbeit**eten** (arbeit**en**)	
Du **arbeitetest** sehr schnell. (*You worked very fast.*)	

Try out your grasp of forming regular verbs in the simple past tense. In this exercise, you see one of the persons (**ich, du, er/sie/es, wir, ihr, sie,** or **Sie**) and the German infinitive form. Fill in the simple past form you need to fit the person indicated.

Q. er _____ arbeiten (*to work*)

A. er **arbeitete**

1. wir _____ (bezahlen)

2. ich _____ (brauchen)

3. es _____ (dauern)

4. Sie _____ (fotografieren)

5. du _____ (hören)

6. sie (*she*) _____ (kaufen)

7. es _____ (kosten)

8. sie (*they*) _____ (lachen)

9. ihr _____ (lernen)

10. ich _____ (machen)

11. Sie _____ (reden)

12. es _____ (regnen)

13. wir _____ (reisen)

14. ihr _____ (sagen)

15. du _____ (tanzen)

16. sie (*she*) _____ (spielen)

17. Sie _____ (wandern)

18. ich _____ (warten)

Forming irregular (strong) verbs in simple past

The group of verbs in this section is called *irregular* because unlike regular verbs, these verbs have a variety of vowel changes in the simple past form. The changes may simply be one vowel change, such as **i** to **a;** with the irregular verb **beginnen** (*to begin*), the simple past stem is **begann** (*began*). You need to memorize the simple past stem for each irregular verb in order to add the simple past endings to it. Fortunately, you encounter many of these verbs often, so you may already know the meaning and be familiar with the present tense form of a number of them.

To conjugate irregular verbs in the simple past, note the following:

✔ These verbs have no endings in **ich** and **er/sie/es** forms.

✔ The other endings, those for **du, wir, ihr, sie,** and **Sie,** are the same as the present tense endings. The endings are nothing, **-st,** nothing, **-en, -t, -en,** and **-en.**

beginnen (*to begin*)	
ich begann	wir begann**en**
du begann**st**	ihr begann**t**
er/sie/es begann	sie begann**en**
Sie begann**en**	
Er **begann** zu laufen. (*He began to run.*)	

Luckily for you, German has only a relatively small number of irregular (strong) verbs for you to worry about when conjugating the simple past tense.

These verbs are relatively easy because with many of them, you can draw on your knowledge of English irregular verbs to help you recognize the German cognates (words that are the same or very close in spelling and meaning in two languages). Table 17-2 lists verbs that are irregular in both English and German; they're cognates or at least verbs that begin with the same letter in English and German and mean nearly the same thing. A couple of verbs — **kommen** (*to come*) and **trinken** (*to drink*) — are different in spelling but quite similar in pronunciation. I give the **er/sie/es** form of the simple past because it doesn't have any endings.

Many irregular verbs are very common verbs, so you can familiarize yourself with them by *reading actively,* which involves thinking beyond the gist of the text. How? By slowing down your reading or by rereading a passage, you may notice how the verb stem is spelled differently from the present tense form. Try writing down the verbs as you come across them and figuring out the corresponding present tense, and then you can familiarize yourself with the various spelling changes in the simple past.

Table 17-2 Simple Past of Irregular Verbs Resembling English Verbs

Infinitive	Simple Past (er/sie/es Form)	Infinitive	Simple Past (er/sie/es Form)
beginnen (*to begin*)	**begann** (*began*)	**lassen** (*to let, allow*)	**ließ** (*let, allowed*)
essen (*to eat*)	**aß** (*ate*)	**liegen** (*to lie [down]*)	**lag** (*lay*)
fallen (*to fall*)	**fiel** (*fell*)	**reiten** (*to ride [a horse or bike]*)	**ritt** (*rode*)
finden (*to find*)	**fand** (*found*)	**schwimmen** (*to swim*)	**schwamm** (*swam*)
fliegen (*to fly*)	**flog** (*flew*)	**sehen** (*to see*)	**sah** (*saw*)
geben (*to give*)	**gab** (*gave*)	**singen** (*to sing*)	**sang** (*sang*)
gehen (*to go*)	**ging** (*went*)	**sitzen** (*to sit*)	**saß** (*sat*)
halten (*to hold, stop*)	**hielt** (*held, stopped*)	**sprechen** (*to speak*)	**sprach** (*spoke*)
kommen (*to come*)	**kam** (*came*)	**trinken** (*to drink*)	**trank** (*drank*)

Before starting this exercise, go over Table 17-2 until you feel confident that you know the verb forms shown and the English meaning. Ready? Now fill in the missing words in this exercise. Many verbs have more than one space to be filled in, including the English meaning. No fair peeking.

Infinitive/Meaning	*Simple Past (er/sie/es Form)*
0. beginnen (*to begin*)	_____
A. beginnen (*to begin*)	**begann**

19. essen (_____) _____

20. _____ (*to fall*) _____

21. _____ (*to find*) fand

22. fliegen (*to fly*) _____

23. geben (_____) _____

24. _____ (*to go*) ging

25. halten (_____) _____

26. kommen (*to come*) _____

27. _____ (*to let, allow*) _____

28. liegen (_____) _____

29. _____ (*to ride*) ritt

30. schwimmen (*to swim*) _____

Table 17-3 lists some irregular verbs that are irregular in both English and German, but they aren't cognates. What these verbs also have in common is that they're high-frequency verbs (verbs you encounter often in German). Try memorizing both the infinitive and simple past forms together.

Table 17-3	Simple Past of Common Irregular Verbs (Non-Cognates)		
Infinitive	*Simple Past (er/sie/es Form)*	*Infinitive*	*Simple Past (er/sie/es Form)*
fahren (*to drive*)	**fuhr** (*drove*)	**tragen** (*to wear, carry*)	**trug** (*wore, carried*)
fangen (*to catch*)	**fing** (*caught*)	**treffen** (*to meet*)	**traf** (*met*)
gewinnen (*to win*)	**gewann** (*won*)	**tun** (*to do*)	**tat** (*did*)
laufen (*to run*)	**lief** (*ran*)	**vergessen** (*to forget*)	**vergaß** (*forgot*)
lesen (*to read*)	**las** (*read*)	**verlieren** (*to lose*)	**verlor** (*lost*)
nehmen (*to take*)	**nahm** (*took*)	**verstehen** (*to understand*)	**verstand** (*understood*)
schneiden (*to cut*)	**schnitt** (*cut*)	**wachsen** (*to grow*)	**wuchs** (*grew*)
schreiben (*to write*)	**schrieb** (*wrote*)	**werden** (*to become*)	**wurde** (*became*)

At the same time you're saying each verb as a chant, demonstrate the action of the verb. For example, with **treffen** (*to meet*), outstretch your hand and pump it up and down as though you're shaking hands with the fireman who just got your kitten out of a tree.

In this exercise, you see the verbs from Table 17-3 with the simple past forms completely missing and around half of the English meanings left out. Try your memory, filling in the blanks without looking at the table.

Infinitive/Meaning	*Simple Past (er/sie/es Form)*
0. fahren (*to drive*)	_____
A. fahren (*to drive*)	**fuhr**
31. fangen (*to catch*)	_____
32. gewinnen (_____)	_____
33. laufen (*to run*)	_____
34. lesen (_____)	_____
35. nehmen (_____)	_____
36. schneiden (*to cut*)	_____
37. schreiben (_____)	_____
38. tragen (*to wear, carry*)	_____
39. treffen (*to meet*)	_____
40. tun (_____)	_____
41. vergessen (_____)	_____
42. verlieren (*to lose*)	_____
43. verstehen (_____)	_____
44. wachsen (*to grow*)	_____
45. werden (_____)	_____
46. werfen (*to throw*)	_____

Forming haben and sein in simple past

When conjugating the two verbs **haben** (*to have*) and **sein** (*to be*), you need to pay extra attention for two reasons:

- **Haben** and **sein** can function as auxiliary or helping verbs. Most verbs use the auxiliary verb **haben** to form the present perfect, but some irregular verbs use **sein**. (See Chapter 16 for more on the present perfect.)

- Although German speakers usually use the present perfect tense in conversations about the past (see Chapter 16), they use the simple past of **haben** and **sein** more frequently in conversation. (They also use the simple past of the modal verbs in conversation; check out the next section.)

You form the simple past of **haben** and **sein** with their respective stems **hatte** and **war.** Similar to the irregular (strong) verbs, the **ich** and **er/sie/es** forms have no verb endings. Look at the two conjugations, with the verb endings in bold.

haben (*to have*)	
ich hatte	wir hatt**en**
du hatt**est**	ihr hatt**et**
er/sie/es hatte	sie hatt**en**
Sie hatt**en**	
Ich **hatte** viel Zeit. (*I had a lot of time.*)	

sein (*to be*)	
ich war	wir war**en**
du war**st**	ihr war**t**
er/sie/es war	sie war**en**
Sie war**en**	
Sie **waren** zu Hause. (*They were at home.*)	

Last month, Helmut and Hannelore drove to Spain for **der Urlaub** (*the vacation*). Hannelore wrote a diary while they were traveling. Read her diary, written in present tense; then fill in in the missing verbs in the German simple past. Some sentences have strong and weak verbs, but the majority contain **sein** and **haben.**

den 11. August

Wir sind in Madrid — endlich! Das Wetter ist absolut wunderbar, und wir haben ein Zimmer in einem sehr schönen Hotel. Wir gehen zum Prado Museum. Am 12. August fahren wir nach Córdoba.

den 13. August

Ich habe viel Glück am 13.! Wir sind in einer billigen, aber netten Pension in Córdoba in der Nähe von der Mezquita (die Moschee im Zentrum). Sie ist sehr, sehr groß! In der Moschee ist es kühler als in der Sonne.

den 14. August

Wir fahren nach Sevilla, aber zuerst bin ich drei Stunden allein. Ich gehe einkaufen. Die Geschäfte sind sehr interessant. Ich suche nach Lederartikeln, aber der Preis für eine Lederjacke ist zu hoch für mich. Der Euro macht alles sehr teuer.

den 15. August

Das Wetter ist schrecklich. Es gibt viel Regen, es ist kühl, und Helmut hat Kopfweh. Wir sind den ganzen Tag in Cafés, essen spanische Spezialitäten, und trinken Rioja.

den 17. August

Der Regen ist zu viel! Helmut hat keine Lust, in Sevilla zu bleiben. Also wir fahren nach Málaga.

den 18. August

Es ist herrlich! In Málaga ist es sonnig und heiß! Ich gehe schwimmen, und Helmut hat eine deutsche Zeitung. Das Leben ist perfekt!

den 11. August

0. Wir _____ (sein) in Madrid — endlich!

A. Wir **waren** in Madrid — endlich! (*We were in Madrid — at last!*)

47. Das Wetter _____ (sein) absolut wunderbar . . .

48. . . . und wir _____ (haben) ein Zimmer in einem sehr schönen Hotel.

49. Am 12. August _____ (fahren) wir nach Córdoba.

den 13. August

50. Wir _____ (sein) in einer billigen, aber netten Pension in Córdoba in der Nähe von der Mezquita (eine Moschee).

51. Sie _____ (sein) sehr, sehr groß!

den 14. August

52. Wir _____ (fahren) nach Sevilla.

den 15. August

53 Das Wetter _____ (sein) schrecklich.

54. Wir _____ (sein) den ganzen Tag in Cafés.

den 17. August

55. Der Regen _____ (sein) zu viel! Helmut _____ (haben) keine Lust, in Sevilla zu bleiben.

56. Also,wir _____ (fahren) nach Málaga.

den 18. August

57. Es _____ (sein) herrlich! In Málaga _____ (sein) es sonnig und heiß!

58. Das Leben _____ (sein) perfekt!

Forming modals in simple past

The modal verbs are the small band of modifying or helping type verbs. (See Chapter 9 for in-depth treatment of the modal verbs.) These verbs modify another verb, although sometimes they can stand alone. The list includes **dürfen** (*to be allowed to*), **können** (*can, to be able to*), **mögen** (*to like*), **müssen** (*to have to, must*), **sollen** (*to be supposed to, should*), and **wollen** (*to want to*). **Note:** Although **möchten** is included in this elite group in the present tense, it falls by the wayside because of its meaning (*would like to*) and joins forces with **mögen** in the simple past tense. Both have the meaning *liked to* in the simple past.

German speakers prefer to use the modal verbs in the simple past form when conversing or telling stories. The modal verbs are reasonably easy to remember in the simple past form because they follow the same criteria:

✔ The past stem changes have no umlaut.

✔ You add the **-te** stem marker onto the simple past stem. The additional endings are as follows: nothing, **-st**, nothing, **-n**, **-t**, **-n**, and **-n**.

Look at Table 17-4, which shows modal verbs in the simple past tense.

Table 17-4		Modal Verbs in Simple Past Tense		
Infinitive	**Past Stem**	**Tense Marker**	**Simple Past (ich, er/sie/es Form)**	**English Equivalent of Simple Past**
dürfen	**durf-**	**-te**	**durfte**	*was allowed to*
können	**konn-**	**-te**	**konnte**	*was able to, could (past-tense meaning)*
mögen	**moch**	**-te**	**mochte**	*liked*
müssen	**muss-**	**-te**	**musste**	*had to*

Infinitive	Past Stem	Tense Marker	Simple Past (ich, er/sie/es Form)	English Equivalent of Simple Past
sollen	**soll-**	**-te**	**sollte**	*was supposed to*
wollen	**woll-**	**-te**	**wollte**	*wanted to*

The following verb table shows the verb **können** conjugated, with the endings in bold, including the **-te** tense marker.

können (*to be able to, can*)	
ich konn**te**	wir konn**ten**
du konn**test**	ihr konn**tet**
er/sie/es konn**te**	sie konn**ten**
Sie konn**ten**	
Nach dem Skiurlaub **konnte** ich besser skifahren. (*I was able to ski better after the skiing vacation.*)	

In the following exercise, some people are talking about a party they went to last week. A lot of things went differently than planned; in fact, it was a comedy of errors. Refer to Table 17-4 and the preceding verb table. Write the correct form of the verb in parentheses.

Q. Wir _____ nur einen halben Kuchen mitbringen. (können)

A. Wir **konnten** nur einen halben Kuchen mitbringen. (können) (*We were able to bring only half a cake.*)

59. Helena _____ früh nach Hause gehen. (müssen)

60. _____ du nicht mit deinem Cousin kommen? (wollen)

61. Marlene und Dieter _____ einen Salat machen. (sollen)

62. Ich _____ den Schweinebraten überhaupt nicht. (mögen)

63. Michael _____ seinen Hund nicht mitbringen. (dürfen)

Contrasting Tenses

In addition to the simple past (**Ich sah** einen rosaroten Elefant — *I saw a pink elephant*), two other verb tenses belong to the past tense club:

- The present perfect: **Ich habe** einen rosaroten Elefant **gesehen.** (*I have seen a pink elephant.*)

- The past perfect: **Ich hatte** einen rosaroten Elefant **gesehen.** (*I had seen a pink elephant.*)

This trio is the mainstay for describing events in the past, in both English and German. However, you can often get away with using the present perfect or even the simple past in describing events that may actually call for the past perfect. In addition, the past perfect isn't used very frequently in either German or English, so it takes a back seat — and that's a good way to remember when it's used: namely to describe events that happened way back before another past event. (Chapter 16 deals in depth with present perfect.)

The past perfect may not be very common, but before relegating the past perfect elephant to oblivion, I want to contrast three past tense verb forms: the simple past, present perfect, and past perfect. Look at Table 17-4. You see how to form these past tenses, their applications (uses), and an example situation.

Table 17-4	German Usage of Past Tenses		
Past Tense	*How to Form*	*Use*	*Example Sentence/Explanation*
Simple past (narrative past)	Use the simple past form of the verb	Used in formal, written language; preferred in spoken language in northern Germany; used with **haben, sein,** and modal verbs	Der Orkan **dauerte** insgesamt zwei Wochen. (*The hurricane lasted two weeks altogether.*) **Dauerte** is the simple past, third-person singular of **dauern** (*to last*).
Present perfect (conversational past)	Combine the present tense of either **haben** or **sein** and a past participle of the verb	Used in casual, informal, spoken language when talking about the past; preferred in southern German-speaking regions	Gestern **haben** wir einen guten Film **gesehen.** (*Yesterday we saw a good movie.*) **Haben** is the present tense, first-person plural of **haben; gesehen** is the past participle of **sehen** (*to see*).
Past perfect	Combine the simple past of either **haben** or **sein** and a past participle of the verb	Used to describe a past event that happened before another past event, often with the two verbs in the same sentence	Nachdem sie das Telefon **aufgelegt hatte,** klingelte es nochmals. (*After she had hung up the phone, it rang again.*) **Hatte** is the simple past tense, third-person singular of **haben,** and **aufgelegt** is the past participle of **auflegen** (*to hang up*).

Answer Key

1 bezahlen (*to pay*)   wir **bezahlten**

2 brauchen (*to need*)   ich **brauchte**

3 dauern (*to last, take [time]*)   es **dauerte**

4 fotografieren (*to take pictures*)   Sie **fotografierten**

5 hören (*to hear, listen to*)   du **hörtest**

6 kaufen (*to buy*)   sie (she) **kaufte**

7 kosten (*to cost*)   es **kostete**

8 lachen (*to laugh*)   sie (they) **lachten**

9 lernen (*to learn*)   ihr **lerntet**

10 machen (*to do, make*)   ich **machte**

11 reden (*to talk, speak*)   Sie **redeten**

12 regnen (*to rain*)   es **regnete**

13 reisen (*to travel*)   wir **reisten**

14 sagen (*to say*)   ihr **sagtet**

15 tanzen (*to dance*)   du **tanztest**

16 spielen (*to play [a game, cards]*)   sie (she) **spielte**

17 wandern (*to hike, wander*)   Sie **wanderten**

18 warten (*to wait*)   ich **wartete**

19 essen **(*to eat*)**   **aß**

20 **fallen** (*to fall*)   **fiel**

21 **finden** (*to find*)   fand

22 fliegen (*to fly*)   **flog**

23 geben **(*to give*)**   **gab**

24 **gehen** (*to go*)   ging

25 halten **(*to hold, stop*)**   **hielt**

26 kommen (*to come*)   **kam**

27 **lassen** (*to let, allow*)   **ließ**

28 liegen (*to lie [down]*)   **lag**

29 **reiten** (*to ride [a horse or bike]*)   ritt

30 schwimmen (*to swim*)   **schwamm**

31 fangen (*to catch*)   **fing**

32 gewinnen (*to win*)   **gewann**

33 laufen (*to run*)   **lief**

34 lesen (*to read*)   **las**

35 nehmen (*to take*)   **nahm**

36 schneiden (*to cut*)   **schnitt**

37 schreiben (*to write*)   **schrieb**

38 tragen (*to wear, carry*)   **trug**

39 treffen (*to meet*)   **traf**

40 tun (*to do*)   **tat**

41 vergessen (*to forget*)   **vergaß**

42 verlieren (*to lose*)   **verlor**

43 verstehen (*to understand*)   **verstand**

44 wachsen (*to grow*)   **wuchs**

45 werden (*to become*)   **wurde**

46 werfen (*to throw*)   **warf**

47 Das Wetter **war** absolut wunderbar . . . (*The weather was absolutely wonderful . . .*)

48 . . . und wir **hatten** ein Zimmer in einem sehr schönen Hotel. (*. . . and we had a room in a very pretty hotel.*)

49 Am 12. August **fuhren** wir nach Córdoba. (*On the 12th of August we drove to Córdoba.*)

50 Wir **waren** in einer billigen, aber netten Pension in Córdoba in der Nähe von der Mezquita, eine Moschee. (*We were in an inexpensive but nice pension in Córdoba, near the Mezquita, a mosque.*) A **pension** is similar to a bed and breakfast.

51 Sie **war** sehr, sehr groß! (*It was very, very big!*)

52 Wir **fuhren** nach Sevilla, (*We drove to Sevilla.*)

53 Das Wetter **war** schrecklich. (*The weather was awful [terrible].*)

54 Wir **waren** den ganzen Tag in Cafés . . . (*We were in cafés the whole day . . .*)

55 Der Regen **war** zu viel! Helmut **hatte** keine Lust, in Sevilla zu bleiben. (*The rain was too much! Helmut didn't feel like staying in Sevilla.*)

56 Also wir **fuhren** nach Málaga. (*So we drove to Málaga.*)

57 Es **war** herrlich! In Málaga **war** es sonnig und heiß! (*It was marvelous! It was sunny and hot in Málaga.*)

58 Das Leben **war** perfekt! (*Life was perfect!*)

59 Helena **musste** früh nach Hause gehen. (*Helena had to go home early.*)

60 **Wolltest** du nicht mit deinem Cousin kommen? (*Didn't you want to come with your cousin?*)

61 Marlene und Dieter **sollten** einen Salat machen. (*Marlene and Dieter were supposed to make a salad.*)

62 Ich **mochte** den Schweinebraten überhaupt nicht. (*I didn't like the roast pork at all.*)

63 Michael **durfte** seinen Hund nicht mitbringen. (*Michael wasn't allowed to bring his dog along.*)

Chapter 18

Looking to the Future (and Avoiding It)

....

In This Chapter

▶ Avoiding the future

▶ Facing the future

....

*W*hether you're the type to face the future head on, no holds barred, or you like to avoid the inevitable at all costs, this chapter has something for you. With all the complications of case endings and the three noun genders in German, at last the future pops up, simple and straightforward.

When you read the chapter title, unless you've been dusting off (and reading) English grammar books lately, you're likely to say that the future is one verb tense, the one associated with *will* + a verb (*I'll get the phone*). Actually, English has several ways to express the future, although in German you're on easy street. Why? In a great deal of situations, you can avoid using the future tense altogether even while describing a future event. In fact, German uses the future verb tenses far less frequently than English does.

Before you travel into the future, though, the first stop is the German present tense. In the beginning of this chapter, you find out how versatile the German present tense is for situations in which English uses various future tenses. Later in the chapter, you jump on the future bus and take a short and smooth ride through the future, looking at how to form it and when to use the future tense. I also include the most frequently used time expressions associated with the future, as well as a short list of adverbs that typically combine with the future tense to express your attitude about a future event.

The Future Is Now: Using the Present Tense Instead

In general, you don't need to use the future in German when the context makes it clear that the action is describing something in future time. Imagine you're standing on the subway platform, and the train is coming into the station at Marienplatz in Munich. You have six bags and a broken arm, and someone behind you says **Ich helfe Ihnen** (Literally: *I help you*). In English, your helper would say *I'll help you*. This German volunteer is not grammar-deficient; he or she is an angel speaking perfectly idiomatic German.

English has a total of four ways to express the future, as opposed to only two future tenses in German. In addition, the future tense usage in German is far less frequent than it is in English. Look at the following breakdown of how German and English express the future:

- First is the present tense used for schedules, like travel plans. This is the same in German: **Die Maschine startet um 7.40 Uhr** (*The plane leaves at 7:40 a.m.*).

- Next is the *going to* future, *going to* + infinitive verb, as in *We're going to visit my cousins this weekend*, which doesn't exist in German. You usually use the German present.

- English also uses the *present continuous* — *to be* + verb with *-ing* ending, as in *I'm taking the dog for a walk* — which is nonexistent in German; you can generally use the present in German for these situations.

- That leaves the *will* future verb form, which is equivalent to the German **werden** (*will*) + *infinitive verb* used to express the future. The usage is less frequent in German because the present tense can punt for the *will* future in a great deal of cases. (Check out the last section in this chapter for more on using **werden** to express the future.)

This section more closely examines how German uses the present to express future actions.

Seeing when German present works perfectly

In English, you encounter all types of situations that require the future tense. But in German, you can state those same situations by simply using the present tense, especially when it's clear that you intend to express future time. (Chapter 5 deals solely with the present tense if you need a refresher.)

The following examples give you an overview of the range of situations where German uses the present to express the future. However, in English, you generally use the future when you include an expression that refers to the future, such as *next week*.

Vielleicht ruft er morgen an. (*Maybe he'll call tomorrow.*) **Morgen** (*tomorrow*) is an adverb of time that expresses the future.

Dieses Wochenende besuchen wir meine Kusinen. (*We're going to visit my cousins this weekend.*) **Dieses Wochenende** (*this weekend*) refers to the coming weekend; also, German has no equivalent to the English verb form *going to* + verb.

Ich bleibe heute etwas länger im Büro. (*I'm staying a bit longer in the office today.*) The reference to **heute** (*today*) in connection with **länger** (*longer*) indicates later on today; also, German has no *-ing* verb equivalent.

Ich glaube/Ich denke, ich bleibe zu Hause. (*I think I'll stay home.*) German uses present tense here, but English expresses a spontaneous decision (*I think I'll . . .*) with the future.

Ich vergesse nicht/Ich werde nicht vergessen. (*I won't forget.*) In English, you use the future for a promise. (If you say *I don't forget,* it's a factual statement, not a promise.) In German, you have both options to make a promise.

Saying when: Using future time expressions with the present tense

When you talk about future events in English, you often include an expression of future time together with one of the future verb forms. Germans also use a wide range of future time expressions such as **heute Abend** (*this evening*) or **morgen früh** (*tomorrow morning*). Here's good news for you: They frequently appear in combination with the present tense.

Take a look at some common time expressions:

- **am Anfang der Woche** (*at the beginning of the week*)
- **am Dienstag** (*on Tuesday*)
- **diese Woche** (*this week*)
- **diesen Monat** (*this month*)
- **dieses Wochenende** (*this weekend*)
- **heute** (*today*)
- **heute Abend** (*this evening*)
- **heute Morgen** (*this morning*)
- **im Frühling** (*in the spring*)
- **in vier Monaten** (*in four months*)
- **in vier Stunden** (*in four hours*)
- **morgen** (*tomorrow*)
- **morgen früh** (*tomorrow morning*)
- **morgen Nachmittag** (*tomorrow afternoon*)
- **nächsten Dienstag** (*next Tuesday*)
- **nächste Woche** (*next week*)
- **übermorgen** (*the day after tomorrow*)

You can express future events in German by simply using a future time expression together with a verb in the present tense — for example, **Ich fliege nächste Woche nach Frankfurt** (*I'm flying to Frankfurt next week*).

German word order is typically *time*, *manner*, and *place*. Look at the breakdown of the word order for a typical sentence:

1. Subject + active verb: **Ich fahre** (*I'm traveling*)
2. Time (when): **morgen Nachmittag** (*tomorrow afternoon*)
3. Manner (how): **mit dem Zug** (*by train*)
4. Place (where): **nach Hamburg** (*to Hamburg*)

Putting it all together, the sentence looks like this: **Ich fahre morgen Nachmittag mit dem Zug nach Hamburg** (*I'm taking the train to Hamburg tomorrow afternoon*).

When you're forming a sentence that has an expression of time such as **am Mittwoch** (*on Wednesday*) or **morgen** (*tomorrow*), as well as an expression of manner and/or place, you may want to be very clear about *when* something is happening. In this case, simply place the time expression at the very beginning of the sentence, followed by the verb and subject. Putting the time expression at the very front of a sentence may also be easier if you have trouble remembering the correct word order for the trio of time, manner, and place. That way, you've taken care of the time, and you have to remember only that manner is before place.

The following example sentences show when various activities take place. All four sentences are in present in German, but they express the future four different ways in English. You may have more than one future-tense alternative for translating the sentences into English, but all are in present tense in German:

> **Ich fliege am Dienstag nach Graz**. (*I'm flying to Graz on Tuesday.*)

> **Ich denke, ich arbeite dieses Wochenende zu Hause.** (*I think I'll work at home this weekend.*)

> **Übermorgen habe ich einen Termin mit einem neuen Kunden.** (*The day after tomorrow I have an appointment with a new customer.*) **Der Kunde** means *the customer*. **Übermorgen** is at the beginning, so the verb comes in second position, followed by the subject.

> **Heute Abend telefoniere ich mit dem chinesischen Lieferanten.** (*This evening I'm going to call the Chinese supplier.*) **Der Lieferant** means *the supplier*. The time element **heute Abend** is first, so the verb follows in second position, followed by the subject.

You work at an international company. Your German boss, Herr Fleischmann, calls you on Monday morning and wants to know your plans for the next three weeks. Using the calendar and some future time expressions, describe what you're doing on the days you've made notes of your activities. Try expressions other than dates (such as **am 20. Oktober**) whenever possible. Note that some questions cover more than one day.

Here's some useful vocabulary: **der Termin** (*the appointment*), **der Abgabetermin** (*the deadline*), **das Meeting** (*the meeting*), and **die Telekonferenz** (*the conference call*).

Note: German calendars begin the week with **Montag** (*Monday*).

Montag	Dienstag	Mittwoch	Donnerstag	Freitag	Samstag	Sonntag
Q. im Büro arbeiten 1. nach Köln fliegen (Abend)	2. in Köln ankommen (früh!) 3. 2 Termine mit Kunden (Nachmittag) 4. Abend: mit dem Kollegen essen (Hotel-Restaurant)	5. nach Düsseldorf zur Messe (trade fair) fahren 6. nach Hause fliegen	7. Telekonferenz mit Herrn Fleischmann & Kollegen	8. Fleischmann den vollen Bericht e-mailen (Nachmittag)	9. bei der Familie	9. bei der Familie
10. Urlaub (vacation)	10. Urlaub	10. Urlaub	10. Urlaub	10. Urlaub	Halloween	Allerheiligen (All Saints Day)
11. mit dem osterreichischen Lieferanten telefonieren			12. Nov. 6: wichtiger Abgabetermin!			

Q. Montag (Monday): im Büro arbeiten

A. **Ich arbeite heute Morgen im Büro.** (*I'm working in the office this morning.*) You can use this standard word order or start with the time element if you find it easier: **Heute Morgen arbeite ich im Büro.** In the Answer Key, I use the standard word order.

1. _____

2. _____

3. _____

4. _____

5. _____

6. _____

7. _____

8. _____

9. _____

10. _____

11. _____

12. _____

Facing the Future with Werden

Sometimes you need to use the future tense in German. German speakers do indeed use the future to describe future events, either with or without a reference to time like **nächstes Jahr** (*next year*), although speakers of German prefer the present tense when they're using a time expression in the same sentence.

When you make no specific mention of when something will happen, you generally use **werden** to express the future. This section shows you how to conjugate the future tense and how to use it correctly in different circumstances.

Forming the future: Werden + infinitive verb

To form the future tense, you conjugate the auxiliary (helping) verb **werden** and add the infinitive form of the verb that you want to express in the future tense: **Ich werde bald nach Hause gehen** (*I'm going home soon*). In this context, **werden** means *going to* or *will*. Notice that the infinitive form, **gehen,** is at the end of the sentence.

werde gehen (*will go, going to go*)	
ich **werde** gehen	wir **werden** gehen
du **wirst** gehen	ihr **werdet** gehen
er/sie/es **wird** gehen	sie **werden** gehen
Sie **werden** gehen	
Ich **werde** bald nach Hause gehen. (*I'm going [to go] home soon.*)	

Werden is a sneaky verb. It has several meanings. In this section, it means *will* or *going to*. However, when **werden** is the main verb, it means *to become* or *get:* **Wir werden immer älter** (*We're always becoming/getting older*).

When some people see **will** in German, they equate it with **werden.** Watch out — *will* indicates the future only in English:

Ich will nach Hause gehen. (*I want to go home.*) **Will** comes from **wollen:** *to want to.* It's a modal verb, which means it modifies the main verb. (For more on modal verbs, see Chapter 9.)

Ich werde nach Hause gehen. (*I will go/am going home.*)

Using the future: Assuming, hoping, and emphasizing intentions

German speakers use the future tense with **werden** in several different situations to express future action. Table 18-1 shows future tense usage, an example sentence in German, and the English equivalent. Notice that the infinitive verb is at the end of the sentence.

Table 18-1	Future Using Werden	
Usage of Future Tense	*German Example Sentence*	*English Equivalent*
Emphasizing intention that an event will take place in the future	Ich **werde** ein erholsames Wochenende zu Hause **verbringen.**	*I'm going to have a restful weekend at home.*
Supposing, assuming, or hoping something will happen, expressed verbally	Ich hoffe, sie **wird** nicht **vergessen.**	*I hope she won't forget.*
Supposing, assuming, or hoping something will happen, expressed with an adverb	Sie **wird** wohl nicht **vergessen.**	*She probably won't forget.*
Giving strong advice or a stern warning	Du **wirst** jetzt ruhig **sein!**	*Be quiet!/You will be quiet!*
Indicating an event will happen after another event stated in the present tense	Joachim studiert sehr fleißig, und er **wird** später ein erfolgreicher Arzt **sein.**	*Joachim is studying very hard, and later he'll be a successful doctor.*

Just as German speakers use the **werden** future to emphasize that something will happen in the future, they also use it to say that something will *not* happen. The two alternatives are **werden** + **nicht** (*will not/won't*) and **werden** + **kein** (*will not/won't*), depending on what you're negating.

Here are clear differences in the usage of **kein** and **nicht** (for further details on **kein** and **nicht,** go to Chapter 7):

✔ **Kein** negates a noun, as in **keine Zeit** (*no time*). It has case and gender endings.

> **Meine Freunde werden kein Geburtstagsfest für mich organisieren.** (*My friends aren't going to organize a birthday party for me.*) **Kein** negates **Geburtstagsfest;** it replaces **ein. Kein** is in the accusative case.

✔ **Nicht** generally negates a verb: **nicht gehen** (*to not go*). It can also negate an adjective, like **nicht lustig** (*not funny*), or an adverb, like **nicht pünktlich** (*not on time*). **Nicht** has no case or gender endings.

> **Ich werde nicht hier bleiben.** (*I won't stay here.*) **Nicht** negates the information **hier bleiben.**

In the following exercise, respond to each prompt by writing a sentence saying that the events will or won't happen. To help you know whether to use **kein** or **nicht,** I underline the word or expression that you negate.

Q. <u>reich</u> sein, wenn ich 70 Jahre alt bin. Ich _____

A. Ich **werde nicht** reich **sein,** wenn ich 70 Jahre alt bin. (*I won't be rich when I'm 70 years old.*) **Reich** is an adjective, so you need to use **nicht.** To express the same information in a positive sentence, leave out **nicht.**

13. <u>ein Haus</u> bauen

    Ich _____

14. in die Politik <u>gehen</u>

    Ich _____

15. mit meiner Familie nach Tehachapi <u>umziehen</u>

    Ich _____

16. <u>reisen</u>, wenn ich Zeit und Geld dazu habe

    Ich _____

17. <u>Adoptivkinder</u> haben

    Ich _____

Using the future to express probability

When you aren't absolutely sure something will or won't happen in the future, you use expressions to describe probability. You may be confident that your favorite team will win a game, but you're not 100 percent certain, so you include words that express high probability together with the future tense. Here are some common expressions:

- ✔ **wohl** (*probably, no doubt, to be sure*): **Wohl** expresses very high probability.

- ✔ **sicher** (*probably, definitely, certainly*): **Sicher** expresses very high probability.

- ✔ **schon** (*probably*): This elusive word can also mean *already* or *yet* or emphasize that you're aware of an event or a fact.

Check out some examples:

> **Die Haffenreffers werden wohl eine neue Garage bauen**. (*The Haffenreffers are probably going to build a new garage.*)

> **Leander Haffenreffer wird sicher ein neues Auto kaufen**. (*Leander Haffenreffer will probably buy a new car.*)

> **Der Nachbar der Haffenreffers wird schon ein riesengroßes Schwimmbecken bauen**. (*The Haffenreffers' neighbor is probably going to build a gigantic swimming pool.*)

Your task in this exercise is twofold. First, arrange the words to make a logical sentence in the correct word order. Second, change the infinitive verb (for example, **machen**) into the correct future form (**ich werde machen, du wirst machen,** and so on).

0. spielen / Monopoly / bis Mitternacht / wir /wohl

A. **Wir werden wohl Monopoly bis Mitternacht spielen.** (*We're probably going to play Monopoly until midnight.*)

18. zu viel / Gerhard Grossmann / Am Freitag Abend / trinken / Bier

_____

19. nicht böse / sein / Frau Grossmann / Ich hoffe,

_____

20. still / ganz / sein! / jetzt / Sie

_____

21. machen / Mit einer Zigarre im Mund / keine Freunde / du / sicher

_____

22. schon / Ihr / Poker / noch zwei Stunden / spielen / mit mir

_____

23. gewinnen / alles / Heute Abend / ich

_____

Answer Key

1 **Ich fliege heute Abend nach Köln.** (*I'm going to fly/I'm flying to Cologne this evening.*)

2 **Ich komme morgen früh/am Dienstag früh in Köln an.** (*I'll arrive in Cologne tomorrow morning/on Tuesday morning.*)

3 **Ich habe morgen Nachmittag/am Dienstagnachmittag zwei Termine mit Kunden.** (*I have two appointments with customers tomorrow afternoon/on Tuesday afternoon.*)

4 **Ich esse morgen Abend/am Dienstagabend mit dem Kollegen im Hotel-Restaurant.** (*I'm having dinner with the colleague in the hotel restaurant tomorrow evening/on Tuesday evening.*)

5 **Ich fahre übermorgen/am Mittwoch nach Düsseldorf zur Messe.** (*I'm going to the trade fair in Düsseldorf the day after tomorrow/on Wednesday.*)

6 Ich fliege **übermorgen/am Mittwoch nach Hause.** (*I'm flying home the day after tomorrow/on Wednesday.*)

7 **Ich habe am Donnerstag eine Telekonferenz mit Herrn Fleischmann und seinen Kollegen.** (*I have a conference call with Herr Fleischmann and his colleagues on Thursday.*)

8 **Ich e-maile Ihnen am Freitag Nachmittag den vollen Bericht.** (*I'll e-mail you the whole report on Friday afternoon.*)

9 **Ich bin dieses Wochenende/am Wochenende bei meiner Familie.** (*I'll be with my family this weekend/on the weekend.*)

10 **Ich habe nächste Woche Urlaub.** (*I'll be/I'm going on vacation next week.*)

11 **Ich telefoniere am Anfang der ersten Woche im November mit dem österreichischen Lieferanten.** (*At the beginning of the first week of November, I'll call the Austrian supplier.*) In German, you telephone **mit** (*with*) someone.

12 **Ich habe am 6. November einen wichtigen Abgabetermin.** (*I have an important deadline on November 6.*)

13 Ich **werde kein** Haus **bauen** / Ich **werde** ein Haus **bauen.** (*I won't/will build a house.*)

14 Ich **werde nicht** in die Politik **gehen.** / Ich **werde** in die Politik **gehen.** (*I won't/will go into politics.*)

15 Ich **werde nicht** mit meiner Familie nicht nach Tehachapi **umziehen.** / Ich **werde** mit meiner Familie nach Tehachapi **umziehen.** (*I won't/will move to Tehachapi with my family.*)

16 Ich **werde nicht reisen,** wenn ich genug Zeit und Geld habe. / Ich **werde reisen,** wenn ich genug Zeit und Geld habe. (*I won't/will travel when I have enough money.*)

17 Ich **werde keine** Adoptivkinder **haben.** / Ich **werde** Adoptivkinder/ein Adoptivkind **haben.** (*I won't/will have [any] adopted children.*)

18 **Am Freitag Abend wird Gerhard Grossmann zu viel Bier trinken.** (*Gerhard Grossmann will drink too much beer on Friday evening.*)

19 **Ich hoffe, Frau Grossmann wird nicht böse sein.** (*I hope Mrs. Grossmann won't be angry.*)

20 **Sie werden jetzt ganz still sein!** (*Be absolutely quiet now!*)

21 **Mit einer Zigarre im Mund wirst du sicher keine Freunde machen.** (*You certainly won't make any friends with a cigar in your mouth.*)

22 **Ihr werdet schon noch zwei Stunden Poker mit mir spielen.** (*For sure you'll play another two hours of poker with me.*)

23 **Heute Abend werde ich alles gewinnen.** (*I'll win everything tonight.*)

Part V
The Part of Tens

The 5th Wave   By Rich Tennant

"Here's something. It's a language school that will teach you to speak German for $500, or for $200 they'll just give you an accent."

In this part . . .

The Part of Tens is one of the most beloved parts of every *For Dummies* book, and this time around, it includes two information-packed chapters. In Chapter 19, I list ten ways to optimize your German. Then comes Chapter 20, in which I counsel you on how to avoid ten major traps that lie along the path of your language endeavors.

Chapter 19

Ten Tips for Optimizing Your German

In This Chapter

▶ Taking your German to the next level

▶ Getting a firm grasp on grammar and vocabulary

Studying a new language can seem daunting at times. You ask what you've gotten yourself into with all those cases, genders, moods, and tenses. No worries, though. In this chapter, I show you ten essential means of optimizing your German. Each tip contains practical guidelines on how to rapidly improve your command of the language. These tips offer you an edge only when you follow through on them. Try some, or try them all; I know you'll reap the benefits.

Think Like a Native Speaker

What happens when you speak or write in your own language? The language flows out of your mouth or onto the page. Now think about what's going on in your mind when you start formulating a sentence in German. It's slower, for one, and it's a piece-meal process. You're concerned about whether the noun is **der, die,** or **das;** you're juggling cases in your mind, and you're mapping out the word order.

In order to overcome all these time-consuming steps, do your level best to think like a native speaker. Here's how:

- ✔ Start thinking in chunks of language. In other words, use the structures that you already know in German and apply them. Every language is filled with frequently used expressions, such as **Viel Spaß!** (*Have fun!*) and **das gefällt mir [nicht]** (*I like/don't like that*). Some language comes in frequently used phrases, like **zum Beispiel** (*for example*) and **mehr oder weniger** (*more or less*).

- ✔ Look for compound words, such as **Umweltverschmutzung** (*environmental pollution*).

- ✔ Get comfortable with flavoring particles and verbal nods of agreement or disagreement: **Wirklich?** (*Really?*), **genau/eben** (*exactly*), and **doch** (verbal nod of disagreement).

- ✔ Become confident using prepositional phrases, such as **bei mir zu Hause** (*at my home*) and subject-verb combinations, such as **ich möchte gern wissen** (*I'd like to know*).

Such expressions are already set up for you; no need to reinvent the wheel by painstakingly translating standard expressions word for word. Just dip into that reservoir.

Break Down Word Combinations

Although at first glance, a German text may seem to be filled with long, complicated words, go for the jugular: Break down those torturously long words and figure out what each part means. Even short words may have two or more parts.

Verbs are the premier culprits in this department. Take the verb **vorhaben;** it looks like the preposition **vor** (*in front of*) combined with **haben** (*to have*). In English, it means *to plan something.* When you think about the literal meaning — *to have something in front* — you can often grasp the figurative meaning as well.

Use What You Know

If German is a mostly purebred language, English is a crafty mutt. Incorporated into English usage are elements of Latin, Greek, German, French, and even Danish. Why not dip into English, and use it in German? German hasn't been averse to using many words that English has borrowed. Both English and German have acquisitions from Native American languages (**Moccasin**), Spanish (**Patio**), Italian (**Ciao**), and so on. *Cognates* — words that share the same ancestor — include the chunk of Germanic-type words known to you in English but with some spelling differences. Be aware of changes such as converting the **v** to *f* (as in **Vater** = *father*) or changing the **d** to *th* (as in **Bad** = *bath*).

Check that a word that *looks* like English actually has the same meaning in German. After all, **der Mist** isn't a thick fog/fine rain; it actually means *dung* in German!

Get Going on Grammar

After you dive into the Grand World of German Grammar, take it slow and easy. Don't panic. There's actually a whole lot of logic in German grammar. As you tread your way through, remember that the following are important parts of German grammar:

- ✔ **Word order:** After you accept the rules of the game, you're all set to cut and paste the words you need to construct a grammatically decent sentence. Check out Chapter 1 for general info on word order.

- ✔ **Case and gender:** You definitely need to know and accept these elements and not fight them. Try to master the ins and outs of one grammar aspect step by step. Consider a two-way preposition like **in (ich gehe ins Hotel** versus **Ich bin im Hotel),** which can be *I'm going in(to) the hotel* (movement) or *I'm in the hotel* (location); then write down some examples you can use that show the difference between the two. Store them in a safe place, and consult them when the going gets tough and you're trying to decide whether to use **im** or **ins.** (For more on prepositions, see Chapter 15.)

Read and Listen Actively

While you're reading or even listening to German, actively think about the grammar and word order. For instance, a word in context may show its gender. As for verbs, notice the location of the verb parts in a sentence. For vocabulary acquisition, try low-brow alternatives such as flashcards or highbrow gadgets like an electronic translator with audio feature. Check out listening material for your car. Watch a German movie.

One of the best ways to improve your German is to take advantage of all the German available to you on the Web. The number of German Web sites is astounding — just look for pages using the **.de** option of your browser (in place of *.com* or other extensions). You can access German newspapers and other German educational sites.

Experiment with What Works Best

If there were ever an easy path to language fluency, the discoverer would make a million. Even so, no two people acquire a language in exactly the same way. You may not be the kind of person who learns to ski by going straight down the steepest slope the first day. You may need some gentle pointers about turning, braking, and knowing how to fall somewhat safely. Make it your mission to figure out what works best for you.

Mentally leaf through the list of any skills you've acquired successfully, even if they're unrelated to language, from tying your shoes to taking apart a car engine. Ask yourself how you did it. You may be the show-me-how-type, the trial-and-error type, or a blend of both. Now try experimenting. Get a dialogue, a text, or anything you want to use later. Try these three methods of gaining fluency and see which works best:

- ✔ **Seeing:** Draw sketches of significant German words. Don't stop at the obvious, such as nouns like **der Baum,** illustrated by a picture of a tree. Draw adjectives that describe emotions (for **unglücklich,** draw an *unhappy* face); indicate a verb such as **wandern** (*to hike*) with a stick figure walking up a mountain (don't forget the **Rucksack!**).

- ✔ **Speaking and hearing:** Practice reading the material to yourself; then record your own voice, listen, and record again until you're reasonably satisfied with your results. Or read in a low voice using a metronome or slow music for rhythm. Also, try singing some German songs.

- ✔ **Doing:** Try reading out loud and walking slowly around your living room (but don't stumble over the dog). As you read through verbs, act out the motions. For **bezahlen** (*to pay*), take an imaginary credit card out of your pocket.

Find what works and implement that technique for improving your German. Go ahead. Be a risk taker! You've got plenty to gain from experimenting — drug free!

Germanify Your Home

To get a firm understanding of German, why not Germanify your home? Whatever you do is bound to pay off down the line. Here are some ideas:

- Make sticky labels for furniture, appliances, objects, or even food items. Concentrate on one room at a time, touching the objects and saying the names out loud.

- Describe daily chores and routines to yourself as you're doing them. Write useful German phrases on a piece of paper and stick it on your bathroom mirror. Repeat the words while brushing your teeth (well, maybe while brushing your hair). Write shopping lists in German, and as you read the ads, mumble the prices to yourself in German, too.

- Write dialogue exchanges on index cards — the question on the front and the answer on the back. Put a stack on your dresser and challenge yourself while you get dressed.

Integrate German into Your Routine

Face it. When you're serious about getting ahead with your German, you need time. But who actually has oodles of leftover hours each day? Try figuring out how to snatch some minutes from your regular routine and devote them to German. Spread out those time bites over a whole day, and take your stuff with you on the road. If you're anything like the average somewhat disorganized Tom, Dick, or Harriet, you're doing yourself a favor by organizing your time for German. Here are some ideas:

- Instead of talking on your cell while stuck in traffic, keep a small notepad and pen handy to jot down some thoughts, words, or phrases in German.

- Take along a word list, a dialogue (enlarge it first), or something you want to master for your morning commute.

- Tuck some good old-fashioned homemade flashcards in your pocket. I know a man in upper-level management who used his cards whenever he was waiting for the elevator.

Embrace the Culture

Your grasp of German is relevant only to the extent to which you're able to integrate language and culture. After all, language is intimately connected with the people who speak it. Broaden your horizons by finding out how German-speaking people think and act. Becoming aware of their hopes and dreams and gaining insight into their way of life is your path to a rich cultural heritage.

Set Goals and Reward Yourself

Set up a modest challenge for yourself by devoting one afternoon a month entirely to pursuing your interest in German language and culture. Give yourself just rewards for your efforts. The idea here is *looking at the bigger picture.* Go online and plan a bicycling trip along the Danube next fall. Go to dinner at a German style restaurant, or try cooking some German specialties for your friends. Go all out: Change careers and learn the beer-brewing trade at **Weihenstephaner Brauerei.** Enjoy even the smallest accomplishments you make. **Tschüß!** Oh, and **viel Spaß!**

Chapter 20

Ten Pitfalls to Avoid in German

*E*veryone makes mistakes while learning a language — some big, some small, some horribly embarrassing, and some riotously funny. As you read this book, you don't have to worry much about making mistakes. But for someone sitting in a language class among peers or traveling in a far-off country, the fear of making a mistake can be strong enough to give a well-adjusted, normally curious person a deflated, get-me-out-of-this-muck type of mindset.

Doing the exercises in this book isn't a substitute for getting out there and talking and writing to as many people as possible — in German. But this book can help you come prepared. This chapter is aimed at helping you sidestep the biggest blunders you're likely to make in German. So never fear . . . help is on the way!

Attempting Word-for-Word Translations

Leave the translating to the translators. It's not your job. (If it were, you'd know instinctively to shy away from word-for-word translations!) The instant online translating tools will never be as accurate as the best simultaneous interpreters at the U.N. Why not? Single words, let alone larger chunks of language, have many shades of meaning. When strung together in sentences, words can even mean something entirely different from the words as separate entities. So please don't try to win a Nobel prize by analyzing German grammar or inventing mathematical equations consisting of German word A + German word B = English word AB.

Word-for-word translations may work, but then again, you may end up the laughing-stock of your listeners or readership. Tell yourself not to succumb to the temptation of thinking a word, expression, sentence structure, or grammar point — *anything at all* — in English is equivalent to something in German, or vice-versa (unless you know for sure that it's a real cognate, a word with the same meaning in two languages). **Butter** *is* what you want on your toast, but **Gift** is (hopefully) *not* what you give someone on his or her birthday — **Gift** means *poison* in German!

Downplaying Gender and Case

By messing up the case and gender endings, you can come up with any number of very embarrassing results! Gender and case are the underpinnings of German grammar. Nouns, pronouns, adjectives, and prepositions are all influenced by gender and case, as well as number. Be sure you know what the three mean:

- *Number* is whether a noun or a pronoun is singular or plural. Not even number is always the same in German and English; for instance, **die Schere** (*the scissors*) is singular in German.

- *Gender* is the triumvirate of **der** (*masculine*), **die** (*feminine*), and **das** (*neuter*), plus the other forms of **der, die,** and **das** that change spelling in various cases.

- *Case* is not related to brief-, suit-, or carrying case; rather, it's the essential tool for putting words together in a sentence to make sense. All four cases — nominative, accusative, dative, and genitive — are in the example sentence **Der Liebhaber gab dem Hund seiner Geliebten eine Leckerei** (*The lover gave his sweetheart's dog a treat*):

  - Nominative: **Der Liebhaber** (*The lover*)

  - Dative: **gab dem Hund** (*gave [to] the dog*)

  - Genitive: **seiner Geliebten** (*[of] his sweetheart/his sweetheart's*)

  - Accusative: **eine Leckerei.** (*a treat.*)

For more info on gender, number, and case, check out Chapter 2.

Wondering Which Word Order

In German, you may frequently get stumped on which word goes where. To avoid mistakes, make sure you know the basics of correct word order. Here's a quick overview of German's three main patterns:

- **Standard:** The order is *subject + verb + other information;* the verb is in second position.

  Bonnie hat viel Geld. (*Bonnie has a lot of money.*)

  Verb in second position is one essential mantra to remember. Look at the example. Substitute **ihr ältester Onkel, Zack Kohle aus Gelsenkirchen** (*her oldest uncle, Zack Kohle from Gelsenkirchen*) for **Bonnie,** and the word order would be the same: **Ihr ältester Onkel, Zack Kohle aus Gelsenkirchen, hat viel Geld.** Why? Because all the information about the uncle counts as one element, namely the subject of the sentence.

- **Inverted:** The verb comes first, as in yes/no questions.

  Hat Bonnie viel Geld? (*Does Bonnie have a lot of money?*)

- **Subordinate clause:** The active verb (the conjugated part) comes at the end of a subordinate clause, preceded by the past participle (if present).

  Bonnie hat viel Geld, weil sie eine Bank überfallen hat. (*Bonnie has a lot of money because she robbed a bank.*) The conjugated verb **hat** is at the end of the sentence, preceded by **überfallen** (*robbed*), the past participle.

The other essential mantra to chant is *time, manner, place.* Look at the sentence **Ich fahre morgen mit dem Fahrrad zum Biergarten** (*Tomorrow I'm bicycling to the beergarden*):

1. *Time,* meaning when something happens, precedes the other two parts: **Morgen** (*tomorrow*).

2. *Manner* describes the *how* of something: **mit dem Fahrrad** (Literally: *with the bicycle*).

3. *Place* refers to where: **zum Biergarten** (*to the beergarden*).

Check out Chapter 1 for more on word order in general.

Think, Thought, Thunk: (Mis)handling Verbs

A sentence is made up of various parts of speech such as nouns, verbs, adjectives, and so on. The single most important part of speech of a sentence that communicates your ideas is the verb. Use the right verb to convey your thoughts, and people are likely to understand your message, even if other factors in your sentence, such as word endings, word order, and who-knows-what-else aren't quite up to snuff. So you select a verb — what next? You need to conjugate the verb correctly and know which verb tense to use; otherwise, people may stare at you as if you just landed from Mars.

You can rattle off **ich habe, du hast, er/sie/es hat** to your heart's content in the shower. But in a restaurant, you're communicating with the server about food, so you're probably better off combining verbs appropriately to order a meal: **Was würden Sie empfehlen?** (*What would you recommend?*).

Here's another thing: Remembering which verbs use **haben** and which use **sein** to build the past tense isn't so terribly difficult. Messing up the modal verbs doesn't have to happen, either. Get as chummy as you can with the gang of six: **dürfen, können, mögen** (and its sidekick **möchten**), **müssen, sollen,** and **wollen.** (Check out Chapter 9 for more info.)

(Mis)Placing Prepositions and Prefixes

Take on the task of tackling both groups of these tricksters — prefixes and prepositions. Prefixes are an important yet sometimes overlooked part of German. They alter the meaning of the word they're attached to, and some prefixes in combination with certain verb tenses are unattached, so they have a quirky word order.

The preppy prepositions make great friends if you put in a fair amount of effort to find out which case you're dealing with. The bottom line is never to underestimate the power of a preposition. They're more influential in deciding the outcome of a noun or adjective's ending than you'd imagine at first. Also, some prepositions — such as **entlang** — are placed after the words they're linked to: **Gehen Sie die Straße entlang** (*Go along this street*).

Prepositions modify the information following them using one of three cases: accusative, dative, or genitive. The words following the preposition, such as **mit** (*in, with*), have case endings corresponding to the dative case. Check out the following sentence:

> Ich fahre gern mit mein**em** alt**en** Kabriolet. (*I like to drive my old convertible [car].*) The case endings for the dative preposition **mit** are in bold.

Some words, such as **ab, an, auf, für,** and **zu,** are both prepositions and prefixes in German; knowing which is which can be a challenge. Many are so short they seem to get hidden at the tail end of other words, or worse, squashed mercilessly in the middle of a verb that's been relegated to the back of the sentence: **nett, Sie kennen zu lernen** (*nice to meet you*). When **zu** is the prefix of the verb **zumachen** (*to close*), it's at the end of the sentence in present tense; for example, **Machen Sie bitte die Tür zu** (*Please close the door*).

Skipping Capitalization and Umlauts

Yield to the speed of lifestyles these days, and you're likely to wish e. e. cummings had gotten his way and eradicated nearly all capitalization. Well, he didn't, and your otherwise passable German can become confusing if you're sloppy about which words to capitalize.

Improper capitalization may just be the easiest blunder to remedy as soon as you realize how few ground rules there are. By now, you probably know to capitalize all nouns, as well as **Sie** (the formal address for *you*) and its sidekicks, **Ihnen** and **Ihr.** The sticklers are the adjectives that function as nouns, such as nationalities and colors. You see nationalities and colors used as nouns and adjectives, but only the nouns are capitalized:

> **Ein Amerikaner** (noun) **fuhr sein deutsches** (adjective) **Auto.** (*An American was driving his German car.*)

> **Er hatte die gelbe** (adjective) **Ampel nicht gesehen, und fuhr bei Rot** (noun) **über die Ampel.** (*He didn't see the yellow light and drove through a red light.*) Although the *red* in *red light* is an adjective in English, it's a noun in German. How can that be? It's alone (**bei Rot**), without mentioning **Ampel,** so it's functioning as a noun.

Like capitalization, umlauts are small typography elements that can have big impact on meaning. Making pronunciation distinctions is one obvious role they play. In addition, German offers five ways of making nouns plural in German, and some of them use umlauts. Should you write **Bruder** (*brother*) when you really mean the plural **Brüder** (*brothers*), the reader may get the math mixed up.

Slipping on Super Slick Sentences

You get your engines revved and you're ready to **Deutsch sprechen oder schreiben** (*speak or write German*), so you figure, why not make a nice, long sentence instead of short, choppy baby sentences like *See Spot run?* Sure . . . if you know how to juggle a million grammar rules faster than the speed of your tongue or keyboard. How about slowing down? The goal of any language is communication, and a lean, clear sentence is more likely to get your point across. You're probably on thin ice grammatically speaking if your sentence runs longer than two lines — unless Goethe is your idol.

Ready for a challenge? You're at the point where you feel confident with your basics that include subject, verb, and object to form a reasonably coherent sentence? Great. Here's how to gradually work your way up to more-complex sentences:

- Think: Is the word order fine? If that's taken care of, consider adding some extra information, a second idea that you connect with **und** (*and*), **oder** (*or*), or **aber** (*but*). Word order with these conjunctions is no issue; just use them as connectors (Chapter 14 explains conjunctions).

- Want to use the present perfect (conversational past) in a sentence and connect it with a second sentence in the present perfect? Still no problem, as long as you

    • Remember the word order for present perfect verbs.

    • Stick to it for both sentence parts you want to link.

    Chapter 16 can fill you in on the present perfect.

- For further challenges, such as using the conjunctions that change word order — like **weil** (*because*), **obwohl** (*although*), and **damit** (*so that*) — build your sentence slowly, thinking about where to place the verbs.

Write down any successful sentence patterns, the ones that have the correct word order using more-complicated wording, and store them. You can use them again by cutting and pasting the necessary words you need into the basic framework of the two-part sentences you construct.

Being Informal on the Wrong Occasion

Being informal on the wrong occasion isn't a matter of wearing jeans to a country-club wedding. It's a matter of using **du** on the wrong occasion. You should show respect, distance, and decorum by addressing your listener or reader as **Sie** when appropriate. That last tidbit — *when appropriate* — is the kicker. In a nutshell, use **Sie** to speak or write to everyone except relatives, children, friends, dogs, cats, and the talking horse.

Try to find out ahead of time whether the business partner, new neighbor, or other German speaker you're talking with or writing to has an academic or medical title of *doctor.* If so, address that person with **Guten Morgen, Herr Doktor Schimmelreiter** over the fence or **Sehr geehrte Frau Doktor Hufnagel** in a letter. Otherwise, **Frau Scherzl** or **Herr Semmeler** is sufficient to keep someone on your good side.

Rejecting Review

Instead of hurrying with your writing, give it a quick read-through again. You can use a plethora of means to check your written language. Go for it. Try a different method for a week and decide which works best for you — maybe use all of them. Here are some options that may be right for you:

✔ Consult native speakers diplomatically (buy them lunch and ask for pointers on the market study you're preparing to implement).

✔ Go to a bookstore that has the kind of coffee you like and peruse the German/English dictionaries . . . and your wallet. Then splurge (I don't mean on the coffee). Next, go online and compare dictionary resources there.

✔ Try using a German spell check.

✔ Use this book to consult the topics that are your weak points.

Do something, anything, but don't click on *send* before you read, review, and revamp.

Giving Up

When working on mastering a new language or a new sport, you may reach a plateau where you get totally discouraged and want to throw in the towel. That's exactly the time to rally, run to the fridge, and grab a smoothie, energy drink, water, or whatever is truthfully going to enable you to get past that stumbling block — and beyond. When you hit that **Mauer aus Ziegelstein** (*brick wall*), simply go around it. Feel good about what you already know.

The minute you start comparing your progress in German to that of a 10-year-old German-speaking kid, stop. Stop, look, and listen to yourself. You're an adult, so be proud that the way you acquire language is far different from kids' bantering on the playground. Adults tend to enjoy analyzing and comparing languages; kids accept and use language, no holds barred. What you know as an adult, you probably won't forget — and if you do, you can implement effective language tools and your mental resources to get back on track. **Viel Glück!** (*Good luck!*)

Part VI
Appendixes

The 5th Wave   By Rich Tennant

"Douglas, it's time we talked about this beer paraphernalia hobby of yours."

In this part . . .

The four appendixes in this part offer you easy access to verbs, cases, and word lists. Appendix A is your reference on forming verbs in the tenses I describe in this book. Use Appendix B as an overview of how case interacts with various parts of speech. In Appendix C, you find an alphabetical English-German list of important words used in this book; Appendix D is its counterpart, with a German-English mini-dictionary.

Appendix A

Verb Charts

• •

*I*n this appendix, I list the conjugations for various verbs in order of the subject pronouns, from first- to third-person singular, then from first- to third-person plural, and finally the formal second-person address: **ich, du, er/sie/es, wir, ihr, sie,** and **Sie.** For the imperative (used for suggestions and commands), the persons are **du, ihr, Sie.** You also find a list that contains the principal parts of high-frequency strong and irregular weak verbs.

Conjugating Verbs in Present and Simple Past Tenses

You conjugate verbs in the present and simple past by combining the appropriate stem and ending for that verb. I list the endings in Table A-1. The patterns are as follows:

✔ **Present tense; simple past tense of weak regular verbs:** Start with the stem (infinitive minus **-en** ending); add the appropriate ending from Table A-1.

✔ **Simple past tense of weak irregular verbs and strong verbs:** Begin with the simple past stem; add the appropriate ending from Table A-1.

Table A-1		Present-Tense and Simple-Past-Tense Verb Endings			
Subject Pronoun	*Present: Most Verbs*	*Present: Stem Ending in d, t, fn, gn*	*Simple Past: Weak Verbs (Regular and Irregular)*	*Simple Past: Weak Verbs, Stem Ending in d, t, fn, gn*	*Simple Past: Strong Verbs*
ich	-e	-e	-te	-ete	-
du	-st	-est	-test	-etest	-st
er/sie/es	-t	-et	-te	-ete	-
wir	-en	-en	-ten	-eten	-en
ihr	-t	-et	-tet	-etet	-t
sie	-en	-en	-ten	-eten	-en
Sie	-en	-en	-ten	-eten	-en

Conjugating Verbs in the Present Perfect, Future, and Subjunctive

The following sections show you how to conjugate verbs so you can use them in your writing and speech.

Present perfect

To form the present perfect, you conjugate the present tense of the auxiliary **haben** (*to have*) or **sein** (*to be*); then add the past participle; for example, **ich habe gesehen** (*I [have] seen*) and **Ich bin gegangen** (*I have gone/went*).

For the past participle of most weak verbs, take the prefix **ge-,** add the infinitive stem (formed by dropping the **-en** from the infinitive), and add the ending **-t.** Example: **ge-** + **wohn-** + **-t = gewohnt** (*lived*). Verbs with the stem ending in **d, t, fn,** or **gn** add **-e** before the final **-t** ending. Example: **ge-** + **arbeit-** + **-et = gearbeitet** (*worked*).

Some verbs don't use the **ge-** prefix. Examples include verbs with the infinitive ending in **-ieren,** such as **informieren** (*to inform*) → **informiert** (*informed*) and **telefonieren** (*to telephone*) → **telefoniert** (*telephoned*). Some inseparable-prefix verbs that don't use the **ge-** prefix include **bekommen** (*to get*), **gehören** (*to belong to*), and **vergessen** (*to forget*).

The past participle of most strong verbs begins with the prefix **ge-** and ends in **-en.** Many past participles have stem vowel changes, and some have both vowel and consonant changes. For example, **sehen** (*to see*) → **gesehen** (*seen*) has no stem change; **finden** (*to find*) → **gefunden** (*found*) has a vowel change; and **sitzen** (*to sit*) → **gesessen** (*sat*) has both vowel and consonant changes. Table A-2, at the end of this chapter, shows the past participles for strong verbs.

The past participles of irregular verbs such as auxiliaries may have different endings. I show these endings separately in the corresponding charts in this appendix.

Future

For the future tense, conjugate the present tense of the auxiliary verb **werden** — **werde, wirst, wird, werden, werdet, werden, werden** — and add the infinitive form of the main verb. Example: **Ich werde fahren** (*I will go/drive*).

Subjunctive

In most cases of the present subjunctive, conjugate the subjunctive of the auxiliary verb **werden** — **würde, würdest, würde, würden, würdet, würden, würden** — and add the infinitive form of the main verb. Example: **Ich würde leben** (*I would live*).

Weak Verbs

Regular verbs (no stem change in the simple past)

wohnen (to live, reside)

> **Present Tense Stem:** wohn-
>
> **Simple Past (1st/3rd-person singular):** wohnte
>
> **Past Participle:** gewohnt; **Auxiliary Verb:** haben
>
> **Present Subjunctive:** würde wohnen
>
> **Present:** wohne, wohnst, wohnt, wohnen, wohnt, wohnen, wohnen
>
> **Simple Past:** wohnte, wohntest, wohnte, wohnten, wohntet, wohnten, wohnten
>
> **Imperative:** wohne, wohnt, wohnen Sie

Some other verbs like this are **brauchen** (*to need*), **feiern** (*to celebrate*), **glauben** (*to believe*), **hören** (*to hear*), **kaufen** (*to buy*), **lachen** (*to laugh*), **lernen** (*to learn*), **machen** (*to make, do*), **sagen** (*to say*), and **spielen** (*to play*).

Regular verbs (with stem ending in -d, -t, -fn or -gn)

arbeiten (to work)

> **Present Tense Stem:** arbeit-
>
> **Simple Past (1st/3rd-person singular):** arbeitete
>
> **Past Participle:** gearbeitet; **Auxiliary Verb:** haben
>
> **Present Subjunctive:** würde arbeiten
>
> **Present:** arbeite, arbeitest, arbeitet, arbeiten, arbeitet, arbeiten, arbeiten
>
> **Simple Past:** arbeitete, arbeitetest, arbeitete, arbeiteten, arbeitetet, arbeiteten, arbeiteten
>
> **Imperative:** arbeite, arbeitet, arbeiten Sie

Some other verbs like this are **kosten** (*to cost*), **öffnen** (*to open*), **reden** (*to talk*), **regnen** (*to rain*), and **warten** (*to wait*).

Irregular weak verbs (stem change in the simple past)

denken (to think)

Present Tense Stem: denk-

Simple Past (1st/3rd-person singular): dachte

Past Participle: gedacht; **Auxiliary Verb:** haben

Present Subjunctive: würde denken

Present: denke, denkst, denkt, denken, denkt, denken, denken

Simple Past: dachte, dachtest, dachte, dachten, dachtet, dachten, dachten

Imperative: denke, denkt, denken Sie

Other verbs like this are listed in Table A-2, at the end of this chapter.

Strong Verbs

Verbs with auxiliary haben

trinken (to drink)

Present Tense Stem: trink-

Simple Past (1st/3rd-person singular): trank

Past Participle: getrunken; **Auxiliary Verb:** haben

Present Subjunctive: würde trinken

Present: trinke, trinkst, trinkt, trinken, trinkt, trinken, trinken

Simple Past: trank, trankst, trank, tranken, trankt, tranken, tranken

Imperative: trinke, trinkt, trinken Sie

Other verbs like this are listed in Table A-2.

Verbs with auxiliary sein

kommen (to come)

Present Tense Stem: komm-

Simple Past (1st/3rd-person singular): kam

Past Participle: gekommen; **Auxiliary Verb:** sein

Present Subjunctive: würde kommen

Present: komme, komm**st**, komm**t**, komm**en**, komm**t**, komm**en**, komm**en**

Simple Past: kam, kam**st**, kam, kam**en**, kam**t**, kam**en**, kam**en**

Imperative: komme, kommt, kommen Sie

Other verbs like this are listed in Table A-2.

Verbs with present-tense vowel change in second- and third-person singular

lesen (to read)

Present Tense Stem: les-; **Present Tense Vowel Change:** liest

Simple Past (1st/3rd-person singular): las

Past Participle: gelesen; **Auxiliary Verb:** haben

Present Subjunctive: würde lesen

Present: lese, **liest**, **liest**, lesen, lest, lesen, lesen

Simple Past: las, las**est**, las, las**en**, last, las**en**, las**en**

Imperative: lies, lest, lesen Sie

Other verbs like this are listed in Table A-2.

Separable-Prefix Verbs

mitbringen (to bring along)

Present Tense Stem: bring- mit

Simple Past (1st/3rd-person singular): brach**te** mit

Past Participle: mitgebracht; **Auxiliary Verb:** haben

Present Subjunctive: würde mitbringen

Present: mitbringe, mitbring**st**, mitbring**t**, mitbring**en**, mitbring**t**, mitbring**en**, mitbring**en**

Simple Past: brach**te** mit, brach**test** mit, brach**te** mit, brach**ten** mit, brach**tet** mit, brach**ten** mit, brach**ten** mit

Imperative: bringe mit, bringt mit, bringen Sie mit

Some other similar verbs are **anhaben** (*to wear*), **anrufen** (*to telephone*), **fernsehen** (*to watch TV*), and **vorhaben** (*to plan*).

Inseparable-Prefix Verbs (without Ge- Prefix in the Past Participle)

Verbs with a past participle ending in -t

bezahlen (to pay)

Present Tense Stem: bezahl-

Simple Past (1st/3rd-person singular): bezahlte

Past Participle: bezahlt; **Auxiliary Verb:** haben

Present Subjunctive: würde bezahlen

Present: bezahle, bezahlst, bezahlt, bezahlen, bezahlt, bezahlen, bezahlen

Simple Past: bezahlte, bezahltest, bezahlte, bezahlten, bezahltet, bezahlten, bezahlten

Imperative: bezahle, bezahlt, bezahlen Sie

Some other verbs like this are **beantworten** (*to answer*), **besuchen** (*to visit*), **erklären** (*to explain*), **gehören** (*to belong to*), and **versuchen** (*to try*).

Verbs with a past participle ending in -en

gefallen (to like)

Present Tense Stem: gefall-

Present-Tense Vowel Change (in 2nd/3rd-person singular): gefäll-

Simple Past (1st/3rd-person singular): gefiel

Past Participle: gefallen; **Auxiliary Verb:** haben

Present Subjunctive: würde gefallen

Present: gefalle, gefällst, gefällt, gefallen, gefallt, gefallen, gefallen

Simple Past: gefiel, gefielst, gefiel, gefielen, gefielt, gefielen, gefielen

Imperative: gefalle, gefallt, gefallen Sie

Other verbs like this are listed in Table A-2, at the end of the chapter.

Auxiliary Verbs Haben, Sein, and Werden

haben (to have)

Present (and auxiliary for verbs using haben in present perfect): habe, hast, hat, haben, habt, haben, haben

Simple Past (1st/3rd-person singular): hatte

Past Participle: gehabt; **Auxiliary Verb:** haben

Present Subjunctive (same as simple past with umlaut): hätte, hättest, hätte, hätten, hättet, hätten, hätten

Simple Past: hatte, hattest, hatte, hatten, hattet, hatten, hatten

Imperative: habe, habt, haben Sie

sein (to be)

Present (and auxiliary for verbs using sein in present perfect): bin, bist, ist, sind, seid, sind, sind

Simple Past (1st/3rd-person singular): war

Past Participle: gewesen; **Auxiliary Verb:** sein

Present Subjunctive: wäre, wärest, wäre, wären, wäret, wären, wären

Simple Past: war, warst, war, waren, wart, waren, waren

Imperative: sei, seid, seien Sie

werden (to become, shall, will)

Present: werde, wirst, wird, werden, werdet, werden

Simple Past (1st/3rd-person singular): wurde

Past Participle: geworden; **Auxiliary Verb:** sein

Present Subjunctive (same as simple past with umlaut): würde, würdest, würde, würden, würdet, würden, würden

Simple Past: wurde, wurdest, wurde, wurden, wurdet, wurden, wurden

Imperative: werde, werdet, werden Sie

Note: The present of **werden** is the auxiliary verb for forming the future tense, and the present subjunctive is the auxiliary verb for many verbs in the present subjunctive.

Modal Auxiliary Verbs

dürfen (to be allowed, may)

Present: darf, darfst, darf, dürfen, dürft, dürfen, dürfen

Simple Past (1st/3rd-person singular): durfte

Past Participle: gedurft; **Auxiliary Verb:** haben

Present Subjunctive (same as simple past with umlaut): dürfte

Simple Past: durfte, durftest, durfte, durften, durftet, durften, durften

können (to be able to, can, to know how to do something)

Present: kann, kannst, kann, können, könnt, können, können

Simple Past (1st/3rd-person singular): konnte

Past Participle: gekonnt; **Auxiliary Verb:** haben

Present Subjunctive (same as simple past with umlaut): könnte

Simple Past: konnte, konntest, konnte, konnten, konntet, konnten, konnten

mögen (to like [to], want to)

Present: mag, magst, mag, mögen, mögt, mögen, mögen

Simple Past (1st/3rd-person singular): mochte

Past Participle: gemocht; **Auxiliary Verb:** haben

Present Subjunctive (same as simple past with umlaut): möchte (*would like to*)

Simple Past: mochte, mochtest, mochte, mochten, mochtet, mochten, mochte

müssen (to have to, must)

Present: muss, musst, muss, müssen, müsst, müssen, müssen

Simple Past (1st/3rd-person singular): musste

Past Participle: gemusst; **Auxiliary Verb:** haben

Present Subjunctive (same as simple past with umlaut): müsste

Simple Past: musste, musstest, musste, mussten, musstet, mussten, mussten

sollen (to be supposed to, should)

Present: soll, sollst, soll, sollen, sollt, sollen, sollen

Simple Past (1st/3rd-person singular): sollte

Past Participle: gesollt; **Auxiliary Verb:** haben

Present Subjunctive (same as simple past): sollte

Simple Past: sollte, solltest, sollte, sollten, solltet, sollten, sollten

wollen (to want to)

Present: will, willst, will, wollen, wollt, wollen, wollen

Simple Past (1st/3rd-person singular): wollte

Past Participle: gewollt; **Auxiliary Verb:** haben

Present Subjunctive (same as simple past): wollte

Simple Past: wollte, wolltest, wollte, wollten, wolltet, wollten, wollten

Principal Parts of Weak Verbs

Table A-2 contains high-frequency strong verbs, irregular weak verbs, modal auxiliaries, common separable-prefix verbs whose base verb is not listed, **haben** (*to have*), and **sein** (*to be*). The past participles that use the auxiliary **sein** are indicated; the others use **haben.**

Table A-2	Principal Parts of Strong and Irregular Weak Verbs			
Infinitive	*Stem Change (3rd-Person Singular Present)*	*Simple Past*	*Past Participle*	*English Meaning*
anfangen	fängt an	fing an	angefangen	*to start, begin*
anrufen		rief an	angerufen	*to telephone*
beginnen		begann	begonnen	*to begin*
bekommen		bekam	bekommen	*to get*
bleiben		blieb	ist geblieben	*to stay*
brechen	bricht	brach	gebrochen	*to break*
bringen		brachte	gebracht	*to bring*
denken		dachte	gedacht	*to think*
dürfen	darf	durfte	gedurft	*to be permitted to, may*
einladen	lädt ein	lud ein	eingeladen	*to invite*
empfehlen	empfiehlt	empfahl	empfohlen	*to recommend*
entscheiden		entschied	entschieden	*to decide*
essen	isst	aß	gegessen	*to eat*
fahren	fährt	fuhr	ist gefahren	*to go, drive, travel*
fallen	fällt	fiel	ist gefallen	*to fall*
finden		fand	gefunden	*to find*
fliegen		flog	ist geflogen	*to fly*
geben	gibt	gab	gegeben	*to give*
gefallen	gefällt	gefiel	gefallen	*to like*
gehen		ging	ist gegangen	*to go*
gewinnen		gewann	gewonnen	*to win*
haben	hat	hatte	gehabt	*to have*
halten	hält	hielt	gehalten	*to hold, stop*
heißen		hieß	geheißen	*to be called, named*
helfen	hilft	half	geholfen	*to help*
kennen		kannte	gekannt	*to know (person)*
kommen		kam	ist gekommen	*to come*
können	kann	konnte	gekonnt	*to be able to, can*
lassen	lässt	ließ	gelassen	*to let*

(continued)

Table A-2 (continued)

Infinitive	Stem Change (3rd-Person Singular Present)	Simple Past	Past Participle	English Meaning
laufen	läuft	lief	ist gelaufen	to run
lesen	liest	las	gelesen	to read
liegen		lag	gelegen	to lie (situated)
mögen	mag	mochte	gemocht	to like
müssen	muss	musste	gemusst	to have to, must
nehmen	nimmt	nahm	genommen	to take
schlafen	schläft	schlief	geschlafen	to sleep
schließen		schloss	geschlossen	to close
schreiben		schrieb	geschrieben	to write
schwimmen		schwamm	ist geschwommen	to swim
sehen	sieht	sah	gesehen	to see
sein	ist	war	ist gewesen	to be
singen		sang	gesungen	to sing
sitzen		saß	gesessen	to sit
sollen	soll	sollte	gesollt	to be supposed to, should
sprechen	spricht	sprach	gesprochen	to speak
stehen		stand	gestanden	to stand
sterben	stirbt	starb	ist gestorben	to die
tragen	trägt	trug	getragen	to wear, carry
treffen	trifft	traf	getroffen	to meet
trinken		trank	getrunken	to drink
tun		tat	getan	to do
vergessen	vergisst	vergaß	vergessen	to forget
verlieren		verlor	verloren	to lose
verstehen		verstand	verstanden	to understand
waschen	wäscht	wusch	gewaschen	to wash
werden	wird	wurde	ist geworden	to become, will
wissen	weiß	wusste	gewusst	to know (fact)
wollen	will	wollte	gewollt	to want (to)

Appendix B

Case Charts

Use these charts as a quick reference guide to articles, pronouns, and adjectives with case, gender, or number endings. You also find prepositions listed by case.

Articles

In this section, you find the definite articles **der, die,** and **das** (*the*) and the indefinite articles **ein** and **eine** (*a, an*). I also list the **ein-** words with the indefinite articles; they have the same case endings.

Definite articles (the)

Table B-1 shows all the ways to say *the* in German.

Table B-1		Definite Articles		
Case	**Masculine**	**Feminine**	**Neuter**	**Plural**
Nominative	der	die	das	die
Accusative	den	die	das	die
Dative	dem	der	dem	den
Genitive	des	der	des	der

Indefinite articles (a, an) and ein- words

Table B-2 shows the indefinite article **ein** (*a, an*) and the **ein-** words, which have the same case endings as **ein**. These words include **kein** (*no, not, not any*) and the possessive adjectives: **mein** (*my*), **dein** (*your*), **sein** (*his/its*), **ihr** (*her*), **unser** (*our*), **euer** (*your*), **ihr** (*their*), and **Ihr** (*your*). Each box in the table includes **ein** and the possessive adjectives **mein** and **unser**. All other possessive adjectives use these same endings. I indicate the case endings for all **ein-** words separately, as well as in each word, in bold.

Note: The word **ein** has no plural, so I put **kein** in the plural slot.

Table B-2		Ein, Kein, and Ein- Words		
Case	*Masculine*	*Feminine*	*Neuter*	*Plural*
Nominative	ein, mein, unser -	eine, meine, unsere -e	ein, mein, unser -	keine, meine, unsere -e
Accusative	einen, meinen, unseren -en	eine, meine, unsere -e	ein, mein, unser -	keine, meine, unsere -e
Dative	einem, meinem, unserem -em	einer, meiner, unserer -er	einem, meinem, unserem -em	keinen, meinen, unseren -en
Genitive	eines, meines, unseres -es	einer, meiner, unserer -er	eines, meines, unseres -es	keiner, meiner, unserer -er

Pronouns

In this section, you find the pronoun group: personal pronouns (in nominative case: *I, you, he/she/it, we, you, they*), relative pronouns (*who, whom, whose, that*), demonstrative pronouns (*this, that, these, those*), reflexive pronouns (*myself, yourself, himself, herself, itself, ourselves, yourselves, themselves*), and the interrogative pronoun *who*.

Personal pronouns

Table B-3 shows the personal pronouns in the three cases: nominative, accusative, and dative. In this section, I list the conjugations in order of the pronouns, from first- to third-person singular, then first- to third-person plural, and finally the formal second-person address (**Sie**). The nominative case is **ich, du, er/sie/es, wir, ihr, sie, Sie.**

Table B-3	Personal Pronouns	
Nominative Case	*Accusative Case*	*Dative Case*
ich (*I*)	**mich** (*me*)	**mir** (*me*)
du (*you*) (s., inf.)	**dich** (*you*)	**dir** (*you*)
er (*he*)	**ihn** (*him*)	**ihm** (*him*)
sie (*she*)	**sie** (*her*)	**ihr** (*her*)
es (*it*)	**es** (*it*)	**ihm** (*it*)
wir (*we*)	**uns** (*us*)	**uns** (*us*)

Nominative Case	Accusative Case	Dative Case
ihr (*you*) (pl., inf.)	**euch** (*you*)	**euch** (*you*)
sie (*they*)	**sie** (*them*)	**ihnen** (*them*)
Sie (*you*) (s. or pl., form.)	**Sie** (*you*)	**Ihnen** (*you*)

Relative and demonstrative pronouns

The relative and demonstrative pronouns are the same in German (see Table B-4). In English, the relative pronouns are *who, whom, whose,* and *that,* and the demonstrative pronouns are *this, that, these,* and *those.*

Table B-4	Relative and Demonstrative Pronouns			
Case	*Masculine*	*Feminine*	*Neuter*	*Plural*
Nominative	**der**	**die**	**das**	**die**
Accusative	**den**	**die**	**das**	**die**
Dative	**dem**	**der**	**dem**	**denen**
Genitive (relative pronouns only)	**dessen**	**deren**	**dessen**	**deren**

Note: Another demonstrative pronoun, **dieser,** also has the same meanings in English: *this, that, these, those.* You can see it in Table B-5 with the **der-** words.

Der- words

The **der-** words all have the same case endings. They include **dieser** (*this, that, these, those*), **jeder** (*each, every*), **mancher** (*some*), **solcher** (*such*), and **welcher** (*which*). Table B-5 shows the endings in bold.

Table B-5	Der- Words			
Case	*Masculine*	*Feminine*	*Neuter*	*Plural*
Nominative	dies**er**	dies**e**	dies**es**	dies**e**
Accusative	dies**en**	dies**e**	dies**es**	dies**e**
Dative	dies**em**	dies**er**	dies**em**	dies**en**
Genitive	dies**es**	dies**er**	dies**es**	dies**er**

Reflexive pronouns

The reflexive pronouns include *myself, yourself, himself, herself, itself, ourselves, yourselves,* and *themselves.* Table B-6 also includes personal pronouns (nominative case) for reference.

Table B-6	Reflexive Pronouns	
Nominative of Personal Pronouns	*Accusative (Reflexive)*	*Dative (Reflexive)*
ich (*I*)	**mich** (*myself*)	**mir** (*myself*)
du (*you*) (s., inf.)	**dich** (*yourself*)	**dir** (*yourself*)
er (*he*)	**sich** (*himself*)	**sich** (*himself*)
sie (*she*)	**sich** (*herself*)	**sich** (*herself*)
es (*it*)	**sich** (*itself*)	**sich** (*itself*)
wir (*we*)	**uns** (*ourselves*)	**uns** (*ourselves*)
ihr (*you*) (pl., inf.)	**euch** (*yourselves*)	**euch** (*yourselves*)
sie (*they*)	**sich** (*themselves*)	**sich** (*themselves*)
Sie (*you*) (s. or pl., form.)	**sich** (*yourself/ yourselves*)	**sich** (*yourself/ yourselves*)

Interrogative pronoun who

Table B-7 shows the interrogative (question) pronoun *who.*

Table B-7	Interrogative Pronoun Who	
Case	*Pronoun*	*English Equivalent*
Nominative	**wer**	*who*
Accusative	**wen**	*whom*
Dative	**wem**	*(to) whom*
Genitive	**wessen**	*whose*

Adjectives

In this section, you find the adjective tables showing case endings for adjectives not preceded by an article and for preceded adjectives (after **der-** words and after **ein-** words). You also find a comparison table for irregular adjectives and adverbs.

Adjectives without der- or ein- words (not preceded)

Table B-8 shows endings for adjectives that aren't preceded by an article (**der/die/das** or **ein/eine**) or other modifiers (**der-** words, such as **dieser** and **solcher**, and **ein-** words, such as **mein** and **kein**). The endings are shown separately in bold.

Table B-8	Adjective Endings Not Preceded			
Case	*Masculine*	*Feminine*	*Neuter*	*Plural*
Nominative	guter Käse (*good cheese*) -er	schmackhafte Wurst (*tasty sausage*) -e	leckeres Brot (*delicious bread*) -es	köstliche Kuchen (*delicious cakes*) -e
Accusative	guten Käse -en	schmackhafte Wurst -e	leckeres Brot -es	köstliche Kuchen -e
Dative	gutem Käse -em	schmackhafter Wurst -er	leckerem Brot -em	köstlichen Kuchen -en
Genitive	guten Käses -en	schmackhafter Wurst -er	leckeren Brotes -en	köstlicher Kuchen -er

Preceded adjectives

Table B-9 shows endings for adjectives that are preceded by an article (**der/die/das** or **ein/eine**) or other modifier (**der-** words or **ein-** words). The adjective endings are shown in bold.

Table B-9	Preceded Adjective Endings			
Case	*Masculine*	*Feminine*	*Neuter*	*Plural*
Nominative	**der** lustige Mann ein lustiger Mann	**die** glückliche Frau eine glückliche Frau	**das** brave Kind ein braves Kind	**die** lustigen Männer keine lustigen Männer
Accusative	**den** lustigen Mann einen lustigen Mann	**die** glückliche Frau eine glückliche Frau	**das** brave Kind ein braves Kind	**die** lustigen Männer keine lustigen Männer

(continued)

Table B-9 *(continued)*

Case	Masculine	Feminine	Neuter	Plural
Dative	**dem** lustig**en** Mann ein**em** lustig**en** Mann	**der** glücklichen Frau ein**er** glücklichen Frau	**dem** brav**en** Kind ein**em** brav**en** Kind	**den** lustig**en** Männer**n** kein**en** lustig**en** Männer**n**
Genitive	**des** lustig**en** Mann**es** ein**es** lustig**en** Mann**es**	**der** glücklichen Frau ein**er** glücklichen Frau	**des** brav**en** Kind**es** ein**es** brav**en** Kind**es**	**der** lustig**en** Männer kein**er** lustig**en** Männer

Note: The plural endings for preceded adjectives are the same in masculine, feminine, and neuter.

Irregular comparison (adjectives and adverbs)

Table B-10 shows how you form the base, comparative, and superlative forms of irregular adjectives and adverbs.

Table B-10	Irregular Comparison Forms	
Base	**Comparative**	**Superlative**
bald (*soon*)	**eher** (*sooner*)	**am ehesten** (*soonest*)
gern (*like/enjoy* [*doing something*])	**lieber** (*prefer*)	**am liebsten** (*like most of all*)
gut (*good*)	**besser** (*better*)	**am besten** (*best*)
hoch (*high*)	**höher** (*higher*)	**am höchsten** (*highest*)
nah (*near*)	**näher** (*nearer*)	**am nächsten** (*nearest*)
viel (*much*)	**mehr** (*more*)	**am meisten** (*most*)

Prepositions

German prepositions have a case: accusative, dative, or genitive. Some prepositions have two cases (accusative and dative). This section gives you the basics.

Accusative, dative, and genitive prepositions

Table B-11 shows accusative prepositions and their English equivalents.

Table B-11		Accusative, Dative, and Genitive Prepositions			
Accusative		**Dative**		**Genitive**	
Preposition	**English Equivalent(s)**	**Preposition**	**English Equivalent(s)**	**Preposition**	**English Equivalent(s)**
bis	*till, until* (also: conjunction *until*)	aus	*from, out of*	(an)statt	*from, out of*
durch	*through, by*	außer	*besides, except for*	außerhalb	*besides, except for*
für	*for*	bei	*at (a home of, a place of business), near, with*	innerhalb	*at (a home of, a place of business), near, with*
gegen	*against, for*	mit	*with, by (means of transportation)*	trotz	*with, by (means of transportation)*
ohne	*without*	nach	*after, past, to* (no article for cities and countries)	während	*after, past, to* (no article for cities and countries)
um	*around, for, at*	seit	*for, since*		
entlang	*along, down*	von	*by, from, of*		
		zu	*to* (with people and certain places)		

Note: **Entlang** (*along, down*) can be an accusative, dative, or genitive preposition.

Note: There's no difference between **anstatt** and **statt** (*instead of*), a genitive prepostion.

Two-way prepositions: Accusative/dative

Table B-12 shows accusative/dative prepositions and their English equivalents. These prepositions can take the accusative case or the dative case, depending on how they're used in a sentence (see Chapter 15 for details).

Table B-12	Accusative/Dative Prepositions
Preposition	*English Equivalent(s)*
an	at, on, to
auf	on, onto, to
hinter	behind, to the back of
in	in, into, to
neben	beside, next to
über	above, over
unter	under, underneath
vor	in front of
zwischen	between

Note: The preposition **entlang** (*along, down*) can take the accusative, dative, and sometimes genitive case. You can place it in front of or after its object.

Appendix C

English-German Dictionary

• •

*H*ere's some of the German vocabulary used throughout this book, arranged alphabetically by the English translation, to help you when reading or listening to German.

a, an: **ein**

(to be) able to, can: **können**

after, to: **nach**

again: **wieder**

all: **alle**

to allow, let: **lassen**

(to be) allowed to: **dürfen**

also: **auch**

although: **obwohl**

always: **immer**

and: **und**

to answer: **antworten**

around, at: **um**

to ask: **fragen**

at: **an, auf, bei, um**

bad: **schlecht**

(to) be: **sein**

to be called, named: **heißen**

because: **da, denn, weil**

because of: **wegen**

to become, will: **werden**

to begin: **anfangen, beginnen**

before: **vor**

behind: **hinter**

between: **zwischen**

to bring: **bringen**

but: **aber, doch**

but rather: **sondern**

to buy: **kaufen**

by: **an, bei**

(to be) called, named: **heißen**

can: **können**

to carry: **tragen**

to come: **kommen**

to cost: **kosten**

to cut: **schneiden**

to dance: **tanzen**

to do: **tun, machen**

to drink: **trinken**

to drive: **fahren**

dry: **trocken**

during: **während**

to eat: **essen**

to enjoy: **gefallen**

except for: **außer**

to fall: **fallen**

few: **wenig(e)**

to find: **finden**

to fit: **passen**

to fly: **fliegen**

for: **für, seit** (time)

to forget: **vergessen**

from where: **woher**

from: **von, aus**

to get: **bekommen**

to give: **geben**

to give (a present): **schenken**

to go: **gehen, fahren**

good: **gut**

happy: **glücklich**

to have: **haben**

to have to, must: **müssen**

he: **er**

to hear: **hören**

to help: **helfen**

her: **sie, ihr**

here: **hier**

high: **hoch**

to hike: **wandern**

him: **ihn, ihm**

his: **sein**

to hold, stop: **halten**

to hope: **hoffen**

how: **wie**

how many: **wie viele**

how much: **wie viel**

I: **ich**

if, whether: **wenn**

if: **ob**

in: **in**

in case: **falls**

in order to: **um . . . zu . . .**

in spite of: **trotz**

inexpensive: **billig**

instead of: **statt**

it; its: **es, ihm; sein**

to know (fact): **wissen**

to know (be familiar with): **kennen**

last: **letzter**

to last: **dauern**

late: **spät**

to laugh: **lachen**

to learn: **lernen**

to let, allow: **lassen**

to like (to): **mögen**

to like, enjoy: **gefallen**

little (quantity): **wenig**

to live: **wohnen, leben**

to lose: **verlieren**

long: **lang**

lovely, gorgeous: **wunderschön**

to make, do: **machen**

may: **dürfen**

me: **mich, mir**

to meet: **treffen**

must: **müssen**

my: **mein**

(to be) named, called: **heißen**

near: **nah, in der Nähe von**

to need: **brauchen**

next: **nächster**

next to: **neben**

nice: **nett**

no: **nein**

not: **kein, nicht**

not only . . . but also: **nicht nur . . . sondern auch**

now: **jetzt**

of course: **gewiss, klar**

often: **oft**

old: **alt**

on: **auf, an**

only: **nur**

or: **oder**

our: **unser**

over: **über**

to pay: **bezahlen, zahlen**

perhaps: **vielleicht**

to play: **spielen**

polite: **höflich**

to put: **stellen, setzen**

to rain: **regnen**

to read: **lesen**

to recommend: **empfehlen**

to run: **laufen**

to say: **sagen**

to see: **sehen**

sensible: **vernünftig**

she, it, they: **sie**

to go shopping: **einkaufen**

should: **sollen**

since: **seit**

to sing: **singen**

to sit down: **setzen**

to sleep: **schlafen**

slow(ly): **langsam**

so; so that: **also; damit**

some, something: **etwas**

to speak: **sprechen**

to stand: **stehen, stellen**

to stay: **bleiben**

still: **noch**

to stop: **halten**

to study: **studieren**

such: **so**

sure: **sicher**

to swim: **schwimmen**

to take: **nehmen**

to talk: **reden, sprechen**

to telephone: **anrufen**

than: **als**

that: **dass**

the: **das** (n.)/**der** (m.)/**die** (f.)

their: **ihr**

them: **sie, ihnen**

then: **dann**

they: **sie**

to: **zu, nach**

to think: **denken**

this, that, these, those: **dies-**

through: **durch**

to throw: **werfen**

to: **zu, nach**

too; too many; too much: **zu; zu viele; zu viel**

to travel: **reisen**

to understand: **verstehen**

us: **uns**

to visit: **besuchen**

to wait: **warten**

to walk: **spazierengehen**

to want (to): **wollen**

to wash: **washen**

to watch TV: **fernsehen**

we: **wir**

to wear: **tragen**

wet: **nass**

what: **was**

what kind of: **was für**

when: **wann, wenn, als**

where: **wo**

where to: **wohin**

whether: **ob, falls**

which: **welch-**

who: **wer**

why: **warum**

will: **werden**

to win: **gewinnen**

with: **mit**

without: **ohne**

to work: **arbeiten**

would like to: **möchten**

to write: **schreiben**

yes: **ja**

you (impersonal), one: **man**

you (inf., pl.): **ihr, euch**

you (form.): **Sie, Ihnen**

you (inf., sing.): **du, dich, dir**

young: **jung**

your (form.): **Ihr**

your (inf., pl.): **euer**

your (inf., sing.): **dein**

Appendix D

German-English Dictionary

• •

*H*ere's some of the German vocabulary used throughout this book, arranged alphabetically by the German translation, to help you when reading or listening to German.

ab: *starting at, away, off*

aber: *but*

alle: *all*

als: *than, when*

an: *at, by, to*

anfangen: *to begin*

anrufen: *to telephone*

antworten: *to answer*

arbeiten: *to work*

auch: *also*

auf: *on*

aus: *from, out of*

außer: *except for*

beginnen: *to begin*

bei: *at, by, to, with*

bekommen: *to get*

besuchen: *to visit*

bezahlen: *to pay*

billig: *cheap, inexpensive*

bis: *by, until*

bleiben: *to stay*

brauchen: *to need*

bringen: *to bring*

da: *because*

damit: *so that*

dann: *then*

das (n.): *the*

dass: *that*

dauern: *to last*

dein (inf., sing.): *your*

denken: *to think*

denn: *for, because*

der (m.): *the*

dich (inf., sing., acc.): *you*

die (f.): *the*

dieser, diese, dieses: *this, that, these, those*

dir (inf., sing., dat.): *you*

doch: *but, nevertheless*

du (inf., sing.): *you*

durch: *through, by*

dürfen: *to be allowed to, may*

ein: *a, an*

einkaufen: *to go shopping*

empfehlen: *to recommend*

er: *he*

es: *it*

essen: *to eat*

etwas: *some, something, a little*

euch (inf., pl., acc./dat.): *you*

euer (inf., pl.): *your*

fahren: *to go, drive, travel*

fallen: *to fall*

falls: *if, whether, in case*

fernsehen: *to watch TV*

finden: *to find*

fliegen: *to fly*

fragen: *to ask*

für: *for*

geben: *to give*

gefallen: *to like, enjoy*

gehen: *to go*

gewinnen: *to win*

gewiss: *of course*

glücklich: *happy*

gut: *good*

haben: *to have*

halten: *to hold, stop*

heißen: *to be called, named*

helfen: *to help*

hier: *here*

hinter: *behind*

hoch: *high*

hoffen: *to hope*

höflich: *polite*

hören: *to hear*

ich: *I*

ihm: *him, it*

ihn: *him*

ihnen: *them*

Ihnen (form.): *you*

ihr: *you* (inf., pl.), *her, their*

Ihr (form.): *your*

immer: *always*

in: *in*

ja: *yes*

jetzt: *now*

jung: *young*

kaufen: *to buy*

kein: *no, not any*

kennen: *to know (be familiar with)*

klar: *of course*

kommen: *to come*

können: *to be able to, can*

kosten: *to cost*

lachen: *to laugh*

lang: *long*

langsam: *slow(ly)*

lassen: *to let, allow*

laufen: *to run*

leben: *to live*

lernen: *to learn*

lesen: *to read*

letzter: *last*

liegen: *to lie (down)*

machen: *to make, do*

man (impersonal): *you*

mein: *my*

mich: *me*

mir: *me*

mit: *with*

möchten: *would like to*

mögen: *to like (to)*

müssen: *to have to, must*

nach: *after, to*

nächster: *next*

nah: *near*

nass: *wet*

neben: *next to*

nehmen: *to take*

nein: *no*

nett: *nice*

nicht: *not*

nicht nur . . . sondern auch: *not only . . . but also*

noch: *still, yet*

nur: *only*

ob: *if, whether*

obwohl: *although*

oder: *or*

oft: *often*

ohne: *without*

passen: *to fit*

reden: *to talk*

regnen: *to rain*

reisen: *to travel*

sagen: *to say*

schenken: *to give (a present)*

schlafen: *to sleep*

schlecht: *bad*

schneiden: *to cut*

schreiben: *to write*

schwimmen: *to swim*

sehen: *to see*

sein: *to be*

sein: *his, its*

seit: *since, for*

setzen: *to sit down, to put*

sicher: *sure, certainly*

sie: *she, her, they, them*

Sie (form.): *you*

singen: *to sing*

so: *such, thus, so, as*

so . . . wie: *as . . . as*

sollen: *should*

sondern: *but rather*

spazierengehen: *to walk*

spielen: *to play*

sprechen: *to speak, talk*

statt: *instead of*

stellen: *to put, stand*

studieren: *to study*

tanzen: *to dance*

tragen: *to wear, carry*

treffen: *to meet*

trinken: *to drink*

trocken: *dry*

trotz: *in spite of*

tun: *to do*

über: *over*

um: *around, at*

um . . . zu . . . : *in order to*

und: *and*

uns: *us*

unser: *our*

vergessen: *to forget*

verlieren: *to lose*

vernünftig: *sensible*

verstehen: *to understand*

vielleicht: *perhaps*

von: *from*

vor: *before, in front of*

während: *during*

wandern: *to hike*

wann: *when*

warten: *to wait*

warum: *why*

was: *what*

was für: *what kind of*

waschen: *to wash*

wegen: *because of*

weil: *because*

welcher, welche, welches: *which*

wenig: *little, few*

wenn: *if, when*

wer: *who*

werden: *to become, will*

werfen: *to throw*

wie: *how*

wie viel: *how much*

wie viele: *how many*

wieder: *again*

wir: *we*

wissen: *to know (fact)*

wo: *where*

woher: *from where*

wohin: *where to*

wohnen: *to live*

wollen: *to want (to)*

wunderschön: *lovely, gorgeous*

zahlen: *to pay*

zu: *to, at, too*

zu viel: *too much*

zu viele: *too many*

zwischen: *between*

Index